J.R.R. TOLKIEN,

Scholar and Storyteller

ESSAYS *IN MEMORIAM*

Professor Tolkien in the gardens of Merton College.
Copyright © Billett Potter.

J.R.R. TOLKIEN,

Scholar and Storyteller

ESSAYS *IN MEMORIAM*

EDITED BY

Mary Salu

and Robert T. Farrell

Cornell University Press

ITHACA AND LONDON

This book has been published with the aid
of a grant from the Hull Memorial
Publication Fund of Cornell University.

First published 1979 by Cornell University Press.
Published in the United Kingdom by Cornell University Press Ltd.,
2–4 Brook Street, London W1Y 1AA.

Second printing 1980

International Standard Book Number 0-8014-1038-X
Library of Congress Catalog Card Number 78-58032

Printed in the United States of America.

*Librarians: Library of Congress cataloging information
appears on the last page of the book.*

Contents

[5

Preface

J. R. R. TOLKIEN has long been known to the world as a superb storyteller. He was also a scholar whose exploration of language and literature made possible important advances in our knowledge of the Middle Ages. This volume is a tribute to a richly learned scholar and storyteller from his students and colleagues.

Part One offers an introduction to the man himself and includes his previously unpublished valedictory address. The essays of Part Two represent Professor Tolkien's major interests— Old Norse, Old English, and Middle English. The quality and range of the contributions are evidence of the inspiration he provided. Part Three examines his popular writings, especially *The Lord of the Rings*. *The Silmarillion*, which was published after these essays were prepared, is not treated.

My colleague John P. White first suggested this volume to me. I am most grateful to Sister Prudence Wilson, my Principal, for allowing me the time necessary to work on it, and to Mr. Christopher Tolkien and Miss Priscilla Tolkien for their help in many ways. I am particularly indebted to Professor Rosemary Cramp for introducing me to Cornell University Press and Professor Robert Farrell; and to Miss Patricia M. Kean for a valuable suggestion. My brother Joseph Salu and Mrs. Eleanor Hubbucks have both helped by taking burdens off my shoulders during the preparation of this book.

Robert Farrell greatly helped to improve the manuscript for publication, with the able assistance of Mrs. Janet Godden of Oxford and several of his graduate students at Cornell University, including Susan Kruse, Susan Straight, and James Barribeau. The editors of Cornell University Press were generous with their time and advice.

We are grateful to the *Heythrop Journal* for permission to reprint, with revisions, the article by William Dowie, and to

[7

George Allen and Unwin Ltd and the Houghton Mifflin Company for permission to reproduce extracts from the three-volume hardcover edition of *The Lord of the Rings* (London and Boston, 1966). The obituary notice of Professor Tolkien is reproduced from *The Times* by permission.

It is with deep regret that I write of the death of Miss Rosemary Estelle Woolf in April 1978. Her declining health brought her great hardship, which she countered with courage and fortitude. I hope the publication of her essay in this book will help to perpetuate the memory of a distinguished and graceful scholar.

MARY SALU

Newcastle upon Tyne

PART ONE

Professor J. R. R. Tolkien

Creator of Hobbits and inventor
of a new mythology

The Times, LONDON, 3 SEPTEMBER 1973

PROFESSOR J. R. R. TOLKIEN, CBE, Rawlinson and Bosworth Professor of Anglo-Saxon at Oxford from 1925 to 1945,
and from 1945 to 1959 Merton Professor of English Language
and Literature, died yesterday at the age of 81.

He was the author of *The Hobbit* and *The Lord of the Rings*,
two much loved and immensely popular books, which sold millions of copies and have been translated into scores of languages.
He was created CBE last year.

John Ronald Reuel Tolkien was born on January 3, 1892, at
Bloemfontein, South Africa, where his father died in 1896. The
family returned to England, where Tolkien's early years were
passed in what was then Worcestershire country, though now
buried in the red brick of outer Birmingham.

He was taught by his mother, from whom he derived all his
bents and early knowledge, linguistic, romantic, and naturalist.
To his descent through her, from the Suffields (originally of
Evesham) he used to attribute that love for the Western Marches
which manifested itself alike in Mercian studies (his primary
philological interest) and in the elvish or "hobbity" strain of his

imagination. In those days he had an "almost idolatrous" love of trees and flowers and a hunger for Arthurian romance, classical mythology, and especially George Macdonald.

In 1903 he went with a scholarship (gained by his mother's teaching) to King Edward's School, Birmingham, of which he reported much good and little evil. His form master, George Brewerton (a "fierce teacher"), introduced him to Chaucer in the correct pronunciation and lent him an Anglo-Saxon grammar; and R. W. Reynolds introduced him to literary criticism. In 1900 he had already, with his mother and brother, been received into the Church of Rome, and on his mother's death in 1904 Fr Francis Morgan, of the Birmingham Oratory, became his guardian. Of Fr Morgan Tolkien always spoke with the warmest gratitude and affection.

In 1910 he won an exhibition at Exeter College, Oxford. By the high standards of King Edward's School the award was tolerable rather than praiseworthy, and indeed Tolkien used to describe himself as "one of the idlest boys Gilson (the Headmaster) ever had." But "idleness" in his case meant private and unaided studies in Gothic, Anglo-Saxon and Welsh, and the first attempt at inventing a language—of which more hereafter.

He came into residence in 1911. Dr Jackson was still Rector and the College had no resident classical tutor until the appointment of E. A. Barber. He came too late to be of much help and Tolkien took only a 2nd in Honour Moderations, having somewhat neglected his studies in favour of "Old Norse, festivity, and classical philology." "My love for the classics," he once said, "took ten years to recover from lectures on Cicero and Demosthenes."

It was at this period that he first came under the influence of Joseph Wright; and he was now busily engaged on the invention of the "Elvish language." This was no arbitrary gibberish but a really possible tongue with consistent roots, sound laws, and inflexions, into which he poured all his imaginative and philological powers; and strange as the exercise may seem it was undoubtedly the source of that unparalleled richness and concreteness which later distinguished him from all other philologists. He had been inside language. He had not gone far with his invention before he discovered that every language pre-supposes a mythology; and at once began to fill in the mythology presupposed by Elvish.

In 1915 he took a First in English. Sisam and Craigie had been his tutors and Napier his professor. Immediately after Schools he entered the Lancashire Fusiliers. In 1916 he married Edith Bratt, whom he had known since boyhood. In 1918 he was back at Oxford, invalided out of the Army, and began to teach for the English School; E. V. Gordon was among his first pupils.

From 1920 to 1925 he worked at Leeds, first as Reader in English and later as Professor of English Language. George Gordon, E. V. Gordon and Lascelles Abercrombie were his colleagues, and some of his best work was done in building up a flourishing department of English Philology from small beginnings.

In 1925 he succeeded Craigie at Oxford as Rawlinson and Bosworth Professor of Anglo-Saxon, and in 1945 vacated that chair to become Merton Professor of English Language and Literature.

His Middle English Vocabulary had appeared in 1922. His edition of *Sir Gawain and the Green Knight* (in collaboration with E. V. Gordon) followed in 1925; *Beowulf: the Monsters and the Critics* in 1937; his Andrew Lang Lecture (on Fairy Tales) in 1939. He became an Hon D Litt of University College, Dublin, and of Liege in 1954.

His most extensive researches were in the West Midland dialect from the Anglo-Saxon period to that of the *Ancrene Riwle*; in this work his most distinguished pupil was Professor d'Ardenne. He retired from the Merton professorship on reaching the age limit in 1959 and was later elected an emeritus fellow of the college.

During the years 1925–35 he was, more than any other single man, responsible for closing the old rift between "literature" and "philology" in English studies at Oxford and thus giving the existing school its characteristic temper. His unique insight at once into the language of poetry and into the poetry of language qualified him for this task.

[13

Thus the private language and its offshoot, the private mythology, were directly connected with some of the most highly practical results he achieved, while they continued in private to burgeon into tales and poems which seldom reached print, though they might have won him fame in almost any period but the twentieth century.

The Hobbit (1937) was in origin a fragment from this cycle adapted for juvenile tastes but with one all important novelty, the Hobbits themselves. It is doubtful how far he realized that these comfort-loving, unambitious, and (in aspiration) unheroic creatures embodied what he loved best in the English character and saw most endangered by the growth of "subtopia," bureaucracy, journalism, and industrialization.

They soon demanded to be united with his heroic myth on a far deeper level than *The Hobbit* had allowed, and by 1936 he was at work on his great romance *The Lord of the Rings*, published in three volumes (1954 and 1955) and often reprinted and translated. The ironic destiny which links the humble happiness of Hobbits to the decision of vast issues which they would gladly ignore, and which even makes civilization itself momentarily dependent on their latent and reluctant courage, is its central theme. It has no allegory.

These things were not devised to reflect any particular situation in the real world. It was the other way round; real events began, horribly, to conform to the pattern he had freely invented. Hence those who heard the growing work read chapter by chapter in the months that followed the fall of France found it as relevant, as stern, and tonic, as Churchill's promise of blood, sweat and tears. It cut right across all contemporary canons of criticism, and its success, when published, surprised and delighted the author and his friends.

Tolkien's spirited farce *Farmer Giles of Ham* (1954) was work of a wholly different type.

Only a tithe of the poems, translations, articles, lectures and notes in which his multifarious interest found expression ever reached the printer. His standard of self criticism was high and the mere suggestion of publication usually set him upon a revision, in the course of which so many new ideas occurred to him that where his friends had hoped for the final text of an old work they actually got the first draft of a new one.

He was a man of "cronies" rather than of general society and was always best after midnight (he had a Johnsonian horror of going to bed) and in some small circle of intimates where the tone was at once Bohemian, literary, and Christian (for he was profoundly religious).

He has been described as "the best and worst talker in Oxford"—worst for the rapidity and indistinctness of his speech, and best for the penetration, learning, humour and "race" of what he said. C. L. Wrenn, R. B. McCallum of Pembroke, H. V. D. Dyson of Merton, C. S. Lewis of Magdalen, and Charles Williams were among those who most often made his audience (and interrupters) on such occasions.

Valedictory Address to the University of Oxford, 5 June 1959

J. R. R. Tolkien

I︎T might be held characteristic that, though I have occupied two chairs (or sat uneasily on the edge of two chairs) in this university, I have not yet delivered an inaugural lecture: I am now about 34 years behind. At the time of my first election I was too astonished (a feeling that has never quite left me) to gather my wits, until I had already given many ordinary lectures as required by statute, and it seemed to me that an inaugural that would not inaugurate was a ceremony better omitted. On the second occasion, my ineffectiveness as a lecturer was already well known, and well-wishers had made sure (by letter or otherwise) that I should know it too; so I thought it unnecessary to give a special exhibition of this unfórtunate defect. And, though twenty years had then gone by, during which this matter of the overdue inaugural had been much on my mind, I had not yet discovered anything special to say.

Fourteen more years have now passed, and I still have nothing special to say. Nothing, that is, of the kind proper to inaugurals—as far as I can judge by those that I have read: the products of minds more sanguine, or more efficient and magisterial than mine. The diagnosis of what is wrong, and the confident prescription of the cure; the wide view, the masterly survey; plans and prophecies: these have never been in my line. I would always rather try to wring the juice out of a single sentence, or explore the implications of one word than try to sum up a period in a lecture, or pot a poet in a paragraph. And I am afraid that what I would rather do is what I have usually done.

For I suppose that, at any rate since the golden days long past when English studies were unorganized, a hobby and not a trade, few more amateurish persons can "by a set of curious circumstances" have been put in a professional position. For thirty-four years my heart has gone out to poor Koko, taken from a county jail; though I had one advantage over him. He was appointed to cut off heads, and did not really like it. Philology was part of my job, and I enjoyed it. I have always found it amusing. But I have never had strong views about it. I do not think it necessary to salvation. I do not think it should be thrust down the throats of the young, as a pill, the more efficacious the nastier it tastes.

But if the ranks of Tuscany should feel inclined to cheer, let me hasten to assure them that I do not think their wares are necessary to salvation either; much of what they offer is peddler's stuff. I have indeed become more, not less, bigoted as a result of experience in the little world of academic English studies.

"Bigoted" is for the Tuscans. Speaking to the Romans, defending the city and the ashes of their fathers, I would say "convinced". Convinced of what? Convinced that Philology is never nasty: except to those deformed in youth or suffering from some congenital deficiency. I do not think that it should be thrust down throats as a pill, because I think that if such a process seems needed, the sufferers should not be here, at least not studying or teaching English letters. Philology is the foundation of humane letters; "misology" is a disqualifying defect or disease.

It is not, in my experience, a defect or disease found in those whose literary learning, wisdom, and critical acumen place them in the highest rank—to which so many in the Oxford School

[17

have in various ways attained. But there are other voices, epigonal rather than ancestral. I must confess that at times in the last thirty odd years I have been aggrieved by them; by those, afflicted in some degree by misology, who have decried what they usually call *language*. Not because they, poor creatures, have evidently lacked the imagination required for its enjoyment, or the knowledge needed for an opinion about it. Dullness is to be pitied. Or so I hope, being myself dull at many points. But dullness should be confessed with humility; and I have therefore felt it a grievance that certain professional persons should suppose their dullness and ignorance to be a human norm, the measure of what is good; and anger when they have sought to impose the limitation of their minds upon younger minds, dissuading those with philological curiosity from their bent, encouraging those without this interest to believe that their lack marked them as minds of a superior order.

But I am, as I say, an amateur. And if that means that I have neglected parts of my large field, devoting myself mainly to those things that I personally *like*, it does also mean that I have tried to awake *liking*, to communicate delight in those things that I find enjoyable. And that without suggesting that they were the only proper source of profit, or pleasure, for students of English.

I have heard sneers at certain elementary kinds of linguistic "research" as mere spelling-counting. Let the phonologist and the orthographer have their swink to them reserved! Of course. And the same to the bibliographer and typographer—still further removed from the living speech of men which is the beginning of all literature. Contemplating the workings of the B.Litt. sausage-machine, I have at times dared to think that some of the *botuli*, or *farcimina*, turned out were hardly either tasty or nourishing, even when claimed to be "literary". But, to use a perhaps more apt simile, the twin peaks of Parnassus are approached through some very dim valleys. If scrambling in these, without any climbing, is sometimes rewarded with a degree, one must hope that one of the peaks at least has been glimpsed from afar.

However, that is not a matter which I wish to explore deeply: that is, "research" and "research degrees" in relation to the ordinary courses of learning—the so-called "postgraduate" activities, which have in recent years shown such rapid growth, forming what one might call our "hydroponic" department. A term which, I fear, I only know from science-fiction, in which it seems to refer to the cultivation of plants without soil in enclosed vehicles far removed from this world.

But all fields of study and enquiry, all great Schools, demand human sacrifice. For their primary object is not culture, and their academic uses are not limited to education. Their roots are in the desire for knowledge, and their life is maintained by those who pursue some love or curiosity for its own sake, without reference even to personal improvement. If this individual love and curiosity fails, their tradition becomes sclerotic.

There is no need, therefore, to despise, no need even to feel pity for months or years of life sacrificed in some minimal enquiry: say, the study of some uninspired mediaeval text and its fumbling dialect; or of some miserable "modern" poetaster and his life (nasty, dreary, and fortunately short)—NOT IF the sacrifice is voluntary, and IF it is inspired by a genuine curiosity, spontaneous or personally felt.

But that being granted, one must feel grave disquiet, when the legitimate inspiration is not there; when the subject or topic of "research" is imposed, or is "found" for a candidate out of some one else's bag of curiosities, or is thought by a committee to be a sufficient exercise for a degree. Whatever may have been found useful in other spheres, there is a distinction between accepting the willing labour of many humble persons in building an English house and the erection of a pyramid with the sweat of degree-slaves.

But the matter is not, of course, as simple as all that. It is not just a question of the degeneration of real curiosity and enthusiasm into a 'planned economy', under which so much research time is stuffed into more or less standard skins and turned out in sausages of a size and shape approved by our own little printed cookery book. Even if that were a sufficient description of the system, I should hesitate to accuse anyone of planning it with foresight, or of approving it wholeheartedly now that we have got it. It has grown, partly by accident, partly by the accumulation of temporary expedients. Much thought has gone into

[19

it, and much devoted and little remunerated labour has been spent in administering it and in mitigating its evils.

It is an attempt to treat an old trouble and a real need with the wrong tool. The old trouble is the loss of the M.A. as a genuine degree. The real need is the desire for knowledge. The wrong tool is a 'research' degree, the proper scope of which is much more limited, and which functions much better when it is limited.

But the M.A. has become a reward for a small "post-graduate" subscription to the university and to a college, and is untouchable. Meanwhile many of the better students—I mean those who have studied English for love, or at least with love as one of their mixed motives—wish to spend *more time* in a university: more time in *learning* things, in a place where that process is (or should be) approved and given facilities. What is more, such students are still at a time of life, soon to pass, and the sooner the less the faculty is exercised, when the acquisition of knowledge is easier, and what is acquired is more permanent, more thoroughly digested and more formative. It is a pity that so often the last of the growing, feeding, years are spent in the premature attempt to add to knowledge, while the vast existing storehouses remain unvisited. Or if they are visited, too often this is done after the manner of research-mice running off with little bits nibbled out of unexplored sacks to build up a little thesis. But alas! those with the more eager minds are not necessarily those who possess more money. The powers that hold the purse-strings require a degree; and those who allot places in an over-crowded university require one too. And we have only a so-called research degree to offer them. This is, or can be, better than nothing. Many would-be learners do well enough at minor research. Some take the chance of using much of their time in reading what they wish, with little reference to their supposed task: that is, in doing on the side, hampered and left-handed, what they should be doing openly and unhindered. But the system cannot be praised for this accidental good that may in spite of it occur within it. It is not necessarily the swifter or wider mind that it is easiest to 'find a subject' for, or to bring down to brass tacks and business to the satisfaction of the Applications Committee. The ability to tackle competently and within approved limits a small subject is, in the early twenties, as likely to belong to a small and limited mind as to a future scholar with the hunger of youth.

If the reform that I always had at heart, if the B.Litt. regulations could have been altered (as I once hoped) to allow an alternative approach by examination, to reward reading and learning at least equally with minor research, I should have left the English School more happily. If even now the School could embrace the newer B.Phil. (an unnecessary and inappropriate additional degree-title), I should regard it as a far greater advance than any remodelling or "new look" given to the Honour syllabus.

As far as my personal experience goes, if I had been allowed to guide the further reading and study of those for whom the Honour School had opened vistas and awakened curiosity, I could have done more good in *less time* than in the so-called supervision of research, done by candidates who had essential territories yet to explore, and who, in the breathless march from Prelim. to Final Schools, had also left much country in rear, only raided and not occupied.

There are always exceptions. I have met some. I have had the good fortune to be associated (the right word) with some able researching graduates, more of them than my small aptitude for the task of supervisor has merited. Some of them took to research like otters to swimming. But they were the apparent exceptions that prove the thesis. They were the natural researchers (the existence of whom I have never denied). They knew what they wanted to do, and the regions that they desired to explore. They acquired new knowledge and organized it quickly, because it was knowledge that they desired to have anyway: it and the particular enquiry were all of one piece; there was no mere mugging up.

I said that I did not wish to explore the matter of the organization of research deeply; but I have nonetheless spoken (for such an occasion) too long about it. Before I stand down finally, I must say something about our main business: the Final Honour School. Not that the topics are unconnected. I think that the possibility of taking a higher, or at least a further, degree for learning things, for acquiring more of the essential parts of the English field, or for digging deeper in some of them, might well have good effects on the Honour School. In brief: if the abler students, the future scholars, commonly took a *third* public examination, it might no longer be felt necessary to arrange in the *second* public examination a four-year syllabus for the reading-time of two years and a bit.[1]

It is in any case, I suppose, obvious that our Honour syllabus is over-crowded, and that the changes that come into force next year have not done much to cure this. The reasons are various. For one thing, related to the situation of the M.A., three years is supposed, in this land, to be quite long enough to play with books in a university, and four years is extravagant. But while the academic *vita* is shortened, the *ars* gets longer. We now have on our hands *one thousand and two hundred years* of recorded English letters, a long unbroken line, indivisible, no part of which can without loss be ignored. The claims of the great nineteenth century will soon be succeeded by the clamour of the twentieth. What is more, to the honour of English but not to the convenience of syllabus-planners, some of the earliest writings show vitality and talent that makes them worthy of study in themselves, quite apart from the special interest of their earliness. So-called Anglo-Saxon cannot be regarded merely as a root, it is already in flower. But it is a root, for it exhibits qualities and characteristics that have remained ever since a steadfast ingredient in English; and it demands therefore at least some first-hand acquaintance from every serious student of English speech and English letters. This demand the Oxford School has up to now always recognized, and has tried to meet.

1. An alternative would be the provision, beside the ordinary Preliminary, of an English Honour Moderations, which would enable the abler or more ambitious to spend four years in reading. It would, I think, be less useful in the English School, the variety and scope of which is little exhibited or understood at earlier stages. Our need is rather to provide for those who first at a university discover what there is to know and do, and what are their true bents and talents.

In such a range divergence of interests, or at any rate of expertise, is inevitable. But the difficulties have not been helped, indeed they have been bedevilled, by the emergence of two legendary figures, the bogeys *Lang* and *Lit*. So I prefer to call them, since the words language and *literature*, though commonly misused among us, should not be thus degraded. Popular mythology seems to believe that *Lang* came from a cuckoo-egg laid in the nest, in which he takes up too much room and usurps the worms of the *Lit*. chicken. Some believe that *Lit* was the cuckoo, bent on extruding her nest-fellow or sitting on him; and they have more support from the actual history of our School. But neither tale is well-founded.

In a Bestiary more nearly reflecting the truth *Lang* and *Lit* would appear as Siamese Twins, Jekyll-Hyde and Hyde-Jekyll, indissolubly joined from birth, with two heads, but only one heart, the health of both being much better when they do not quarrel. This allegory at least resembles more closely our older statute: *Every candidate will be expected to show a competent knowledge of both sides of the subject, and equal weight in the examination will be attached to each.*

What the "sides" were was to be deduced from the title of the School which we still bear: *The Honour School of English Language and Literature*. Though this becomes in the running headline: *English Language, etc.* And that I have always thought a more just title; not that we require the *etc.* The full title was, I think, a mistake; and it has in any case had some unfortunate results. *Language* and *Literature* appear as "sides" of one subject. That was harmless enough, and indeed true enough, as long as "sides" meant, as it should, aspects and emphases, which since they were of "equal weight" in the subject as a whole, were neither of them normally exclusive, neither the sole property of this or that scholar, nor the sole object of any one course of study.

But alas! "sides" suggested "parties", and too many then took sides. And thus there entered in *Lang* and *Lit*, the uneasy nest-fellows, each trying to grab more of the candidates' time, whatever the candidates might think.

I first joined the School in 1912—by the generosity of Exeter College to one who had been up to then an unprofitable exhibitioner; if he learned anything at all, he learned it at the wrong time: I did most of my undergraduate work on the Germanic languages before Honour Moderations; when English and its kindred became my job, I turned to other tongues, even to Latin and Greek; and I took a liking to *Lit* as soon as I had joined the side of *Lang*. Certainly I joined the side of *Lang*, and I found the party-breach already wide; and unless my recollections are mistaken, it went on widening for some time. When I came back from Leeds in 1925, WE no longer meant students of English, it meant adherents of *Lang* or of *Lit*. THEY meant all those on the other side: people of infinite guile, who needed constant watching, lest THEY should down US. And, the rascals, so they did!

For if you have Sides with labels, you will have Partisans. Faction fights, of course, are often fun, especially to the bellicose; but it is not clear that they do any good, any more good in Oxford than in Verona. Things may to some have seemed duller in the long period during which the hostility was damped; and to such they may seem livelier if the smoulder breaks out again. I hope not. It would have been better if it had never been kindled.

Removal of the misunderstanding of words may sometimes produce amity. So though the time left is short, I will now consider the misuse of *language* and *literature* in our School. I think the initial mistake was made when *The School of English Language and Literature* was first adopted as our title. Those who love it call it the *School of English* or the *English School*—in which, if I may intrude a *Lang* remark, the word *English* is not an adjective, but a noun in loose composition. This simple title, *School of English*, is sufficient. And if any should say "English what?", I would answer: "For a thousand recorded years *English* as a noun has meant only one thing: the English Language."

If the title then is made explicit, it should be *The School of English Language*. The parallel formula is held good enough for our peers, for French and Italian and others. But lest it be thought that this is a partisan choice, let me say that actually, for reasons that I will give, I should be well content with *Literature* —if *Letters* is now too archaic.

We hold, I suppose, that the study of *Letters* in all languages that possess them is "humane", but that Latin and Greek are 'more humane'. It may, however, be observed that the first part of the School of humaner letters is stated to be "The Greek and Latin Languages"; and that is defined as including "the minute critical study of authors . . . the history of Ancient Literature" (that is *Lit*) "and Comparative Philology as illustrating the Greek and Latin Languages" (that is *Lang*).

But of course it can be objected that English, in an English-speaking university, is in a different position from other Letters. The English language is assumed to be, and usually is, the native language of the students (if not always in a Standard form that would have been approved by my predecessor). They do not have to learn it. As a venerable professor of Chemistry once said to me—I hasten to add that he is dead, and did not belong to Oxford—"I do not know why you want a department of English Language; I know English, but I also know some chemistry."

Nonetheless I think that it was a mistake to intrude *Language* into our title in order to mark this difference, or to warn the ignorant. Not least because *Language* is thus given, as indeed I suspect was intended, an artificially limited and pseudo-technical sense which separates this technical thing from *Literature*. This separation is false, and this use of the word "language" is false.

The right and natural sense of Language includes Literature, just as Literature includes the study of the language of literary works. *Litteratura*, proceeding from the elementary sense "a collection of letters; an alphabet", was used as an equivalent of Greek *grammatike* and *philologia*: that is, the study of grammar and idiom, and the critical study of authors (largely of linguistic kind). Those things it should always still include. But even if some now wish to use the word "literature" more narrowly, to mean the study of writings that have artistic purpose or form, with as little reference as possible to *grammatike* or *philologia*, this

[25

"literature" remains an operation of Language. Literature is, maybe, the highest operation or function of Language, but it is nonetheless Language. We may except only certain subsidiaries and adminicles: such as those enquiries concerned with the physical forms in which writings have been preserved or propagated, epigraphy, palaeography, printing, and publishing. These may be, and often are, carried on without reference to content or meaning, and as such are neither Language nor Literature; though they may furnish evidence to both.

Only *one* of these words, *Language* and *Literature*, is therefore needed in a reasonable title. *Language* as the larger term is a natural choice. To choose *Literature* would be to indicate, rightly as I think, that the *central* (central if not sole) business of Philology in the Oxford School is the study of the language of *literary* texts, or of those that illuminate the history of the English literary language. We do not include some parts of linguistic study. We do not, for instance, teach directly "the language as it is spoken and written at the present day", as is done in Schools concerned with modern languages other than English. Nor are our students made to compose verses or to write proses in the archaic idioms that they are expected to learn, as are students of the Greek and Latin languages.

But whatever may be thought or done about the title of our School, I wish fervently that this abuse in local slang of the word *language* might be for ever abandoned! It suggests, and is used to suggest, that certain kinds of knowledge concerning authors and their medium of expression is unnecessary and "unliterary" the interest only of cranks not of cultured or sensitive minds. And even so it is misapplied in time. In local parlance it is used to cover everything, within our historical range, that is mediaeval or older—except "Chaucer and his Contemporaries". It thus contrives to smear some of the tar not only on Mediaeval philology but also on Mediaeval literature. Except of course Chaucer. His merits as a major poet are too obvious to be obscured; though it was in fact Language, or Philology, that demonstrated, as only Language could, two things of first-rate literary importance: that he was not a fumbling beginner, but a master of metrical technique; and that he was an inheritor, a middle point, and not a "father". Nonetheless, it is in the backward dark of "Anglo-Saxon" and "Semi-Saxon" that Language, now reduced to bogey *Lang*, is supposed to have his lair. Though alas! he may come down like Grendel from the moors to raid the "literary" fields. He has (for instance) theories about puns and rhymes!

But this popular picture is of course absurd. It is the product of ignorance and muddled thinking. It confuses three things, quite different. Two of them are confined to no period and to no "Side"; and one though it may attract specialist attention (as do other departments of English studies) is also confined to no period, is neither dark, nor mediaeval, nor modern, but universal.

We have *first:* the linguistic effort and attention required for the reading of all texts with intelligence, even those in so-called "modern" English. Of course this effort increases as we go back in time, as does the effort (with which it goes hand in hand) to appreciate the art, the thought and feeling, or the allusions of an author. Both reach their climax in "Anglo-Saxon", which has become almost a foreign language. But this learning of an idiom and its implications, in order to understand and enjoy literary or historical texts, is no more "language", as an enemy of "literature", *Lang* as opposed to *Lit*, than the reading of, say, Vergil or Dante. And it is at least arguable that *some* exercise of that kind of effort and attention is specially needed in a School in which so much of the literature read seems (to the careless and insensitive) to be sufficiently interpreted by the current colloquial speech.

We have *second:* actual technical philology, and linguistic history. But this is confined to no period, and is concerned with all aspects of written or living speech at any time: with the barbarous forms of English that may be met today as much as with the refined forms that may be found a thousand years ago. It may be "technical", as are all departments of our studies, but it is not incompatible with a love of literature, nor is the acquisition of its technique fatal to the sensibility either of critics or of authors. If it seems too much concerned with "sounds", with the audible structure of words, that is because this aspect is basic: one must know one's letters before one can read. If it seems most exercised in the older periods, that is because any historical enquiry must

begin with the earliest available evidence. But there is also another reason, which leads to the *third* thing.

The *third* thing is the use of the findings of a special enquiry,
not specifically "literary", for other and more literary purposes.
Technical philology can serve the purposes of textual and literary criticism at all times. If it seems most exercised in the
older periods, if the scholars who deal with them make most use
of philology, that is because it was Philology that rescued these
things from oblivion and ignorance, that presented to lovers of
poetry and history fragments of a noble past that without it
would have remained for ever dead and dark. But it can also
rescue many things that it is valuable to know from a past far
nearer than the Old English period. It seems strange that the use
of it seems by some to be regarded as less 'literary' than the use
of the evidence provided by other studies not directly concerned
with literature or literary criticism; not only major matters such
as the history of art and thought and religion, but even minor
matters such as bibliography. Which is nearer akin to a poem, its
metre or the paper on which it is printed? Which will bring
more to life poetry, rhetoric, dramatic speech or even plain
prose: some knowledge of the language, even of the pronunciation, of its period, or the typographical details of its
printed form?

Mediaeval spelling remains just a dull department of *Lang*.
Milton's spelling seems now to have become part of *Lit*. Almost
the whole of the introduction in the *Everyman* edition of his
poems, which is recommended to the students for our Preliminary, is devoted to it. But even if not all of those who deal with
this facet of Milton criticism show an expert grasp of the history
of English sounds and spelling, enquiry into his orthography
and its relation to his metre remains just *Lang*, though it may be
employed in the service of criticism.

Some divisions in our School are inevitable, because the
very length of the history of English Letters makes mastery all
along the line difficult even to the widest sympathy and taste.
These divisions should not be by *Lang* and *Lit*, they should only
be by period. All scholars should be to an adequate if not to an
expert degree, within their own special period both *Lang* and

Lit, that is both philologists and critics. We say in our Regulations that all candidates taking papers in English Literature (from *Beowulf* to A.D. 1900) "will be expected to show such knowledge of the history of England as is necessary for the profitable study of the authors and periods which they offer." And if the candidates, the teachers too, one may suppose. But if the history of England, which though profitable is more remote, why not the history of English?

No doubt this point of view is more widely understood than it once was. But minds are still confused. Let us glance again at Chaucer, that old poet out in the No-man's land of debate. There was knifework, axe-work, out there between the barbed wire of *Lang* and *Lit* in days not so far back. When I was a young and enthusiastic examiner, to relieve the burden of my literary colleagues (at which they loudly groaned), I offered to set the Chaucer paper, or to help in reading the scripts. I was astonished at the heat and hostility with which I was refused. My fingers were dirty: I was *Lang*.

That hostility has now happily died down; there is some fraternization between the barbed wire. But it was that hostility which, in the reformed syllabus of the early thirties (still in essentials surviving), made necessary the prescription of *two* papers dealing with Chaucer and his chief contemporaries. *Lit* would not allow the greedy hands of *Lang* to soil the poet. *Lang* could not accept the flimsy and superficial papers set by *Lit*. But now, with the latest reform, or mild modification, that comes into force next year, once more Chaucer is presented in one common paper. Rightly, I should have said. But alas! What do we see? "Candidates for Courses I and II may be required to answer questions on language"!

Here we have hallowed in print this pernicious slang misuse. Not "*his* language", or "*their* language", or even "the language of the period"; just "language". What in the name of scholarship, or poetry, or reason, can that here mean? It *should* mean, in English fit to appear in documents of the University of Oxford, that certain candidates may be asked questions of general linguistic import, without limitation of time or place, on a paper testing knowledge of the great poetry of the Fourteenth Cen-

[29

tury, under the general heading "English Literature". But since that is lunatic, one must suppose that something else is meant.

What kind of question can it mean which no candidate of Course III need ever touch? Is it wicked to enquire, in paper or *viva voce*, what here or there Chaucer really meant, by word or form, or idiom? Is metre and verse-technique of no concern to sensitive literary minds? Must nothing in any way related to Chaucer's medium of expression be ever allowed to disturb the cotton wool of poor Course III? Then why not add that only Courses I and II may be required to answer questions that refer to history or politics or religion?

The logical result of this attitude, indeed its only rational expression would be this direction: "Courses I and II may be expected to show knowledge of Chaucer in the original; Course III will use a translation into our contemporary idiom". *But*, if this translation, as may well happen, should at any point be erroneous, this may *not* be mentioned. That would be "language".

I have once or twice, not so long ago, been asked to explain or defend this *language:* to say how it can possibly be profitable or enjoyable. As if I were some curious wizard with arcane knowledge, with a secret recipe that I was unwilling to divulge. To compare the less with the greater, is not that rather like asking an astronomer what he finds in mathematics? Or a theologian what is the interest of the textual criticism of Scripture? As in Andrew Lang's fable a missionary turned on a critic with the words: "Did Paul know Greek?"

I did not accept the challenge. I did not answer, for I knew no answer that would not appear uncivil. But I might have said: "If you do not know any *language*, learn some—or try to. You should have done so long ago. The knowledge is not hidden. If you cannot learn, or find the stuff distasteful, then keep humbly quiet. You are a deaf man at a concert. If you do not specially enjoy old wine of a good vintage, drink some. Drink again. Persevere. Take it with your other meats—and perhaps cut down on whiskey!" Grammar is for all, though not all may rise to star-spangled grammar.

I have said enough, perhaps more than enough for this occasion. I must now get out of the chair and finally stand down. I have not made any effective *apologia pro consulatu meo*, for none is really possible. Probably my best act in it is in the leaving of it— especially in handing it on to its elected occupant, Norman Davis. Already one of the chairborne, he will know that in the cosy cushions, which legend furnishes for professorial seats, many thorns lurk among the stuffing. But as Henry Cecil Wyld replied when I wrote to congratulate him on his election: "if there are any *dyrne gastas* still about, I will deal with them." Alas! He was not Beowulf.

If we consider what Merton College and what the Oxford School of English owes to the Antipodes, to the Southern Hemisphere, especially to scholars born in Australia and New Zealand, it may well be felt that it is only just that one of them should now ascend an Oxford chair of English. Indeed it may be thought that justice has been delayed since 1925. There are of course other lands under the Southern Cross. I was born in one; though I do not claim to be the most learned of those who have come hither from the far end of the Dark Continent. But I have the hatred of *apartheid* in my bones; and most of all I detest the segregation or separation of Language and Literature. I do not care which of them you think White.

But even as I step off—not quite the condemned criminal, I hope, that the phrase suggests—I cannot help recalling some of the salient moments in my academic past. The vastness of Joe Wright's dining-room table (when I sat alone at one end learning the elements of Greek philology from glinting glasses in the further gloom); the kindness of William Craigie to a jobless soldier in 1918; the privilege of knowing even the sunset of the days of Henry Bradley; my first glimpse of the unique and dominant figure of Charles Talbut Onions, darkly surveying me, a fledgling prentice in the Dictionary Room (then fiddling with the slips for WAG and WALRUS and WAMPUM); serving under the generous captaincy of George Gordon in Leeds; seeing Henry Cecil Wyld wreck a table in the Cadena Cafe with the vigour of his representation of Finnish minstrels chanting the

Kalevala. And of course many other moments, not forgotten if not mentioned: and many other men and women of the Studium Anglicanum: some dead, some venerable, some retired, some translated elsewhither, some yet young and very much with us still; but all (or nearly all—I cannot say fairer than that and remain honest) nearly all dear to my heart.

If then with understanding I contemplate this venerable foundation, I now myself *frod on ferðe* am moved to exclaim:

> Hwǽr cwóm mearh, hwǽr cwóm mago? Hwǽr cwóm maðumgyfa?
> Hwǽr cwóm symbla gesetu? Hwǽr sindon seledréamas?
> Ealá, beorht bune! Ealá, byrnwiga!
> Ealá, þéodnes þrym! Hú seo þrág gewát,
> Genáp under niht-helm, swa heo nó wǽre!

> (But that is 'Language')

> Ai! laurië lantar lassi súrinen!
> Yéni unótime ve rámar aldaron!
> Yéni ve linte yuldar vánier —
> Sí man i yulma nin enquantuva?[2]

> (But that is 'Nonsense')

In 1925 when I was untimely elevated to the *stól* of Anglo-Saxon, I was inclined to add:

> Nearon nu cyningas ne cáseras
> Ne goldgiefan swylce iú wǽron!

But now when I survey with eye or mind those who may be called my pupils, though rather in the sense of the 'apples of my eyes'; those who have taught me much (not least *trawþe*, that is, fidelity), who have gone on to a learning to which I have not attained; or when I see how many scholars could more than worthily have succeeded me; then I perceive with gladness that the *duguð* has not yet fallen by the wall, and the *dréam* is not yet silenced.

2. Alas! as gold fall the leaves in the wind:
   Years innumerable as the wings of trees!
   Years like swift draughts of wine have passed away—
   Who now will fill again the cup for me?

I

The Man and the Scholar

S. T. R. O. d'Ardenne

UNIVERSITY OF LIEGE

WHEN I was asked to contribute to the Tolkien memorial volume I felt greatly honoured, but at the same time greatly embarrassed. Tolkien's personality was so rich, so diverse, so vast and so elusive, that I was quite at a loss to choose which aspect of it to study.

Now there was in Tolkien's personality such *humanity* that I thought I might try my hand there. But as soon as I broached the subject, so many aspects of him were revealed that I was left still more perplexed: should it be the Christian, or the friend, the artist or the humanist, the father or the teacher? I hesitated between the last two, for they have in common the same paternal quality.

Thus my contribution to the Tolkien memorial volume is based on the vivid memories I have kept of several visits I paid to his house, and on a friendship which extended over forty years —a long span indeed. During these visits I gained firsthand knowledge of the man and the scholar. Hence the title of this modest contribution.

Among the different aspects of Tolkien's *humanity*, there is one which deserves special attention, that of the *paterfamilias*. All his letters, extending over about forty years, tell of his concern about his children's health, their comfort, their future; how best he could help them to succeed in life, and how to make their lives as perfect as possible. He started by giving them a most pleasant childhood, creating for them the deep sense of home, which had been denied to him, as he lost his father when he was a small child, and his splendid mother a few years later. And to provide all this Tolkien accepted the heavy and tedious burden of examining in several English universities, which, of course, took up much time that he might have devoted to his research. But, however busy he was, he always found time to rush home and kiss his younger children goodnight.

And it was this great love of his children that prompted him to invent and create the delightful hobbits and their mythology. They were wildly discussed at the breakfast table and in the nursery. Finally, Father Christmas heard of them, and took a great interest in them—so much so that every Christmas brought a letter, written in Tolkien's beautiful (but shaky) hand and adorned with beautiful paintings illustrating the adventures which had happened to the hobbits during the year. And Father Christmas was very particular that his letters should not go astray. He delivered them himself, leaving on the spotlessly clean carpet a very dirty and disreputable footprint as his signature, an irrefutable proof of the authenticity of the letters.

Those lovely letters were the origin of *The Hobbit*, which soon made Tolkien famous, and the starting point of the later 'fairy tale for grown-ups', the great trilogy of *The Lord of the Rings*.

Now, they are not fairy tales of the usual type—very attractive, easily read and still more easily forgotten, leaving no indelible mark on the reader or on the teller. What makes them so unusual and powerful was that, among other things, Tolkien was a genuine philologist. And it was as such that W. H. Auden hailed him in his 'Short Ode to a Philologist' (*English and Medieval Studies* [London, 1962], pp. 11–12), and did not hesitate to call him 'a bard to Anglo-Saxon', that is, 'a true lover of the word', endowed with boundless imagination. I said to him once: 'You broke the veil, didn't you, and passed through?' which in fact he did and which he readily admitted. No wonder therefore that he could recapture the language of the fairies, and he mastered it so completely that he was able (and dared) to write 'fairy poems' worthy to be read at Oberon's Court.

34]

Tolkien belonged to that very rare class of linguists, now becoming extinct, who like the Grimm brothers could understand and recapture the glamour of 'the word'. 'In the beginning was the Word, and the Word was with God, and the Word was God'.

This love of the Word led him to study languages wherever he could find them,[1] with the result that his knowledge of languages other than his native English was amazing, and filled his students with wonder mingled with awe: he was so learned! Old Celtic, Old Welsh, Old Norse, Old French among many others, to say nothing of the profound knowledge of Greek and Latin— he was proud to claim that he 'was brought up on the classics'— were familiar to him, and not only the languages themselves, but their remote dialects! One day he took my breath away. He had been lecturing on Chaucer. After the lecture, he suddenly said to me: 'In your native Eastern Walloon dialect, the French word *beau* must be pronounced *bê* (*bę̀*), with a slack low *ę̀* as in French *bête*, or the first element of the vocalic part of Modern English *bêar*', which indeed is its right pronunciation. I was so surprised that my answer could only be expressed in my native dialect: '*Vos-estez on bê*, which means, *mutatis mutandis:* 'You are a fine fellow!' Finding a new language aroused in Tolkien the same enthusiasm as that described by Max Müller[2] and Goethe when Sanskrit was newly discovered. For instance he told us that the discovery of Gothic[3] took him by storm, a sensation as full of delight as that aroused by 'first looking into Chapman's Homer', 'though', he added, 'I did not write a sonnet about it'. No, he simply 'tried to invent Gothic words'. This was indeed the first step towards the creation of a new language, with its own consistent spelling and strict grammar, with its own rhythm and metre, spelt with its own letters, which appears in *The Lord of the Rings*. Masefield's words on Chaucer can well be applied to Tolkien: 'Some tale of an unreal world is always wanted: to create it

1. "English and Welsh," *Angles and Britons: The O'Donnell Lectures* (Cardiff, 1963).

2. Friedrich Müller, *India, What Can It Teach Us* (New York, 1883), pp. 28–29. Cf. J. Mansion, *Esquisse d'une histoire de la langue sanskrite* (Paris, 1931), pp. 20–21.

3. "English and Welsh," p. 38.

is rapture, and to read it such fun'.[4] But a great part of the fun
he reserved for one group of readers who enjoyed the fact that
'the names of persons and places in this story [*The Lord of the
Rings*] were mainly composed from patterns deliberately modelled on those of Welsh (closely similar but not identical), which,
he added, 'probably has given more pleasure to a certain class of
readers than anything else in it'.[5] No wonder that Welsh, which
was supposed to have been the language of heaven, exerted a
special influence on him! In *The Hobbit*, however, the name of
the 'dwarves' and of Gandalf have come straight from *Völuspá*,
which gives to the work a tremendous sense of authenticity.

But when did Tolkien acquire that extraordinary knowledge
of languages so well described in his essay on 'English and
Welsh' (cited above)? Although I stayed at his house frequently,
I never knew when he got any sleep at night, for as has been said
'he had a Johnsonian horror of going to bed'. With Chaucer,
whom he knew so well, he must have muttered:

> And also domb as any stoon
> Thou sittest at another book
> Tyl fully daswed ys thy look.

So many books were left unfinished; so many were never
printed, unless some extracts from them appeared sporadically
in prefaces or as commentaries in other scholars' works, as for
instance his verse translation of *Beowulf*, never published; extracts appeared in his preface to the revised version of Clark
Hall's translation of *Beowulf and the Finnesburg Fragment*.[6] They
were printed to illustrate the important chapter on the metre,
which is indeed a very clear and original description of that
difficult part of Old English literature, which every student interested in Old English should read. Other translations of Old
English poems into Modern English are found in the second
volume of Tolkien's great trilogy, *The Two Towers*. He was not
only a *grant translateur:* he could write a long poem in Modern
English on 'The Homecoming of Beorhtnoth, Beorhthelm's

4. "Chaucer" in *The Leslie Stephens Lectures* (Cambridge, 1931), p. 13.
5. "English and Welsh," p. 41.
6. (London, 1940), pp. xxvi–xli.

Son," using Old English metre and illustrating the old English *Weltanschauung* that *līf is lǣne*.

In all his works, scientific and fiction, the philologist keeps peeping in and out: Tolkien was first and foremost a linguist. No doubt the Comic Muse, sitting as usual by his side, must have compressed her lips when she heard that the C.B.E. had been given to him 'for services to literature'; to him who throughout his academic career had 'fought the long defeat against the hostility and the malice of the devotees of English'.[7] Unless, of course, a more malign spirit had something to do with it; for his literary works and fiction, quite unique in English Literature, brought something new into English letters: a humorist caught at his own trick!

We, his students, friends and admirers, regret all the more that his great work on *Silmarillion* was left unfinished—a work which in his own words 'will not be a retreat into "Fairyland", which is only a trivial and contemptuous word'. I am sure that I express the sincere wish of all his friends when, quoting his own words to them when he left them, we might say to Him:

> Nai hiruvalye Valimar
> Nai elye hiruva.[8]

7. See his Valedictory Speech.
8. "Maybe thou shalt find Valimar. Maybe even thou shalt find it." The end of Galadriel's lament in Lothlórien, *The Lord of the Rings* (London, 1966), I, 394.

PART TWO

2

Beowulf, Lines 3074–3075

A. J. Bliss

UNIVERSITY COLLEGE, DUBLIN

næs he goldhwæte gearwor hæfde
agendes est ær gescearwod

(*Beowulf*, 3074–3075)

ONE of the most notoriously difficult passages in *Beowulf* is to be found in lines 3074–3075: very widely different interpretations are current, and each has its supporters. Though the passage is short, nearly all the words in it are difficult or ambiguous, and the resolution of the ambiguity is made more difficult by the fact that "the situation which the poet is representing is not clear as a whole."[1] The solution of the crux must therefore be sought along two parallel lines: on the one hand, the syntax and the vocabulary must be scrutinised yet again, to reduce the area of doubt to a minimum; on the other hand, the context must be carefully examined in an attempt to find a framework for the resolution of the remaining ambiguities.

1. G. V. Smithers, "Five Notes on Old English Texts," *English and Germanic Studies* 4 (1951–52), 75. I am much indebted to Professor E. G. Stanley for illuminating comments on an early draft of this paper.

[41

The general context of the passage is Beowulf's ill-fated contest with the dragon. The antecedents of the fight are described in lines 2200–2354, the fight itself in lines 2510–2711, and Beowulf's final speeches and death in lines 2711–2820. At line 3030, as the Geats go to visit the scene of the contest, the poet begins a retrospective commentary on the whole episode; the passage beginning at line 3051 is so important that it must be discussed in detail, and for the convenience of the reader it is reproduced below. The text is Dobbie's,[2] but the punctuation has been adjusted in the light of the discussion which follows; the letters in the left-hand margin are explained on p. 51.

A Þonne wæs þæt yrfe   eacencræftig,
   iumonna gold,   galdre bewunden,
   þæt ðam hringsele   hrinan ne moste
   gumena ænig,

B   nefne God sylfa,
   sigora Soðcyning,   sealde þam ðe He wolde   3055
   (He is manna gehyld)   hord openian,
   efne swa hwylcum manna   swa Him gemet ðuhte.

C   Þa wæs gesyne   þæt se sið ne ðah
   þam ðe unrihte   inne gehydde
   wræte under wealle—   weard ær ofsloh   3060
   feara sumne—   þa sio fæhð gewearð
   gewrecen wraðlice.

D   Wundur hwar þonne
   eorl ellenrof   ende gefere
   lifgesceafta,   þonne leng ne mæg
   mon mid his [ma]gum   meduseld buan.   3065

(A)   Swa wæs Biowulfe,
C   þa he biorges weard
   sohte, searoniðas—

D   seolfa ne cuðe
   þurh hwæt his worulde gedal   weorðan sceolde—

---

2. *The Anglo-Saxon Poetic Records*, ed. George P. Krapp and E. V. K. Dobbie, 6 vols. (New York, 1931-53) IV. All quotations from Old English poetic texts are taken from *ASPR* (with adjustment of the punctuation where appropriate).

A   swa hit oð domes dæg   diope benemdon
         þeodnas mære   þa ðæt þær dydon,   3070
         þæt se secg wære   synnum scildig,
         hergum geheaðerod,   hellbendum fæst,
         wommum gewitnad,   se ðone wong strude:

B   næs he goldhwæte   gearwor hæfde
         Agendes est   ær gesceawod.   3075

The interpretation of this passage has for a great many years been bedevilled by a mistranslation of the word *benemdon* in line 3069, apparently provoked by a failure to understand the function of the word *hit* in the same line; and in turn the mistranslation has provoked extensive misconceptions about the syntactic structure of the passage. Since before 1900 the vast majority of interpretations have rendered *benemdon* as "placed under a spell."[3] This rendering, however, is without any authority at all:[4] *benemnan* means "declare." The word is not common in Old English poetry: apart from this instance it occurs only five times, in *Husband's Message* 49, *Beowulf* 1097, *Paris*

3. Cf. J. Earle, *The Deeds of Beowulf* (Oxford, 1892, pp. 100–101: "had uttered a deep spell to hold till doomsday". So C. G. Child, *Beowulf and the Finnsburgh Fragment* (London, 1904), p. 83: "so laid it under a deep curse till Doomsday." The wide popularity of this interpretation is no doubt due to its adoption in the influential editions of Friedrich Klaeber, ed. (*Beowulf and the Flight at Finnsburg*, 3d. ed. [Boston, 1936]) and C. L. Wrenn, ed. (*Beowulf with the Finnsburg Fragment* [London, 1953; 2d ed. rev. by W. F. Bolton, 1973]). There were dissentient voices. In the glossaries, A. J. Wyatt and R. W. Chambers, eds. (*Beowulf with the Finnsburg Fragment* [1914]) give "declare solemnly" (though the note on lines 3062 ff. translates "laid the spell"; W. J. Sedgefield, ed. (*Beowulf* [Manchester, 1913; 3d ed. 1935]) gives "solemnly declare"; E. von Schaubert, ed. (*Heyne-Schückings Beowulf, 2 Teil: Kommentar*, 17th ed., [Paderborn, 1961]) gives "feierlich etwas aussprechen, erklären, bestimmen"; Bolton's revision of Wrenn gives "solemnly pronounced." Some recent translations have also abandoned the spell: K. Crossley-Holland (*Beowulf* [London, 1968]) gives "solemnly pronounced." G. N. Garmonsway and J. Simpson (*Beowulf and Its Analogues* [London, 1968]) give "had spoken solemn words over it."

4. Klaeber, ed., *Beowulf*, cites *begalan* in support of his rendering "lay a curse on s. th."; but *begalan* is hardly comparable, since the stem *gal-* itself has magical connotations which are totally lacking from the stem *nemn-* (cf. *galdre* in line 3052). In his Supplementary Glossary (1941) he cites the *Paris Psalter* 88.43 (see below) without explicitly withdrawing his previous gloss.

Psalter 88.3, 43, and *Paris Psalter* 94.11; in all these instances it occurs in conjunction with *að* or *aðswaru*, and in the *Psalms* it invariably glosses *jurare*. In *Paris Psalter* 88.43 it occurs in conjunction with *deope:*[5]

> þe þu mancynne
> and Dauide   deope aðe
> þurh þines sylfes   soð benemdest.

Here *deope aðe . . . benemdest* (glossing *jurasti*) means "declared with a solemn oath"; it seems scarcely possible that in *Beowulf* 3069 *diope benemdon* means anything but "solemnly declared."

The imaginary meaning "placed under a spell" seems to have been invented in order to explain the function of *hit*, taken as referring to the treasure—though editors do not explain why the pronoun should be *hit* in line 3069 and *þæt* in the following line.[6] Since *benemdon* means "declared," the *þæt*-clause in lines 3071–3073 must be a noun clause, and *hit* is a proleptic pronoun anticipating the noun clause.[7] Proleptic pronouns are very common in Old English poetry, particularly if a clause intervenes between the verb and the noun clause. The pronoun is usually *þæt*, which may be either in the nominative or (more commonly) in the accusative case. Instances in *Beowulf* with *þæt* in the nominative are 705, 1846, 2682, 2836;[8] with *þæt* in the accusative, 290, 377, 415, 435, 535, 632, 750, 809, 942, 1345, 1497, 1591, 1700, 1826, 2219, 2300, 2713, 2864. The proleptic use of *hit* is much rarer: in the nominative it occurs in 83, 1753, 3174, in the accusative only in 1671. This latter

5. See also the *Paris Psalter* 131.11 where *deopne að . . . aswor* glosses *juravit*.

6. In line 3070 *þæt* probably does refer to the treasure. There is no need to look for a specific antecedent: S. O. Andrew (*Postscript on Beowulf* [Cambridge, 1948]) § 41, points out that *þæt* is a pronoun of much more general reference than *hit*. It is even possible that *ðæt . . . dydon* means "did (all) that," i.e. were responsible for laying the curse on the treasure, as described in lines 3051–54.

7. Sedgefield seems to be the only editor to make this clear: in his third edition the note on line 3069 says that "*hit* is explained by the *þæt*-clause, lines 3071–73." In his second edition he had said "*hit*, the treasure."

8. A similar but not identical usage is to be found in lines 716, 932, 1304, 1361, 1463, 2532.

instance, however, is so close to the use in 3069 that it is worth quoting:

> Ic hit þe þonne gehate,   þæt þu on Heorote most
> sorhleas swefan   mid þinra secga gedryht . . .[9]

The meaning "promise" is not far removed from "declare," and the construction is identical with that of 3069–3073. If the *þæt*-clause in lines 3071–3073 is a noun clause, the subjunctive *wære* offers no difficulty, since the subjunctive is the appropriate mood for the "future-in-the-past" in dependent statements;[10] but if the *þæt*-clause is not a noun clause, the subjunctive poses difficult problems.

For editors who mistakenly believe that *benemdon* means "placed under a spell," the *þæt*-clause in lines 3071–3073 cannot be a noun clause; they have to seek for another interpretation, and their efforts are uniformly unconvincing. Whether taken on its own or in conjunction with *swa* in line 3066,[11] *þæt* must introduce an adverb clause. In either case the difficulty is the subjunctive verb. If *þæt* is taken on its own, it must introduce either a consecutive or a final clause: in a consecutive clause the verb is in the indicative, in a final clause it is in the subjunctive.[12] The subjunctive *wære* therefore presupposes a final clause; yet the context clearly requires a consecutive clause. The glorious chieftains did not devise a curse *in order that* the man who should plunder the place should be guilty of sin—their primary purpose was not to punish the plunderer but to protect the hoard; they imposed the curse, and *as a result* the man who plundered the hoard was guilty of sin. Hence if the *þæt*-clause is adverbial the subjunctive is inappropriate. There are two ways in which *þæt* can be taken in conjunction with *swa: swa* might be

9. "I promise to you, then, that you may sleep carefree in Heorot with a band of your warriors."

10. R. B. Mitchell, "An Old English Syntactical Reverie," *Neuphilologische Mitteilungen* 67 (1967) 145. There is a clear example of this usage in 1096–99: *benemde þæt he . . . heolde.*

11. Cf. Klaeber, ed., *Beowulf*, note on 3069a: "*Swa* is to be connected with *þæt* 3071." So Child, *Beowulf*, p. 83: "The mighty prince who had placed the treasure there so laid it under a deep curse till Doomsday, that the man. . . ."

12. R. B. Mitchell, *A Guide to Old English*, 2d ed. (Oxford, 1968), § 175.

absolute, or it might qualify an adjective or an adverb.[13] In either case, *swa* . . . *þæt* introduces a consecutive clause, and is therefore followed by the indicative;[14] the subjunctive *wære* is an insuperable obstacle.

If *swa* in line 3069 is not to be taken in conjunction with *þæt*, how is it to be interpreted? *Swa* is often used retrospectively, to introduce "an individual exemplification of the preceding general observation".[15] In line 3066 this meaning would fit very well, as Chambers's translation shows:[16] "It is a subject for wonder [i.e. it is uncertain] where a man will end his life, when he may no longer dwell on this earth. Even so was it with Beowulf —*he* knew not. . . ." In line 3069, however, it will not do at all: the curse on the treasure has not been mentioned for twelve lines, and the intervening matter has no direct relevance to it; in any case, the statement of the curse in lines 3069–3073 is no more specific than the statement in lines 3051–3057. However, the inappropriateness of a retrospective meaning has not deterred some translators from rendering *swa* as "thus,"[17] and W. J. Sedgefield in his Glossary includes this reference under instances of *swa* "introd[ucing] special instance." Sometimes *swa* can mean "since, because," and this is presumably what is intended by the translators who render *swa* as "for."[18] However, this rendering does not give an acceptable meaning. If *swa* means "because," the principal clause must be the clause in lines 3067b–3068. Beowulf, the text would then tell us, did not know in what circumstances his passing from the world was to come about, *because* the glorious chieftains had placed a curse on

13. E. T. Donaldson, *Beowulf: a New Prose Translation* (New York, 1966), p. 53, takes *swa* with *diope* in the same line: "The great princes who had put it [the treasure] there had laid on it so deep a curse. . . ."

14. Mitchell, *Guide to Old English*, § 175.

15. Klaeber, ed., *Beowulf*, note on line 1769.

16. Wyatt and Chambers, eds., *Beowulf*, note on lines 3062 ff.

17. E.g. R. K. Gordon, *Anglo-Saxon Poetry* (1926), p. 68.

18. E.g. D. Wright, *Beowulf* (1957), p. 99; C. B. Hieatt, *Beowulf and Other Old English Poems* (New York, 1967), pp. 83–84; Garmonsway and Simpson, *Beowulf and Its Analogues*, p. 80. It is curious that all these translators put a full stop before *For*, thereby producing a sentence with no principal clause; can it be that they were unhappy about the non sequitur, and tried to reduce its impact with a full stop?

the treasure. This cannot be true: Beowulf did not know the circumstances of his death, not because there *was* a curse, but because he did not *know* that there was a curse.

Else von Schaubert suggested an original and ingenious interpretation of *swa* in line 3069:[19] "Das *swa* in V.3069 ist hier als modale Konjunction gefasst, *swa hit . . . benemdon* also wie *þurh hwæt . . . weorðan sceolde* von *ne cuðe* abhängig gedacht: Als Beowulf auszog, den Drachen zu bekämpfen, wusste er nicht, dass auch seine Seele—infolge des auf dem Schatze lastenden Fluches—furchtbarste Gefahr lief. Zur Konstruktion vgl. 1233ff."[20] It seems that *swa* is to be translated "how": "he himself did not know in what circumstances his passing from the world was to come about, [nor] how the glorious chieftains. . . ." This gives excellent sense, but there is no justification at all for the supposition that *swa* can mean "how," in fact, it is difficult not to think that this mistranslation depends on the fact that German *wie* means both "as" and "how." It may further be doubted whether such a construction would not require rather *wisse* than *cuðe*.

The only other way in which *swa* in line 3069 can be interpreted is by taking it as correlative with *swa* in line 3066. This solution might, indeed, have been reached with much less discussion; but, since correlation gives a meaning which many readers of the poem are likely to find repugnant, it seemed necessary to show in detail that no other solution is possible without violating the canons of Old English syntax and semantics. The assumption of correlation here is by no means new: Holthausen in 1905 adopted a punctuation presupposing correlation;[21] Chambers in 1914 tentatively suggested correlation, "with *seolfa . . . sceolde* forming a parenthesis";[22] and the necessity for cor-

19. E. von Schaubert, ed., *Heyne-Schückings Beowulf,* note on lines 3066 ff.

20. "The *swa* in line 3069 is here taken as a modal conjunction, and thus *swa hit . . . benemdon* (like *þurh hwæt . . . weorðan sceolde*) is taken as dependent on *ne cuðe:* when Beowulf went out to fight the dragon he did not know that his soul too —because of the curse on the treasure—was incurring the most terrible danger. For the construction cf. 1233 ff."

21. F. Holthausen, ed., *Beowulf nebst dem Finnsburg Fragment* (Heidelberg, 1905), p. 99.

22. Wyatt and Chambers, eds., *Beowulf* note on lines 3062 ff.

[47

relation was argued by S. O. Andrew in three separate places.[23] Before we consider the implications of this interpretation, I must point out that there is another example of correlation, apparently overlooked by all editors and commentators, in the passage under discussion: the correlation of *þa . . . þa* in lines 3058–3061. Correlation gives excellent sense. Without it, the use of *gesyne* in line 3058 is inexplicable: why was it "obvious" that the course of action had been of no profit? If the second *þa*-clause is taken as subordinate, it provides the explanation of *gesyne*: "it was obvious that that course of action had been of no profit . . . when that feud was savagely avenged." In each of these two instances of correlation the second clause is separated from the first by a parenthesis describing an explanatory or concomitant circumstance. This is quite a common pattern, and it can be argued that it is the presence of a parenthesis that makes the use of correlation desirable, so that the relationship between the preceding and the following clauses may not be obscured.

We have already seen that a common use of *swa* is to introduce "an individual exemplification of the preceding general observation";[24] if the general observation *follows* instead of preceding the individual exemplification, correlation seems particularly appropriate, and this is what we find in lines 3066a and 3069–3073. Beowulf, the poet tells us, became subject to the curse imposed on the man who should plunder the hoard; that is, he incurred damnation. It has sometimes been doubted whether Beowulf can properly be said to have plundered the hoard, and of course in a literal sense he did not, since he never laid a hand on the treasure. In lines 2773–2774 we are told that it was Wiglaf who plundered the hoard:

> Ða ic on hlæwe gefrægn   hord reafian,
> eald enta geweorc,   anne mannan . . .[25]

23. S. O. Andrew, "Three Textual Cruxes in *Beowulf*," *Medium Ævum* 8 (1939), 207; Andrew, *Syntax and Style in Old English* (Cambridge, 1940), p. 111; Andrew, *Postscript on Beowulf*, p. 28. There are marginal differences between the three translations given.

24. Klaeber, ed., *Beowulf*, note on line 1769.

25. "Then I heard that a certain man plundered the treasure in the mound, the ancient handiwork of giants."

Wiglaf, however, had acted in pursuance of Beowulf's explicit instructions in lines 2743–2751; though the hand was Wiglaf's, the responsibility was Beowulf's.[26]

Many readers of Beowulf find it difficult to accept the conclusion that Beowulf was damned, and to refute it it is customary to cite lines 2819–2820:

> him of hreðre gewat
> sawol secean   soðfæstra dom.[27]

Translations of *soðfæstra dom* vary, but Tolkien's interpretation may be taken as typical:[28] "the glory that belongs (in eternity) to the just, or the judgment of God upon the just." Of course, if Beowulf was "just" in this sense it is not possible that he can have been damned. In fact the standard translation of *soðfæstra dom* can hardly be defended. Tolkien himself notes that "*soðfæstra dom* could by itself have meant simply the 'esteem of the true-judging', that *dom* which Beowulf as a young man had declared to be the prime motive of noble conduct";[29] it would be more accurate to say that this is what the phrase *must* mean. *Dom* is a common word in Old English poetry, and it is very frequently preceded by a qualifying genitive; in every single instance the qualifying genitive specifies the author of the judgment, not its subject—the judger, not the judged. Usually the qualifying genitive is singular, as in the frequent collocation *Dryhtnes dom* "the judgment of the Lord"; apart from *Beowulf* 2820 there are only three instances of a qualifying genitive in the plural. In *Beowulf* 1098 and *Juliana* 98 the phrase is *witena dom* "the judgment of

26. Cf. E. G. Stanley, "Hæthenra Hyht in Beowulf," *Studies in Old English Literature in Honor of Arthur G. Brodeur*, ed. Stanley B. Greenfield (Eugene, Ore., 1963), p. 146: "Though he does not actually perform the deed himself, his order that it be performed makes him accountable for it."

27. See for instance A. G. Brodeur, *The Art of Beowulf* (Berkeley and Los Angeles, 1959), p. 217, and Mitchell in Crossley-Holland, *Beowulf*, p. 22.

28. J. R. R. Tolkien, "Beowulf: The Monster and the Critics," *Proceedings of the British Academy*, 22 (1936), 42.

29. Ibid., pp. 41–42, Cf. C. Donahue, "Beowulf and Christian Tradition," *Traditio* 21 (1965), 110: *Soðfæstra dom* can mean good repute among right thinking men. But *dom* meant also the judgement of God and *soðfæstra dom* meant the judgement accorded to the righteous." Donahue takes the phrase as "a deeply serious pun."

[49

the counsellors"; in *feonda dom* in *Exodus* 571 *dom* means "power," but the construction is the same. In the light of these parallels it can hardly be doubted that the *soðfæste* must be those who are judging. This conclusion is strikingly confirmed by the fact that *soðfæst* is an adjective traditionally applied to those who judge: *soðfæst dema* or *dema soðfæst* is a formula (*Lord's Prayer II* 37, 121, *Paris Psalter* 93.20). Tolkien argues that the combination with *gewat secean* excludes this meaning,[30] but it is difficult to see why. In *Beowulf* the word *sawol* is not used in a Christian sense: it normally means "life-spirit," that which leaves the body at death. The collocation of *sawol* and *secean* is therefore not very different from the collocation of *myne* and *sohte* in *Beowulf* 2570–2572:

> Scyld wel gebearg
> life ond lice   læssan hwile
> mærum þeodne   þonne his myne sohte.[31]

There seems to be no reason at all why we should not translate lines 2819–2820 as follows: "his spirit departed from his breast, hoping for the esteem of the true-judging." The concept of esteem after death is, of course, a common one in Old English poetry, as in *Beowulf* 884–85:

> Sigemunde gesprong
> æfter deaðdæge   dom unlytel.[32]

A still closer parallel to the *Beowulf* passage is to be found in *Seafarer* 72–73:

> Forþon þæt bið eorla gehwam   æftercweþendra
> lof lifgendra   lastworda betst . . .[33]

Here the phrase *lof lifgendra* corresponds closely to *soðfæstra dom*. Beowulf believes that he has done well, and that posterity will judge him as favourably as his own retainers do; but in fact he is

30. Tolkien, "Beowulf: The Monster and the Critics," p. 42.
31. "The shield protected life and limb for the famous prince for a shorter time than he had hoped [*or*, expected]."
32. "Not a little glory sprang up for Sigemund after the day of his death."
33. "Assuredly that is the best of epitaphs for every warrior, the praise of those who live and speak after him."

heading for the damnation which he has incurred by un-
wittingly rendering himself liable to the curse.

Lines 3069–3073 refer back to lines 3051–3054a, but this
is not the only reference back in lines 3051–3074; in fact, there
are four recurring thematic elements which can be summarized
as follows:

A   The curse on the treasure[34]
B   Exemption from the curse through the intervention of God
C   Conflict with the dragon
D   The unpredictability of a hero's death.

In lines 3051–3065 the four themes are stated, and in lines
3066–3075 each is applied to Beowulf. The poet has adopted a
chiastic pattern, which can be illustrated by the following
diagram:

$$
\begin{array}{llll}
A & 3051-54a & C & 3066b-67a \\
B & 3054b-57 & D & 3067b-68 \\
C & 3058-62a & A & (3066a),\ 3069-73 \\
D & 3062b-65 & B & 3074-75
\end{array}
$$

The patterning has not been overlooked in the past, though no
single critic has seen all of it. The AB parallelism was explicitly
pointed out by Bartlett, who described it as an "envelope pattern."[35] Sedgefield claimed that "The order of sentences in this
passage, ll. 3058–75, points to a lack of consecutiveness ob-
servable in other parts of the poem. The lines 3069–75 would
perhaps be more in place if they directly followed l. 3057."[36]

34. There is a discrepancy between the two accounts of the curse given in
lines 3053–57 and 3071–73. According to the first account, no man would be
permitted to touch the treasure-chamber, unless God granted him permission.
According to the second account, the man who should plunder the place would
be guilty of sin. The second passage envisages the possibility that the hoard will
be plundered; according to the first, this could happen only if the plunderer had
received God's permission; if he had received God's permission he could not
possibly be guilty of sin. It seems that the first passage must be understood to
mean that no man might touch the treasure-chamber *with impunity* unless God
granted him permission.

35. A. C. Bartlett, *The Larger Rhetorical Patterns in Anglo-Saxon Poetry*
(New York, 1935), pp. 28–29. It is surprising that Miss Bartlett did not
observe the complete pattern, which is similar to one she illustrates on page 10
of her book.

36. Sedgefield, ed., *Beowulf* (3d ed., 1935), note on lines 3058 ff.

[51

The same parallelism probably underlies the popularity of the emendation of *næs (he)* in line 3074 to *næfne* (cf. *nefne* in line 3054), and the misinterpretation of *benemnan* discussed above. The D parallelism is implicit in the popularity of translations which explicitly refer Beowulf's uncertainty about the circumstances of his death back to the general statement in lines 3062b–3065. The C parallelism has not previously been noticed, perhaps because of misunderstandings of lines 3058–3062a, perhaps because of the brevity of the recapitulation in lines 3066b–3067a.

The significance of the chiastic pattern for the present investigation is that the meaning of lines 3074–3075 must correspond in some way to that of lines 3054b–3057: that is, these lines must have some relevance to the possibility of Beowulf's exemption from the effects of the curse through the intervention of God. We already know that Beowulf *did* become subject to the effects of the curse, so that the poet has no need to tell us that God did not intervene on his behalf; what we still need to know is *why* God did not intervene. We may therefore expect lines 3074–3075 to make some statement about Beowulf's relationship to God, perhaps in general, or perhaps especially in connection with treasure. It remains to be seen whether the wording of these two lines is susceptible of any such interpretation.

Nearly every word in lines 3074–3075 calls for comment. The first word *næs*, either by itself or in conjunction with *he*, has often been emended to *næfne*,[37] in order to complete the parallelism with lines 3054b–3057; but this is to misunderstand the nature of the parallelism. If the manuscript reading *næs* is to be retained, there are two ways of interpreting it. It might be a contraction of *ne wæs* "was not": the difficulty is that there is already a finite verb, *hæfde*, in line 3074, so that the first half of the line, *næs he goldhwæte*, would have to form a separate clause: and there is no meaning that can plausibly be given to *goldhwæte* which would make it a satisfactory complement to *næs he*. Alternatively, *næs* might be the emphatic negative "not at all, by no

37. E.g. Holthausen, ed., *Beowulf*; W. W. Lawrence, "The Dragon and His Lair in *Beowulf*," *PMLA* 33 (1918) 561–62; Friedrich Klaeber, "Beowulfiana," *Anglia* 50 (1926), 221–22.

means," equivalent to *nealles, nalæs,* etc., and this seems to be the only acceptable rendering. In Old English poetry the function of *nalæs* (here used as a convenient standard form) is to make a positive assertion by emphatically rejecting its contrary. In *Beowulf* there are twenty-eight instances of *nalæs;* in ten of these the *nalæs*-clause is followed by a clause introduced by *ac* in the sense of "on the contrary," in which the alternative is made explicit.[38] Sometimes the *nalæs*-clause rejects the contrary of something that has already been asserted;[39] sometimes the contrary is implicit in the general context.[40] We are therefore entitled to assume that lines 3074–3075 emphatically reject some possibility the untruth of which is obvious in the light of the context, either immediate or remote.

The word *goldhwæte* has given rise to a great deal of discussion, all of which has been rendered obsolete by the work of Professor G. V. Smithers. In an erudite and convincing study[41] Smithers demonstrated beyond reasonable doubt that *goldhwæte* must be read as *goldhwǣte;* that it must be construed with *est;* and that it means "gold-bestowing." The word *est* is qualified by *agendes,* and the meaning of this has also been disputed: does it mean 'owner' in general, or does it refer to God? Apart from instances in which it is qualified by a dependent genitive, *agend* occurs only three times in Old English poetry: once here, once in *Genesis* 1353, where it means "owner," and once in *Exodus* 295, where it means "God." The qualifying genitives found in conjunction with *agend* are *wuldres, lifes, sigores,* and *swegles;* in each instance the complete phrase refers to God. The weight of the evidence, therefore, is in favour of the meaning "God," since there is only a single instance in which *agend* refers to an owner other than God.[42] This conclusion is strongly reinforced by a

38. Lines 338, 562, 2145, 2179, 2221, 2503, 2596, 2832, 3015, 3023.
39. E.g. lines 1493, 1529, 1749, 1811.
40. E.g. lines 43, 1076, 2873.
41. Smithers, "Five Notes," pp. 75–84.
42. Stanley, "Hæthenra Hyht," pp. 143–44, has called attention to the use of *agend* in the early Kentish laws to mean "owner as opposed to possessor" in cases of robbery, and concludes that in line 3075 "it must refer to the dragon." However, the relevance of prose usage to poetic usage must be considered very dubious, especially when prose usage is effectively limited to legal contexts.

[53

consideration of the collocations in which *est* occurs in Old English poetry. Leaving aside examples of the adverbial use of *estum*, there are sixteen instances of *est*, and in eleven of these the word is qualified by a dependent genitive singular: six instances of *Metodes est*, three of *est Godes*,[43] and one each of *æðelinges est* and *agendes est*. Again the weight of the evidence strongly supports the view that *agend* in line 3075 means "God."

The word *est* is most commonly translated "favour"; it is related to *unnan*, and its etymological meaning is "granting." In Old English prose *est* often means "(divine) grace," and this meaning seems to be called for in *Gifts of Men* 87. In general, however, the etymological meaning seems to survive in the poetry, to a greater or lesser degree. The most frequent collocations are *ofer Metodes est* (*Genesis* 1251, *Daniel* 174, *Andreas* 517, *Metres of Boethius* 11.25) and *ofer est Godes* (*Phoenix* 403);[44] the natural translation here is "against God's will," but the basic idea is rather "contrary to God's intention," "without God's permission." In the collocations *þurh est Godes* (*Guthlac* 826, *Phoenix* 46) and *þurh Meotodes est* (*Elene* 985) the idea of "granting" is stronger: each of the events referred to (the birth of Adam, the exemption of the happy land from the effects of the flood, the finding of the cross) is seen as the result of the direct intervention of God. In the remaining instances, where God is not involved, the idea of "grant" or "gift" is wholly dominant. So in *Genesis* 2444–45: *Hie on þanc curon / æðelinges est* "they gratefully accepted the prince's offer." In *Beowulf* 2157 the detailed interpretation is obscure, but it is obvious that *est* refers to Hrothgar's gift of the *hildesceorp*. *Andreas* 337–39 has been fully discussed by Smithers,[45] who demonstrates that the phrase *est ahwettan* is precisely equivalent to *unnan*, and, like *unnan*, is construed with a dependent genitive. In *Beowulf* 2165 the phrase *est geteon*, also construed with a dependent genitive, seems to

43. The difference in word-order is dictated by the metre: *Godes est* would not be an acceptable ending to a half-line.

44. Of the two occurrences of *ofer mine est* (*Andreas* 1215, 1374) the first refers to God, the second to the Devil.

45. Smithers, "Five Notes," pp. 78–79. Smithers points out that *ahwettan* is formed from the same stem as (*gold-*) *hwæte*.

mean "make a present (of)." In the light of these usages the phrase *goldhwæte* . . . *Agendes est* is perhaps best translated "the gold-bestowing favour of God"; but for purposes of interpretation it is important to bear in mind the underlying ideas of "grant, gift, intention, permission."

The word *gearwor* is the comparative of the adverb *gear(w)e* "fully," a word of very restricted usage: in Old English poetry, outside *Beowulf* and the *Psalms,* it occurs only in conjunction with the verbs *witan* and *cunnan.* The occurrences in the *Psalms* are of special interest, since the Vulgate text is available to indicate the sense the word had for the Anglo-Saxon poet. The other instances (apart from two in *Beowulf* which will be examined below) are as follows: with *witan, Genesis* 41, 655, 1098, 2344, 2626, *Exodus* 291, *Elene* 419, 719, 859, 1239, *Azarius* 170, *Beowulf* 246, 878, 2339, 2656, 2725, *Metres of Boethius* 20.94; with *cunnan, Genesis* 583, *Elene* 167, 399, 531, 648, *Christ* 573, *Guthlac* 1045, *Wanderer* 69, 71, *Beowulf* 2062, 2070.[46] In the *Psalms* it is interesting to observe that *gear(w)e* usually glosses nothing at all: that is, it is frequently added with any verb, apparently for the sake of the alliteration, often with *God.* So with *gehyran,* 53.2, 61.11; with *gewenan,* 55.4, 68.3, 70.1; with *lician,* 55.10; with *wacian,* 62.1; with *hycgan,* 90.2; with *atreddan,* 138.2; with *ongietan,* 139.12. In 107.7 *gearwe* is used without a verb. With the verb *witan* whole phrases are freely used where there is nothing corresponding in the Latin: *ic (ful) gearwe wat* 135.1, 3, 117.28; *wat ic (eac swiðe) gearwe* 101.5, 118.118; *þu . . . wistest gearuwe* 118.21. There are no more than three instances in which it is possible to think that *gearwe* has any special meaning, and even in these it seems to be no more than a rather vague intensive: *canst mine ædre ealle gearuwe* "quia tu possedisti renes meos" 138.11; *do me wegas wise, þæt ic wite gearwe / on hwylcne ic gange* "notam fac mihi viam, in qua ambulem" 142.9; *onginnað ge Drihtne geare andettan* "præcinite Domino in confessione" 146.7. In *Beowulf* 265 *gear(w)e* is used with *gemunan,* in *Beowulf* 2748 with *sceawian;* this

---

46. The comparative *gearwor* occurs three times (*Andreas* 932, *Elene* 945, *Juliana* 556), each time in conjunction with *witan,* and each time preceded by *þe* or *þi.* The superlative *gearwost* occurs twice, once with *witan* (*Beowulf* 715) and once with *cunnan* (*Elene* 328).

latter usage is discussed below, p. 58.[47] The basic meaning of *sceawian* is "to see"; but in line 3075 this meaning must be modified by the collocation with *gearwe*, which is normally used only with verbs of knowing; the full meaning here must be something like "see and perceive," "see and understand."

The function of the comparative in line 3074 is not immediately clear. Certainly there is no direct comparison, since there is no *þonne* to introduce the standard of comparison. However, there are very many instances of the use of the comparative without *þonne*, and those in Beowulf have been discussed by Klaeber.[48] There are, indeed, a few unmistakable instances of the "absolute comparative," e.g. *syllicran wiht* 3038 (cf. *Dream of the Rood* 4); but in most cases the comparison, though not explicit, is more or less clearly implied by the context. So, for instance, in line 915:

> He þær eallum wearð,
> mæg Higelaces,   manna cynne,
> freondum gefægra.[49]

So again in line 980:

> Da wæs swigra secg,   sunu Eclafes,
> on gylpspræce   guðgeweorca . . .[50]

It is possible, therefore, that the use of the comparative *gearwor* may be justified by the context; and the presence of the word *ær*

47. This list of occurrences of *gear(w)e* does not include instances of the spelling *geara*. This spelling is limited to the *Psalms*, apart from one instance in *Metres of Boethius* 9.9 and one in a very obscure passage in *Maxims I* 191. One difficulty here is that there are a number of instances in which it is impossible to distinguish with certainty between *geara* "clearly" and *gēara* "long ago"; another is that some instances seem to call for an adjective rather than an adverb, as in two instances of *geara andfencgea* glossing "susceptor" (*Paris Psalter* 58.9, 18). In *Paris Psalter* 141.4 *geara* is used with *sceawade* "considerabam," but since it alliterates with *gearwe* (adjective) it seems scarcely possible that it can stand for *gearwe* (adverb).

48. Friedrich Klaeber, "Studies in the Textual Interpretation of Beowulf," *Modern Philology* 3 (1905), 251–52.

49. "The kinsman of Hygelac became more pleasing to all mankind and to his friends [than he had been before]."

50. "Then the son of Ecglaf was more silent in boastful speech of deeds of battle [than he had been before]".

in the next line suggests that, as in the two examples just cited, the standard of comparison is temporal. The word *ær* properly means "previously, in the past," but it is often used in conjunction with a past tense to form a pluperfect, as in line 3060. Here it is used with the compound pluperfect *hæfde . . . gesceawod;* since *ær* in this case cannot be used to form a pluperfect, the meaning "in the past" seems certain.[51] A literal translation of lines 3074–3075 must therefore run; "In the past he had not at all seen and understood the gold-bestowing favour of God more clearly [than he did now]."

Unfortunately, negative statements of this kind are basically ambiguous.[52] In the first place, it is never certain which element in the statement is being negated: the poet may be saying "not this, but that," or "not thus, but otherwise," and so on. In the second place, there may be more than one possible alternative to the element being negated. The translation given above is not in itself new—it is not very different, for instance, from the translation given by Chambers:[53] "Not before had he (Beowulf) beheld more fully the gold-abounding grace of the Lord." The crucial step is still to be taken: to choose between the many possible *interpretations* of the translation, in the light of comparable usages elsewhere in Old English poetry, and above all with due consideration of the context. The use of *nalæs* with a comparative is very rare in Old English poetry, but fortunately there is an enlightening instance in *Beowulf* 43–46:

Nalæs hi hine læssan   lacum teodan,
þeodgestreonum,   þon þa dydon
þe hine æt frumsceafte   forð onsendon
ænne ofer yðe   umborwesende.[54]

51. Cf. lines 3164–65, in which *ær* is used with the pluperfect *genumen hæfdon.*

52. On the ambiguity of negative statements see R. A. Williams, *The Finn Episode in Beowulf* (Cambridge, 1924), pp. 26–28. The occasion of the discussion is line 1071, in which *ne huru* performs a function similar to that of *nalæs;* see also lines 182, 862, 1465.

53. Wyatt and Chambers, eds., *Beowulf,* note on lines 3074–3075.

54. "By no means did they provide him less with gifts, with princely treasures, than those did who sent him forth at the beginning alone across the ocean as a child."

[57

Here the implication is plainly "not less, but more": his retainers provided the dead Scyld with *more* treasure than those did who had sent him forth in the beginning.[55] It seems reasonable to suppose, therefore, that the implication of lines 3074–3075 is "not more, but less." If we apply this interpretation to the translation given above, we arrive at the following: "In the past he had seen and understood the gold-bestowing favour of God much less clearly than he did now."

If the interpretation is correct, this statement ought to be obviously true in the light of the context, either immediate or remote; and the poet has given us an important clue to the part of the context we should look at. The collocation of *gear(w)e* and *sceawian* in lines 3074–3075 is paralleled in lines 2747–2751:

> Bio nu on ofoste, þæt ic ærwelan,
> goldæht ongite, gearo sceawige
> swegle searogimmas, þæt ic ðy seft mæge
> æfter maððumwelan min alætan
> lif ond leodscipe, þone ic longe heold.[56]

Beowulf, already wounded to the death, tells Wiglaf to bring the treasure so that he can see it; then he will be able to die easy. It is not enough for him to *know* that the treasure is now his, he must also *see* it; this is plainly an improper attitude towards treasure, and unmistakably savours of avarice. Later, in his dying speech, Beowulf adopts a different attitude (lines 2794–2796):

> Ic ðara frætwa Frean ealles ðanc,
> Wuldurcyninge, wordum secge,
> ecum Dryhtne, þe ic her on starie.[57]

55. The implication of the only other instance of *nalæs* with the comparative (*Andreas* 1042) is not so clear: *Nalæs leng bidon/ in þam gnornhofe guðgeþingo.*

56. "Make haste now, so that I may perceive the ancient wealth, the treasure of gold, and plainly see the gleaming jewels, so that after seeing the abundant treasure I can the more easily give up my life and the people that I have ruled for a long time." Stanley, "Hæthenra Hyht," p. 146, called attention to this parallelism to support a different interpretation of lines 3074–75.

57. "I express my thanks to the Lord of all, the King of Glory, the eternal Lord, for the treasures that I gaze on here."

This time Beowulf's attitude is irreproachable: he thanks God for bestowing the gold on him. Now he sees clearly the gold-bestowing favour of God; previously he had not done so. The contrast between the two speeches corresponds precisely to the two states of mind implied by lines 3074–3075.

Furthermore, the meaning here postulated for lines 3074–3075 amply fulfills the expectation created by the chiastic pattern adopted by the poet. We know that Beowulf has incurred damnation in making himself subject to the curse by ordering the plundering of the hoard. We know, therefore, that God did not intervene to exempt him from the operation of the curse. Now at last we know why God did not intervene: it was because Beowulf had never, until his dying moments, sufficiently recognised the fact that the bestowing of gold on man is at the sole discretion of God. To facilitate the further consideration of the implications of the poet's statement it may be useful to give here a full translation of lines 3051–3075, in accordance with the conclusions reached above:[58]

> Moreover that mighty heritage, the gold of men of old, had been encircled with a spell, so that no man might touch that treasure-chamber, unless God Himself, the true King of victories (He is the protector of men) should grant it to whom He wished, to whatever man seemed fit to Him, to open up the hoard.
>
> It was obvious that his course of action had been of no profit to the creature that had wrongfully kept the treasure hidden under the wall —the guardian had killed a man with few peers—when that feud was savagely avenged. It is a mystery in what circumstances a warrior famed for valour may reach the end of his allotted span, when a man can no longer dwell in the mead-hall with his kinsmen.
>
> When Beowulf went to meet the guardian of the barrow and his subtle enmity—*he* did not know in what circumstances his passing from the world was to come about—it happened to him just as the glorious chieftains who had put the treasure there had solemnly decreed it, that until doomsday the man who should plunder the place should be guilty of sin, confined in heathen precincts, held fast in hell's bonds, and cruelly tormented: in the past he had seen and understood the gold-bestowing favour of God much less clearly than he did now.

58. I have borrowed felicitous phrases from a variety of sources.

A. J. BLISS

The curse on the treasure has troubled many critics of *Beowulf*. According to Brodeur,[59] the poet represents the operation of the curse as "undeserved, but inevitable." Mrs. Goldsmith's view of the curse[60] is that "like Piers Plowman's pardon, it tells the hearer what he knew all along: that coveting the gold is wrong, that stealing is sinful, and that, short of a special dispensation from God himself, the sinful thief will end in hell." Elsewhere Mrs. Goldsmith is highly critical of the poet:[61] "The oddity about the curse is that the poet makes no good use of it, and it becomes a literary blemish. Without it, there is a satisfying moral sequence; with it, there is a conflict of causes which obscures the circumstances of Beowulf's end." No doubt the reluctance of readers of the poem to accept that Beowulf is damned is due in part to their feeling that the curse is too arbitrary to be acceptable: it is unfair that Beowulf should incur damnation because of an ancient curse of which he knows nothing. These views overlook the symbolism of the curse, which lines 3074–3075 make explicit. The curse symbolises the corrupting power of the gold (*hæðen gold* as it is called in line 2276), which the poet has described explicitly in lines 2764–2766:

> Sinc eaðe mæg,
> gold on grund[e],   gumcynnes gehwone
> oferhigian,   hyde se ðe wylle.[62]

The exemption from the curse symbolises the possibility of escaping the corrupting power of gold through a proper recognition of the fact that it comes to man only by the favour of God. Far from being arbitrary, the curse is a direct consequence of Beowulf's avarice; far from introducing "a conflict of causes," the curse provides a clear explanation of Beowulf's end.

It has become a commonplace of *Beowulf* criticism that Hrothgar's "Sermon" holds a central place in the plan of the

59. Brodeur, *The Art of Beowulf*, p. 239.
60. M. Goldsmith, *The Mode and Meaning of Beowulf* (London, 1970), p. 228.
61. Ibid., p. 95.
62. "Treasure, gold in the earth, can easily get the better of any man, no matter who hides it."

poem. It is indeed in many ways a surprising passage. The context seems to demand praise of Beowulf; yet, of the eighty-five lines of the "Sermon" (lines 1700–1784), no more than sixteen consist of praise. In lines 1709b–1722a, Hrothgar summarises the history of Heremod, who displayed ferocity ("him on ferhþe greow / breosthord blodreow") and avarice ("nallas beagas geaf / Denum æfter dome"). In lines 1722b–1724a he applies this story specifically to Beowulf:

> Đu þe lær be þon,
> gumcyste ongit; ic þis gid be þe
> awræc wintrum frod.[63]

In lines 1724b–1757 he describes a hypothetical ruler who is overcome by arrogance (*oferhygd*, line 1740) and avarice (lines 1748–1752), and again the lesson is applied specifically to Beowulf in lines 1758–1760:

> Bebeorh þe ðone bealonið, Beowulf leofa,
> secg betsta, ond þe þæt selre geceos,
> ece rædas.[64]

In the following clause Beowulf is specifically warned against arrogance:

> oferhyda ne gym,
> mære cempa.[65]

Much later in the poem, in lines 2345–2347, a verbal reminiscence emphasises the fact that Beowulf did not heed this warning, and did succumb to arrogance:

> Oferhogode ða hringa fengel
> þæt he þone widflogan weorode gesohte
> sidan herge.[66]

63. "Learn a lesson from that, recognise manly virtues; wise in my old age I have related this story for your sake."
64. "Dear Beowulf, best of men, guard yourself against that wickedness and choose for yourself the better way, eternal counsels."
65. "Pay no heed to arrogance, glorious warrior."
66. "Then the prince of rings scorned to attack the dragon with a band of warriors, a great army."

"He will not deign to lead a force against a dragon, as wisdom might direct even a hero to do";[67] and because he will not, he goes to his death in single combat. Lines 3051–3075 tell us that he also succumbed to avarice. Far from being "a hero without a tragic flaw,"[68] he is a hero with two tragic flaws.

It is true enough that these flaws can readily be seen as the consequences of the near-impossible demands made on a man by the heroic code. Leyerle has convincingly documented the way in which the code's emphasis on personal valour could lead to the irresponsibility of *ofermod* or *oferhygd;*[69] similarly the emphasis on the duty of the chieftain to distribute rings to his retainers could lead to excessive preoccupation with material wealth. In heroic society avarice appears in two aspects, one positive and the other negative, and both are described by Hrothgar in lines 1749–1751. The positive aspect is the desire for greater wealth:

> þinceð him to lytel   þæt he lange heold,
> gytsað gromhydig. . . .[70]

The negative aspect is reluctance to give away existing possessions:

> nallas on gylp seleð
> fædde beagas.[71]

It is this negative aspect which is emphasised later in line 1756: the miser will be succeeded by someone "se þe unmurnlice madmas dæleþ."[72] There is no suggestion anywhere in the poem that Beowulf was reluctant to distribute what treasure he had; on the contrary, two of Beowulf's retainers describe him as the lord "ðe us (ðas) beagas geaf" (2635, 3009), and the poet refers to him as "þone þe him hringas geaf" (3034).[73] Nevertheless, the obligation

67. J. R. R. Tolkien, "The Homecoming of Beorhtnoth Beorhthelm's Son," *Essays and Studies* (1953), p. 14.

68. Brodeur, *The Art of Beowulf*, p. 105.

69. J. Leyerle, "Beowulf the Hero and the King," *Medium Ævum* 34 (1965), 97–102.

70. "What he has possessed for a long time seems to him too little, he is furiously avaricious . . . ."

71. "By no means does he honourably give away decorated rings."

72. "Who distributes treasures without reluctance."

73. See also lines 2640, 2865.

to distribute rings must inevitably have caused the chieftain to be concerned about the replenishment of his supply of treasure. No doubt Hygelac's ill-fated expedition against the Frisians, mentioned no less than four times in the poem,[74] was undertaken in order to secure more rings for distribution; indeed, this is clearly implied by the poet's comment in lines 2919–2920, "nalles frætwe geaf / ealdor dugoðe," an ironical reminiscence of the crime alleged against Heremod in lines 1719–1720, "nallas beagas geaf / Denum æfter dome." It is unlikely to be a coincidence that the second account of Hygelac's raid follows immediately after the description of Beowulf's preparations for battle with the dragon: part, at least, of Beowulf's motive in undertaking the conflict was his desire to secure more treasure for his people, as he himself says in lines 2797–2798, when he thanks God

> þæs ðe ic moste   minum leodum
> ær swyltdæge   swylc gestrynan.[75]

Beowulf cannot be criticised for his desire to secure treasure for his people, any more than he can be criticised for wishing to save them from the ravages of the dragon: it is the impurity of his motives which lays him open to criticism. Just as his arrogance led him into the error of attacking the dragon single-handed, so his avarice led him to forget that the granting of wealth to men is the prerogative of God alone. If Beowulf had paid heed to Hrothgar's warnings, he might have lived on to rule his people with honour; because he neglected them he discovered that the wages of arrogance is death, and the wages of avarice is damnation.

74. Lines 1202–1214, 2354–2366, 2501–2508, 2913–2920.
75. "Because before the day of my death I was permitted to obtain such a thing for my people."

3

Laȝamon's English Sources

P. J. Frankis

UNIVERSITY OF NEWCASTLE UPON TYNE

THE general situation regarding Laȝamon's sources is well known:[1] his poem, *Brut*, derives its material from *Le Roman de Brut* of Wace, but his writing is shaped in metre and poetic language by the Anglo-Saxon tradition.[2] The exact nature of Laȝamon's knowledge and use of English sources is still problematic, however, and although there has been a good deal of theorizing, specific examples of the incontrovertible use of Old English material have been lacking. Laȝamon's use of certain passages from Ælfric's homilies is therefore of some interest.

The first of these is in Laȝamon's account of the Temple of Diana visited by Brutus after the fall of Troy (lines 569–637).[3] In Geoffrey of Monmouth (*Historia Regum Britanniae* I.11) this

1. The basic studies are R. Wülcker, "Über die Quellen Layamons," *Beiträge zur Geschichte der deutschen Sprache* 3 (1876) 524–55, and R. Imelmann, *Layamon: Versuch über seine Quellen* (Berlin, 1906); important later studies, giving details of intervening work, are J. S. P. Tatlock, *The Legendary History of Britain* (Berkeley, Calif., 1950), and H. Pilch, *Layamons 'Brut'*, Anglistische Forschungen 91 (Heidelberg, 1960). Most of the material in the present paper was presented in a somewhat different form in a research seminar at the University of Newcastle upon Tyne in 1972.

2. See H. Ringbom, *Studies in the Narrative Technique of 'Beowulf' and Lawman's Brut*, Acta Academiae Aboensis, Ser. A, Humaniora, Vol. 36, no. 2 (Åbo, 1968), as well as the classic studies of Wyld and Tatlock therein cited.

3. References are as far as possible to *Laȝamon's Brut*, ed. G. L. Brook and R. F. Leslie, Early English Text Society (hereafter EETS), 250 (London, 1963); for the second half of the poem I refer to *Layamon's Brut*, ed. F. Madden (London, 1847), prefixing such references with M. Unless otherwise stated, quotations are from the Caligula text, and I supply my own punctuation.

64]

episode is recounted with historical detachment, as if there were no reproach attaching to the consultation of a pagan oracle. Wace, however, introduces a note of Christian censure:

> L'image ert d'une deuesse,
> Diane, une divineresse:
> Diables esteit, ki la gent
> Decevait par enchantement. [635–38][4]

This condemnation of idolatry is considerably amplified by Laȝamon, and for this purpose he draws on Ælfric's homily *De Falsis Diis*.[5] The similarities are of a kind that suggest the poet's recollection of an earlier reading of the homily rather than his writing with a copy of the Old English text beside him: the correspondences, that is to say, are not exact, and none of them in isolation would be conclusive, but cumulatively the evidence is convincing. The following verbal parallels are the most important, and the syntactical parallel (in the use of the present participle) between *Brut* 582 and *De Falsis Diis* 104 is also striking:

Laȝamon, *Brut*	Ælfric, *De Falsis Diis*
575, þe Deouel heo luuede	162, þe þa leahtras lufodan, þe liciað þam deofle
578, a þon heðene lawen me heold heo for hehne godd	128, þisne wurðodan þa hæðenan for healicne god
(cf.4030, heo heolden hine for hæhne godd)	(cf.136, þone macodan þa hæþenan him to mæran gode
	and 114, Iuno, swiðe healic gyden)
582, þe wile þeo on þan eitlonde wes folc woniende	104, An man wæs eardiende on þam ilande
583, heo wurðeden þat anlicnes	208–9, for þære anlicnysse . . . he wurðode hi for god
635–36, wrchen hire ane temple and on licnesse [*Otho:* on anlicnesse] of ræde golde.	190–94, Hi worhtan eac anlicnyssa þam arwurþum godum, sume of smætum golde . . . and him hus arærdon,

4. References are to *Le Roman de Brut*, ed. I. Arnold, Société des anciens textes français (Paris, 1938). "The image was of a goddess, Diana, a sorceress: she was a devil who deceived people by magic." (635–38).

5. *The Homilies of Ælfric*, ed. J. C. Pope, Vol. II, EETS, 260 (London, 1968), no. XXI.

[65

þæt hi heton tempel.[6]

In the last example Laȝamon's recollection of Ælfric was perhaps prompted by Wace's use of the word *temple (Roman de Brut* 697, *Temple e image li fereit).*

The second passage is Laȝamon's account of Vortigern's attempt to build a tower and the divination to which he resorted to overcome his difficulties (lines 7721–7880). It is possible that the source-reference to the sacrificial killing of a child without a father (*Hist. Reg. Brit.* VI.17, repeated in Wace 7347–54) reminded Laȝamon of Ælfric's condemnation of the killing of illegitimate children in the homily *In Laetania Maiore* (also known as *De Auguriis*), lines 151–6;[7] however this may be, Laȝamon's expansion of the theme of witchcraft and divination at this point has a number of parallels with the portion of Ælfric's homily immediately preceding this condemnation. As in the previous case, the parallels are scattered and inexact, suggesting a vague memory of earlier reading rather than reference to a text readily at hand. In addition to the general thematic similarities the following verbal parallels may be noted:

Laȝamon, *Brut*	Ælfric, *De Auguriis*
7734, 7740, leoten weorpen	80, hleotað 84, hleotan
7739, summe heo wenden to þan wude,	129–30, Sume men synd swa ablende þæt hi bringað heora lac . . . to treowum

6. *Brut:* 575, "she loved the devil"; 578, "in the heathen laws she was held to be a high god"; 4030, "they held him to be a high god"; 582–83, "At that time there were people living on the island: they honoured the image"; 635–36, "make her a temple and an image of red gold."
Ælfric: 162, "who loved the sins that please the devil"; 128, "the heathens honoured him as a high god"; 136, "the heathens made him into a famous god"; 114, "Juno, a very high goddess"; 104, "a man was dwelling on that island"; 208–9, "concerning that image . . . he honoured it as a god"; 190–94, "they also made images for the honoured gods, some of pure gold . . . and raised for them a building that they called a temple."
7. Ed. W. W. Skeat, *Ælfric's Lives of Saints,* no. XVII, EETS, 76, 82 (London, 1881, 1887): see p. 374. Skeat's subtitle *De Auguriis* is appropriate only to the middle section (lines 67–207), which uses material from the pseudo-Augustinian homily of that title (see *Patrologia Latina* 39, cols. 2268–70), actually by Caesarius Arlatensis: see D. G. Morin, *Corpus Christianorum* 103 (1953), 235–40.

summe to weien-læten	148, Eac sume gewitlease wif
	farað to wega gelætum
7880, wigeling	70, 87, 99, 100, wiglung[8]

There is a reference to crossroads as places sacred to Mercury in *De Falsis Diis* (137, *and æt wega gelætum him lac offrodan*),[9] but the lines from *De Auguriis* are closer to Laȝamon in that they use a similar construction with *sume* and likewise refer to woods (trees) as well as to crossroads as places of pagan rituals. The theme of the sacrifice of boys (*Brut* 7747–51, from Wace 7347–54) also appears in *De Falsis Diis* 565–67, a coincidence that may have served to strengthen the associations with Ælfric in Laȝamon's mind as he reworked his main source. A further reminiscence of *De Falsis Diis* may well underlie Laȝamon's account of the destruction of pagan idols by King Luces, a theme not present in Geoffrey (*Hist. Reg. Brit.* IV.19) or Wace (5245–48), who refer only to the Christian consecration of pagan temples:

Brut 5079–81	*De Falsis Diis* 556–59
þa nomen anlicnes þe Mahun weoren ihatene,	Man toheow þa sticmælum þone sceoccenan god, and mid
heo letten heom draȝen vt oðer bi hondes oðer bi fot,	langum rapum his lima toferode; his heafod hi drogon
heo heom letten swalen inne swærte fure.	mid hospe geond þa burh, and his lima forbærndon.[10]

With this evidence that Laȝamon's writing was liable at times to reflect a knowledge of Ælfric's homilies, we may with more confidence postulate the same influence in isolated words and

8. *Brut:* 7734, 7740, "cast lots"; 7739, "some go to the wood, some to crossroads"; 7880, "sorcery."

Ælfric: 80, 84, "cast lots"; 129–30, "some people are so blind that they take their offerings . . . to trees"; 148, "also some stupid women go to crossroads"; 70, 87, 99, 100, "divination, sorcery."

9. 137, "and made him offerings at crossroads."

10. *Brut*, 5079–81, "they took the images that were called *Mahoun*, they had them dragged out by the hands or by the foot, they had them burnt in a black fire."

Ælfric, 556–59, "then they chopped the devilish god to pieces and pulled his limbs off with long ropes; they dragged his head contemptuously through the town and burned his limbs."

phrases which, taken by themselves, would hardly seem significant. For example, Laʒamon's choice of the word *feðerhome* in his account of Bladud's attempt to fly (1436–38) may have been influenced by Ælfric's use of *fiðerhama* in his retelling of the somewhat similar story of Simon Magus: in each case a man attempts to fly and falls to his death.[11] Again, although Laʒamon's account of the pagan temple in London and the sacrifices of Cassibellaune (4025–37) follows Wace fairly closely, Laʒamon supplies a name for the idol which is not found in Wace or Geoffrey of Monmouth:

> biforen heore mahun þe heom þuhte mære,
> Apolin was ihaten, heo heolden hine for hæhne godd.[12]

As we have already seen, this last phrase recalls *De Falsis Diis* 128, so we may also see in the preceding phrase an echo of *De Falsis Diis* 582, *þe wæs gehaten Apollo.* The supplying of the name *Dagon* (2695; not in Wace or Geoffrey) may also reflect Laʒamon's reading of *De Falsis Diis* 224–33 rather than the apparently more obvious biblical source. Likewise, Laʒamon's account of the plague in Britain (1943–50) may have been influenced, particularly in his use of the word *monqualm* (1950), by Ælfric's account of the plague (*manncwealm*) that afflicted the Philistines in *De Falsis Diis* 236–41.[13] Further, Laʒamon's version of the story of Pope Gregory and the English slaves—generally thought to have been drawn from Bede's *Historia Ecclesiastica*— introduces a reference to a street that has no counterpart in either the Latin or the Old English Bede:

11. See Ælfric's homily "Passio Apostolorum Petri et Pauli," ed. B. Thorpe, *The Sermones Catholici or Homilies of Ælfric*, 2 vols. (London, 1844–46) (commonly known as *The Catholic Homilies*, hereafter abbreviated *CH*), I.380. The same homily contains the phrase *Godes wiðersaca* (*CH* I.376) used by Laʒamon in *Brut* 906.

12. *Brut* 4029–30, "before their *Mahoun*, who seemed glorious to them; he was called Apollin, they held him to be a high god."

13. Wace, following Geoffrey of Monmouth, refers to a plague of flies that killed many men: *E tel plenté de musches crut / Dunt mainte gent d'engrot morut* (2127–28); perhaps influenced by the biblical plague of flies with its concomitant destruction of the land (Exodus VIII.24, *corruptaque est terra hujuscemodi muscis*) Laʒamon adds the line *swulc fare of fleoʒen her was þat heo freten þet corn & þat græs* (1948). Ælfric's account of the plague that afflicted the Philistines has *Him comon eac mys to, manega geond þæt land, and heora æceras aweston,*

þa com he in are strete þat strahte to Rome,
þa isah he leden of Englisce leoden. [M.29453–54][14]

Here again we have a clue to Laȝamon's reading of Ælfric since a
similar phrase occurs in Ælfric's homily on St. Gregory:

brohton heora ware to Romana byrig, and Gregorius eode be ðære
stræt to ðam Engliscum mannum.[15]

Since this story of Gregory is generally held to be Laȝamon's
only certain use of Bede, the dependence on Ælfric for this detail
calls into question Laȝamon's claim (*Brut* 17) to have used the
Old English Bede as a source.[16]

Laȝamon's *Brut* frequently shows independent additions that
have no counterpart in Wace or Geoffrey of Monmouth, and the

---

and þone eard fordydon (*De Falsis Diis* 240–41), but the Old Norse translation of
this homily in Hauksbók (see Pope, *The Homilies of Ælfric*, pp. 669–70) expands
this to *Mys . . . a lande þvi ato korn alt firir monnum oc grasretr*. There is no reason
to suppose that the Norse translator worked from an English text that included
any mention of corn and grass, and it is hardly conceivable that Laȝamon
should have had any knowledge of the Old Norse translation; the reference to
the eating of corn and grass that is shared by Laȝamon and the Old Norse text
must therefore be a coincidence to be explained in terms of common attitudes
in early medieval agricultural societies. As mentioned above, Ælfric's *of
smætum golde* (*De Falsis Diis* 191) corresponds to Laȝamon's *of ræde gold* (636),
and here the Old Norse translation of *De Falsis Diis* has *or rauðu gulli;* in this case
the coincidence is due to the long-standing collocation "red gold" in both
English and Norse, so that Laȝamon and the Norse translator independently
accommodate Ælfric's phrase to a formulaic tradition.

14. *Brut* M. 29453–54, "then he came into a street that led to Rome, and
he saw some English people being led there."

15. In the homily *Sci. Gregorii Pape Urbis Romane Incliti*, ed. Thorpe, *CH*
II.120; this parallel is noted by Pilch, *Layamons 'Brut'*, p. 67, n. 218ᵃ. Ælfric:
"they brought their wares to the city of Rome, and Gregory went along the street
to the Englishmen."

16. See Tatlock, *Legendary History*, p. 488, n. 10. Ælfric's homily on St.
Gregory follows the Old English Bede very closely, retaining numerous phrases
verbatim; the phrase quoted above is one of the few independent additions by
Ælfric. Laȝamon also used some other source, as appears in his reference to *three*
English slaves: this detail is not in Bede or Ælfric, but appears in the Life of St.
Gregory in the *South English Legendary*, line 21, *swete children þreo*: see *The Early
South English Legendary*, ed. C. Horstmann, EETS 87 (London, 1887), 357, and
The South English Legendary, ed. C. D'Evelyn and A. J. Mill, EETS 235 (London,
1956), 81.

foregoing examples (which in no way aim at completeness) suggest that sources for these additions may sometimes be found in Anglo-Saxon religious writings. Laȝamon presumably had access to sources that are beyond our recovery, including, it is often suggested, orally transmitted popular poetry; hypothetical lost sources are, however, a dangerously open-ended category, and one should perhaps be cautious about accepting, for example, C. S. Lewis's admittedly attractive suggestion of a source in lost Anglo-Saxon legend for Laȝamon's story of the East Anglian heroes Eðelbald and Ælfwald (6114–49), who liberated their country by murdering a tyrant while he was hunting (a story most inappropriately placed in Roman Britain).[17] The story of a king killed while hunting was familiar to Englishmen in the century following the death of William Rufus; and, more pertinently, the story of a king falsely induced to go out hunting so that he might be murdered was especially popular in Laȝamon's part of the country in the legend of the West Mercian saint Kenelm,[18] but Laȝamon's tale of the death of Gratien may even be based on nothing more specific than the fact that kings were more vulnerable while hunting than at other times.[19] The names Æðelbald and Ælfwald might have been taken quite prosaically from a literary source, and one in which they both appear in connection with East Anglia is Felix's *Life of Guthlac*.[20] In this case there

17. See *Selections from Laȝamon's Brut*, ed. G. L. Brook (Oxford, 1963), Introduction by C. S. Lewis, p. xi.

18. See the *South English Legendary*, ed. Horstmann, p. 349, and ed. D'Evelyn and Mill, p. 284.

19. Compare the account of the murder of Chilperic in Gregory of Tours, *History of the Franks* VI.46. The Life of St. Edward the Elder in the *South English Legendary* likewise places the murder of Edward during a hunting expedition (a detail not mentioned in the Anglo-Saxon Chronicle *sub anno* 978): see ed. Horstmann, p. 48, line 45, and ed. D'Evelyn and Mill, p. 111, line 41.

20. See *Felix's Life of Guthlac*, ed. B. Colgrave (Cambridge, 1956); the Life is dedicated to *Ælfwaldo regi Orientalium Anglorum* (p. 60), refers to the East Anglian milieu of Crowland (p. 126, *in Orientalium Anglorum terminis*), and narrates how the exiled Æthelbald visited Guthlac there (p. 148). The same details are also in the Old English translation of Felix's Life: see *Das altenglische Prosa-Leben des hl. Guthlac*, ed. P. Gonser (*Anglistische Forschungen* 27, [1909]), 100, 152 ff. The names Æðelbald and Ælfwald also occur together in the Anglo-Saxon Chronicle (E: *sub anno* 778) and in the letters of St. Boniface (*Die Briefe des hl. Bonifatius*, ed. M. Tangl, *Monumenta Germaniae Historica, Epistolae Selectae* I, nos. 73–75 and 81), but none of these associates Æðelbald with East Anglia.

must remain a good deal of doubt about the exact nature of Laȝamon's source, but something dully bookish is marginally more plausible than the exciting possibility of a lost patriotic legend. It may indeed be worth considering the question of La-ȝamon's sources in the light of what is known about books that were available in Worcester in the thirteenth century, since Worcester held a large library of Old English manuscripts and was within walking distance (about eleven miles) of Laȝamon's home in Areley Kings: in Worcester Laȝamon could have had access to Ælfric's *Catholic Homilies* and *Lives of Saints*, including *De Auguriis* and *De Falsis Diis*, and also Felix's Latin *Life of Guthlac*.[21]

The wider implications of this use of material from Ælfric's homilies may be considered in relation to recent studies by Professor N. Blake and Professor E. G. Stanley. Professor Blake has rightly pointed out that the rigid modern distinction between verse and prose is not valid throughout much of the Old and Middle English periods, and he conjectures that the origins of Laȝamon's alliterative metre are to be found in the rhythmic prose (or "rhythmic alliteration," as Blake prefers to call it) of the homilies of Ælfric and Wulfstan and of certain early Middle English works like the *Life of St. Katherine* rather than in classical Old English verse or a hypothetical popular verse.[22] Certainly it is important to see rhythmic alliteration as a contributory factor in Laȝamon's verse, and the foregoing examples of borrowing from Ælfric support Blake's view in so far as they show that Laȝamon was familiar with this literary form. On the other hand, it must be admitted that in the passages cited above where Laȝamon leans most heavily on Ælfric the alliterative patterning and the rhythm show certain differences, while Laȝamon also uses elsewhere, particularly in his rhyming passages, rhythmic forms that are

21. Manuscripts known to have been in Worcester in the thirteenth century include large numbers of Ælfric's homilies (see N. R. Ker, *Catalogue of Manuscripts Containing Anglo-Saxon* [Oxford, 1957], for full details); Ker 41 (Corpus Christi College, Cambridge, MS 178/162) and 333 (Bodleian MS Hatton 116) contain both *De Auguriis* and *De Falsis Diis*; Ker 331 (Hatton 113–14) and 48 (CCCC 198) contain the homily on St. Gregory; Ker 29 (Cotton Nero E.1) contains Felix's *Guthlac* (with some Old English glosses).

22. See N. F. Blake, "Rhythmical Alliteration," *Modern Philology* 67 (1969–70), 118–24; on "rhythmic prose" see especially Pope, *The Homilies of Ælfric*, I, 105–36. Blake objects to the term "rhythmic prose" on the grounds that it classifies as prose a form of writing that is neither prose nor verse.

much more remote from Old English rhythmic prose. The tradition of rhythmical alliterative prose from Ælfric to St. *Katherine* was clearly among the literary forms that contributed to Laȝamon's verse-form, but other models, both English and French, are likely to have been involved too. This whole question, which deserves further discussion, lies outside the scope of the present study.

Professor Stanley has pointed out that the revised ascription of MS Cotton Caligula A.ix to the late rather than the early thirteenth century means that we need no longer accept the traditional date of *c*. 1200 for the composition of Laȝamon's *Brut*. Although the *terminus a quo* still stands at 1189, the *terminus ante quem* (the date of the Caligula MS) is almost a century later.[23] Laȝamon's borrowings from Ælfric may now throw some light on the balance of probabilities within this extended time-span, though they must be considered together with Professor Stanley's further comments on the archaistic nature of Laȝamon's language.[24] The time-span allows, of course, a range of possible interpretations, but if we take its two termini, we obtain rather different interpretations of Laȝamon's use of Ælfric. On one hand, assuming that Laȝamon wrote at a date not long before the compilation of the two extant manuscripts of the poem (during, say, the 1260s), he would appear to be a writer who had access to Old English manuscripts of which he could not have understood very much, and who attempted to give his poem a superficial Old Englishness (what Stanley calls "putting up *ye olde* signs") by taking from these manuscripts isolated old words and phrases for inclusion in his poem; his borrowings might thus be expected to be orthographic (perhaps accurately so) and lexical rather than generally thematic. On the other hand, accepting the traditional dating of *c*. 1200, Laȝamon would appear as a man who had received his education at some time in the second half of the twelfth century, perhaps in a place where the reading and copying of Old English manuscripts was still actively practised, plausibly in Worcester, and who read Ælfric's homilies as part of his

23. See E. G. Stanley, "The Date of Laȝamon's *Brut*," *Notes and Queries* 213 (1968), 85–88.

24. See E. G. Stanley, "Laȝamon's Antiquarian Sentiments," *Medium Ævum* 38 (1969), 23–37.

clerical training; at some later date, we may conjecture, when he came to write the *Brut*, his earlier reading came to mind, mostly in the form of memories of subject-matter, but with a few odd words and phrases preserved intact, to be embodied in his poem. Some of the borrowings I have referred to (the use of isolated words and names) might seem to fit the first of these interpretations, but the most important (the recollection of Ælfric's attacks on paganism and sorcery) belong more plausibly to the second, as presumably do Laȝamon's erratic quasi-Old English spellings and the other linguistic archaisms discussed by Professor Stanley:[25] all these look like the products of a vague and confused memory of an early—and conceivably extensive—reading of Old English texts rather than archaisms culled from manuscripts that were readily available but no longer easily comprehensible; that is to say, they look like the work of a man in the first rather than the second half of the thirteenth century.

Professor Stanley's perceptive comparison of Laȝamon and the possessor of the famous Worcester "tremulous hand" points to the different kinds of antiquarianism of these two men, who came from the same area and who may have been contemporaries; whether either knew of the other's work or existence is not known, but two manuscripts that contain copies of homilies used by Laȝamon also contain glosses in the "tremulous hand" (Corpus Christi College Cambridge MS 178 and Bodleian MS Hatton 116); indeed, all the passages from *De Falsis Diis* that Laȝamon drew on contain "tremulous" glosses in CCCC 178, though we have no reason to believe that the glossator's Latin would have been more comprehensible than Ælfric's Old English to Laȝamon. Professor Stanley justly challenges Laȝamon's claim (*Brut* 13–14) to have used a Latin book by Albin and Augustine of Canterbury, and he concludes his consideration of this claim

25. For the probable relationship of the spelling of Caligula to Laȝamon's own spelling see ibid., pp. 26–27. Since completing this paper I have seen A. F. Cameron's important study, "Middle English in Old English Manuscripts," in *Chaucer and Middle English*, ed. B. Rowland (London, 1974), pp. 218–29; Cameron's demonstration that "the ability to read Old English never died out completely in England" (p. 226) does not invalidate my general argument here, though statements about the lack of understanding of Old English in the late thirteenth century need to be formulated more carefully in the light of Cameron's findings.

[73

with the words, "Perhaps Laȝamon had really seen some book containing works by both Albin/Alcuin and St. Augustine (of Hippo presumably) for such books existed, even in the vernacular, e.g. University Library Cambridge Ii.i.33."[26] The provenance of this last manuscript is unknown, but as it happens the two Worcester manuscripts just mentioned also meet this description, for both contain not only Ælfric's translation of Alcuin's *Interrogationes Sigewulfi*, beginning "Sum geþungen lareow . . . albinus gehaten" (the work generally held to be responsible for the famous phrase in the *First Worcester Fragment*, "Ælfric abbod þe we Alquin hoteþ"), but also the two homilies especially used by Laȝamon, *De Falsis Diis* (incomplete in the Hatton MS) and *De Auguriis*, the latter of which claims to quote Augustine (line 67, "Augustinus se snotera biscop sæde eac on sumere boc . . .").[27] To substitute for Laȝamon's Latin book by St. Albin and St. Augustine of Canterbury an English book with pieces deriving from Alcuin and St. Augustine of Hippo (or rather pseudo-Augustine, the actual source of *De Auguriis* being Caesarius Arlatensis) may seem cavalier, but it may not be an unjustifiable assumption for a world in which Ælfric and Alcuin were interpreted as variant names for the same person. One does not even have to agree with Stanley's opinion that "there is something sham rather than honestly erroneous about Laȝamon's antiquarian learning", for *Brut* 13–14 could represent a hazy memory of a book such as CCCC 178 that Laȝamon had seen at some time in the past. Alternatively, one may prefer to interpret Laȝamon's claims to have used books by Bede, Albin, and Augustine in a more imaginative way, for by the first half of the thirteenth century there was a well-established tradition for writers on Arthurian themes to refer to vague and unverifiable sources, often of an apparently fictitious nature, and Laȝamon's debt to Bede, Albin, and Augustine may be no more real than Geoffrey of Monmouth's to his mysterious book in the British

26. Stanley, "Laȝamon's Antiquarian Sentiments," p. 32.

27. Ælfric: "Augustine the wise bishop also said in a certain book." See ed. Skeat, *Ælfric's Lives of Saints*, no. XVII, p. 368; on the *Worcester Fragment* see Stanley, "Laȝamon's Antiquarian Sentiments," p. 31, and the works there cited.

language (*Hist. Reg. Brit.* I.i), or Chrétien's to his book from Beauvais (*Cligés* 1–44), or Wolfram's to his book by "Kîot" (*Parzival* VIII.416, IX.453, XVI.827), to mention only the more prominent among the numerous fictions by which Arthurian authors contrived to endow their writings with authority and romantic antiquarianism: in some cases, like Laȝamon's reference to Wace (*Brut* 15–19), such claims may be more or less true, but their function is not so much to impart truth as to prepare a certain mood of receptiveness in the reader. Whether terms like "sham" and "honest" are appropriate in this area of literary criticism is perhaps not important (we have Sir Philip Sidney's word for it that poets do not tell lies because they do not claim to tell the truth), what is more important is that Laȝamon is now emerging as a very much less simple sort of poet than used often to be thought.[28]

28. Claims to fictitious sources are by no means confined to Arthurian writings, particularly in the later Middle Ages (Chaucer's Lollius is not unique); before Laȝamon's time they are less common outside the Arthurian field, but a striking claim to the use of a fictitious Old English source is in Marie de France's statement that her *Fables* (apparently based on well-known Latin collections) are translated from an English version by King Alfred; there is no evidence for the existence of such a version, and indeed no evidence that manuscripts of fables ever circulated at all in pre-Conquest England; Marie was presumably aware of a popular tradition of the kind that subsequently gave rise to *The Proverbs of Alfred*, featuring the king as a repository of popular wisdom.

For the sake of conformity with other contributors to this volume I have referred to the poet as *Laȝamon*, the form of the name used in MS Cotton Caligula A.ix. The disadvantage of this form is obvious: the obsolete letter ȝ is not commonly available in modern type, and the arguments concerning its phonetic realization are familiar only to experts. Dissatisfaction with the Caligula form gave rise to the widespread form *Layamon*, which is of course linguistically unjustifiable. The other manuscript of the poem, Otho C.xiii, has the more evolved form *Laweman*, and it is reasonable to take this as a basis and to refer to the poet in Modern English as *Lawman*. This was recommended by Tatlock, *Legendary History*, p. 484, in 1950, and independently by F. Mossé in his *Manuel de l'anglais du moyen age*, II, *Moyen-anglais*, p. 183 (Paris, 1949). Mossé's arguments, together with the form *Lawman*, were retained in the English translation of his work: F. Mossé, *A Handbook of Middle English*, translated by J. A. Walker (Baltimore, 1952). The form *Lawman* is also used by T. F. Mustanoja in his *Middle English Syntax* (Helsinki, 1961): it is perhaps time that English scholars adopted this excellent American and continental practice.

4

God, Death, and Loyalty in *The Battle of Maldon*

Fred C. Robinson

YALE UNIVERSITY

I N *The Battle of Maldon*, said Humphrey Wanley, "celebratur virtus bellica Beorhtnothi Ealdormanni, Offae et aliorum Anglo-Saxonum, in praelio cum Danis,"[1] and two and a half centuries later another great Anglo-Saxon scholar summed up the traditional interpretation of the poem in terms which, though fuller, are not essentially different: "The words of Beorhtwold [*Maldon* 312–19] have been held to be the finest expression of the northern heroic spirit, Norse or English; the clearest statement of the doctrine of uttermost endurance in the service of indomitable will. The poem as a whole has been called 'the only purely heroic poem extant in Old English.' "[2] Most (though not all[3]) readers still view the poem as primarily a celebration of heroism

This essay was prepared during a year when a fellowship from the John Simon Guggenheim Foundation made it possible for me to devote my time to studies in English philology and literary interpretation. I have benefited from suggestions and encouragement generously offered by Professors Robert T. Farrell, Thomas D. Hill, and Robert E. Kaske of Cornell University.

1. *Antiquae Literaturae Septentrionalis Liber Alter seu Humphredi Wanleii Librorum Vett. Septentrionalium, qui in Angliae Bibliothecis extant,* . . . *Catalogus Historico-Criticus* (Oxford, 1705), p. 232.

2. J. R. R. Tolkien, "The Homecoming of Beorhtnoth Beorhthelm's Son," *Essays and Studies* 6 (1953), 13–14. This statement of the traditional view

rather than a homiletic or hagiographical exercise, and yet this view involves some theoretical difficulties which have hitherto been dealt with, as far as I am aware, only indirectly if at all. The first difficulty is that *Maldon* was written out of a culture whose fundamental assumptions about God and death were incompatible with a heroic sense of life. The second is that the ideal which motivates the heroes' sacrifice seems (from previous interpreters' accounts of it) too narrow and parochial to sustain *Maldon*'s significance beyond its own age, a great heroic poem requiring a theme of more universal significance than "comitatus loyalty." By confronting these difficulties in the present essay, I hope to confirm *Maldon*'s status as "the finest expression of the northern heroic spirit" and to deepen in some measure our understanding of the poem's meaning.

I

The battle of Maldon was fought and the poem about it was written at a time when the Heroic Age of England and the conditions which made that age possible lay in the distant past. The Anglo-Saxons had embraced Christianity centuries before, and the period of monastic reform which preceded the battle had been effective in rejuvenating men's faith and in renewing Chris-

---

of the poem is the starting point for Tolkien's own argument that *Maldon* specifically celebrates "the heroism of obedience and love" which is "the most heroic and the most moving" of all heroic gestures (p. 16), a view which is accepted and expanded in the closing pages of my essay.

3. Bernard F. Huppé, *Doctrine and Poetry, Augustine's Influence on Old English Poetry* (New York, 1959), pp. 23–38; N. F. Blake, "The Battle of Maldon," *Neophilologus* 49 (1965), 332–45; and W. F. Bolton, "Byrhtnoth in the Wilderness," *Modern Language Review* 64 (1969), 481–90, all argue in varying ways that Christian doctrine has displaced concern with secular heroism in the poem, a view which is vigorously opposed by, among others, George Clark, "*The Battle of Maldon:* A Heroic Poem," *Speculum* 43 (1968), 52–71. J. E. Cross supports Clark's position in general, although he differs with him over some particulars, in "Mainly on Philology and the Interpretative Criticism of *Maldon*," in *Old English Studies in Honour of John C. Pope*, ed. E. B. Irving and R. B. Burlin (Toronto, 1974), 235–53. See also Cross essay "Oswald and Byrhtnoth: A Christian Saint and a Hero Who Is Christian," *English Studies* 46 (1965), 93–109.

tianity's pervasive enrichment of the vernacular literature of the
Anglo-Saxons. In the range of literary conventions at their dis-
posal, however, their commitment to the church entailed losses
as well as gains. The Christian world-view, with its assumption
of a just God presiding over the affairs of men and its promise of
a joyous life after death for all believing and obedient Christians,
was not a world-view congenial to heroic narrative. Among the
cultural historians who have observed this fact, R. W. Southern, in his essay "Epic and Romance," has stated the matter with
particular clarity:

> [T]he monastic life—or for that matter the Christian life in any form
> —could never be merely "heroic" in its quality. That fatal struggle of
> man against superior forces, that meaninglessness of fate, and the
> purely resigned, defensive and heroic attitude of man in the face of
> fate could not, on a Christian view, be the whole story. As Europe
> became Christianized the epic was bound to decline, for it left out the
> personal and secret tie between man and God.[4]

Viewed through the uncolored lens of history, the Anglo-
Saxons at Maldon in August of 991 would appear to have been
anything but resigned, heroic men waging a struggle in the face
of a meaningless fate. They were Christians fighting heathens,
and they were led by a man who was exceptionally devout. The
personal tie between these men and their God would seem to
have been indissoluble, and we could imagine their looking forward to the happy afterlife which, as the Anglo-Saxon homilists
so often proclaimed, awaits those who suffer martyrdom for the
Lord. Indeed, as we reflect on the men at Maldon in 991, their
deaths seem less and less like acts of heroic daring and more and
more like a joyous witness to the faith.

But when we turn our eyes from the historical battle and
consider its depiction in the poem, the dying soldiers do not
seem to be Christian Martyrs on the threshold of Paradise but
valiant warriors enacting a grim and terribly meaningful heroic
sacrifice for heroic ideals. They appear to be oblivious of the
Christian assurances which were available to men in their predicament, and it is this that gives the poem that curiously ancient quality remarked so often by the critics. "But for a few
phrases it might, as far as the matter is concerned, have been

4. *The Making of the Middle Ages* (New Haven and London, 1953), p. 224.

written before the conversion of England," observed W. P. Ker
in 1896,[5] and a later critic amplifies his statement to absurdity:
"In *Maldon* for the last time in our literature the old epic strain is
. . . revived. Once again flames out in a Christian epoch the
spirit of the old pagan lays. It was doubtless the work of a
Christian, but of a Christian in whom the defence of home and
kindred against the Danish sea-robbers, 'the wolves of blood,'
had roused the smouldering pagan fires."[6] Almost everyone who
has meditated over the poem has sensed something archaic and
stern in it—"the old epic strain," if you will. But the
"smouldering pagan fires" are an embarrassing relic from nineteenth-century Romantic scholarship. Indeed, the central question, both for the *Maldon* poet and for us, is how can a poem
revive an "old epic strain" (posited on the fatal struggle of man
against superior and unfriendly forces) when there are no pagan
fires smoldering? I believe an answer to this question may lie in
the poet's portrayal of God and death in his narrative, for it is a
portrayal which evokes an aspect of the Christian thought-world
congenial to the heroic temper.

There is in the poem only one detailed account of a warrior's
death, and that is the slaying of Byrhtnoth, which therefore
becomes a type and emblem of all the many death-agonies suffered by Englishmen in the battle. Lines 130–72 recount the
manner of Byrhtnoth's slaying, and in lines 173–80 appears his
much-discussed death-prayer:

> "Geþancie þe, ðeoda waldend,
> ealra þæra wynna þe ic on worulde gebad.
> Nu ic ah, milde metod, mæste þearfe
> þæt þu minum gaste godes geunne,
> þæt min sawul to ðe siðian mote
> on þin geweald, þeoden engla,
> mid friþe ferian Ic eom frymdi to þe
> þæt hi helsceaðan hynan ne moton."[7]

5. *Epic and Romance* (London and New York, 1897), 2d ed. (Oxford,
1908), p. 55.

6. W. MacNeile Dixon, *English Epic and Heroic Poetry* (London, 1912), p.
86.

7. Quotations from *Maldon* and other Old English poems are drawn from
The Anglo-Saxon Poetic Records (hereafter *ASPR*), ed. George P. Krapp and
E. V. K. Dobbie, 6 vols. (New York, 1931–53).

Before Morton Bloomfield's discerning essay "Patristics and Old English Literature,"[8] readers paid scant attention to what this speech actually says, regarding it as no more than a vaguely pious prayer. In fact, it is a specific allusion to the *judicium particulare*—a literal, physical struggle between devils and angels for possession of the soul as it leaves the body of a dying man. Having identified the motif, Bloomfield goes on to suggest that this evocation of the "patristic" notion of the death-struggle bespeaks a religious dimension in the characterization of Byrhtnoth and that the "speech would suggest a consciousness of [Byrhtnoth's] martyrdom." Proceeding from Bloomfield's conclusion, other scholars have arrived at allegorical or hagiographical interpretations of the entire poem.[9] In contrast to this view, I shall argue that the motif which Bloomfield identified has the opposite effect, that instead of Christianizing the poem the death-speech of Byrhtnoth subtly de-Christianizes the cosmic setting of *Maldon* and in doing so helps to create the conditions necessary for a heroic narrative.

While it is true that the supernatural struggle for a dying man's soul may be found in the writings of the Fathers,[10] it is by no means limited to patristic contexts. To the *Maldon* poet, I suspect, this curious conception would have seemed a popular rather than a patristic tradition and hence would have introduced no particular suggestion of formal Christian theology into the poem. For the motif occurs much more widely than has been

8. *Studies in Old English Literature in Honor of Arthur G. Brodeur*, ed. Stanley B. Greenfield (Eugene, Ore., 1963), pp. 37–38.

9. Bolton, "Byrhtnoth in the Wilderness," p. 489, Blake, "Battle of Maldon," p. 339. Cf. Huppé, *Doctrine and Poetry*, pp. 237–38. The first scholar to suggest a hagiographic reading of *Maldon* was Bernhard ten Brink, and it is interesting to note that in his translation of Byrhtnoth's death-prayer he silently deletes any reference to the devils who will strive with the angels for Byrhtnoth's soul. See his *Geschichte der englischen Litteratur* (Berlin, 1877), I, 120. Very likely ten Brink sensed that the squabbling demons detracted from the religious dimension which he wanted to see in the poem.

10. See G. Rivière, "Rôle du démon au jugement particulier chez les Pères," *Revue des Sciences Religieuses* 4 (1924), 43 ff., and Alfred C. Rush, "An Echo of Christian Antiquity in St. Gregory the Great: Death a Struggle with the Devil," *Traditio* 3 (1945), 369–80. For a wider survey of the occurrences of the theme, see now Ute Schwab, "Ær-Æfter. Das Memento Mori Bedas als Christliche Kontrafaktur. Eine philologische Interpretation," in *Studi di Letteratura Religiosa Tedesca in Memoria Sergio Lupi* (Florence, 1972), pp. 91–100.

noticed heretofore. It is the subject of a text called "Freondlic Mynegung" which appears in Bodleian MS Ashmole 328 at the end of Byrhtferth's *Manual*, and it is developed vividly in an eighth-century Latin letter from Wynfrith to Eadburga, which was translated into Old English in the late tenth century.[11] Many Old English homilists describe how the soul will be attacked when it passes from the body,[12] sometimes in phrasing reminiscent of Byrhtnoth's prayer in *Maldon*.[13] Several accounts of the death-struggle occur in Old English translations of Apocrypha,[14] and of Gregory's *Dialogues*,[15] while formulas alluding to it appear in the penitential texts published by Max Förster.[16] Bede's *Historia Ecclesiastica* depicts the struggle for the soul in his accounts of Furseus and Dryhthelm, and these were excerpted and translated into Old English as exempla by his countrymen.[17] Vernacular poems allude to the death-struggle, as

11. See Kenneth Sisam, *Studies in the History of Old English Literature* (Oxford, 1953), pp. 199–224.

12. See *Wulfstan: Sammlung der ihm zugeschriebenen Homilien*, ed. Arthur Napier (Berlin, 1883), pp. 140–41, 235–37, 249–50; (also in *Byrhtferth's Manual*, ed. S. J. Crawford, Early English Text Society, [hereafter EETS], o.s. 177 [London, 1929], 249–50); *Homilies of Ælfric*, ed. Benjamin Thorpe (London, 1846), II, 336–38, 350–52; *Early English Homilies from the Twelfth-Century Manuscript Vespasian D.XIV*, ed. R. D.-N. Warner, EETS, o.s. 150 (London, 1917), 110–13; *Ancient Laws and Institutes of England* (London, 1840), II, 466–69; *The Blickling Homilies*, ed. R. Morris, EETS, o.s. 73 (London, 1880), 209, and cf. 149–51. See also *Homilies of Ælfric: A Supplementary Collection*, ed. John C. Pope, EETS, o.s. 260 (London, 1968), II, 776–79.

13. Compare, for example, *Maldon* 173–74 and *Wulfstan*, ed. Napier, p. 237, lines 4–6; *Maldon* 180 and *The Blickling Homilies*, ed. Morris, p. 209, line 28.

14. Rudolph Willard, *Two Apocrypha in Old English Homilies*, Beiträge zur englischen Philologie 30 (Leipzig, 1935), 38 ff., 126 ff., et passim; and Milton McCormick Gatch, "Two Uses of Apocrypha in Old English Homilies," *Church History* 33 (1964), 379–91 (especially his discussion of the Apocalypse of Paul).

15. *Bischof Wærferths von Worcester Übersetzung der Dialoge Gregors des Grossen*, ed. Hans Hecht, Bibliothek der angelsächsischen Prosa 5 (Hamburg, 1907), pp. 316–21.

16. "Zur Liturgik der angelsächsischen Kirche," *Anglia* 66 (1942), 29 and 35.

17. *Venerabilis Baedae Opera Historica*, ed. C. Plummer (Oxford, 1894), I, 164–67, 303–10. For the Old English versions see *Homilies of Ælfric*, ed. Thorpe, II, 332–58.

[81

does at least one entry in the *Anglo-Saxon Chronicle*—that for A.D. 959 containing the half-metrical obituary for King Eadwig.[18] A vivid illustration of St. Peter fighting with a devil over the soul of a dead Christian appears in an Anglo-Saxon manuscript which has been dated to 1031—just forty years after the battle of Maldon.[19] There are many descriptions of the death-struggle in Latin works from the British Isles,[20] and the theme is attested in vernacular literature across the English Channel. The ninth-century Old High German *Muspilli* 1–30 gives a particularly somber description of the clash of angels and devils, and there is a reference to it in *Gíslasaga*. Jacob Grimm cites numerous occurrences of the motif in later vernacular literature and suggests parallels between the Christian version of the death-struggle and pagan Germanic visions of the Valkyries descending to catch up the souls of the slain.[21] Though never as widespread as the more conventional Christian conceptions of death and judgment,[22] the contest of angels and devils at a *judicium particulare* was clearly an alternative explanation which was available in popular tradition.[23]

18. *Two of the Saxon Chronicles Parallel*, ed. C. Plummer (Oxford, 1892–99), I, 115, lines 14–16. Among the poems, see *Resignation* 49–56 and *A Prayer* 74–76; cf. *Guthlac* lines 6–7, 22–25.

19. British Library MS. Stowe 944, fol. 7ʳ. The setting in this instance, it should be mentioned, is the last judgment.

20. Rudolph Willard, "The Latin Texts of the Three Utterances of the Soul," *Speculum* 12 (1937), 147–66; *Adomnan's Life of St. Columba*, ed. Alan Orr Anderson and Marjorie O. Anderson (London, 1961), pp. 477–79; see also n. 17, above.

21. *Teutonic Mythology*, trans. J. S. Stallybrass, II (London, 1883), 836–38; IV (1888), 1551.

22. The prevailing view, as expressed repeatedly by Ælfric and others, was that the souls of good to mediocre Christians repose with God or in some kind of vaguely conceived purgatory until the last judgment, while evil Christians await everlasting punishment in hell. (See, for example, *Homilies of Ælfric*, ed. Pope, I, 425–28, and *Byrhtferth's Manual*, ed. Crawford, p. 249.) Milton McCormick Gatch has rightly observed that the contrary view suggested by Byrhtnoth's prayer was somewhat eccentric. "By far the more usual sort of prayer," says Gatch in *Loyalties and Traditions: Man and His World in Old English Literature* (New York, 1971), p. 143, "is that which Cynewulf wove into the conclusion of the *Ascension*: that men would pray for him so that he might be accepted at the Judgment as a thegn of Christ."

23. The point of uncertainty which lay between the two explanations of

What is most striking about these various accounts of devils and angels struggling over the souls of the dying is the stark terror which they bring to the experience of death and their apparent negation of the usual Christian consolations for death. The souls of good men as well as of evil ones are repeatedly described as cowering in the corpses which they ought to have abandoned,[24] afraid to venture outside where "all this air is filled with hellish devils which travel throughout the world."[25] A frequent motif is the dying Christian's fear that during his lifetime he may have committed sins of which he was unaware—unwitting sins which could tip the balance of the battle between the angels and the devils in the direction of the swarming demons. This is especially noticeable in the poem *Resignation* 75–82, where the speaker's mention of "þara synna þe ic me sylf ne conn / ongietan gleawlice" brings to a climax his anxieties over the fortunes of his departing soul.[26] It is these same anxieties which moved the saintly Bede to speak "de terribili exitu animarum e corpore" when he utters his *Death-Song,*[27] and which add poignancy to the melancholy forebodings in his *De die judicii.* If a pious man like Bede feared the moment of Divine decision, then how much more terrible should that moment be to a soldier at Maldon with his enemy's gore on his hands?

In the other accounts of Byrhtnoth's slaying which have

---

the soul's passage to the next life was the question as to where the soul abided between death and Judgment. Gregory deals with this question at some length in Book IV of the *Dialogues.* For a survey of Anglo-Saxon views, see Milton McC. Gatch, "Eschatology in the Anonymous Old English Homilies," *Traditio* 21 (1965), 124–28.

24. See for example *Wulfstan,* ed. Napier, pp. 140–41, and *Homilies of Ælfric,* ed. Pope, II, 776–79.

25. *Wulfstan,* ed. Napier, p. 250: "eall þis lyft ys full hellicra deofla, þa geondscriðað ealne middangeard." The statement occurs in the context of a description of the "mycel gewinn betweox deoflum and englum" on the day of one's death. Cf. *Byrhtferth's Manual,* ed. Crawford, p. 249.

26. Anxiety over sins unconsciously committed is also a motif in some of the prose accounts of the war with the demons for a man's soul. Thus in Wynfrith's letter (Sisam, *Studies,* p. 216) a dying man saw that "manige synna þær cirmdon swiðe egeslice wið hine þa þe he næfre ne wende þæt hio to synnum oðlengdon; and þa awyrigdan gastas wæron geswege eallum þam synnum." See n. 31 below.

27. *Venerabilis Baedae Opera Historica,* ed. Plummer, I, clxi.

[83

come down to us along with *The Battle of Maldon* there is nothing
like the disturbing image of struggle which darkens his last moments in the English poem. The nearly contemporary *Vita Os-
waldi* draws on the more conventional religious doctrines when
it tells us that at Maldon Byrhtnoth was supported by "the man-
ifold love of the Lord—because he was deserving." All "the alms
and holy masses he had donated comforted him," and his
"prayers and his [former] good deeds lifted him up."[28] The later
History of Ely also emphasizes his "righteous life and deeds," and,
most interestingly, observes that he was "free from the fear of
death" ("sine respectu et timore mortis"). The account of the
monks' tender care for the corpse of "this active and pious man"
brings the narrative to a close with distinct overtones of the
conventional saint's life.[29] Indeed, it is the strikingly similar
death of St. Boniface which comes most readily to mind when
we read the Latin accounts of Byrhtnoth's death. Boniface's joyous death-speech to his comrades as they are about to be cut
down by the pagan Frisians is just what we might have expected
Byrhtnoth to say: "Now is the day for which we have long
yearned, and the moment of our release, which we have desired,
is at hand. . . . Do not be frightened by these who kill our
bodies, for they cannot slay the soul, which is immortal; rejoice,
rather, in the Lord, . . . because in a moment He will give you a
reward of everlasting recompense and a seat with the angels in
the heavenly hall."[30]

28. "Stabat ipse, statura procerus, eminens super caeteros, cujus manum
non Aaron et Hur sustentabant, *sed multimoda pietas Domini fulciebat, quoniam
ipse dignus erat. . . . elemosinae et sacrae Missae eum confortabant. . . . Protegebat se
. . . quem orationes et bonae actiones elevabant."* See *Historians of the Church of York and
Its Archbishops*, ed. James Raine, I (London, 1879), 456.

29. *Liber Eliensis*, ed. E. O. Blake, Camden 3d ser., XCII (London,
1962), 134.

30. *Vitae Sancti Bonifatii Archiepiscopi Moguntini*, ed. Wilhelm Levison in
*Scriptorum Rerum Germanicarum in usum scholarum ex Monumentis Germaniae Histo-
ricis separatim editi* (Hannover and Leipzig, 1905), pp. 49–50 (my translation).
Other good Christians of the period end their lives like Boniface and Oswald
"with a happy slaying" ("felici cede" in ibid., p. 50). Thus St. Edmund, who,
like Byrhtnoth, was slain by Vikings and beheaded, sees his "happy soul travel
to Christ" the moment he is cut down (W. W. Skeat, ed., *Ælfric's Lives of Saints*,
EETS, o.s. 114, II, 32). Felix says that Guthlac at his death declared that

Instead of these reassurances, the poet of *Maldon* evokes the anxieties of the supernatural struggle for the soul as Byrhtnoth takes leave of his life, and his last words are a pathetic plea to God not to let the demons prevail in the contest. We are not told why this good and generous benefactor of monasteries should feel so uncertain about the fate of his soul. Perhaps we are to assume that he, like the speaker in *Resignation*, feared that he might have committed unawares some grievous sins which would leave his soul prey to the rapacious devils.[31] Or again, he may have had a more immediate cause for anxiety. Anglo-Saxon penitentials state that homicide on the field of battle is not exempted from all ecclesiastical censure but must be atoned: even soldiers who have fought "pro aecclesiastica justitia" or who were defending their homeland against pagan invaders ("incursio paganorum") are forbidden entry to the church for specified periods of time.[32] Byrhtnoth and his troops had good reason to fear death at Maldon, and the poet was not violating the letter of current beliefs when he adopted as his image of death in the poem a conception which emphasizes all man's un-

---

"the spirit is eager to travel to its infinite joy," while the Old English poet in lines 1266–68 describes the saint's soul as "yearning for its exit hence to nobler homes." On every hand the contrast with Byrhtnoth's death is striking.

31. Such morbid fears are but an extreme expression of the orthodox Christian view that mortals must never presume to know what God's judgment of any human being will be. Gregory the Great's interlocutor Peter gives expression to this feeling in Book IV of the *Dialogues*, the Old English translation of which is this: "Hwylc man is, þe him ne ondræde, þonne he cymð to ænde, swa unasecgendlicne cwyde þære hynðe ond þæs wites, þe þu rehtest, sy swa hwylces weorces ond geearnunge man swa hit sy, forþon þe þeah he eallunga wite, hu he lifde ond hwæt he dyde ær, he swa þeah nat þonne gyt, hu smealice his dæde sceolon beon gedemde beforan Godes eagum?" to which Gregory answers, "Swa hit is swa þu sægst. . . ." See *Bischof Wærferths Übersetzung*, ed. Hecht, p. 377.

32. See J. E. Cross, "The Ethic of War in Old English," in *England before the Conquest: Studies in Primary Sources Presented to Dorothy Whitelock*, ed. Peter Clemoes and Kathleen Hughes (Cambridge, 1971), pp. 280–81. It should also be mentioned that in the instances of the war for dying men's souls which are cited above, one of the commonest motifs is the warning that men who had not confessed their sins were especially vulnerable to the host of demons who came for the soul. It seems unlikely that the men at Maldon had all been safely shriven before the battle.

certainties and anxieties over dying and thus recalls a thought-world more like that of Homer or the sagas. The poet was careful, moreover, in his timing of the allusion. It is immediately after he has evoked the image of the *judicium particulare* that the cowards break and run for their lives; it is in the face of this disturbing vision of death that the heroes of the poem make their decision to stand and die.

Even before we come to Byrhtnoth's death-prayer, however, the poet has begun to hint subtly at an ominous uncertainty in God's disposition of events in this world. Besides Byrhtnoth's prayer there are but three allusions to the Deity. The first occurs when Byrhtnoth, having rashly granted the Viking horde free passage through the Panta to his own army's position, muses over the outcome of the battle to which he has committed his troops: "God ana wat / hwa þære wælstowe wealdan mote" (lines 94–95). At first glance this statement seems to be a mere formula for acknowledging an uncertainty, but in the context of the poem and of history it is darkened with tragic irony, for readers of *Maldon* have always shared God's foreknowledge of how the battle was to end: He granted victory to the heathens and allowed His faithful Christians to be massacred. This bitter irony restores to the formula some of the meaning which it bore in an earlier gnomic phrasing:

	Meotod ana wat
hwyder seo sawul sceal	syððan hweorfan . . .
æfter deaðdæge. . . .	
	Is seo forðgesceaft
digol and dyrne;	drihten ana wat . . . [*Maxims* II.57–62]

The next allusion to God occurs at the moment when Byrhtnoth drives his spear through the heart of a Viking. He rejoices briefly[33] and thanks God for the success he has had. And then, as if in sardonic reply to his prayer of thanksgiving, the next line

---

33. The poet says (line 147) "hloh þa, modi man," and both the phrasing and the situation are echoed elsewhere in early English literature in a way that suggests that the words are a narrative formula. In *Judith* 23–26, Holofernes "hloh ond hlydde, . . . modig ond medugal" before Judith decapitates him. Later, in *Layamon's Brut*, ed. F. Madden (London, 1847) II, 203, line 13, we are told that "þa king loh" at the very moment when, unbeknownst to him,

of the poem tells us that a Viking spear immediately pierced the Christian, wounding him mortally. Here again a startling juxtaposition of narrative details throws an ominous shadow on a prayer of Byrhtnoth's. The final allusion to God is near the end of the poem where the Christian warriors offer prayers to God that He allow them to punish the heathen slayers of Byrhtnoth —prayers which, once again, God seems not to have granted. These allusions to God in the poem, along with the dying prayer of Byrhtnoth, suggest a world devoid of the certainties which orthodox Christianity is usually thought to bring and one in which heroism is achieved at a dear price and is rich with meaning.

The poet's artful evocation of a cultural attitude which makes heroic narrative possible in no way implies that he criticized or rejected standard Christian beliefs. His strategy, rather, is to select from the available Christian attitudes those which depict the world in the bleakest perspective possible. We should remember that pessimism and uncertainty over the Divine scheme of things were not uncommon around the year 1000 and in the immediately succeeding centuries. The entries in the *Anglo-Saxon Chronicle* from the time of the battle of Maldon to the end of the twelfth century make surprisingly few references to God working through history, and such allusions as do occur often carry a tone of bewilderment at the Deity's permitting the horrors which seem to prevail throughout that period. "A more sorrowful deed was not done in this country since the Danes came and peace was made with them here," says the *Chronicle* poem for the year 1036 (referring to Godwin's mutilation and murder of Alfred's retainers), and he adds uncertainly, "Now one must trust to the beloved God that they will be happy and peaceful with Christ who were so miserably murdered without any guilt."[34] Three times in this period an entry closes with a

---

Rowenna is pouring poison into his cup. This laugh may be a conventional dramatic signal that a mortal blow is imminent at the moment when the threatened person least expects it.

34. "The Death of Alfred," lines 11–15. Although Dobbie (*ASPR*, vi, 24), following Plummer (*Two of the Saxon Chronicles Parallel*, I, 158, and II, 211), prints the first part of this entry as prose, it is clear that the Chronicler intended it all to be poetry, the first lines in alliterative verse (of very poor quality) and the rest in a combined alliterative-rhyming form.

form of the gloomy refrain, "God hit bete þa his wille beð," and this mood culminates in the Peterborough chronicler's observation on the prevailing despair of the English: "And the land was all destroyed by such deeds, and men were saying openly that Christ and his saints were asleep."[35] Henry of Huntingdon (who is among the chroniclers who recorded the story of Byrhtnoth's death) also speaks of Englishmen saying that God slept,[36] while William of Newburgh reports the view that "the Deity seemed to be sleeping and not caring for the things of men."[37]

God's apparent condonation of human suffering had long troubled the Anglo-Saxons, of course, and the homilist Wulfstan is typical of many churchmen in his frequent insistence that England's calamities were God's punishment for the sins of the English. But as the innocent appeared increasingly to be those who suffered most, this explanation of God's purpose lost persuasiveness among some writers. The *Peterborough Chronicle* of Hugh Candidus contains a powerful description of the horrors of the Viking invasions, in which innocent Christians were butchered by bloodthirsty pagans, and then, at the close of his account, the author turns indignantly on "men of perverse mind who persist in saying that these things are visited upon men because of their own sins." Hugh seeks among seven alternative reasons why God might afflict the innocent, but in the end he concludes stoically that Christians must assign calamities "to the mysterious judgments of God"[38]—a view which seems to bring us back to the Anglo-Saxon gnomic reflection cited above: "God alone knows . . . future destiny is hidden and mysterious; God alone knows."

35. *The Peterborough Chronicle,* 1070–1154, ed. Cecily Clark (Oxford, 1958), p. 56.

36. *Henrici Archidiaconi Huntendunensis Historia Anglorum,* ed. Thomas Arnold (London, 1879), p. 277.

37. *Historia Rerum Anglicanum,* in *Chronicles of the Reigns of Stephen, Henry II, and Richard I,* I, ed. Richard Howlett (London, 1884), 45.

38. *The Chronicle of Hugh Candidus, a Monk of Peterborough,* ed. W. T. Mellows (London, 1949), pp. 23–27. Hugh lived more than a century after the battle of Maldon, but, as the editor has shown in his introduction, his Chronicle often draws on Old English sources.

God, Death, and Loyalty in *The Battle of Maldon*

It was in this world where God was inscrutable—or simply asleep—that the poet of *Maldon* recognized a viable analogue to the cosmic outlook of a Heroic Age. He portrayed the actions of his heroes against a background of divine remoteness and indifference which many Englishmen were at that time beginning to sense, and which gave deep meaning to heroic sacrifice. In doing so, the *Maldon* poet was solving in a new way the problem that an earlier English poet had solved with equal success in a quite different way. The author of *Beowulf*, who was also a Christian, used the simple device of placing his heroic narrative in the lost world of Germanic paganism, thereby lending a dark grandeur and heroic meaning to deeds which, had they been performed by devout Christians in a Christian setting, would have been merely exemplary.[39]

II

While the poet's portrayal of God and death may provide the conditions necessary for a heroic poem, it does not in itself provide a heroic poem. For no matter how bravely men die, they do not achieve heroic stature unless they sacrifice themselves for some purpose which readers can recognize as significant and worthy. To most readers there has never been doubt that it is loyalty that inspires the English to fight and die in *The Battle of Maldon*, but the poet has stressed and characterized that particular ideal of loyalty more fully, I believe, than previous students of the poem have noticed.[40] By focusing

39. The classic work on this subject is J. R. R. Tolkien's *"Beowulf: The Monsters and the Critics,"* Sir Israel Gollancz Memorial Lecture, 1936, *Proceedings of the British Academy* 22 (1936), 245–95.

40. Most previous discussion of the ideal of loyalty in *Maldon* has centered on the question whether it was a poetic anachronism (suggestive of the customs described in Tacitus's *Germania*) or an actuality of the late tenth century. Edward B. Irving, "The Heroic Style in *The Battle of Maldon*," *Studies in Philology* 58 (1961), 460, speaks of "the antique virtues husbanded over the centuries in the worn formulas of poetic diction," and this seems to me to account adequately for the highly traditional form which the theme assumes in the poem. T. D. Hill, "History and Heroic Ethic in *Maldon*," *Neophilologus* 54 (1970), 291–96, and M. J. Swanton, *"The Battle of Maldon: A Literary Caveat,"* *JEGP* 67 (1968), 441–50, see the ideals governing the heroic action as

on the Viking messenger's speech, the speeches of the dying Englishmen, and other narrative details in the poem, I shall try to show first how central the theme of loyalty is in *Maldon* and second how the poet has expanded the significance of that theme so that it justifies the heroic sacrifices of the English.

It is the superb arrogance of the Viking's challenge (lines 29–41) which is usually noticed, and that arrogance may have been given an especially sharp edge by the poet's use of Scandinavicisms to characterize the speaker (a device which would make this the first instance of literary dialect in English[41]). But these features merely supplement the central point of the speech, which is to challenge the Englishmen's loyalty to their leader. This challenge becomes clear when we attend to those grammatical forms in the speech which have troubled scholars in the past. "The use of singular and plural in this passage is puzzling," says Margaret Ashdown, and in her translation she uses modern English *you* for both singular and plural.[42] But the poet's shifts in number are his sign that the Viking does not address himself exclusively to the leader Byrhtnoth, as protocol would dictate, but speaks alternately to Byrhtnoth and to his men. Taking for granted that all Englishmen are disloyal cowards at heart, he presumes to negotiate directly with the troops themselves. The opening sharp demand is directed to Byrhtnoth alone ("þu most sendan raðe beagas wið gebeorge"), but the speech

genuinely anachronistic and argue that the poet is critical of Byrhtnoth for adhering to them. Hans Kuhn, on the other hand, feels that the comitatus was a living system which the Essex Englishmen had adopted from their Scandinavian neighbors in the Danelaw: see "Die Grenzen der germanischen Gefolgschaft," *Zeitschrift der Savigny-Stiftung für Rechtsgeschichte*, Germ. Abt. 86 (1956), 1–83, esp. p. 45, as well as the rejoinder by Walter Schlesinger, "Randbemerkungen zu drei Aufsätzen über Sippe, Gefolgschaft und Treue," *Alteuropa und die Moderne Gesellschaft: Festschrift für Otto Brunner*, Herausgegeben vom Historischen Seminar der Universität Hamburg (Gottingen, 1963), pp. 21–41. František Graus's startling claim, "Eine typische germanische Treue gibt es (ausser in der Historiographie) nicht," in "Über die sogenannte germanische Treue," *Historica* 1 (1959), 120, is effectively rebutted by Schlesinger, pp. 41–59.

41. My evidence for this supposition is set forth in "Some Aspects of the *Maldon* Poet's Artistry," *JEGP* 75 (1976), 25–40.

42. *English and Norse Historical Documents* (Cambridge, 1930), p. 74.

softens as the messenger turns away from the leader to speak directly with the troops ("eow betere is . . ."). At line 34, or possibly even at line 33, the Viking actually slips into a comradely first-person plural ("ne þurfe we us spillan"), implying that the soldiers in the field, both Viking and English, are united in their desire for peace, which is obstructed only by the selfish leader Byrhtnoth. When he returns to the second-person singular and addresses Byrhtnoth again, he talks as if he were the spokesman for both English soldiers and Vikings: "Gyf þu þat gerædest, þe her ricost eart . . . ," and his plea with the leader to "deliver" or "ransom" his men (*lysan*) is barbed with a stinging double entente: The sense of *ricost* addressed to Byrhtnoth is "most powerful" (i.e. the one in authority), while the sense addressed to the Englishmen under arms is "wealthiest"—insinuating that it is Byrhtnoth, not they, who stands to lose the most if peace is purchased from the Vikings. The last clause in the speech is once again a friendly plural addressed over Byrhtnoth's head to his men: "We willaþ . . . eow friþes healdan."

To these divisive innuendoes Byrhtnoth replies appropriately in the name of his army,

Gehyrst þu, sælida,   hwæt þis folc segeð?

The ensuing plurals of his rejoinder unite the English and their leader decisively and thus answer the challenge to his men's honor. Byrhtnoth underscores the strength of the bonds of loyalty by emphasizing that he is himself but the loyal servant of his own lord, Æthelred (line 53), and thus expects no more from his troops than his own lord expects from him. Byrhtnoth's assertion (line 51), "here stands an undishonored earl with his army," affirms that the traditional bond between men and leader remains intact.

The exchange of speeches is, then, a rhetorical prelude rehearsing the test of loyalty soon to be enacted on the battlefield in deadly earnest. At another passage of high rhetoric near the end of the poem the dramatics of speechmaking serve again as a vehicle for the poet's central theme. The sequence of the speakers in lines 209–60 has evoked several alternative explanations. R. W. V. Elliott perceived the speeches as "a picture of confused hurling of words as of spears" and thought of "the random style of the cine-camera."[43] N. F. Blake surmised that the variety of warriors from various regions and social stations was intended "to imply that the defenders in the battle were a microcosm of the whole of England," while O. D. Macrae-Gibson sees the speeches at the end of the poem progressing steadily from active cries for vengeance to passive statements of the speaker's willingness to die.[44] It seems to me, however, that the speeches from lines 209–60 are arranged in a sequence determined by the poem's theme of loyalty, a sequence which dramatizes the increasing power which the ideal of loyalty exerts among the loyal English at the close of the poem. The first speaker, Ælfwine, explains that in his case the claims of loyalty are the most tangible and urgent of all, for "he wæs ægðer min mæg ond min hlaford" (line 224). The rhetorical emphasis upon *min* forced by the meter emphasizes Ælfwine's special obligations to live up to the heroic ideal.[45] Offa, the next speaker, does not share Ælfwine's double tie of kinship and fealty, but he is clearly the most overtly obligated of all the other retainers, having been portrayed throughout the poem (esp. lines 198–201, 289–93) as a specially close friend and lieutenant of Byrhtnoth's—probably even his second in command. Leofsunu is a less distinguished retainer, and his homely boast is that the steadfast soldiers whom he knows back at the pool near Sturmer[46] will find no reason to taunt him for disloyalty. He shares neither kinship nor close friendship with Byrhtnoth, but the principle of loyalty, conceived of in broad social terms rather than personal terms, motivates him to make the same noble sacrifice as Ælfwine and Offa have vowed to make. Next, the churl Dunnere, a fyrd man who is not even a member of Byrhtnoth's comitatus, is fired by the ideal of loyalty and, in two simple verses, demonstrates that

43. "Byrhtnoth and Hildebrand: A Study in Heroic Technique," in *Studies in Old English Literature*, ed. Greenfield, p. 64.

44. Blake, "Battle of Maldon," p. 338; Macrae-Gibson, "*Maldon:* The Literary Structure of the Later Part," *Neuphilologische Mitteilungen* 71 (1970), 192–96.

45. See John C. Pope, *Seven Old English Poems* (Indianapolis, 1966), p. 78.

46. See Gordon, ed., *Battle of Maldon*, Methuen's Old English Library (London, 1937) p.85, on the meaning of *Sturmere*.

the inspiring example of the previous speakers has elevated him to the company of Byrhtnoth's comrades in performance of duty.[47] There is yet one further climax in this sequence, for the example of Dunnere seems to have been infectious itself. First, the noble *hired* is inspired by his example (line 261), and then the one man among the Anglo-Saxons who had least obligation of all to die with Byrhtferth joins the loyal heroes: the Northumbrian hostage Æscferth at this point surges forward to fight and die for the fallen Essex leader.[48] At the end of this sequence of speeches the poet has demonstrated in strong dramatic terms that the remaining Englishmen on every hand have withstood the challenge to their loyalty, and we know precisely the motivation for the deaths in the remaining lines of the poem, where the poet records the name of each Englishman as he falls under the Vikings' axes.

The force of the heroes' commitment to the ideal of loyalty is further dramatized by the poet in quite another way. Throughout the poem there emerge several partial justifications for an Englishman's taking flight. First, Byrhtnoth is clearly stated to have made an error when he committed his troops to a battle in which the enemy were allowed to have free passage across the river and take up positions before the Englishmen could begin their defense. One may argue over the meanings of *lytegian* and *ofermod* (although Professor Helmut Gneuss has now provided virtually certain evidence that the latter word means "pride" and that the poet's use of *ofermod* signals a criticism of Byrhtnoth's generalship),[49] but the phrase *londes to fela* admits of

47. The name *Dunnere* may be related to *Dunne*, which Henry Bosley Woolf cites as the name of a peasant in his *Old Germanic Principles of Name-Giving* (Baltimore, 1939), p. 140. W. J. Sedgefield, *The Battle of Maldon* (Boston, 1904), inadvisedly emends the name to Dunhere, thus obscuring its humbler origins.

48. Sedgefield, finding it incredible that a hostage held by Byrhtferth should die fighting for him, reasons that "Æscferð was doubtless a hostage who had escaped from the enemy" (*Battle of Maldon*, p. 38). That a hostage could be inspired by the example of his captor's loyal retainers to join in the fight for their leader is demonstrated, however, by the British hostage in the famous *Chronicle* entry for 755.

49. See H. Gneuss's discussion in *"The Battle of Maldon* 89: Byrhtnoth's *ofermod* Once Again," *Studies in Philology* 73 (1976), 117–37.

no doubt. Byrhtnoth erred, and the men at Maldon were free to meditate over this fact as they considered whether or not to remain and die out of loyalty to the man whose misjudgment had brought them to this hard decision. They might further have reflected that Byrhtnoth's misjudgment was probably the basis for his retainers' decision to flee. At least some of the cowards were among Byrhtnoth's closest household thanes (see lines 200–201), and if these high-ranking men thought it right to leave the field, then surely the hostage Æscferth and humble fellows like Dunnere might be excused for leaving. Finally, the poet's pointed references to Æthelred throughout the poem would clearly have carried some irony, for Æthelred was at this time becoming the national symbol for English unwillingness to stand and fight.[50] A king who set an example for craveness, a leader who had blundered, and lieutenants who withdrew from the field might well provide soldiers with a basis for reassessing the force of their own sworn loyalties. But the heroes at Maldon, though presumably aware of these possible justifications for flight, scorned them, and the nobility of their stand is accordingly enhanced.

However inspiring their gesture, it remains to be asked whether the "narrow Germanic convention of honor and loyalty"[51] is a sufficiently serious theme to warrant the poet's celebration of it. Soldiers fighting loyally to the death are not necessarily an exalting spectacle; indeed, without some clearly perceived higher purpose their struggles might be, as Milton disdainfully observed, no "more worth . . . then to Chronicle the Wars of Kites, or Crows, flocking and fighting in the Air."[52]

50. In the paper mentioned in note 41 I argue that *The Battle of Maldon* was composed long enough after the death of Byrhtnoth for its audience to have appreciated the historical ironies created by Æthelred's ineffectual warfaring in succeeding decades. The frequent assumption that *Maldon* was composed almost before the dust of battle had settled has little to support or recommend it. As Tolkien observed ("Homecoming," p. 16), the poem "is certainly not a work of hot haste."

51. *The Oxford Anthology of English Literature*, I, ed. J. B. Trapp et al. (London, 1973), 106: "The poet's theme turns on this narrow Germanic convention of honor and loyalty." See n. 40 above.

52. *The History of Britain* in *The Works of John Milton*, ed. F. A. Patterson et al. (New York, 1932), p. 191. The reference is to earlier wars of the Anglo-Saxons.

Why was the loyalty of the Maldon Englishmen worth the poet's writing a poem on the subject, and what is that poem's claim on our interest and sympathy today?

More than a mere tribal custom, the interlocking bonds of loyalty were the principle on which Anglo-Saxon civilization rested, the only bulwark against primitive chaos and anarchy.[53] Wulfstan's most famous sermon is in large part a catalogue of the horrors that befall a people once the principle of loyalty is forgotten,[54] and the *Chronicle* entry for 1010 illustrates how the absence of loyalty between leaders and men induces anarchy: "Ultimately," says the chronicler, "no captain would raise an army, but each man took flight as best he could, and at the last one shire wouldn't even support the other."[55] Like respect for the law today, loyalty in pre-Conquest society was the sine qua non, and its absence marked the difference between civilization and primeval disorder. The concept in this enlarged sense was extended by poets even into the theological realm. As has often been remarked, portrayals of Christ in *The Dream of the Rood* and other Old English poems suggest that it was not merely love, but rather that unique combination of loyalty and affection which Anglo-Saxons felt for their chosen leaders that seems to bind the Christian to his Lord. And as the poem *Genesis* makes clear, Satan emerges in the Anglo-Saxon view as an unworthy thane whose disloyalty to God introduced disorder and evil into the world. To Christians elsewhere, the primal sin of Lucifer was pride; to the Christian Anglo-Saxon it seems more often to have been disloyalty.

That disloyalty reduces human society to ungoverned misery is stated overtly by more than one poet. The doom-laden prediction of Wiglaf makes the connection directly:

53. See Dorothy Whitelock, *The Beginnings of English Society* (Harmondsworth, Middlesex, 1952), pp. 29–47, and Gatch, *Loyalties and Traditions*, pp. 129–41. Gatch's discussion of *Maldon* on pp. 129–35, which anticipates in part some of my own arguments, seems to me to be the best existing account of the theme of loyalty in the poem.
54. *Sermo Lupi ad Anglos*, ed. Dorothy Whitelock, reprinted with additions to the bibliography (New York, 1966).
55. *Two of the Saxon Chronicles Parallel*, ed. Plummer, I, 140–41. Clark, "*The Battle of Maldon*," p. 59, cites this passage.

Londrihtes mot
þære mægburge   monna æghwylc
idel hweorfan,   syððan æðelingas
feorran gefricgean   fleam eowerne,
domleasan dæd.   [*Beowulf* 2886–90]

In *Maldon* the connection is dramatized rather than stated. As long as the Anglo-Saxons stand fast in their loyalty to Byrhtnoth, the English line holds, and the English warriors are as one. But at the climax of the poem, where the cowards break and run, all is suddenly transformed. The cowards' behavior is depicted not merely as a panic but specifically as personal disloyalty leading to anarchic disorder: Godric usurps the horse and trappings of his leader, and this induces immediate chaos in the English ranks, for, as Offa explains in lines 237–42, some men mistook the fleeing Godric for their lord and so were deceived into thinking Byrhtnoth was leading them in a retreat. "The people were dispersed," laments Offa, "and the shieldwall was shattered" by Godric's violation of the oaths that bound him to Byrhtnoth.

The shieldwall itself is another eloquent symbol of the link between personal loyalty and social order, for this formation was the perfect physical expression both of loyalty to the leader and of mutual loyalty among men. At the leader's command, "the front rank of men held their shields before their breasts and the ranks behind held theirs over their heads to protect both those in front and themselves."[56] As long as each man stands fast (as Byrhtnoth repeatedly urges his men to do), the formation is virtually impregnable,[57] but if a section of the rank gives way, the battle order is lost and the soldiers become isolated and helpless, vulnerable to massacre. Twice in the poem we see Byrhtnoth ordering the men to form and hold the shieldwall (lines 19–21, 101–2), and twice we are told how it was broken by the disloyal retreat of the cowards (lines 193–95, 241–42). The cowards' disloyalty not only severs the bond of love and

56. Gordon, ed., *Battle of Maldon*, p. 50.
57. Albert S. Cook, *Judith* (Boston, 1904), p. 26, collects passages from Roman historians attesting to the difficulty of penetrating a Germanic shieldwall. (Gordon, ed., *Battle of Maldon*, p. 50, calls attention to Cook's note.)

obedience between men and their leaders; it also disrupts the bonds between men and men and reduces a harmonious community to primitive anarchy.

It is a comprehensive principle of human loyalty and civilized order which the English heroes choose to preserve on the battlefield of Maldon when they regroup to fight the enemy in a last desperate stand. They uphold this ideal despite the plausible rationalizations for flight which the poet suggests were available to them, and they uphold it in the face of a death to which the poem has lent renewed and ominous meaning. When the Englishmen decide to die, each man reasoning out his decision in a speech, they are not dying under orders, for their leader is dead. They are not dying in a frenzy of hatred for the enemy, for the poet has been careful to portray the Vikings as anonymous rather than hateful.[58] They are not even dying for victory, since it is clear after the rout of the cowards that no hope of victory remains. As the details and emphases of the poem make clear, the soldiers are dying together,[59] loyal both to their lord and to each other, for the principle which underlay all that was positive and good in life as they understood it.[60] The principle can be upheld on the field of battle only if man's mind and spirit are brought to assert the superior importance of the ideal over physical life and physical strength. And it is this assertion that Byrhtwold makes in the name of the fallen and falling Englishmen in words that are more meaningful the more literally they are understood: "The mind must be the firmer, the heart the stronger, the spirit must be the greater, as our body's strength

58. Clark (*"The Battle of Maldon,"* p. 58) has stated this point well: "The vikings are simply a force impelling the decisions to pay or fight, to flee or die; they are not objects of interest in themselves." See also my remarks in *Philological Essays in Honor of Herbert Dean Meritt* (The Hague, 1970), pp. 100–101, and in "Some Aspects of the *Maldon* Poet's Artistry," *JEGP* 75 (1976), 25–40.

59. The orderly solidarity of the dying heroes stands in eloquent contrast with the pell mell, *sauve qui peut* flight of the deserters. Brave men die in good company; the oldest proverb in English tells us how cowards die: *suuyltit thi ana.*

60. In their speeches the Englishmen do not, of course, enunciate an abstract principle of loyalty. They speak rather to the particular vows which are the concrete manifestations of that principle of loyalty within their own lives.

declines."[61] In making this statement against the background of cosmic uncertainty which the poem's details suggest, *Maldon* is a supremely heroic poem, in a sense more heroic than the poems with which it is so often compared—*The Iliad*, the Eddic lays, and *The Song of Roland*.

61. *Maldon* 312–13. F. Th. Visser, *An Historical Syntax of the English Language*, Part One. (Leiden, 1963), pp. 162–63, makes the interesting suggestion that *sceal* is gnomic in this passage. But his translation of the verb ("is proper," "ought to be") seems weak. Context implies the normal meaning "must be."

5

Geoweorþa:
"Once Held in High Esteem"

E. G. Stanley

PEMBROKE COLLEGE, OXFORD

Aspelling in the Old English *Orosius*[1] has long been singled
out as of great philological interest—that for the name of the
king of the Numidians *Iugurtha* in Latin, *Geoweorþa* in the Anglo-
Saxon translation. There is no doubt at all about the spelling,
with either *þ* or *ð* and in oblique cases with inflexional final *n;* but
what matters is that Latin *Iu-* of the first syllable is always spelt
geo- in the translation, and the second syllable always has Old
English *-weorþ-* or *weorð-* for Latin *-gurth-*. Two manuscripts containing the name survive, the Lauderdale or Tollemache MS,
now British Library MS Addit. 47967, to which N. R. Ker
assigns the date "s.X¹," i.e. about the middle of the first half of
the tenth century, and British Library MS Cotton Tiberius B.i,
the first article of which, the *Orosius*, is written in four hands, all
assigned a date by Ker a century later than that of the Lau-

1. The translation was formerly attributed to King Alfred, but differences
in syntax and vocabulary between the *Orosius* and Alfred's genuine works make
that attribution untenable. For references to work demonstrating these differences see E. G. Stanley, "Studies in the Prosaic Vocabulary of Old English
Verse," *Neuphilologische Mitteilungen* 72 (1971), 408 n.; and especially J. M.
Bately, "King Alfred and the Old English Translation of Orosius," *Anglia* 88
(1970), 433–60, whose own contribution to the question of attribution is
important.

[99

E. G. Stanley

derdale MS.[2] The Lauderdale MS is available in facsimile; it was edited by Henry Sweet in 1883; the Cotton MS was edited by Joseph Bosworth in 1859 and collated by Sweet in his edition.[3] Bosworth thought that the Cotton MS was copied from the Lauderdale MS;[4] but some readings correct in the Cotton MS and wrong in the Lauderdale MS would presuppose uncommonly intelligent scribes for the Cotton MS if Bosworth were right, and it is better to reject Bosworth's view and to accept the view that the two extant manuscripts are independent copies of the same lost antecedent, shared errors making it unlikely that the lost manuscript was the translator's original.[5] Clearly, the *geoweorþa* spellings of Iugurtha go back to the common antecedent, faithfully copied into the two extant manuscripts, but in giving figures to show that the spelling is to be relied on it is best to ignore the Cotton MS rather than double the figures obtained from the Lauderdale MS alone. In the Contents (ed. Sweet, p. 5.28) *geoweorþan* comes once; in the body of the *History* (pp. 228, 230) that form comes ten times; uninflected *geoweorþa* comes three times with þ and twice with ð. There is no other name in the *Orosius* with which to compare the second half of the name, the -*gurth-* rendered by *weorþ-*, though there are many oddities of spelling in the names, admirably discussed by Miss Janet Bately in connection with her demonstration that there is Welsh linguistic influence.[6] The first half of the name is, however, readily comparable with other names in the work, yet none of them manifests a similar spelling of *geo-* for initial *Iu-* or *Io-*. Thus we find in the Lauderdale MS spellings like *Iulius, Iulianus,* and

2. N. R. Ker, *Catalogue of Manuscripts Containing Anglo-Saxon* (Oxford, 1957), nos. 133 and 191.

3. A. Campbell, ed., *The Tollemache Orosius*, Early English Manuscripts in Facsimile, III (Copenhagen, 1953); Henry Sweet, ed., *King Alfred's Orosius* Early English Text Society (hereafter EETS), o.s. 79 (London, 1883); Joseph Bosworth, *King Alfred's Anglo-Saxon Version of the Compendious History of the World by Orosius* (London, 1859).

4. Bosworth, *Orosius*, pp. xxi f.

5. See Campbell, *The Tollemache Orosius*, p. 23.

6. "The Old English Orosius: The Question of Dictation," *Anglia* 84 (1966), 255–304; see especially pp. 270–72.

Iosep, as well as for the Latin name *Iouianus* a range of not very good spellings, like *Iuuinianus* (ed. Sweet, p. 7.8), *Iuninianus* (p. 286.24), *Iuninius* (p. 288.1), with the Cotton MS giving better forms, like *Iuuianus* (ed. Bosworth, p. 14.33), *Iuuinianus* (p. 129.2), as well as *Iuuinius* (p. 129.12, and notes p. 30).[7]

The Old English form for the name Iugurtha is, therefore, truly remarkable. It has received much linguistic comment. *Geoweorþa* has been regarded as providing, in general terms, a good example for the fact that spellings are not an unequivocal guide to the pronunciation of a dead language; and more particularly, the form seems to furnish evidence, by a double use of inverted spelling, that two specific phonological developments are only imperfectly represented by the Anglo-Saxon system of spelling. That imperfect representation in the written form of words of the vowel sound in them is attested to also in spelling doublets of the type *iu* beside *geo*, *iung* beside *geong*, *iuguð* beside *geoguð*, in which it is far from certain that a distinction was made, not merely in spelling, but also in pronunciation; and secondly, doublets of the type *wurð* beside *weorð*, *swurd* beside *sweord*, *wurpan* beside *weorpan*. In both halves of the form *Geoweorþa*, so it seems, that spelling of two possible variants has been used which is the less like the Latin spelling though the pronunciation of the vowel could be that corresponding in each half to the *u* of the Latin.

Moreover, in the belief, first advanced by Schilling and only recently shown to be untenable, that the *Orosius* was translated by King Alfred himself, the form *Geoweorþa* was adduced as evidence for the theory that scribes took down the work from dictation.[8] Now the theory of dictation has been abandoned too, yet some explanation is still needed for a form in the translated text so far removed from the Latin text that aural transmission of the text was apparently best able to explain it; it does

---

7. Sweet and Bosworth conflict in their reading of the Cotton MS on *n* or *u* after *iu-* in the name, but that is not relevant to the present discussion.

8. H. Schilling, *König Ælfred's ags. Bearbeitung der Weltgeschichte des Orosius* (Halle, 1886), see especially pp. 57 f. on the evidence provided by *Geoweorþa* for dictation. For a refutation of the argument that the oddly spelt names provide evidence for dictation see Bately, "The Old English Orosius."

not seem entirely convincing to put down *w* in *Geoweorþa* to the Welsh connection discussed by Miss Bately.[9]

In the standard grammars, the phonological and orthographic problems connected with *Geoweorþa* are attributed to the conflict between conservative spelling and what Campbell § 172 fn. 1[10] calls "the natural W-S pronunciation of *Iugurtha*," and Luick § 169.1[11] reminds his readers in connection with *geo-* for *iu-* that the form is found "in der wahrscheinlich nach einem Diktat geschriebenen Handschrift des Orosius."[12] Luick is even more explicit on the second half of the form; he connects, § 286.1 and especially Anm. 1, the spelling *-weorþa* for *-gurtha* with the change which led from *weorð* to *wurð*, first evidenced in Alfred's West-Saxon; Campbell § 321 draws attention to *wurþ* in the *Pastoral Care*. Luick's Anmerkung is on the conservatism of spellings with special reference to *Geoweorþa* (which seems a most unconservative, or at least unconventional spelling for the name Iugurtha): "As early as the *Orosius* we meet the spelling *Geoweorþa* for Jugurtha, which obviously presupposes a text taken down from dictation, and proves that at the end of the ninth century the letter sequence *weor* was connected with the sound value [wur], in other words that the sound-change *weor-* to *wur-* had taken place by then, even though the spelling was still *weor-*."

The form *Geoweorþa* as a whole, therefore, provides evidence —if it stands simply for *Iugurtha* as pronounced by an Anglo-Saxon—for the distance between spelling and pronunciation. But the two halves of the word do not point in the same direction. The first half with *geo-* for *iu-* has a new spelling for the sound sequence *iu* which seems to have been retained through-

9. She discusses the form in "The Old English Orosius," pp. 270–72; she regards the form of the name with *w* for *ʒ* as "most satisfactorily explained in terms of Old Welsh pronunciation and scribal tradition."

10. A. Campbell, *Old English Grammar* (Oxford, 1959).

11. K. Luick, *Historische Grammatik der englischen Sprache* (Leipzig, 1914–40; reprinted Oxford and Stuttgart, 1964).

12. In addition to Luick and Campbell, see A. Pogatscher, *Zur Lautlehre der griechischen, lateinischen und romanischen Lehnworte im Altenglischen*, Quellen und Forschungen zur Sprach- und Culturgeschichte der germanischen Völker, LXIV (Strasburg, 1888), 177, 180.

out Old English and later, though perhaps not always, in such words as *iu, iung, iuguð,* also spelt *geo, geong,* and *geoguð:* in these words the initial sound is the Germanic palatal semi-vowel *j.* In Primitive Old English initial ʒ before a front vowel was palatalized to the same sound. A glide developed in some cases after the sound *j,* in other cases diphthongs developed through other combinatory sound-changes, and there is evidence that in some cases a rising diphthong developed from a falling diphthong, making it hazardous to assert that in the words *geo, geong,* and *geoguð,* for example, there never was a genuine diphthong in any dialect at any time. It does, however, seem to be true that undiphthongized forms never died out.[13] Unlike the relationship of sound to spelling in the first half of *Geoweorþa,* that in the second half of the form shows an old spelling retained for what is in words like *weorð > wurð* a new sound sequence, but in the name *Iugurtha* is the unchanged pronunciation of the Latin by an Anglo-Saxon.

The third element of importance in the strange spelling *Geoweorþa* is the *w* for Latin *g.* We may presume that in pronouncing the Latin an Anglo-Saxon would have used the voiced velar spirant for the *g,* the sound which he would have used in a native word with spelling *g* between two back vowels, e.g. *iuguð.* Very much later, certainly not before the twelfth century,[14] that sound became *w,* such a sound being regarded as a necessary intermediate stage between the velar spirant and its vocalization (leading to MnE. *youth,* for example). It is quite unlikely that a manuscript of the first half of the tenth century could provide genuine evidence in spelling for the sound-change that gave, as it

13. See Luick, *Historische Grammatik,* §§ 168–77; Campbell, *Grammar,* §§ 170–89.

14. See Luick, *Historische Grammatik,* §§ 402 [cf. for northern dialects 406, which is not relevant], 711; R. Jordan, *Handbuch der mittelenglischen Grammatik* (Heidelberg, 1934; reprinted 1968), § 186. If anything, the evidence is later than is suggested in the standard grammars, because of the palaeographical redating of what used to be regarded as the earlier of the two extant manuscripts of Laʒamon's *Brut:* see N. R. Ker's introduction, pp. ix–xx, to the facsimile of *The Owl and the Nightingale,* EETS, 251 (London, 1963); I discuss some of the implications of that redating in *Notes and Queries* 213 (1968), 85–88, and *Medium Ævum* 38 (1969), 25–37.

is thought, a *w* in positions that look remarkably like the position of *g* in *Iugurtha*.

A further step is required. Campbell § 321 suggests as an explanation of the -*weorþa* that it is "with assimilation of the second part of the name to the adj. *weorþ* worth, and this presupposes a form *wurþ*"—of which he provides a genuine Alfredian example. Why that assimilation should have taken place is not explained by Campbell. As we have seen, the two manuscripts nowhere, in such names as Iulius, Iulianus, Ioseph, and (with other errors) Iouianus, assimilate initial *Iu*- or *Io*- to vernacular *geo*, except in *Geoweorþa*. I presume that the process that took Latin *Iugurtha* by association through some similarity of sound to Old English *Geoweorþa* was a pun on the name, and a bad pun if the medial *g* of the Latin cannot have had the sound of *w* required by the Old English. In Old English, *iu*, alternatively spelt *geo*, means "formerly," and *weorþa*, with which Latin -*gurtha* seems to have been punningly identified, means "worthy" weak masculine singular.

When it comes to punning the cry is soon, "Un œuf is as good as a feast." And that very example illustrates Charles Lamb's principle, smuggled in by him under the general heading of "Popular Fallacies," viz. "That the Worst Puns are the Best."

> If by worst be only meant the most far-fetched and startling, we agree to it. A pun is not bound by the laws which limit nicer wit. It is a pistol let off at the ear; not a feather to tickle the intellect. It is an antic which does not stand upon manners, but comes bounding into the presence, and does not show the less comic for being dragged in sometimes by the head and shoulders. What though it limp a little, or prove defective in one leg?[15]

Lamb's Law may be expressed less whimsically: a pun gives special pleasure when it requires a leap to be made from one word to another disparate in sense yet suddenly brought close by a sufficient similarity of sound in a context where each of the

15. *Last Essays of Elia*, ed. T. Hutchinson, *Works in Prose and Verse of Charles and Mary Lamb* (Oxford, 1908), I, 792.

two words can operate. Identity of sound does not require a great leap to be made, and it is the leap that is enjoyable.

In his chapters on Shakespeare's puns, Helge Kökeritz[16] distinguishes between homonymic puns and jingles, though he may at times seem to enlarge the area of homonymity at the expense of the jingles. He treats as homonymic puns such Shakespearean word-play on names as "Aufidius: so fiddious'd" (whatever that may mean) *Coriolanus* II.i.139–45; "Jupiter: Jibbetmaker" *Timon of Athens* IV.iii.79–85, which is brought nearer to homonymity by the knowledge that, as Kökeritz (p. 119) says, "Q spells the name Jubiter," and (p. 297) that there is good evidence of *b* being widespread in the name; "Ninnies toombe: Ninus tombe" *Midsummer Night's Dream* III.i.99–100, where Quince's correction of the pronunciation makes it clear that the pun was not homonymous to him. Among jingles on names Kökeritz gives "infranchise: one Francis" *Love's Labour's Lost* III.i.121–23; "Mortimer: Bricklayer" *2 Henry VI* IV.ii.41–43, where Butcher understands Cade's father to have had dealings with mortar like a bricklayer, as the clown in *Timon* thinks that Jupiter's trade is in *gibbets;* "Suffolkes duke: suffocate" *2 Henry VI* I.i.124.

Some of the jingles are no more than playful linking of a kind far removed from punning; in others the effectiveness of the pun is advanced rather than inhibited by the distance in pronunciation of the two words involved, though in some cases one variety of pronunciation may bring the words nearer to each other in sound than in a more formal variety. Lamb's Law operates well in Shakespeare, and may even have been formulated (with characteristic whimsy) with an eye on the puns of Shakespeare and his contemporary dramatists of which Lamb had a better knowledge than most.

In recent years the word-play of a much earlier period, that of the Anglo-Saxons, has been subjected to searching scrutiny. Professor Roberta Frank has examined Old English scriptural

16. H. Kökeritz, *Shakespeare's Pronunciation* (New Haven, 1953; reprinted 1960), pp. 51–157.

verse,[17] whose examples include a wide range of paronomastic sound-effects such as proceed readily from alliterative verse which, by definition, relies on like initial sounds for its prosodic linking. Names, especially biblical names, are in the tradition of exegesis, and that is not so much a matter of sound or echo, but rather of sense and moral implication revealed by patristic and later medieval inquiry into the derivation of names, discussed in an illuminating excursus by E. R. Curtius, "Etymology as a Category of Thought."[18] Professor Fred C. Robinson has shown how such established etymologies of biblical names have their place in Old English vernacular writing, both prose and verse.[19] In verse we find, for example, *sædberendes Sethes lice* (*Genesis* 1145) and that had been introduced (line 1133) by *sedes* used for *Sethes*,[20] an extension into vernacular expression of a traditional etymology, enshrining it in an Old English–Latin jingle, an inexact pun, which, though, of course, not designed for laughter, may have involved that special pleasure of requiring a leap for recognition, such as Lamb speaks of for modern puns: the voiced dental stop *d* of *sedes* is not likely to have been identical with the dental spirant *th* of *Sethes*, voiced by the Anglo-Saxons between vowels.[21]

17. "Paronomasia in Old English Scriptural Verse," *Speculum* 47 (1972), 207–26, based on her important and stimulating Harvard doctoral dissertation "Wordplay in Old English Poetry" (1968) which she has allowed me to read. For a full range of references to other writings on Old English word-play and related subjects, see the footnotes to her article, especially footnote 5.

18. E. R. Curtius, *European Literature and the Latin Middle Ages* (London, 1953), pp. 495–500.

19. "The Significance of Names in Old English Literature," *Anglia* 86 (1968), 14–58. See also Fred C. Robinson, "Some Uses of Name-meanings in Old English Poetry," *Neuphilologische Mitteilungen* 69 (1968), 161–71. I am very grateful to Professor Robinson for reading this article in typescript and making a number of valuable improvements in it.

20. See Robinson, "Significance of Names," pp. 29–32; Professor Robinson, however, regards *sēd* for *Seth* as a substitution of the name-meaning, with a fortuitous similarity of sounds. On the extension into the vernacular of sacred etymology, see Frank, "Paronomasia," p. 223.

21. It seems that Latin *d* in some positions became *ð* when the word was borrowed into English, as Campbell, *Grammar*, § 530 says; but the relationship of the pun on Seth is in the opposite direction, and I doubt if it was exact. For the

In a way the pun on Seth and OE. *sæd* is untypical of Old English puns on names, for the obvious reason that typical Anglo-Saxon names are of two elements. Before turning to more familiar examples, I may perhaps mention a drawing to which Dr. A. Heimann of the Warburg Institute has drawn my attention, though I alone bear the blame for the punning interpretation. On fol. 64r of British Library MS Harley 603, the drawings of which have been discussed, especially by the late Professor Francis Wormald, who assigns the hand to "the early years of the second quarter of the 11th century",[22] is a drawing of a winged bowman shooting three arrows into what looks like a cairn. It is inscribed *ægelmund*, perhaps the artist's name. I take the drawing to stand for the bowman Egil, known to us in Old English as *Ægili* from the Franks Casket,[23] with *Ægil, Ægel* in the Harley MS for the name-element *Æþel*. The name-element is found in many forms, *oeþel* "homeland" for example, but also *Ægel* leading later to Anglo-Norman *Ail, Ael*.[24] The second part of the rebus on Æþelmund is phonologically easier. Instead of *mund* "hand, protection" we must understand, as we look at the cairn, *munt* "hill, mount" [< Latin *mont-em*]. In such loan-words *u* for *o* is normal,[25] and spellings with *d* can be paralleled in the form *Mund-iu* found in Ælfric,[26] so that perhaps in some pro-

special problem of names involving *ð* for classical *d* in the Old English *Orosius* (see Campbell, *Grammar*, § 530, footnote), cf. Bately, "The Old English Orosius," pp. 264–67.

22. Francis Wormald, *English Drawings of the 10th and 11th Centuries* (London, 1952), pp. 69–70. The drawing is with, but marked off from, a psalter illustration proper between Psalms 118 and 119.

23. See A. S. Napier, "The Franks Casket," *An Old English Miscellany Presented to Dr. Furnivall* (Oxford, 1901), pp. 365–67 and Plate I: ÆGILI. See also J. Hoops, *Reallexikon der Germanischen Altertumskunde*, I (Strasburg, 1913), s.v. *Egill*, § 2; F. J. Child, *English and Scottish Popular Ballads*, III (Boston, 1888), 16.

24. See W. G. Searle, *Onomasticon Anglo-Saxonicum* (Cambridge, 1897), pp. 33–61; and especially O. von Feilitzen, *The Pre-Conquest Personal Names of Domesday Book*, Nomina Germanica 3 (Upsala, 1937), pp. 102–6.

25. See Pogatscher, *Zur Lautlehre der . . . Lehnworte*, pp. 103 f.; Luick, *Historische Grammatik*, § 213.2; Campbell, *Grammar*, § 501.

26. J. C. Pope, *Homilies of Ælfric*, EETS, 263 (London, 1967), 708 (XXI.578), has the form *Mundiu*, with *Mund-* for *Munt-*; cf. Glossary, s.n.;

nunciations *munt* came close to *mund*. In this rebus, therefore, though we may feel at several points that the bowman of Germanic mythology and the mount of Latin derivation have to be dragged in by head and shoulders, it is, to use Lamb's conception, a *good pun* for being bad; and at the same time it shows how in punning on an Anglo-Saxon name use has to be made of the two elements.

Such use is made, of course, in punning on *Guthlac* in the versified saint's life, literally *guð* "battle, warfare" + *lac* "gift, offering," or "belli munus" according to the writer of his Latin life, the Anglo-Saxon Felix, as Professor Fred C. Robinson has adduced, before going on to delve further into etymological meanings of the names in *Beowulf*, though he was not the first to do so, as his footnotes show.[27] If the spelling *Geoweorþa* is to be interpreted by word-play as if it were a vernacular name it forms a counterpart to Gregory the Great's bilingual punning on Angles and angels, etc., which Professor Robinson discusses in his article.[28] The meaning derived from the name by learned etymological playfulness, not of course "folk-etymology," is "once held in high esteem." That amounts to a moral judgement on Iugurtha, and not one that is derived fully from the accounts of Iugurtha given in the Anglo-Saxon *Orosius*:[29]

---

perhaps as a result of sporadic unvoicing of final voiced stops (see Luick, *Historische Grammatik*, § 653; Campbell, *Grammar*, § 450) some interchange of *d* and *t* may have become possible, at least to some extent.

27. "Significance of Names," pp. 35–57, deals with vernacular names. See also Fred C. Robinson, on the name Unferð, "Elements of the Marvellous in the Characterization of Beowulf: A Reconsideration of the Textual Evidence," *Old English Studies in Honour of John C. Pope*, ed. Robert B. Burlin and Edward B. Irving, Jr. (Toronto, 1974), pp. 119–37. See also his "Personal Names in Medieval Narrative and the Name of Unferth in *Beowulf*," in *Essays in Honor of Richebourg Gaillard McWilliams*, ed. Howard Creed (Birmingham, Ala., 1970), pp. 43–48.

28. Robinson, "Significance of Names," pp. 36–38.

29. The following is a translation of the account of Geoweorþa as it appears in the *Orosius*, ed. Sweet, pp. 228–30. The Old English table of contents, ibid., p. 5, has further "How the Romans were [Cotton MS "fought", accepted by Sweet] against Geoweorþa, king of the Numidians." In the translation I normalise all names.

Six hundred and thirty-five *years after Rome was built, when Scipio Nasica and Lucius Calpurnius were consuls in Rome, the Romans fought against Iugurtha, King of the Numidians. The same Iugurtha was* a kinsman *of Micipsa, King of the Numidians, and he received him in his youth, and ordered him to be fed and brought up with his two sons.* And when the king died *he ordered his two sons to give a* third of the realm *to Iugurtha.* But after that third share was in his power he deceived both the sons: *he slew one and expelled the other,* and he [scil. the elder of the two brothers] then went to the Romans for his protection; and *they sent the Consul Calpurnius with him* together with an army. But Iugurtha obtained from the Consul *against payment of money* that he [scil. the Consul] should achieve little in the war. *Afterwards Iugurtha came to Rome, and* secretly *bought* [Latin *corrupit*] the Senate, one by one, till they were *all at variance in what they said* about him. *When he was going home from the City he blamed* the Romans *and mocked them greatly with his speeches, saying that no city could be bought more easily* with money *if anyone were to buy it.*

The following year the Romans sent the Consul Aulus Postumius with sixty *thousand* against Iugurtha. *They met at the city of Calama, and the Romans were defeated there;* and a little later they made peace between them, and then *almost all* the *Africans joined Iugurtha. After that* the Romans sent *Metellus* with an army back against Iugurtha, and he [scil. Metellus] *was victorious on two occasions, and on the third* he drove out Iugurtha into *Numidia, his own country, and forced him* to give to the Romans *three hundred hostages.* And yet *he afterwards harried* the Romans. Then they sent *the Consul Marius* in his turn against Iugurtha, *as cunning* and as wily *a man as he* [scil. Iugurtha] was; and he [scil. Marius] marched to *a city* very much as if it were his intention to storm it. But as soon as Iugurtha had led his army to the city against Marius, Marius abandoned that fortress and went to another where he had ascertained that Iugurtha's gold-*treasure* was, and he *wearied*[30] the citizens so that they

30. Perhaps Sweet is right not to prefer *gemedde* of the Lauderdale MS to *genydde* of the Cotton MS; for he has no entry for a verb from which *gemedde* might be derived in his *The Student's Dictionary of Anglo-Saxon* (Oxford, 1897). There is, however, a possibility that *gemedde* translates the Latin *fatigauit* used a little later of Iugurtha and Bocchus wearying Marius' army; the Latin is not followed at all closely by the Old English here. A second-class weak verb *ge-með(g)ian* is recorded, but not a first-class weak **ge-mēðan*, though such a form would be possible—cf. the cognate MHG. *müeden*, MDutch *moeden*, presumably from unrecorded **muodjan*, **modjan*. For the preterite *gemedde* with *þd > dd* see Campbell, *Grammar*, §§ 481.7 and 751(2). That form would explain *genydde* of the Cotton MS.

submitted to him and gave him all the ready money which was in the city. *Then Iugurtha did not trust his own people any more,* but *allied himself with Bocchus, King of the Mauritanians,* and he joined him with a great force of men, and *often advanced* stealthily upon the Romans till they decided on battle between their hosts. *Bocchus reinforced Iugurtha* for that battle *with sixty thousand horse* as well as foot-soldiers. *Never* before or since *was there with the Romans so hard a battle,* because *they were encircled all round,* and *moreover* most perished because the encounter was on a sandy hill, so that *they could not see for dust* how they should act. Besides, both *thirst and heat afflicted them,* and all day long they were having to put up with that *till night. The next day* they did *the same,* and again were *encircled all round* as they had been before. And when they doubted very much *if they could escape* they decided that they should defend their rear, and some should break out through all those forces if at all possible. When they had done so a great *rain* came, and the Mauritanians were greatly worn out by that because their *shields* were covered *with elephant hide* so that *few of them could lift them* on account of that wet,[31] and they were therefore put to flight; for an *elephant's hide will drink wet just as a sponge does.* Sixty *thousand* and one hundred of the Mauritanians were *slain.* After that *Bocchus made peace* with the Romans, and *handed Iugurtha over* to them *bound,* and they put him *in prison* then *together with his two sons* till they all perished there.

In presenting this translation of the Lauderdale text I have italicised those parts taken over from the Latin, inverting the method used by Sweet of printing in roman those parts of the Latin used by the translator. At times I have been slightly more generous than Sweet in relating the Old English to the Latin; but the account of the battles in the Old English remains imprecisely related to the source. It might be tempting to look elsewhere, in Sallust's *De bello Iugurthino* especially, for some of the touches supplied correctly in the Old English though not derived direct from the Latin source. Thus the fact that Iugurtha was a kinsman of Micipsa is explicitly stated in the Old English as well as in Sallust, but not in the Latin of Orosius, might seem significant; I think, however, that it is implicit in the Latin and that nothing should be based on it. The same is true to a lesser extent of the clear statement that Iugurtha bribed the

31. *for þam wætan* (Cotton MS), as emended in Sweet's text of the Lauderdale MS.

Senate one by one, much as we are told by Sallust (13.7 and 15.2), but not by Orosius; and thirdly, in the vague Old English account of the battles it clearly emerges that Marius intended to storm a city, or to make it seem that he had that intention; Sallust (89.6) tells how Marius had the intention to capture the city of Capsa, but even that seems to me insufficiently clear in its relationship to the brief account of the taking of unnamed cities in the Old English, and it seems best not to infer that at times, when the translator departs from his source, he goes to Sallust. Orosius himself, in what is clearly a reference to Sallust's *De bello Iugurthino* among others, makes a statement not included in the Old English translation that he is hurrying over the story of Iugurtha on the grounds that it is given by historians in sufficient detail.

Neither from Orosius' Latin account nor from the briefer Old English translation is it possible to extract more than a muted sense of honour turned to dishonour, such as is implicit in the word-play on the anglo-saxonised name *Geoweorpa*, "once held in high esteem." Like Orosius' Latin, the Anglo-Saxon translation, though briefer, dwells longest on those sections that bring out the generalship of Iugurtha. The translator renders, imprecisely, the utterance "O city for sale and about to perish if it finds a buyer!" for which, in variant forms, Iugurtha is famous through the writings of the historians, including Plutarch and Appian in Greek and Sallust and Livy in Latin.[32] The translator does not even translate into Old English the highly derogatory summary of Iugurtha's character which his source, the Latin of Orosius, provides: "unsteadfast of disposition and unbearable, and especially as wily in his dealings as he was energetic in his

32. Plutarch, *Lives*, C. Marius XII.3–4 (Loeb edition, IX [London, 1920], 493–95;) Appian, *Roman History*, VIII.ii.I (Loeb edition, II [London, 1912], 3); Sallust, *De bello Iugurthino*, 35.10 (Loeb edition [London, 1920], 212); Livy, *History*, LXIV (Loeb edition, XIV, [London, 1959], 76–77). The most common form of the utterance in the Latin writers is "O urbem venalem et mature perituram, si emptorem invenerit!"

For Orosius, *Historiarum adversum Paganos Libri VII*, I have used Karl Zangemeister's edition in CSEL, V (1882), 308–14, to supplement Sweet's incomplete text of the Latin.

deeds"; coming near the beginning of Orosius' account, that summary takes away not a little from the honour assumed by the word-play as the starting point of *Geoweorþa*'s career.

Orosius himself, in the tradition of Sallust, tells the story of Iugurtha to bring out something of Iugurtha's knowledge of Rome and of the Romans, especially their readiness to be bought, resulting in his readiness to bribe them. The Anglo-Saxon translator, and perhaps his language, is innocent of the technical terms of venality, and *geceapian* + *to* does duty for "to corrupt" in a way not elsewhere recorded for either *geceapian* or *geciepan*.

For a full history of the rise of Iugurtha we must go to Sallust. Though his birth of a concubine does not promise well for Iugurtha's future and leads to his exclusion from what he would have been entitled to if he had been legitimate,[33] that is only a temporary hindrance to his ambitions. What follows, especially his early manhood, fully confirms that he was at first held in high esteem. Sallust says:

> As soon as Iugurtha grew up, mighty in strength and of handsome appearance, but, most important of all, of powerful intellect, he did not give himself over to be corrupted by luxury and idleness, but practised the pursuits of his people, riding, throwing the javelin, contending in races with men of his age; and though he excelled them all in glory, yet he was dear to all. He spent the greater part of his time in hunting, and was always the first or among the first at the killing of lions or other big game. He did a great deal, but he said very little about it.[34]

Sallust dwells on his popularity (7.1), and relates how in the war in Spain he proved himself an excellent soldier—well able to size up both his commanding officer and the enemy—an intelligent tactician, always hardworking and dutiful, unassuming and very brave, "so that he became passionately dear to our men and the terror of the Numentines" (7.4). He possessed that rare combination that he was both energetic in battle and wise in council (7.5); his liberality and *ingeni sollertia* "dexterity of mind" gained him close friendships among the Romans (7.7). In Sallust's tell-

33. *De bello Iugurthino*, 5.7.
34. Ibid., 6.1.

ing the esteem in which Iugurtha was held in his early manhood is seen clearly to be the result of rare endowments, great strength, and a nimble intelligence, used single-mindedly to advance himself, chiefly by ingratiating himself to upstarts and nobles, who, valuing riches more than right and honour, were susceptible to corruption and fired Iugurtha's ambitious spirit by assuring him that he would achieve high rank for two reasons, "his own very great qualities and because at Rome all things can be bought" (8.1).

Iugurtha's commander in the field, Publius Scipio, later Africanus, commended the young man to the head of his family, his uncle Micipsa, because Iugurtha had distinguished himself in the war above all others: "To me he is dear for his merits, and I will endeavour by the greatest exertion that he shall be as dear to the Senate and people of Rome" (9.2). Privately, however, Scipio had warned Iugurtha that if he was not content to wait for the advancement which would assuredly come to him in due course, the glory and the sway, and if he urged matters on more speedily, his very own money would bring about his downfall (8.2).

In Sallust's account of the advice of Scipio we have not merely the end of Iugurtha's glorious youth, but the beginning, only as a warning, of the crime-stained road to death in the Roman dungeons. The rise of Iugurtha exemplifies Roman venality and the mind of an unscrupulous man who knew how to exploit it, as he knew how to exploit for his own advantage every weakness in others. To Sallust very probably, and to the twentieth-century reader certainly, there is a special interest in Iugurtha as "one of the greatest corruption scandals of world-history."[35] Sallust provides in his history of the age of Iugurtha

35. W. Schur, *Sallust als Historiker* (Stuttgart, 1934), p. 140. Throughout this part of my study I have greatly profited from A. D. Leeman, *A Systematic Bibliography of Sallust*, Mnemosyne Bibliotheca Classica Batava, Suppl. IV (Leiden, 1965). I find it difficult to believe, however, that Sallust's account of Iugurtha should be thought to give the reader no hint of anything in him other than virtue till he discovers Micipsa's hypocritical words on his deathbed (11.1), together with Hiempsal's insulting words at that time (11.6–7), as suggested by Leeman, "Aufbau und Absicht von Sallusts Bellum Iugurthinum," *Mededeelingen der Koninklijke Nederlandse Akademie van Wetenschappen*, Afd. Letterkunde, N. R. 20, 8 (1957), 7. See also n. 40 below.

a warning to his countrymen on the vice of corruption. He does not linger on the brutality of Iugurtha's death. For that we must read Plutarch:

Marius came across the sea from Africa with his army, and on the very Calends of January . . . assumed the consulship and celebrated his triumph, exhibiting to the Romans Jugurtha in chains. This was a sight which they had despaired of beholding, nor could any one have expected, while Jugurtha was alive, to conquer the enemy; so versatile was he at adapting himself to the turns of fortune, and so great craft did he combine with his courage. But we are told that when he had been led in triumph he lost his reason; and that when, after the triumph, he was cast into prison, where some tore his tunic from his body, and others were so eager to snatch away his golden ear-ring that they tore off with it the lobe of his ear, and when he had been thrust down naked into the dungeon pit, in utter bewilderment and with a grin on his lips he said: "Hercules! How cold this Roman bath is!" but the wretch, after struggling with hunger for six days and up to the last moment clinging to the desire of life paid the penalty which his crimes deserved.[36]

If one wished to delineate how pride has its fall or crime its punishment one could not do better than to look at Plutarch's description of Iugurtha in chains and prison. Such a moral view might well have been pleasing to the Anglo-Saxons, but there is no evidence that they had access to it in the history of Iugurtha. There is no reason for supposing that they knew Plutarch. Sallust's De bello Iugurthino, however, seems to have been a fairly widely distributed work,[37] and though there is no extant manuscript or manuscript fragment of English provenance of a date early enough for it to underlie the account of Geoweorpa in the Old English Orosius, a fragment of a probably continental eleventh-century manuscript is preserved in the flyleaves of a manuscript,

36. Plutarch, Lives, C. Marius, XII. I quote the Loeb translation by J. C. Rolfe, 493–95.

. 37. The indexes to the three volumes of M. Manitius, Geschichte der lateinischen Literatur im Mittelalter (Munich, 1911, 1923, and 1931), give an excellent idea in summary form of how widespread in the Middle Ages was the knowledge of Sallust's writings, and open up a vast range of medieval reference, most of it, however, later than the tenth century; cf. F. Vogel, Quaestionum Sallustianarum pars II, Acta Seminarii Philologici Erlangensis, II (Erlangen, 1881), 413–26.

Corpus Christi College Cambridge, MS 309, of the twelfth to thirteenth centuries, originally from St. Mary's, York; the flyleaves could have been in England earlier than the date of the manuscript in which they are preserved.[38]

The treatment of the name Iugurtha in the spelling of the Old English *Orosius* is, as we have seen, different from spellings of comparable names in that work, involving, I think, a play on the sound of the Latin name to Anglo-Saxon ears, and though we have no hard evidence that Sallust's book was available to a southern English translator of Orosius in the early tenth century, it is not an unreasonable assumption that the paronomastic orthography of the name is unrelated to the study of Orosius in Anglo-Saxon times, but related to their understanding of the rise and fall of Iugurtha as told by Sallust, with special emphasis on the glorious youth of Iugurtha in peace and war: there is no trace of punning in the spellings of non-English names in the Old English *Orosius* discussed from their different points of view by Schilling and Miss Bately.[39] Orosius' Latin does not furnish the material for the vernacular pun, though the translation leaves out Orosius' summary of Iugurtha's character which would have undermined the pun from the start. I believe, therefore, that the form *Geoweorpa* was imported into the Old English *Orosius* because it was already to hand.

The very absence of the means of expression in Old English for the subtleties of Roman venality makes it unlikely that the Anglo-Saxons would have read *De bello Iugurthino* in the spirit in which it is thought, by modern writers on Sallust,[40] that Sallust

38. See J. D. A. Ogilvie, *Books Known to the English, 597–1066* (Cambridge, Mass., 1967), p. 237 (British Library MS Harley 5412, listed by Ogilvie as of uncertain provenance, is not English). For CCCC MS 309 see M. R. James, *Descriptive Catalogue of the Manuscripts in the Library of Corpus Christi College Cambridge* (Cambridge, 1912), II, 109; and cf. N. R. Ker, *Medieval Libraries of Great Britain* (London, 1964), p. 217.

39. See n. 8, above.

40. In addition to Schur and Leeman, whose work is referred to in n. 28, above, the following are particularly illuminating: K. Büchner, *Sallust* (Heidelberg, 1960); D. C. Earl, *The Political Thought of Sallust* (Cambridge, 1961), especially pp. 60–81; Sir R. Syme, *Sallust* (Berkeley, Calif., 1964), especially chaps. X–XI; and the symposium collected by V. Pöschl, *Sallust*, Wege der Forschung, XCIV (Darmstadt, 1970).

wrote. Instead we may perhaps speculate that the Anglo-Saxons would have read the story of Iugurtha as fitting a different pattern, that of an evil king. Much of the rich fabric of *Beowulf*, those strands especially to which earlier scholars gave the name "digressions," is concerned with evil kingship typified by Heremod and Hrothulf. Kingship came early to both, to Heremod as far as we know by honest accession. The allusive accounts in the poem (ll. 901–15, cf. 1709–22, 2177–83), always in contrast with or at least with reference to Beowulf himself, make clear that Heremod was endowed with qualities beyond all men (ll. 1716–18): "though mighty God had exalted him with joys of power, with strengths, had advanced him above all men." His strength in war—*Heremodes hild . . . eafoð*[41] *ond ellen* (ll. 901 f.)— led many a wise man of the Danish people to have high hopes of him once they had elected him to succeed his father (ll. 908–13): "many a wise man who had looked to him for a remedy from afflictions, had believed that that prince's son was destined to prosper, to receive his father's noble rank, to rule the nation, the treasure and the citadel, a realm of heroes, the homeland of Scyldings." Youthful glory giving way to crime—*hine fyren onwod* (l. 914)—is the pattern of Heremod. Sallust's account of Iugurtha's birth and youth, however, contains facts and bitter ironies stronger than hints that from the start the concubine's son was out for all he could get by clever deployment of his various great gifts. Heremod, seen from outside, undergoes what looks like a sudden change, and the trust of his people, equally suddenly, turns to fear.

Nearer to some aspects of the accession of Iugurtha is that of Hrothulf, if the hints in *Beowulf* (ll. 1014–19, 1162–65, 1177–87, and 1228–31) may be interpreted as stronger condemnation of his disloyalty than seems suggested by the glory attached to him in the Scandinavian analogues, where Hrolfr Kraki (or in Latin Roluo) continues his admirable heroic role— "the most glorious among ancient kings, the first among them for generosity, valour and simplicity," in Snorri's words[42]—for

41. MS *earfoð*.
42. Snorri's *Edda, Skáldskaparmál*, chap. 53; see G. N. Garmonsway and J. Simpson, *Beowulf and Its Analogues* (London, 1968), p. 177. Hrothmund does

in *Beowulf* we see only the *adoptivus*, to use a word for Iugurtha in the Latin of Orosius passed over by the Anglo-Saxon translator, who usurped the throne, a cuckoo in the nest, a ruthless ingrate. Wealhtheow's forebodings, as her words to Hrothulf (ll. 1180–87) are usually, and I think rightly, interpreted, resemble the fears Iugurtha's uncle Micipsa has for his young sons from the increasing power of the adopted Iugurtha (Sallust, *De bello Iugurthino*, 6.2–3). The eighth chapter, devoted to Prince Hrothulf, in John Gardner's recent novel *Grendel*,[43] brings out well Wealhtheow's fears for her own sons Hrethric and Hrothmund as their cousin, the adopted Hrothulf, dissembles ideal kinship among them; there will be cause for envy:

> The babes you comfort when they weep
> Will soon by birthright have
>
> All these gold rings! Ah, then, then
> Your almost-brother love will cool;
> The cousin smile must grind out lean
> Where younger cousins rule.[44]

These are close parallels to Iugurtha: Heremod is morally like him in pattern, and Hrothulf pursues the same road of usurpation of cousins. The word-play *Geoweorþa* "once held in high esteem" fits Heremod well, and probably the English Hrothulf too, though not the analogues—and in any case, even the English account of Hrothulf is less one of high honour brought low through crime in kingship as one of that supreme act of ingratitude, the usurpation by an adopted son of the throne which by right belongs to weaker heirs.

Beowulf is filled with the lives of kings, both centrally in the narrative and contrapuntally in the "digressions." Implicit in almost each one is the idea of change either from high to low because glory came too soon or from low to high because too pessimistic a view was taken of unpromising or even cruel begin-

---

not come in the Scandinavian story, but Hrethric (Roricus) does, and Hrothulf's (Roluo) slaying of him is justified in Saxo's account by Roricus' ignoble avarice; see Garmonsway and Simpson, *Beowulf*, pp. 207–11.

43. New York, 1971; Ballantine Books (New York, 1972).

44. "The Queen Beside Hrothulf's Bed. Wealtheow speaks," p. 101.

nings. In a vague sense of the term, there is Boethianism apparent in that, vague because a direct indebtedness to Boethius need not be assumed. What we are dealing with is the contemplation through medieval eyes of "the up and down of dynasties," as F. P. Pickering has spoken of it (without reference to Old English literature) in his stimulating study of two contrasting medieval views, the Boethian and the Augustinian.[45]

The underlying principle, "Reversal of fortune" as the classification of such story-motifs is headed by Stith Thompson,[46] is the same, but the movement can be in one of two directions: *Geoweorþa*, the glorious youth of a prince leading to tyranny and a violent end, in short leading from love and honour to fear and hatred; and the opposite to which one might give the made-up label *Geo-heana* "once held in low esteem," leading from cruel or unpromising beginning to kingship in a land at peace, in short leading from contempt to love and honour.

It was pointed out long ago by Sophus Bugge[47] that the poet uses Heremod in contrast to Beowulf. The first account of Heremod makes that explicit (ll. 913–15), the kinsman of Hygelac, Beowulf, grew dearer (if that is what *gefægra* means)[48] to all mankind, his friends; sin entered Heremod. Hrothgar, giving counsel to Beowulf (ll. 1709–24), specifically tells of Heremod for the benefit of Beowulf, for him to gain a true understanding of *gumcyst* "manly virtue." But, from the starting point of *Geoweorþa*, the third, merely allusive mention of Heremod is the most instructive. It comes at the climax of the homecoming of Beowulf immediately after the ceremonial handing over to his king, Hygelac of the Geats, of all that the grateful Danish king Hrothgar had given him, and before some of it was given back to

45. *Augustinus oder Boethius?*, Philologische Quellen und Studien 39, (Berlin, 1967), see especially pp. 18–25.

46. *Motif-Index of Folk-Literature* (Bloomington, Ind., 1955; reprinted 1966), V, 6–26. The folk-tale motifs in *Beowulf* were discussed most fully in F. Panzer, *Studien zur germanischen Sagengeschichte*, I: *Beowulf* (Munich, 1910), pp. 29–39, 269 (and references given there are especially relevant).

47. "Studien über das Beowulfepos," *Beiträge zur Geschichte der deutschen Sprache und Literatur* 12 (1887), 39.

48. See Friedrich Klaeber's note to the passage, *Beowulf and the Fight at Finnsburg*, 3d ed. (Boston, 1936; rpt. 1950), p. 166.

Beowulf by the munificent Hygelac. Recent criticism that I have seen has made less of the significance of that highly symbolic ceremonial than should be made of it; for here are brought together in acts of homage and reward the two halves of the poem as Danish triumphs honour the Geatish throne. In the middle of that, lines 2177–89, the pattern of noblest kingship is adumbrated in the life of Beowulf, and Heremod is contrasted with him. We learn how Beowulf was famed in battles and good deeds, how he bore himself *æfter dome*, whatever that may mean exactly—"to gain glory" or "in accordance with accepted principles of what is right"[49]—and then the poet goes on to speak of Heremod without naming him, how he when drunk slew his hearth-companions. Then there is praise of Beowulf again, the first mention of his gentle disposition which is the note on which the poem ends, and at the same time Beowulf's great strength is referred to again (as it is insisted on throughout the poem from the first mention of the hero), "he held the greatest strength of mankind, the ample gift which God had given him" (ll. 2181–83). And then the opposite of the *Geoweorþa* motif: "For a long time he was held in low esteem, in that the sons of the Geats had not thought him noble, nor had the lord of the Weder-Geats wished to do him honour on the mead-bench with great possessions. They very much thought that he was slothful, a princely ne'er-do-well. A change came to that glorious and happy man reversing every one of his troubles."

We have moved a long way from the Old English orthographic peculiarity in the *Orosius*. It seems to me that one of the patterns of kingship, best seen by us now in Old English literature by exemplification and contrast in the many lives of kings which form the single theme of much that is various and digressive in *Beowulf*, has affected the spelling of Iugurtha, king of the Numidians. The word-play points the moral. Perhaps it also points another moral: *Geoweorþa* was once held in high esteem by phonologists, but sense intervenes to mar what at first seemed sound.

---

49. See the note to l. 1720 in ibid., p. 191. The editors incline strongly to the former sense, but there is no reason why both should not be applicable here.

6

Narrative Insight in
Laxdœla Saga

Ursula Dronke

LINACRE COLLEGE, OXFORD

J. R. R. TOLKIEN taught many of us both Norse texts and Chaucer. In memory of him, and of the love of both subjects that his teaching inspired, I should like to offer this essay. For it was growing familiarity with the narrative art of Chaucer that first helped me to see comparable subtleties of structure in the greatest of the Icelandic sagas, above all in *Laxdæla* and *Njála*.

> Hold of thi matere
> the forme alwey,

Pandare advises, with the authority of Horace behind him, and, as Chaucer knew, the same "matere" is capable of many forms. It can be turned in the light of the story-teller's imagination to cast different shadows, display different surfaces, textures, structures, in response to the teller's purpose and his kind of vision. Chaucer could survey the forms that matter took in the hands of earlier tellers of his tales, and he turned the existing forms (as he saw them in his sources) and the potential forms (as he saw how those sources could be altered) in the light of his own imagination, until he was satisfied that he had a narrative whose matter embodied the form he had envisaged. In the same way, I suggest, the greatest saga-writers contemplated the story-traditions they wished to recreate, seeking for a fresh form, a new harmony, within the old matter.

The author of *Laxdœla Saga* knew many versions of the theme that he has made central to his story, the theme of the woman with two lovers, who unwillingly marries the one she does not care for, the lesser man. So tense does the situation become that it can only be resolved by her husband's killing of the other man. In some versions, a rivalry between the two men grows up after the marriage, in which the husband is increasingly humiliated by the other man: jealousy and humiliation drive the husband to kill him (so it is in *Bjarnar Saga Hítdœlakappa*). In other versions of the theme, the woman's jealousy of the other man's wife makes her force her husband to kill him (as in the Norse legends of Brynhildr). The variant of the theme that the author of *Laxdœla Saga* chose (or created) shows a unique synthesis of motifs from different versions of the theme:

(1) His tragic comedians, Kjartan and Guðrún, far excel other men and women in beauty and elegance and all the accomplishments that make for social brilliance. Not only common talk, but their own self-esteem establishes them as the rightful, almost the ordained, partners for each other (as the fearless hero Sigurðr is the fit and destined prince for the valkyrie Brynhildr).

(2) The lesser man, Bolli, who marries Guðrún, is cousin and foster-brother of Kjartan, and dreads harming him (as Gunnarr, who marries Brynhildr, is the sworn brother and brother-in-law of Sigurðr, and recoils from killing him with his own hand).

(3) The responsibility for the marriage of Guðrún to the "wrong man" lies entirely with the "right man," with Kjartan himself. We cannot blame a scheming mother-in-law (such as Grímhildr, who gives Sigurðr a magic potion so that he forgets his betrothed Brynhildr), nor an envious rival, who tells the girl that her lover is dead (as in *Bjarnar Saga*), nor a witch's curse (as in *Kormaks Saga*); nor can we even blame Óláfr Tryggvason (as some critics do), because he held Kjartan hostage in Norway, for Kjartan could easily have overcome this difficulty with Bolli as his messenger. Kjartan alone is responsible, and here the only parallel I know is that of Hallfreðr Vandræðaskáld, who refuses point-blank to marry his sweetheart when her father demands

that he should. The only reason the saga-writer gives us is that Hallfreðr does not want to marry, *vildi eigi kvænask.*

The form of *Laxdæla Saga* is, I suggest, determined by the emotional content of these three motifs. The full story of the saga stretches for nearly two hundred years, from the first settlement of the "Dales" of Breiðafjǫrðr by the great ancestress, Unnr "of the Deep Thoughts," to the death of Guðrún Ósvífrsdóttir's youngest son. Near the mid-point of these years, at the time of the change of faith from the religion of Þórr to that of Christ, the tale of Guðrún, Kjartan, and Bolli is set. The preceding history prepares us for this tale, the following history distances us from it. By the art of selection, by the kind of incident he includes or omits, by the warmth—or lack of it—in his telling, the saga-writer constructs an anatomy of human actions, in which we may investigate, ponder about, the working of human motives. At the heart of this anatomy, controlling its life, is the story of Kjartan.

The saga-writer has analysed the emotions in this story as being of two kinds, those that are related to social status, reputation, self-esteem, and those that are not, namely, family affection, loyalty between friends, love between men and women. In the story of Guðrún, Kjartan, and Bolli these two kinds of emotion affect the action in different ways at different moments, and the crossplay of both brings about Kjartan's voluntary death. The narrative that leads up to the story of Kjartan and his death is alive with impulsive feeling: vigorous personalities and sharp scenes stand out—Auðr wearing breeches and stabbing her faithless husband in the breast, Jórunn jealous of her royal Irish slave-girl and hitting her with her stockings, Stígandi the outlaw caught sleeping on the lap of the shepherdess and stoned to death—as if the writer were deliberately crowding the life that tradition preserved of all those years into the chronicle's course. Our involvement with these people, which the saga-writer has secured by his art, prepares us for involvement with the story of Kjartan, so that when he flings away his life, we feel a dullness has come upon the world. Bolli is left with his status and his repentance.

As many critics note, the glow fades from the narrative in the second half of the saga. Has the saga-writer lost his skill, or does he mean us to see that a change has come over the action itself? Kjartan was killed by a man who was his dearest friend. Bolli is killed by a man who had no reason whatever to avenge Kjartan except that he happened to be staying with his brother-in-law, who was an old friend of Kjartan's father, at the time that Kjartan's brothers were summoning all the support they could get. This man, Helgi Harðbeinsson—a brave and decent person—is killed in vengeance for Bolli, more than twelve years later, by Bolli's twelve-year-old son, who was not born when his father died. Though the boy Bolli kills his father's killer dutifully with the same sword that killed Kjartan, and with noble instinct spares the young son of Helgi, these heroically correct acts cannot lend dignity to the motley collection of people who accompany Bolli's young sons on their task of vengeance. Their chief supporter is a man who has been duped into believing Guðrún will marry him if he helps to avenge her last husband; two others are men who actually accompanied Helgi Harð-beinsson in the attack on Bolli (and one of these was Helgi's own brother-in-law, who involved him in the killing of Bolli in the first place); and another is a hanger-on, a furtive, clownish, thieving fellow, with darting eyes, who boastfully joins their enterprise and is killed by Helgi's spear at the outset. But convention is satisfied, Bolli Þorleiksson is avenged, and his son becomes "Magnificent"—*Bolli inn prúði*—wearing only scarlet and furs, buying his way to social eminence (*vildi vera fyrir ǫðrum mǫnnum; honum tóksk ok svá, því at maðrinn var ǫrlátr*, as the saga-writer says sardonically), and even ornamenting splendidly with gold the plain sword with the walrus-tusk hilt and the steel blade that never rusted, with which Kjartan and Helgi had been killed. What was passionate and cruel in the past has become encrusted with wealth, and otiose: a subject for comfortable speculation: "Whom did you love most, mother?"

Fate plays no part in *Laxdœla Saga*. Men and women may dream about their "fate," as Guðrún dreams about her four future husbands, or be haunted by premonitions of death, as the lacrymose Gestr, seeing the happy youths sporting in the river, prophesies that Bolli will "stand over the crown of Kjartan" and be his killer. But the saga-writer deploys these banal theatricalities as a foil to his existential treatment of human action. People's "fates" are the consequence of their own decisions. But what prompts their decisions? And how have the situations arisen in which they must decide? Are not they too the product of human choice? These are the questions that preoccupy the author of *Laxdæla Saga* and lead him into an analysis of the human feelings which prompt men to act as they do, and so create the situations in which they find themselves. Through his own decisions Kjartan is responsible for losing Guðrún as his wife, and his failure to marry her is the main cause of his death. As the saga-writer presents it, his death is his last decision. But Kjartan is helped towards his tragic end by the blundering benevolence of his father. Long before any actions of Kjartan concern us, Óláfr the Peacock is influencing his future. I should like to trace this theme of responsibility as the saga-writer unfolds it in the lives of Óláfr and Kjartan.

As a young man, Óláfr pursued a golden career of success: politely refusing an Irish kingdom; with quiet imperturbability winning a well-born bride, bastard though he is, and establishing the most lavishly stocked farm in Iceland. He began, seemingly, with nothing, a bondwoman's child, but he rose to the top by the magic of royal blood in his veins, as if by destiny. His great fortunes are delicately crowned by the hint that he has the wholesome power of the hero who can exorcise evil: he builds his farm on haunted ground, but when the vicious ghost haunts his cow-byres, he plunges his spear through it and it sinks straightway into the earth. Up to his settlement in wealth and ease, all Óláfr's actions have been forthright, unhedged by doubts, greeted by success. But once he is caught in the web of family affairs, encountering wills that run contrary to his own, he begins to lose his golden touch and make mistakes. He becomes, in effect, one of the chief agents of his own son's death.

The saga-writer makes it plain that on four occasions Óláfr the Peacock takes a decision, or directs action, in a way that leads to the killing of Kjartan. Sometimes the motives that lead

to these decisions are not wholly laudable (though they are so
wholly human that we do not think at the time that they might
be productive of ill); sometimes superstitious anxiety confuses
his judgment and weakens his principles. These are the
occasions:

(1) To compliment and make peace with his envious and
touchy brother, Þorleikr, Óláfr offers to adopt Þorleikr's three-
year-old son, Bolli. So Bolli becomes the shadow, emulator, and
eventually the killer of Kjartan. Why did Óláfr adopt him? It
was the price his conscience told him he ought to pay for de-
priving his elder, and legitimate, brother of the heirlooms that
should by rights have been his, the golden armlet and gilded
sword that their father Hǫskuldr had been given by the earl of
Norway. By a trick, an ambiguity in the words he uses, the
dying Hǫskuldr gets Þorleikr's consent to the bequeathing of
these treasures to Óláfr. Óláfr accepts the two treasures, saying
he will risk Þorleikr's displeasure, *kvazk til mundu hætta;* and he
even repeats his fear that some danger is involved: "I'll risk being
able to keep them" (*mun ek til þess hætta, hvárt ek fæ haldit*). Þorleikr
is indeed angry, but what has Óláfr to fear from him? His apprehension springs, I suggest, from a prick of conscience, an
awareness that it would have been more fitting, and less cov-
etous, to surrender the treasures to the oldest son. But he cannot
bring himself to do this, though he knows he should. In his
heart of hearts he probably feels he suits them, and deserves
them, better—"so well born as he is on his mother's side," as
Hǫskuldr says. To rid himself of the sense that he has done
something a little reprehensible, as well as to conciliate his
brother, Óláfr offers, not to give him the glamorous golden treasures, but to foster the three-year-old Bolli. It was an offence
against Þorleikr's status to take the ring and sword; Óláfr restores
the balance by this fostering, "for," as he says pointedly, "he
who fosters another's child is always thought the lesser man."

(2) The second unfortunate (though again generous) decision
that Óláfr takes is when he refuses to insist that his harsh son-in-
law Geirmundr the Norwegian should leave money to support
his wife and baby daughter, when after three quarrelsome years
of married life in Iceland he decides to return home without

them. Óláfr—always a peace-loving man—even gives him a well-rigged ship to go in. Furious at her husband's meanness, and no doubt also at her father's refusal to insist on her rights, the young Þúríðr rows after Geirmundr at night, steps into his ship, where it waits for a wind, tucks the baby daughter beside him in his sleeping-bag, and snatches his beloved sword Leg-biter, *Fótbítr*. When she is already rowing away from his ship, Geirmundr wakes with the baby's howls and begs for his sword at any price. Precisely because he values it so, Þúríðr refuses, and when she gets home she gives Legbiter to Bolli, "because she loved him no less than her own brothers." It is with this sword that Bolli kills Kjartan.

This episode tells us more than the history of the sword: it shows us the confused behavior of Óláfr, now taking a strong line, now a weak, towards his womenfolk. His wife Þorgerðr had not wanted him to go to Norway in the first place (where he picked up Geirmundr), but Óláfr had made up his mind (*kvazk ráða mundu*). Þorgerðr wants Geirmundr as a son-in-law, because he has bribed her with a great deal of money; Óláfr does not want him, but gives in to Þorgerðr, declaring, "I shall not go against you in this, any more than in any other matter." But when mother and daughter pester him to extort some compensation from Geirmundr before he leaves, Óláfr is adamant: "they got nowhere with him" (*kómu þær engu á leið við Ólaf*). Had he either followed his own instinct in refusing Geirmundr's suit, or agreed with Þorgerðr (as he said he always did) in demanding compensation from him, Legbiter would never have come into Bolli's hands. Óláfr wanted to score off his wife and teach her a lesson, showing her how inferior her judgment is compared with his, how he feels such importunacy in demanding compensation to be beneath his dignity. He teases her, reminding her of the bribe she took: "Does the Norwegian not seem so lavish now as once he did?" Óláfr would also have observed that the quarrels in the marriage were as much of Þúríðr's making as Geirmundr's (as the saga-writer tells us they were: *var svá af beggja þeira hendi*), and, having some experience of the wrong-headedness of women, he may have felt that Geirmundr was not without justification in refusing to pay any more for his wife.

Any sword that Bolli wielded would, at that moment, have served to kill Kjartan (for Kjartan threw away his weapons); but the fact that it was Geirmundr's sword in retrospect makes every move in the story of the sword's acquisition bitterly significant. At the climax of this cruel and ignoble episode, Geirmundr's flash of prophetic insight—"that sword will kill the darling of your family"—comes almost as a curse, and one that could lightly have been avoided, had wilful actions been different.

(3) The third occasion when a decision of Óláfr's has disastrous consequences is, most obviously, his refusal to prevent Bolli's marriage to Guðrún. For, of course, Bolli consults his eminent foster-father. "I want to have no part in this," says Óláfr. "You know what talk there has been of the love between Kjartan and Guðrún." Yet immediately he promises to put no hindrance in Bolli's way (*mun ek leggja engan meinleika til*), and washes his hands of the whole matter by adding that Bolli may do as he likes (*kvað hann með mundu fara, sem honum líkaði*). Why does Óláfr not make the slightest attempt to safeguard Kjartan's interests? Why does he not insist that Bolli should wait at least until there is definite news about Kjartan's return or non-return? He does not do so, I suggest, because he has always had a strange premonition that harm will come to Kjartan from his friendship with Guðrún, as he tells Kjartan during the days when Kjartan is frequenting Laugar. And behind these premonitions is the force of a fearsome nightmare Óláfr had, that a huge and irate woman came to him in his sleep and threatened to show him his own son all bloody, because Óláfr had just killed her son, a magnificent but aged ox which he had slaughtered that autumn. With these dreads haunting his mind, Óláfr lets Bolli's marriage to Guðrún take place, because he thinks it is a way of saving his son. Fear makes him act unworthily.

(4) Even so, Óláfr has one more chance to keep Kjartan out of danger, but he ignores that chance. After Kjartan's return from Norway, he insists that Kjartan should accompany him on the yearly family visit to Laugar, though Bolli and Guðrún are now there as man and wife. "Directly you and your cousin see each other again, you'll be friends once more," he says in his simple, peace-loving way. There are two visits, one before

Kjartan is married, one after, and both times Kjartan begs to be excused (*kvazk mundu heima vera at gæta bús. . . . Kjartan var trauðr til*), but he yields to his father's persistence. Second only to Macbeth in his failure to interpret omens correctly, Óláfr had concluded that the one thing that was fatal for Kjartan was marriage to Guðrún, whereas his presentiment had been precisely of enmity between the two families: "that our family and the men of Laugar will not carry good luck with us to the very end of our dealings with each other" (*vér frændr ok Laugamenn berim eigi allsendis gæfu til um vár skipti*). Not even the stealing of Kjartan's royal sword by Guðrún's brothers was sufficient to warn Óláfr of the folly of thrusting the young people together again; and after the theft of the gold-woven headdress, on the second visit to Laugar, there is no holding back the deeds of hatred on both sides.

Against the pattern of Óláfr's behaviour, with its transparent motivation, the saga-writer sets that of Kjartan. For his young hero he envisages a totally different mentality and he presents this mentality enigmatically, even cryptically, so that we shall be led deep into Kjartan's own self-absorption as we retrace the thoughts that could have caused him to speak or act as he does. For Kjartan is grandly secretive. How few people he confides in—not his father, not Bolli, not Guðrún. Perhaps only to Ingibjǫrg, the King's sister, does he ever unburden a little of his heart. He is determined to have independence; the darling of a prosperous family, he wants to cut his own channel of life. He begins at the top—where can he now climb to? If he confides his ambitions to others, he may be inhibited in pursuing them; and in any case they are not yet sharply defined, even to himself.

The first act of independence that we see is Kjartan's refusal to stop visiting Guðrún at Laugar, at the time of their earliest acquaintance. She is fashionable, lovely, and a clever talker (*málsnjǫll*). His father hints (with his superstitious mind, he will not venture to prophesy—*eigi vil ek þess spá*) that these visits may lead to trouble. Politely, but deviously, Kjartan evades his attempt to "protect" him, saying that he will always comply with any wish of his father's, "in so far as that lay within his power" (*þat er hann mætti við gera*), and he is sure all will end better than his father anticipates. And he continues his visits to Laugar.

Next, however, he makes firm arrangements to sail to Norway, buying the half-share of a ship. He does not mention his plans either to his father or to Guðrún until they are completed. Ólafr will not stand in his way, though he thinks Kjartan has been over-hasty. When Guðrún is told, it is clear that she is deeply offended. In this brief exchange between the lovers, we become aware at once how much they did not know about each other.

"Such a swift decision," she says, and adds some words—we are not told what they are—which (the saga-writer says) reveal her displeasure. Was he planning all this, while he talked so warmly and, seemingly, openly during his visits to Laugar? Does she count for so little in his life that he does not even tell her? Must not these have been her thoughts?

Kjartan evidently anticipated some vexation on her part, for he says, to humour her and rouse her curiosity: "Don't be annoyed by what I have done. I shall do something else (*annan hlut*) that will reconcile you to it." He speaks with a touch of jocularity (that might be thought patronizing) because the "something else" he has in mind is a proposal that she shall pledge herself to wait for him for three years: a tacit betrothal. But before he can utter this proposition (which he obviously considers she will be delighted to accept), Guðrún seizes swiftly upon his words.

"That something else you offer to do to please me, be prepared for it, because I shall tell you at once what it is." And to his consternation he hears that she means to go with him.

"Take me with you, then you will have more than made up for presenting me with such a startling decision, for I have no love for Iceland" (*ekki ann ek Íslandi*).

How much already she thinks she owns him! How quickly she identifies her soaring and supercilious spirit with his in her longing to see and be seen in a grander world than that of the farmers of Iceland. She has grown from—but not wholly outgrown—that girl of fifteen for whom it was laid down in her marriage settlement that her unprepossessing husband must buy every jewel and piece of finery that came within his reach, in order to make her the best-dressed wife in Breiðafjọrdr. But by seizing upon Kjartan as her way to fulfilment in a nobler society, she kills all the comparable hopes he himself had been cherishing. He wanted to try his fortunes in a new world, pit his excellence against unknown strengths. How can he be free to try himself, if Guðrún is beside him, possessive and self-willed, as her marital history alone could tell him? And with wounding alacrity he refuses her outright. "Impossible," he says, and offers every reason except the true one. After this, his suggestion that she wait three years for him falls upon cold ears, and she will promise nothing. His clumsiness has succeeded only in showing her very clearly that he is less keen to possess her than she is to possess him.

Had he had a little of his father's tact, or some imagination for the thoughts and feelings of others, Kjartan could have secured a warm promise from Guðrún before he left. But if she is never consulted, how can she approve?

On a second occasion Kjartan could have secured her as his wife, but again he does not. When he is held as a hostage in Norway, waiting for Iceland to accept Christianity, why does he not give Bolli a message for Guðrún, asking her to wait for him another winter? As Bolli himself points out to Guðrún: "He could well have entrusted me with a message about this, if he had thought it mattered." Yet Bolli himself was partly to blame for this (though he probably was not aware of it), for he tried to induce Kjartan to declare his mind by oblique suggestion and a hint of criticism: "I doubt if the king will ever let you leave Norway, and in any case we think you forget all the joys that Iceland can offer when you sit talking with Ingibjǫrg, the king's sister." Kjartan is a man who will clench his teeth against such interference in his private affairs, and feel a disdainful repulsion at the sudden revelation of gossip that guesses at his chances, his plans, his privacy. And he may in his heart feel the deep injustice of Bolli's words. The saga-writer gives us some indication that when Kjartan sat talking with Princess Ingibjǫrg it was sometimes about Guðrún that he spoke. A man often finds it easier to talk about the women in his life to another woman, rather than to a man (partly, no doubt, because that is what the other woman is most interested in asking him). It is possible, then, that when Princess Ingibjǫrg, cold with disappointment, but dignified, sends a superlative bridal gift expressly to Guðrún Ósvífrsdóttir (adding, with a touch of sarcasm, that it is "exceedingly grand for her to wrap round her head," *kvað Guðrúnu Ósvífrsdóttur hólzti gott at vefja honum at hǫfði sér*), she is making her own guess from what Kjartan has told her about the women of Iceland. Clear in his own mind that he is still retaining his freedom of choice, despite the attractions of Ingibjǫrg, Kjartan rebuffs Bolli, his closest and oldest friend, for inquisitiveness and unworthy insinuation: "Do not speak like that. Just greet my family from me, and my friends too."

The same refined reaction to vulgar suggestion can be seen in Kjartan on a later occasion, when his young wife Hrefna goads him with coarse gossip. He and his men have been besieging Laugar for three days, humiliating the household by preventing them from reaching the outdoor privies. When he returns home, Hrefna greets him laughingly, saying she has been told for certain that he talked with Guðrún and "she was wearing the gold headdress and it suited her extremely well." "That did not happen as far as I could see, Hrefna. Guðrún would not need to put on a headdress to look more handsome than all other women." The saga-writer tells us that Kjartan was angered at her mocking flippancy, and Hrefna silenced by his crushing rebuke. It must have given her a painful insight into the admiration for the other woman that he has never lost, despite the year of very happy marriage he has enjoyed with her. His rooted fastidiousness, his resentment of criticism, of attempts to spy into his actions or probe into his heart make him unfeeling and relentless both to his wife and to his friend.

If Guðrún could have heard Kjartan's casual greeting "to all his friends" in Iceland, she would hardly have been pleased. Kjartan could not (and almost certainly did not) expect Bolli to *invent* a special message for Guðrún from him. And how could Bolli do so? He honestly believed that Kjartan was playing a double game, winning Guðrún's love in Iceland and Princess Ingibjǫrg's in Norway. He is hurt on Guðrún's behalf by Kjartan's behaviour, as the touch of bitterness in his words implies. Had Kjartan reassured him: "I have not forgotten Iceland—greet Guðrún for me," can we doubt that Bolli would have delivered his message honourably, or that Guðrún would have received it with joy? For despite the coolness with which she and Kjartan parted, despite the lack of any message from him, she still tells Bolli plainly: "I will marry no man as long as Kjartan is alive." Bolli ostensibly does well for Kjartan, making him appear a pawn of politics: the king values Kjartan so much that "he would rather marry him to his sister than let him leave." But Bolli's thoughts are divided. He convinces himself that Kjartan will not return to Iceland (and tells Guðrún so repeatedly); yet why does he press on so hastily with his wooing of Guðrún, unless he secretly fears that Kjartan may return the next summer? At home, in Iceland, as his self-importance grows without Kjartan beside him to dwarf it, he dreams of marrying "the most celebrated woman of the land" (*hon er frægst kvenna*). In his new vanity he expresses his interest in Guðrún in terms of status, not of love. But it may well have been the belief that he valued her more than Kjartan, the princess's paramour (and therefore deserved her more than Kjartan), that first made him determined to ask for her hand. Later, when they are man and wife, it is only after Guðrún has threatened to end all sexual intercourse with him—*mun lokit okkrum samførum*—that he can force himself to work up a hatred for Kjartan— *miklaði Bolli fyrir sér fjándskap allan á hendi Kjartani ok sakar*—and join in the attack: Bolli's need to have Guðrún as his wife has become so great. Possession of her represents the sum of his ambition as a man. But had Kjartan answered him differently in Norway, he would never have married her.

Why does Kjartan return to Iceland? He contended with the king at swimming, and almost won. He held out against the king's missionary zeal until he could accept Christianity almost on his own terms. He forced the king to respect his fierce independence, recklessly admitting, "Yes, it was I who planned to burn you in your hall"—and not being put to death for it; kicking grimly against coercion: "I shall only become a Christian in Norway if I find next winter in Iceland that I do not care so much for Þórr." He recognizes in the king a man he can admire, against whom he can measure himself. Significantly, the king's scarlet clothes fit Kjartan, for "men said they were of equal height, when their measurements were taken, Óláfr the king and Kjartan." What more did Kjartan come to Norway for than to be assured of his own stature? If he stays, he is the king's vassal, a royal lady's consort, a servant of politics indeed. Though the common games of Iceland are less polished entertainment than is found at the king's court—*annat var tíðara með Óláfi konungi*—Kjartan chooses to return to them. Princess Ingibjǫrg recognizes the emotional implication of his going—"It is your own choice: no one else has urged you to leave us!"—and gives him the bridal gift for Guðrún.

We are never told that Kjartan cared that he had lost Guðrún; we are left to guess at his disappointment, his sense of emptiness and hurt pride, from the brusqueness with which he woos Hrefna. As she sits among the unloaded cargo, trying on the gold-woven headdress intended for Guðrún, Kjartan swiftly appreciates her prettiness: "It suits you well, Hrefna—I think it may be most appropriate if I own the whole thing, the headdress and the girl in it." But when she flirtatiously flatters him in return—"you'll get any woman you ask for, if ever you do want to marry"—he quenches the gaiety of the moment, as if a sudden cloud had come over him, by saying stolidly (the saga-writer changes here to reported speech) it did not matter whom he married, but he would not hang around waiting for any woman's answer for long—*lézk engrar skyldu lengi vánbiðill vera* (and this from the young man who was prepared to keep Guðrún waiting for four years!)

He spends the winter before he marries Hrefna in great depression of spirit, morose and silent: *nutu menn lítt tal hans*. We assume that he is brooding over Bolli's behaviour as much as over any regret for Guðrún, for when he visits Laugar with Óláfr for the first time after his return from Norway, there is no mention at all of his first meeting with Guðrún after her marriage, though Guðrún must have been there. Only Bolli is making a great show of gaiety and generosity: *Bolli er við þá inn kátasti;* but Kjartan will not touch his superb gift of a stud of rare horses: "I'm not a stableman" (*kvazk engi vera hrossamaðr, ok vildi eigi þiggja*). And when Kjartan is provoked to his greatest act of enmity against the family at Laugar, it is against Bolli that he directs it. Bolli has presumed to usurp Kjartan's status, marrying the most celebrated woman in Iceland. But Bolli's wife must take second place always to Kjartan's wife, and Bolli is not going to be allowed any aggrandisement as a landowner in the district. Kjartan annuls Bolli's contract for a purchase of land and takes that land himself. The gentle farmer (who was only selling his land in order to escape the quarrels he saw brewing in the district) is obliged to submit to Kjartan's powerful injustice, allowing himself one ironic comment: "I must prize *my lord's* word in this matter—*dýrt mun mér verða dróttins orð um þetta mál*—though I would rather keep to my contract with Bolli." Although in Iceland Kjartan observed his Christian faith rigorously, as King Óláfr asked him to—*"þess vil ek biðja þik, Kjartan, at þú haldir vel trú þína"*—even becoming the marvel of Iceland by fasting in Lent (people came from miles away to watch him "living without food for so long"), he could still behave with a savage autocracy worthy of the saintly king himself.

What reaction did Kjartan expect from Bolli when he humiliated him so publicly (for the news of his ruthless infringement of Bolli's rights would spread like wild-fire with a gossip such as Þorhalla scurrying from farm to farm)? Kjartan appears to have had two expectations in mind: first, that Guðrún's brothers would try to ambush him, and second, that Bolli would never join them. He calmly ensures that the household at Laugar shall be perfectly informed of all his movements by supplying Þorhalla the gossip with every detail she asks concerning his journey through the Laugar district: when he rides north, how long he will stay, what day he rides back. Yet he says, as he dismisses the friends who would have protected him on the last part of his journey home: "Bolli my cousin will have no part in any plan to kill me" (*Eigi mun Bolli, frændi min, slá banaráðum við mik*). Is Kjartan by his repeated humiliations of Bolli and his provocation of open conflict challenging Bolli once and for all to break with the family at Laugar, to surrender to him in friendship and take second place as he used to? When he sees Bolli at the fight, holding back, despite the urging of Guðrún's brothers, he seems to think—or ironically to suggest—that Bolli still has the choice open to him to join him against

Guðrún's family: "Now is the right moment to give your help to one side or the other." (*er þat nú vænst, at veita ǫðrumhvárum*). When he sees that his faith in Bolli's old love and admiration is an illusion—for Bolli is drawing his sword upon him—he throws away his defence. He will not finally drive home his superiority by killing him. If this "other self," as once he was, does not wish him to live, then Kjartan will not fight for his life. There is no thought of Guðrún in Kjartan's mind, though Bolli kills him for her sake.

Between these two men what role does Guðrún play? None, until her social existence is threatened. The saga-writer makes this quite clear. Only when she has heard Kjartan say deliberately in her presence that the high seat of honour among the women shall be given to Hrefna "as long as I live" (*á meðan ek em á lífi*) does the consequence of her marriage become quite clear to her. The wife of the lesser man must take second place. The price of change is Kjartan's death. Once she has seen the gold-woven headdress—the rarest treasure that anyone in Iceland had ever gazed on—and guessed who had sent it, and to whom—her acts become vicious and ignoble: the attempted destruction of Kjartan's great sword, the burning of the peerless headdress. The meanness of the acts reflects the ugliness and pain of her feelings: envy, jealousy, humiliation, rage. She is fighting for her rights, hammering against the door that has been shut upon her, and she uses what means she can. Why should she bear inferiority? When Bolli suffers shamefacedly every insult thrown upon him, Guðrún seizes the matter into her own hands. Assuming the determined role of the egging woman of the old tales, uttering the time-honoured formula with which women pour scorn on their menfolk—and which Þorgerðr too employs when she eggs on her sons to kill Bolli—"surely you are your father's daughters, not his sons"—Guðrún drives her brothers out of their beds at dawn to intercept Kjartan on his homeward ride. She acts her part so vigorously and with so sharp a turn of phrase (such sluggards in vengeance have "pigs' memories," she declares) that she seems the perfect embodiment of the archetypal vengeful woman, "whose violent emotions both in hate and in love demand their tribute of blood among the men in her life" (as one critic has put it). The conventional pattern of her behaviour, however, and the studied calm with which she receives Bolli after the killing: "What time is it?", and above all the artificiality of the manner in which she seems to make light of the killing: "How different our morning's work has been—I have spun wool for twelve ells and you have killed Kjartan," shows that she is making her lips say what she has planned them to say, not that they are speaking from the heart. She is *málsnjǫll* and knows how to shape her words, but her face is drained of colour, as Bolli sees. And now that her ordeal is over, she can see, and feel for, the anguish in Bolli's face too; she turns to him with the first semblance of tenderness and thanks him: he has proved that he will be a slave to her wishes (*þikki mér nú þat vitat, at þú vill ekki gera í móti skapi mínu*). Later that year, their first son is born.

We never see Guðrún so deeply moved again until she is a very old woman: certainly not after the callous slaughter of Bolli (nine men against one, when he casts away his sword, as Kjartan did, as soon as he sees a weapon capable of killing him), nor, twelve years later, when she spreads out the blood-soaked clothes of Bolli—linen underwear, shirt, breeches—in her kitchen garden, to goad her young sons (with perfunctory words) to vengeance. Did she keep those clothes out of calculation, in the first place, or out of tenderness? And why did she smile at Helgi Harðbeinsson as he wiped Bolli's blood from his great spear on to the fringed end of the blue-embroidered wrap she had draped over her pregnant figure? Why not call down curses on the murderers, like the true wife Vígdís Markússdóttir in 1244, when her husband's brutal beheader dried his sword on her clothes, as recorded in *Sturlunga*? If we saw that scene between Helgi and Guðrún enacted on the stage, would we not sense a fleeting complicity of understanding between the two? Helgi's act is both a blood-offering for Kjartan and an imposition of the duty to avenge Bolli. He has relieved her of her husband, of the last burden of feeling from the past. Her smile accepts the service and the duty. As if to protect the enigma within, her outward appearance, a stately front to the world, is described for the first and only time in the saga: the tall headdress, close-fitting bodice, rare robes of foreign weave (*mjǫk*

136]

fyrir ǫðrum konum um allan skǫrungsskap). In her old age she becomes very devout, and blind; the finery she used to love can have no more meaning for her. She holds long vigils at night in the church, weeping such warm tears that the heathen ghost beneath the floorboards feels scalded and begs her to stop. When Guðrún prayed and wept all night in the church, what was she repenting? Was it the inner turmoil of vain and jealous thoughts that prompted her actions in the past, the terrible rage that made her want Kjartan killed, as Brynhildr wanted Sigurðr killed? She modelled her behaviour on heathen patterns once, now she strives to wipe away that past. She greets the ghost's request as a good omen, and has the evil-smelling bones (the skeleton of a heathen sibyl, complete with magic staff) removed far from human paths. It is a symbol of the removal of her own bad deeds, a token of forgiveness.

Did the saga-writer himself invent this story of the heathen *vǫlva's* ghost in order to evoke for us the significance of Guðrún's prayers? Did he invent the detail that Bolli Bollason had the plain steely sword *Fótbítr* made florid with gold? Did he invent the legend that Kjartan and King Ólafr Tryggvason could wear the same suit of clothes, so perfectly were they matched? Did he invent the exemplary story of how King Óláfr Haraldsson tried to cut the presumptuous Þorkell Eyjólfsson, and his church-timbers, down to size? I suspect that he did. He wanted to show not merely what happened in the past, but the quality of the happening, the texture of motive, feeling, doubt, decision; the grain of a personality as it could be felt in a saying or an act. He had a metaphorical turn of mind, as Chaucer had, and could build from the incidents of a story a pattern that the intellect could perceive. Every detail in the saga can be seen as a strand in the pattern, and with each detail the pattern is strengthened and given depth. By means of the old Nibelung story he has re-enacted for his own time a golden age of passionate expectations and has shown it pass into a settled, elderly, repentant age of pewter. His saga is a paradigm of past and present.

Note: The English "citations" of direct speech from *Laxdæla Saga* are, in a few instances, not literal translations of the Icelandic, but abbreviated paraphrases to convey more succinctly my interpretation of the text.

7

Nosce te ipsum: Some Medieval Interpretations

J. A. W. Bennett

MAGDALENE COLLEGE, CAMBRIDGE

T HE history of the oracular γνῶθι ϛεαυτον from classical to medieval times, or at least from Delphi to Cîteaux, has lately been traced by Pierre Courcelle in two authoritative volumes.[1] Courcelle has left not a single patristic or neoplatonic text unturned, so that for the present purpose we need note only that the stages in the Augustinian and Plotinian interpretations of the precept are pretty clearly marked, and that they carry one as far from Socrates as from the common Greek understanding of it: if Socrates made it the basis of philosophy, for Xenophon it meant

1. *Connais-toi toi-même de Socrate à Saint Bernard*, I (Paris, 1974). I have had only intermittent access to this volume, and I have seen only a summary of Vol. II (1975). Preliminary studies appeared in *Le Neoplatonisme* (Paris, 1971) and elsewhere. Leon Brunschvicg's *De la connaissance de soi* (Paris, 1931) is concerned rather with modern than medieval thought. I have in general eschewed study of Plotinian teaching on the topic; it is summarised by Elmer O'Brien, *The Essential Plotinus* (New York, 1964), pp. 28–29. I have tried to avoid trespassing on the territory marked out by Colin Morris in *The Discovery of the Individual* 1050–1200 (London, 1972); but I owe to him my knowledge of the passage in Damian and the inscription cited on p. 141 below.

hardly more than "know your own limitations, your chances of success" (*Memorabilia* LV.ii.26). It is not till the twelfth century that a Christian Socratism develops.

Two passages from Augustine will serve to illustrate differences between classical and Christian views.[2] In *De Trinitate* iv.7 the pupil asks: "In what manner does the human soul know itself?"; and the answer is: "It has consciousness of being but does not know *what* it is." In the *Confessiones* he applies this to himself: "nec ego ipse capio totum, quod sum"; and speaking of confession, he asks: "Quid est enim a te audire de se nisi cognoscere se? Quis porro cognoscit et dicit 'falsum est', nisi ipse mentiatur" (X.3).[3] Two chapters later he returns to this point: "Tu enim, domine, diiudicas me, quia . . . est aliquid hominis, quod nec ipse scit spiritus hominis, qui in ipso est, tu autem, domine, scis eius omnia, qui fecisti eum . . . tamen aliquid de te scio, quod de me nescio."[4]

Gregory of Nazanzien had said that Man can know himself only if he knows God, and like his namesake of Nyssa had affirmed that God alone can fully comprehend what He is. John Scotus Eriugena had related the theme to that of man as a microcosm, citing in support the verse of Cant. i.7 ("si ignoras te . . .") that later writers were to apply rather differently. Man before the Fall both knew himself and loved the knowledge of self, for *esse, nosse, amare* were one. The neoplatonic developments began with Plotinus, who first makes the association with

2. Augustine would know the precept in its Ciceronian context (*Tuscul. Disp.* I, i,22,32) and from Juvenal (see p. 143 below). The Greek form of the phrase was corrupted by the early Middle Ages to *notis elitos*, which according to Courcelle was often interpreted as "habite avec soi-même"; it appears in the English *Secreta Secretorum* as *Notis clotos;* for another bizarre variant see below p. 152. In Trinity College Cambridge MS 72, fol. 258, it is cited as 'neocoleton.' For other fifteenth-century variants see C. F. Buhler, *Early Books and Manuscripts* (New York, 1973), p. 351.

3. "What is it to hear from thee of themselves, but to know themselves? And who is he that, knowing himself, can say that it is false unless he himself lies?"

4. "For thou, O Lord, dost judge me: because . . . there is something of man that the very spirit of man that is in him knoweth not. But thou knowest all of him who has made him. . . . Yet I know something of thee, which I know not of myself."

the origins of man that we shall find in Gower: "He who knows who he is will know also whence he comes." For Plotinus self-knowledge is knowledge of universal forms—a view that enabled Christian Platonism to associate self-knowledge with God. Porphyry read the Delphic motto as a warning to the supplicant, who would not obtain what he desired unless he attained self-knowledge and thus put himself in harmony with the gods; and Porphyry proffers three interpretations of his own: To know oneself is (1) to recognise the *nous* as essence; (2) to recognise man as a microcosm who fittingly prepares himself to contemplate the macrocosm, the universe; and (3) to philosophise. As if developing this third aspect Iamblichus states that the first duty of a philosopher is to perfect his *nous*, and then to attach himself to the gods. Julian, conforming rather to Gregory of Nyssa, claims that the gods know themselves perfectly. By the sixth century the neoplatonists could assert that all men were capable of self-knowledge, though most did not realise its practicability. For Olympiodorus the precept had the function of the mirror set at the approaches to Egyptian sanctuaries—and the mirror-figure will appear in similar contexts several centuries later. The Pseudo-Dionysius conceived of self-knowledge as a preparatory stage in the process of purification that the powers he identifies with the angels of Christian thought help to accomplish. St. Thomas was to incorporate this conception into his discussion of the intellect of the first man: "There are three degrees of movement in the soul, as Dionysius says. The first is by the soul passing from exterior things to concentrate its powers on itself; the second is by the soul ascending so as to be associated with . . . the angels; the third is when the soul is led on yet further to the supreme good, that is, to God" (*Summa Theologica* 1, Q. 94, art. 2). But, he continues, the soul, the human intellect, can know itself only as regards intellectual operations; the soul of the first man was not able to arrive at the knowledge of separate substances by means of its self-knowledge. As always, a limiting note is sounded.

In Boethius's *Consolatio* the chief charge that Philosophy brings against her interlocutor is self-ignorance: "quid ipse sis, nosse desisti" (I.pr.vi.40); which Chaucer will translate as

"Thou has left for to knowen thyselve, what thou art." The passage leads on (at the beginning of Book II) to a discussion of Fortuna; and Fortuna and self-ignorance are themes not infrequently conjoined in later literature. Colin Morris, in his study of twelfth-century "inwardness" (see n. 2) duly cites Boethius. But it is to be doubted whether Peter Damian was consciously following the *Consolatio* when in the middle of the eleventh century he wrote: "Let sterile attention to business cease. Let the mind return within itself." Probably before Damian died there was carved on the doorway of Saint Angelo in Formis the inscription: "You will climb to heaven if you know yourself."

By the time of Anselm the interpretation that was to dominate the later Middle Ages had taken shape: in the *Monologion* he says that the more the rational soul tries to know itself the more it approaches the knowledge of God. The soul is a mirror in which the image of God can be contemplated. These concepts are supplemented and developed in the Victorine writings of the twelfth century, notably in Hugh of St. Victor, who in *De Sacramentis* states: "mens rationalis se ipsam videt" and in the *Didascalicon:* "sapientia illuminat hominem ut se ipsum agnoscat." Elsewhere he writes: "ascendere ad deum hoc est intrare ad semetipsum et non solum ad se intrare sed ineffabili quodam modo in intimis etiam se ipsum transire."[5] Achard of St. Victor takes up the notion of the journey homeward to oneself: the promised land is the interior man (*Sermo ix*). The figure is Augustine's ("Noli foras ire, in te ipsum redi; in interiori homine habitat veritas"[6] [*De vera religione* 29]) and it will recur repeatedly in Bernardine literature. Again in the *Benjamin Minor*, of Richard of St. Victor, self-knowledge is a step towards the knowledge of God (cf. ME version in C. Horstman, *Yorkshire Writers*, London 1895 I, 171): "If Plato and Aristotle had known themselves they would never have worshipped idols"; but whilst in the flesh man

5. "The rational mind sees itself. . . . Wisdom enlightens man so that he may know himself. To ascend to God is to enter into oneself and not only to enter but in an inexpressible way to penetrate into one's inmost being."

6. "Do not roam abroad, return unto thyself. Truth dwells in the inner man."

J. A. W. BENNETT

cannot see the substance of his soul full except by revelation. William of Thierry returns to Origen's interpretation of Cant. i.7: "If you do not know yourself it is because you have left yourself." The *De Contemplatione* reads the precept as emphasising that man is made from mire; to know oneself is to learn in what virtue consists.

For St. Bernard self-knowledge was primarily an exercise in humility. In the thirty-sixth sermon on the Canticles he writes:

> The soul can find no motive more effective or more powerful for humility than a thorough knowledge of itself as it really is, only it must be honest in purpose and without guile, and standing in presence of itself must ignore nothing that it beholds. . . . Then it will find itself different from what it believed itself to be, laden with sins, heavily burdened with its mortal body, involved in earthly cares, infected with the corruption of carnal desires, blind, bent earthwards, weak, entangled with many errors, exposed to a thousand perils, trembling with a thousand fears, struggling with a thousand difficulties, the subject of a thousand suspicions and a thousand distressing necessities, prone to vices and to virtue slow and backward. [*Works*, trans. S. J. Eales (London, 1896), IV, 237; *Opera*, ed. J. Mabillon (Paris, 1690), I. 1395]

Exhaustive and discursive as Bernard's exposition of the Canticles is, he does not dwell, curiously enough, on the opening phrase of Cant. i.7 ("Si ignoras te" . . .). Indeed, in commenting on it in *Sermo* 35, (and 34), he appears to read it as "si ignoras:" hence his later allusion to Psalm xlviii.13, which he interprets as meaning that man became devoid of honour because he did not understand (para. 6). But he cites *cautus illud Græcorum* elsewhere: once in expounding Cant. i.3 (*Sermo* 23): he does not presume to know what the chamber (*cellaria*) of that verse is; "being careful, according to that proverb of the Greeks, to know myself (*'scire me ipsum'*) and to know as did the Psalmist that such knowledge is too wonderful for me" (*Works*, IV. 136; *Opera*, I.1342); and a second time in *Sermo* 40 *De Diversis*: "*Prima semita et primus gradus in via ista est Cognitio sui. De caelo cecidit ista sententia nosce te ipsum, homo. Vide si non et Sponsus in amoris Cantico sponsae idem loquatur. Si ignoras te, inquit, o pulchra* [etc.]. *Cognitio*

sui stat in tribus, ut cognoscat homo quid fecit, quid meruit, quid amisit" (*Opera*, I.1166).[7]
Here is Bernard's doctrine of self-knowledge in a nutshell. Not everyone will realise that it is based on Juvenal as much as on the Canticles: "E caelo descendit γνῶθι σεαυτόν" (Satires xi.27). The line had been given currency by Macrobius, who quotes it, without revealing its source, in his Commentary on *Somnium Scipionis*, adding: 'nam et Delphici vox haec fertur oraculi. Consulenti ad beatitatem quo itinere perveniret: si te, inquit, agnoveris. Sed et ipsius fronti templi haec inscripta sententia est. Homini autem, ut diximus, una est agnitio sui, si originis natalisque principii exordia prima respexerit, nec se quaesiverit extra.'[8] Macrobius gave the line a Platonic reading, Richard of St. Victor (as Courcelle shows) a Christian one.

But the twelfth century was the century not only of St. Bernard and the abbey of Cîteaux but of Abelard and the schools of Chartres. To Chartres went John of Salisbury; and in

7. "The first stage on the road is self-knowledge. It was from heaven that the maxim came: Man, Know Thyself. And does not the Bridegroom in the Lovesong for his Bride say, likewise: 'If thou knowest not thyself'' (etc.) Self-knowledge has three aspects: that a man should recognise what he has done, what he has deserved, and what he has lost."
Self-knowledge is the medicine for Pride in *Cursor Mundi* 2750–52 (and note Judas's belated self-knowledge, 15998). The grace of "knowyng to knowe þi self" is described at length in *Jacob's Well*, Pt. I, ed. A. Brandeis, EETS, o.s.115 (London, 1900), 275–76: "it techeth þe noȝt of þe sterrys. . . . But it techeth þe to kun þeself, whanne þouart synfulle, and whanne þu art riȝtfull (etc.)."
8. "For this is said also to have been the utterance of the Delphic oracle. When answering him who enquired by what means he might attain to happiness, it replied, "If you have known yourself." And this maxim is likewise written across the entrance to the temple. But as we have said, a man has only one way of knowing himself; if he looks back to his beginning and origin and does not search for himself elsewhere." (*Commentarii in somnium Scipionis*, ed. J. Willis [Leipzig, 1963], p. 40). Stahl compares Porphyry, *Sententiae* xxxii. 8, and Adelard of Bath [*De edodem et diverso*], 16-17, passages on which Courcelle draws. Stahl also notes the allusion to Persius's *Nec quaesiveris extra* and Macrobius's other reference to the inscription as being on the doorpost of the temple at Delphi: *Commentary in the Dream of Scipio*, translated by W. H. Stahl (New York, 1952), p. 124.

his *Metalogicon*, that strenuous defence of the arts of the Trivium, the English writer taps very different sources from St. Bernard's, such as Aristotle and Cicero. Chapter XXII, Book IV of the *Metalogicon* is devoted to "the cognition, simplicity, and immortality of the soul, according to Cicero"; and amongst the citations from the *Tusculan Disputations* (i.28.9: cf. n. 2) is the following: 'The thinking soul cannot fully know itself. Still, like the eye, it beholds other things without seeing itself. Perhaps it is true that it does not see its own form, which is not an important defect. Although possibly it even sees this. But whatever the case, the thinking soul certainly perceives its own force, sagacity, memory, activity and quickness' (*Metalogicon*, trans. Daniel D. McGarry [Berkeley and Los Angeles, 1955], p. 233).

Nothing could be further from St. Bernard's teaching than this. Whether it is borne out or developed by the authors cited later in the same chapter—they include Claudianus Mamertus and Nemesius—is not our concern. But we may note that the *Metalogicon* was addressed to schoolmen not to religious (and its influence was the less far-reaching on that account). Yet in his final chapter—which includes a revealing reference to *ignorantia invincibilis* of such mysteries as the Trinity, following Abelard's *Scito te ipsum* c.xiv[9]—John manages to conjoin Cicero and the great Cistercian. For its theme is that it is futile to know many things if the one thing needful is lacking. The pagan philosophers, preoccupied with investigating all things under the sun, became vain in their thought. "To know oneself is according to Apollo practically the highest wisdom" (the quotation is again from Cicero: *De Finibus* v.16.44). "Of what use is it to understand the nature of the elements, . . . to speculate about the opposition of virtues and vices . . . to dispute with probability on all sorts of points, if, meanwhile, one remains ignorant of himself? . . . However, he who . . . takes into account his own imperfection (which is scarcely able to understand a few things) . . . checks, represses, or extinguishes the lusts of his flesh; endeavours diligently to form again in himself the image of God,

9. Abelard's interpretation of the phrase is summarised by M. de Gandillac in a passage cited by Jacques Le Goff, *Les Intellectuels au Moyen Age* (Paris, 1957), p. 53.

which has been disfigured by vice; . . . such a one is truly philosophizing" (ed. cit. p. 270).

With this kind of gloss our precept was to prove palatable to many sorts and conditions of men, as evidence from fourteenth-century English verse will show. But it is to ascetical writers that it owes its earliest dissemination in England. One of them is Ailred of Rievaulx, who in his sermon on Cant. i.7 interprets that verse much as Bernard did, and in his *Speculum Caritatis* describes self-knowledge as distinguishing man from animals (Courcelle, I 285). If the *Middle English Dictionary* is to be trusted it is in the *Trinity Homilies* (c. 1200) that the phrase first appears in an English form: "man is understondinde þe him seluen cnoweð and gode leueð." What this meant for the preacher he indicates when he translates: "Ille seipsum cognoscit qui considerat in speculo mentis quantus sit . . . expositus miseriis. Ut pote natus in merore" as "þe man cnoweð him seluen þe þencheð of wu medeme [vile] þinge he is shapen."[10] This is as traditional in its emphasis as a passage in the *Ayenbite of Inwyt* one hundred and fifty years later: "Prede . . . ablent men   zuo þet hi ham-zelve ne knaweþ ne ne zyeþ."[11]

More interesting on several counts is its appearance in the text that was Tolkien's abiding love, *Ancrene Wisse*. Whatever reassessment of the originality of this work has to be made in the light of the newly identified *Moralia* of Alexander of Bath, it will remain true that a pervasive influence is the teaching of St. Bernard, and in particular his Sermons on the Canticles. Early in Part II of *Ancrene Wisse* the writer cites the verse we have already encountered, Cant. i.7: "Si ignoras te o pulcra inter mulieres, egredere et abi post uestigia gregum tuorum et pasce edos tuos iuxta tabernacula pastorum"; which he expounds thus: "ʒef þu ne cnawest te seolf he seið ure lauerd.   neomeð nu gode ʒeme. þet is ʒef þu nast hwas spuse þu art. þet tu art cwen of heouene. ʒef þu art me treowe as spuse ah to beonne. ʒef þu þis hauest forʒeten and telest her to lutel wend ut and ga . . . ʒef þu hauest

10. "That man knows himself who considers of what vile matter he is made" (*O. E. Homilies*, ed. W. Morris, EETS, o.s.53 [London, 1876]), p. 121.

11. "Pride blinds men so that they do not know or see themselves" (W. Morris, EETS, o.s.28 [London, 1866], p. 16).

forȝete nu þi wurðfule leafdischipe, ga and folhe þeos geat. folhe flesches lustes."[12] (*Ancrene Wisse* Corpus Christi College Cambridge), ed. J. R. R. Tolkien, EETS, 249 (London, 1962), 53–54, 28 ff.). The kids (*hœdos*) of the Canticles are identified with the wandering senses, as in St. Bernard.

In Part IV of the same text is another allusion to the desirability of self-knowledge, in the discussion of illness which "makeð mon to understonden hwet he is. to cnawen hím seoluen."[13] Through illness man learns his human frailty—a view certainly consonant with the saint's teaching. In that teaching the opposition of self-knowledge to *curiositas* is constant. For the kids of the Canticles symbolise *curiositas* as well as the troublous desires of the flesh. The theme was taken up by the anonymous disciple who wrote the *Meditationes Piissimœ de cognitione humanœ conditionis*, sometimes attributed to St. Bernard himself; and it was the Anonymous who picked up a phrase used by Peter Damian when reproaching certain monks—"cum multa sciant se nesciant"[14]—and gave it (in his opening sentences) epigrammatic formulation: "Multi multa sciunt et seipsos nesciunt. Alios inspiciunt, et seipsos deserunt. Deum quærunt per ista exteriora, quibus interior est Deus. Idcirco ab exterioribus redeam ad interiora, et ab inferioribus ad superiora ascendam. . . ."[15] In *Piers Plowman* Scripture will apply this condemnation to the Dreamer:

12. "If thou knowest not thyself, o fairest among women, go forth and follow the tracks of the flocks and feed thy kids beside the herdsmens' tents": 'If thou knowest not thyself," says Our Lord. Take careful note. This means: if thou knowest not whose spouse thou art and hast forgotten that thou art queen of heaven (if thou art true to me as a spouse should be) go and follow these goats, follow the lusts of the flesh."

13. "Causes a man to understand what he is, and to know himself" (*Ancrene Wisse*, ed. Tolkien, p. 95).

14. "Many know much yet are ignorant of themselves. They examine others and neglect themselves, seeking the God within externals, and disregarding their own inner state. Wherefore let me turn from outward things to things within and ascend from the lower to the higher" (*Opera*, ed. Mabillon, II, 319).

15. "Though they may know much, they may not know themselves" (*Patrologia Latina*, 144, 921 BC). I owe this reference to P. Courcelle but he does not discuss Damian's curious supporting quotation from 1 Cor. XV. 38 (*Unicuique seminum proprium corpus*).

Thanne Scripture scorned me and a skile tolde,
And lakked me in Latyne and liȝte by me she sette,
And seyde multi multa sciunt et seipsos nesciunt,
                                    [B, XI. 1–3, cf. XII. 113–116]

The rebuke becomes less cryptic if we read the preceding passus as exposing the dreamer's *curiositas;* and the appearance of *Concupiscentia Carnis* (as handmaid of Fortune) in the following scene is wholly in line with St. Bernard's thought as illustrated in the sermon cited above: if one does not know oneself one will be a prey to the troublous claims of the flesh, as the Dreamer is in the Land of the Longing:

> *Concupiscentia-carnis* culled me aboute the nekke,
> And seyde 'thou art ȝonge and ȝepe and hast ȝeres ȝnowe . . .'
>   [B, XI. 16–17]

The mirror of Middelerd in which the Dreamer can see wonders (XI. 9 ff) is to be thought of as diverting the Dreamer's gaze from the mirror in his own mind. The intent of this part of the poem is to suggest the perils of *curiositas*, exactly as St. Bernard had done. But whereas for the Saint the perils were embodied in Abelard and his followers, for Langland they took the form of sophisticated speculation in the Schools on the nature of the Trinity, Predestination, and Divine Foreknowledge.

The dichotomy between *curiositas* and self-knowledge is found at the same time in a poet who had none of Langland's religious preoccupations, John Gower. Gower adverts to the theme in each of his major works. In the *Mirour de l'omme* "Veine curiosite" is thus characterised:

> . . . est d'orguillouse fantasie;
> Car tous jours serche l'autri vie,
> et de soy ne s'est remembré:
> Trop se fait sage et surquidée,
> Quant sciet et jugge en son degré
> Tous autres, et soy ne sciet mie.
> Dont Bernard dist "Trop ad torné
> Sa sapience en vanité,
> Cil q'autri sciet et soy oublie." [lines 1612–20]

Macaulay suggested that Gower may have had in mind a passage in the *Meditationes Piissimæ*, which Gower may well have attributed to St. Bernard: "Stude cognoscere te: quam multo melior et laudabilior es si te cognoscis quam si te neglecto cognesceres cursum siderum."[16] In fact, many other passages quite as close in thought to Gower's might be cited, all doubtless deriving ultimately from the chapter in Augustine's *Confessiones* cited above: "Et eunt homines mirari alta montium, et ingentes fluctus maris, et latissimos lapsus fluminum, et Oceani ambitum, et gyros siderum, et relinquunt se ipsos"[17] (X.viii); and the contrast between study of the stars and study of the self will reappear in such contexts for several centuries. In *Confessio amantis* a marginal gloss attributing to "Bernardus" a variant form of the maxim—"Plures plura sciunt et seipsos nesciunt"—appears opposite a generalising passage rather oddly inserted in the tale of Ulysses and Telegonus in Book VI:

> Men sein, a man hath knowleching
> Save of himself of alle thing;
> His oghne chance noman knoweth,
> Bot as fortune it on him throweth:
> Was nevere yit so wys a clerk
> Which mihte knowe al goddes werk
> Ne the secret which god hath set
> Ayein a man mai noght be let.   [1567–74]

This is at once more "absolute" than St. Bernard—in that it is applied to all men—and less concerned with spiritual self-knowledge: the ignorance is simply that of a man's future fortune; as it is in the tale of Nectanabus, where the contrast with the *cursus siderum* is illustrated very literally. Nectanabus takes the young Alexander to view the stars from a tower:

> And seith what ech of hem amonteth,
> As thogh he knew of alle thing:

16. "Study to know thyself. How much better and more estimable it is if thou knowest thyself than if thou study the courses of the constellations and neglect thyself."

17. "And men go forth to consider with wonder the loftiness of mountains, the great waves of the sea, the length of rivers, the compass of the Ocean, the courses of the constellations and yet pay no attention to themselves."

> But yet hath he no knowleching
> What schal unto himself befalle.   [*Confessio amantis* vi.2294–97]

The stars could not tell him that Alexander would suddenly push him over the wall, saying:

> Thou knewe all othre mennes chance
> And of thiself hast ignorance:
> That thou has seid amonges alle
> Of thi persone, is noght befalle   [2313–15]

Gower's third adaptation of the phrase occurs in a passage in *Vox clamantis* on man as the microcosm: a context in which it can be found from patristic times. Here, indeed, we come closer to the twelfth-century emphasis on self-knowledge as prerequisite for the knowledge and love of God:

> Si minor est mundus, que sunt primordia mundi
> Si meditetur, agit vnde sit et quid homo.
> Si se nesciret, nec eum cognosceret, a quo
> Vel per quem factus est, nec amaret eum.[18]   [vii.671–74]

Here Gower's *cognosceret* reminds one that the *Meditationes Piissime* distinguishes between *cognoscere* and *intelligere:* "Ex me intelligo quam incomprehensibilis sit Deus: quoniam me ipsum intelligere non possum, quem ipse fecit": to "know" God is not to comprehend him. And Gower's phrasing suggests that he was indeed familiar with the *Meditationes*, in which the intention is: "ut possim cognoscere unde venio aut quo vado: quid sum vel unde sum; et ita per cognitionem mei valeam pervenire ad congitionem Dei."[19] Langland seems to have this passage in mind when presenting Anima, who at one stage of the dreamer's progress in self-discovery

> tolde me whyder I shulde,
> And whereof I cam and of what kynde.   [B XV.13–14]

18. "If he is a lesser world and meditates on the origins of the world, he considers what man is and whence he comes. If he know not himself neither will he come to know Him by whom or through whom he was made, nor to love Him."

19. "So that I may be able to discover whence I come and whither I go; what I am or whence I came: and so by learning about myself come to arrive at the knowledge of God."

J. A. W. BENNETT

That self-knowledge involves awareness of man's origins and destiny is a prominent theme in the one Middle English poem devoted specifically to our precept, the refrain-stanzas in the Vernon MS that begin as an exposition of the first six words of 1 Thess. iv.4: "*ut sciat unusquisque vestrum vas suum* . . ." ("that every one of you should know [how to possess] his vessel"). The superficial verbal similarity with the classical precept provides the impetus for nine twelve-line stanzas linked by the same refrain:

> In a Pistel þat Poul wrouȝt
> I fond hit writen & seide riht þis:
> Vche cristne creature knowen himself ouȝt
> His oune vessel; and soþ hit is.
> Nere help of him that vs deore bouȝt,
> We weoren bore to lytel blis,
> Whon al þi gode dedes beþ þorw-souȝt,
> Seche, and þou shalt fynden Amis.
> Eueri mon scholde I-knowen his,
> And that is luitel, as I trowe;
> To teche vs self, crist vs wis,
> For vche mon ouȝte himself to knowe.[20]

Here the Pauline text seems to have been deliberately wrested to fit into a traditional interpretation of the precept, which is at once glossed by means of the *unde, quo, quid* formula:

> Knowe þi-self what þou ware,
> Whon þou were of þi moder born,
> Ho was þi moder þat þe bare,
> And ho was þi fader þer-bi-foren.
> Knowe hou þei beþ forþ-fare,
> So schaltou þeiȝ þou hed sworen . . .

"Knowe þi lyf, hit may not last"; worldly goods waste away, sin slays the soul; amend, and know thyself; recognise what God has done for you as creator and savior. The last verse identifies self-inquiry with Conscience:

20. *Religious Lyrics of the Fourteenth Century*, ed. Carleton Brown (Oxford, 1936) no. 100.

Þi Conscience schal þe save and deme,
Wheþer þat þou beo ille or good:
Grope aboute and tak good ʒeme,
Þer maiʒt þou wite, but þou beo wood . . .

The verses probably come from the same pen as another poem
in the Vernon MS, with the refrain "þis world fareþ as a Fantasy":
an extended warning against *curiositas:*

Whar-to wilne we forte knowe
þe poyntes of Godes priuete?
More þen him lustes forte schowe
We schulde not knowe in no degre . . .
[*Religious Lyrics*, no. 106, lines 85–88]

Everything suggests that by the end of the fourteenth century
the precept had become a preacher's commonplace to be applied
in bringing home a sense of sin. The Prologue to the *Prick of
Conscience* states:

He þat right ordir of lyfyng wil luke
Sulde bygyn þus, as says þe boke;
To knaw first what hym-self es,
Swa may he tvttest come to mekenes.

and so accordingly withdraw from sin and vanities.[21] "The soul
that knows itself humbles himself," wrote Catherine of Siena to
Gregory XI.[22] Humility, says Chaucer's Parson—apparently

---

21. Ed. R. Morris (London, 1863), lines 205–8. The passage continues:

For if he hym-self knew kyndely,
He suld haf knawyng of God almyghty
And of his endyng thynk suld he
And of þe day þat last sal be. [lines 221–24]

It includes the customary contrast with knowledge of *aliena* and we are not
surprised to find St. Bernard cited on the four things that make man forget
himself: *forma, fervor populi, fervor juvenilis opesque/ surripuere tibi noscere quid sit
homo.*

22. The phrase recurs in St. Catherine's *Dialogues*, in a passage on the
torments of the damned, the English version of which reads: "in sich a siʒt þei
knowen hemsilf moore fully þan þei dide, for þere þei se þat þoru her owne
defautis þei ben worþi to haue þo turmentis" (*The Orchard of Syon*, ed. P.
Hodgson, EETS 258 [London, 1960], p. 89, lines 6–8).

without referring to Peraldus—"is a virtue thurgh which a man hath verray knoweleche of hymself and holdeth of hymself no pris ne deyntee, as in regard of his desertes, considerynge evere his freletee" (*The Canterbury Tales*, I. 475).[23]

Chaucer's other explicit reference is at first sight more cryptic. Commenting on the tale of Hercules, his Monk says

> Ful wys is he that kan hymselven knowe;
> [*Canterbury Tales*, B* 3329]

but to anyone familiar with Gower's juxtaposition of Fortune and worldly wisdom (see above) the implication is plain: no one is wise enough to reckon with the "unwar stroke" of Fortune; and it is perhaps worth noting that in some traditions Hercules figures as an example of *curiositas*. The moral had been popularised by the *Gesta Romanorum*, which gives the story (found first in Jerome) of a Roman Triumph, of which Mirk's *Festial* provides a fourteenth-century English version:

> But when he [the Roman general] come þrogh any cyte, þer schuld a man stond by hym in þe char, and bete hym in þe mowth wyth a branche of olyf, saying thus; "Anothe selitos": þat is to say: "Know thyselfe". As þogh he sayde to hym þus: þagh þou haue þe victory now, hit may happen þat þou schalt anoþyr tyme have þe wors, and so turne þe in as moch vyleny as now þis doþe to worschip: *wher for be not prowde* of þyselfe. [*Festial*, ed. Erbe, EETS, p. 116; my italics; for *Anothe Selitos* see n. 2, p. 139, above.]

The same juxtaposition, but with a different emphasis, is made by Lydgate:

> Fortune hath cast hem from ther sees
> Namly such as koude hemselff not knowe.   [*Fall of Princes*, I, 6907]

The apparent hint of our precept in the Clerk's tale (*Canterbury Tales*, E 474) is of no significance. There the marquis is reminding Griselda that he took her "in poor estate":

> "For any wele ye moot yourselven knowe."

However we construe this line—which has no basis in Petrarch

23. All quotations from Chaucer are from F. N. Robinson's edition.

or the French version of Petrarch—it is hard to read into it any ethical emphasis: her present prosperity is not to blind her to her humble origins. More to our purpose is the couplet inserted into the Chaucerian version of the *Roman de la Rose* at the point where in the French text Raison cautions the man who relies on riches:

> But he amende him of that vice
> And knowe hymself, he is not wyse. [5379–80]

At this point Raison is following closely the lines laid down in Boethius's *Consolatio* II.pr.viii. But the English lines have no equivalent in the Latin or in the *Roman*.

It is not, however, in verbal renderings of the time-worn injunction that we must look for evidence of its real impact on medieval thought. The spiritual self-examination recommended by St. Bernard had its secular counterpart in the interior monologues that entered European Romance first in the Old French *Eneas* and later in the poems of Chrétien. Henceforth we have to do with protagonists who think about themselves as well as their actions. In English romance, *Gawain and the Green Knight*, even more than *Troilus*, represents this new self-consciousness (and it is no accident that in the former poem much hinges on the confession scene). A history of the English novel could be written entirely in terms of the characters who are shown as struggling towards, or indifferent to, the self-knowledge that humbles and enlightens. *Emma* or *The Egoist* provide two obvious examples, but the theme is never far from Conrad's concerns, and in our own day Graham Greene and Patrick White answer to this touchstone. In these two novelists at least it appears in a form wholly unaffected by the revolutionary developments in self-analysis initiated by Freud.

The concept of individuality, of personal uniqueness, has replaced the generalisations of medieval thought, and began to do so just as autobiography, and self-portraiture, were developing as distinct genres. But the names we first associate with autobiography are of those writers who took *nosce te ipsum* most to heart: Augustine, Abelard, Petrarch. In a famous letter (*Epistolæ Familiares* iv) Petrarch cites Augustine's "nec ipse capio quod sum"; and in the *De Remediis* he makes a more positive association between self-knowledge and Fortune than that glanced at above: "to know oneself in the most secret closet of the mind is the last help to the acceptance of Fortune." (As for self-portraiture, whether in prose or in paint, it is not always proof of self-knowledge. As Nietszche wrote, in a passage cited by Brunschvicg (p. 23): "L'observation directe de soi est loin de suffire pour apprendre à se connaître."

Even before the end of the fourteenth century the precept, freed from its earlier associations with Bernardine ascetism, had appeared in a wholly secular context. In *Mum, Sothsegger* self-knowledge is synonymous with mental maturity, for it is said of the young Richard II, who ascended the throne at the age of ten: "ȝe come to ȝoure kyngdom er ȝe ȝoure-self knewe." And the *Secreta Secretorum*, which was read primarily as a mirror for princes, was expanded by James Yonge in 1422 by the addition of a passage translated from the *Breviloquium de quatuor virtutibus cardinalibus* of the Franciscan John of Wales: at the beginning of the passage on "The second part of Prudence" the expanded text runs: "Amonge all thynges that byth to vndyrstonde, Oone soveraynly nedyth, that a man knowe hym-selfe. For in vayne othyr thynges hym paynyth to know, that hymselfe wolde foryete." It is duly followed by Jerome's story of the Roman Triumph, and—what is more interesting—by a gloss on the very verse in the Psalms that Bernard had cited in *Sermo* 35: "Dauid the Profete sayth of men that in honoure byth and knowyth not ham-selfe, *Homo cum in honore esset non intellexit*, etc."[24]

The mystic's understanding of self-knowledge is a theme that demands immersion in Dionysian doctrine, and this is not the place to consider how such doctrine came within the purview of Walter Hilton or Julian of Norwich. But a passage from Hilton's *Scale of Perfection* will indicate the points of contact with Bernardine teaching:

A soul which wants to have knowledge of spiritual things must first have knowledge of itself. It cannot understand a nature superior to its own, unless it first understands itself. And it is by self-knowledge that the soul can attain to a spiritual knowledge of God. I do not say . . .

24. *Secreta Secretorum*, ed. R. Steele, EETS, e.s. 75 (London, 1898), 154–55.

that *you* need to occupy yourselves with this matter and are bound to do so: but I do say to those who feel themselves moved by grace to undertake it. . . .[25]

This might suggest that the attainment of self-knowledge was a special grace; and indeed Hilton goes on to speak of the various graces by which men are saved. Yet he soon adds: "But there is one thing which is profitable to us all to do, and that is to know our own souls. Man's soul is a life, made of three powers—that is, memory, reason, and will—in the likeness of the glorious Trinity."[26] By the Fall this likeness was perverted into forgetfulness or ignorance of God, and an animal delight in ourselves and other creatures:

> Go, if you first wish to find your own soul, withdraw yourself from all bodily outward things, . . . and from the exercise of all your senses, as much as is possible: and reflect on the spiritual nature of a rational soul; . . . the more that you can see what is the nature of a rational soul and what are its functions, the better you know yourself. We ought to recognise God and spiritual things by the soul's understanding, not by our imagination. Just as the soul sees, by understanding, that the nature of justice is in giving to everything that which is its due, so, in the same way, the soul can see itself by understanding, and by doing so it will see how God can be recognised.[27]

If this is Dionysian in language it is wholly orthodox in its conclusion: "To see and to know Jesus, God and man . . . may be called the reforming of the soul in faith and in feeling . . . the more that the soul knows itself, through grace and by its visions of truth . . . and the less that the soul thinks that it is loving God, the closer it comes to perceiving God's gift of His blessed love for the soul."[28]

25. Quotations are from the section of the *Scale* that is included in the fifteenth-century "Westminster" *Florilegium*, printed in a modernised version under the title *The Knowledge of Ourselves and God*, ed. James Walsh and Eric Colledge (London, 1961), pp. 23 ff. The quotations from Canticles in the section, and their application, further show Hilton's affinities with St. Bernard.
26. Ibid.
27. Ibid.
28. Ibid.

It is in the light of the medieval traditions so variously illustrated in English verse and in Hilton's prose that we should read
Sir John Davies's long poem *Nosce te ipsum* (1599). Its subtitle, *of
Human Knowledge*, at once suggests what the nexus will be; and
indeed it opens on the same sceptical note as *In a Pistel:* When all
the learned volumes have been turned, what can we know? Error chokes the windows of the mind. Reason's lamp, which first
"throughout Man's little world her beams did spread" has now
become a mere spark. How may we attain to other things when
none of us understands his own soul? The oracle's *Know thyself* is
the Devil's mockery of our curious brain. Why believe the soul
when she cannot say how, whence, where, or what she is?

> We seek to know the moving of each sphere,
> and the strange cause of the ebbs and floods of Nile;
> But of that clock within our breasts we bear,
> The subtle motions we forget the while.
>
> We that acquaint ourselves with every Zone
> And pass both Tropics and behold the Poles,
> When we come home are to ourselves unknown,
> And unacquainted still with our own souls.

The mind is frightened by her own image. It is Affection that
teaches us to know ourselves beyond all books. The Divine
Powers infused an inward light, whereby the soul, as by a mirror, may take a perfect sight of her own form;

> But as the sharpest eye discerneth nought
> Except the sunbeams in the air do shine
> So the best soul with her reflecting thought
> Sees not herself without some light divine.

The soul learns the outward form of things by the senses which
enroll them on the fantasy. But in judging between good and ill,
false and true, the soul views in her own mirror.

This figure of the *speculum mentis* has its own history. It
appears (though it is not translated) in the Trinity Homily cited
above (p. 145). It was known to Chaucer, for in the gloss to
Boethius Book V m.iv.7–9 he writes: "Thilke stoiciens wenden
þat þe soule hadde ben naked of itself, as a mirour or clene parch-

emyn" (cf. Aristotle's *tabula rasa*).[29] But Root's quotation of
Chaucer's gloss in his notes on *Troilus* I.365 is inappropriate:
Troilus is there simply recreating in his mind's eye the figure of
Criseyde, and using the terms by which Chaucer had filled out
the lines in the *Roman de la Rose* (2653–54) describing the activity
of Douz Pensers, who

> au devant li met
> les iaus rianz, le nes traits:

> For Thought anon thanne shall bygynne
> As fer, God wot, as he can fynde,
> To make a mirrour of his mynde.
> For to behold he wole not lette.
> Hir persone he shall afor hym sette . . .
> [*Romaunt of the Rose* 2804–8]

The mirror as a figure for self-scrutiny I have not found in
English before Lydgate, who begins a poem: "Look in thy mirror, Consule quisquis eris"; but it can probably be traced to
Narcissus gazing at his own reflexion. In the OF *Narcisus* it is
only by means of his image that he comes to know himself, to
know the self-love that was implicit in his conduct towards
Dane.[30]

Davies's use of the figure in contrast is deliberate and precise; and he repeats it in the section on the immortality of the
soul:

> But whoso makes a mirror of his mind
> And doth with patience view himself therein,
> His Soul's eternity shall clearly find,
> Though the other beauties be defaced with sin.

One recalls that in the first English Emblem book, Geoffrey
Whitney's *A Choice of Emblems* (1586), the device for our "golden

29. For Paracelsus's application of the figure, see E. Cassirer, *The Individual and the Cosmos* (Oxford, 1963), p. 112; E. Barkan (*Nature's Work of Art*
[New Haven, 1975], p. 39), claims that "the most significant correspondence
within [Paracelsus's] system is between cosmology and self-knowledge",
though I confess that I cannot see that this is borne out by the passages cited in
Cassirer that Barkan refers to.

30. Cf. Helen Laurie, "*Narcisus*," *Medium Ævum* 35 (1966), 114.

sentence" (there, as sometimes elsewhere, attributed to Chilon) is a mirror.

The ode *Of Our Sense of Sinne* that Grierson admitted to the Donne Canon, though later editors have rejected it, testifies by its title as well as its content to the persistence of the association of a realisation of sin with true self-awareness. The first two stanzas dwell on human incapacity to perceive one's faults. The last alludes both to the mirror-image and to the ancient assertion that complete self-knowledge is an attribute peculiar to the deity:

> But we know ourselves least; mere outward shows
>> Our minds so store
> That our soules, no more than our eyes, disclose
> But form and colour. Only He who knowes
>> Himself, knows more[31]

Isabella's speech in *Measure for Measure* gives this view its supreme formulation:

> Man, proud man,
> Drest in a little brief authority,
> Most ignorant of what he's most assured,
> His glassy essence, like an angry ape,
> Plays such fantastic tricks before high heaven
> As make the angels weep.   [II,ii,121]

Thus England's greatest poet harks back to Bernard and Boethius.

31. Certainly the stanzas contain nothing contrary to Donne's philosophy; and possibly they have some bearing on the second stanza of his most cryptic poem, *Negative Love*, which reaches its climax in the lines:

> If any who deciphers best,
> What we know not, our selves, can know,
> Let him teach mee that nothing;

H. J. C. Grierson (*The Poems of John Donne* [London, 1912], ii 50) quotes on these lines a passage from Donne's *Sermons* (p. 563): "In that (Adam) gave no name to himself, it may be by some perhaps argued that he understood himself lesse then he did other creatures." St. Thomas did not accept this argument. See *Summa Theologica* 1, Q. 94, art. 3. In Sermon XLIV (*John Donne*, ed. John Hayward (London, 1932), p. 720, we have: *"veniet dies, quae me revelabit*, comes that day that shall show me to myselfe; here I never saw myselfe, but in disguises."

8

Chaucer's Man of Law and His Tale: The Eccentric Design

Robert T. Farrell

CORNELL UNIVERSITY

C HAUCER'S Man of Law and his tale have received much attention in recent years, most of it devoted to showing that the Man of Law is something less than admirable, while admitting that the tale has a certain limited effectiveness. Two major pieces on the subject have been given to us by Professors Alfred David and Chauncey Wood. David sees the Man of Law as "something of a fool and perhaps something of a knave," who tells a tale that is "impeccably moral." If we believe David's further arguments, the Man of Law is an incompetent critic, who provides in his Prologue "a pronouncement on Chaucer's works." He goes on to state, "The lawyer's discussion of poetry can be construed as a humorous projection—with serious implications—of Chaucer's own search for fit materials to carry out

While this paper is of course intended to honor the memory of Professor Tolkien, I have taken the second element of my title from one of the books of my friend and teacher Marius Bewley, as a mark of respect. I am grateful to my colleague Peter Wetherbee, who read over this paper in draft and made many useful suggestions for its improvement, and to my assistant, Marilyn Migiel, who helped in the checking of references.

[159

his great plan [*i.e.*, *The Canterbury Tales*]." As I hope to show, this interpretation makes much of a very brief passage, belittles a great work, and does not account for all the elements which compose the "matter" of the Man of Law.[1] Chauncey Wood sees the Man of Law as satirizing himself in a tale that is "anti-Boethian, anti-humanistic and anti-religious," while the lawyer himself is a disturbingly limited character who at every opportunity fails to understand the difference between divine and human capacity and perspective: "Chaucer has created here a character who is constant in his perversity, and whose misinterpretations of literature, moral essays, astral influence and the spiritual welfare of merchants are logical and easily anticipated developments of his central concern for worldly prosperity."[2] One cannot easily summarize the various critical positions held on the Man of Law and his tale, but the main trends are clear. Paull F. Baum, whose gifts for incisive and controversial criticism long invigorated medieval studies, summed up the ultimate negative view succinctly:

> The real "critical problem" of the poem is why at any date (unless *very* early) Chaucer should have occupied himself with such a crude implausible tale. . . . Chaucer approached it in a spirit midway between what you might call low seriousness and levity. His generally ironic attitude would recognize the absurdities of the tale; his naturally medieval attitude would not wholly condemn it, since no author is wholly detached from the spirit of his age. To rework such crude popular material and see what can be done with it might well seem amusing.[3]

1. His very title clarifies the limits of his study: "The Man of Law vs. Chaucer: A Case in Poetics," *PMLA* 82 (1967), 217–25. Professor David's arguments have been well received in some quarters; Rodney Delasanta starts a more recent essay: "Praise be to Alfred David for finally coming up with a credible motive for the *Man of Law's Tale*" ("And of Great Reverence: Chaucer's Man of Law," *Chaucer Review* 5 [1970–71], 288–310).

2. Chauncey Wood, "Chaucer's Man of Law as Interpreter," *Traditio* 23 (1967), 149–90, quotations pp. 151 and 188. Professor Wood's study is a masterly and detailed analysis of how the Man of Law's manner, matter, and method interrelate with philosophical and theological notions current in Chaucer's time; I respectfully disagree with him, but only because I am viewing the matter from a different stance.

3. Paull F. Baum, "The Man of Law's Tale," *MLN* 64 (1949), 12–14. The assumption here, that as Chaucer is more "medieval" he is less artful, less

To my mind, one of the most successful and detailed comments on the *Man of Law's Tale* is Edward A. Block's "Originality, Controlling Purpose, and Craftsmanship in Chaucer's *Man of Law's Tale*."[4] Block makes a painstakingly detailed study of the relation of Chaucer's story of Constance to Trivet's Anglo-Norman *Chronicle*. He points out that Chaucer omitted the mass of specifying detail that Trivet had included to give credence to his "history." Dates, numbers, precise indications of time are all excised, as is the gore that pervades Trivet's work.[5] Block tells us that the cumulative effect of these changes lifts Trivet's story "into the realms of romance, remote in time and space."[6] Chaucer's *additions*, Block points out, act in two directions. The dignity and pathos of the story are increased by rhetorical apostrophes, and certain characters, notably Constance herself, are made more human by sharp focus on reaction in emotional circumstances. There are then two movements, one to the dreamlike state, the other toward a reality of personality achieved through vivid use of character, situation, and detail. Block sees these two movements producing an "irreconcilable dualism of purpose."[7] Though he qualifies this dualism, he does not resolve it:

The dualism is, I think, understandable even though in this particular instance it does expose [Chaucer] to the imputation of being guilty of

accomplished, is unacceptable. For other negative views, see Marchette Chute, *Geoffrey Chaucer of England* (London, 1951), and Robert O. Payne, *The Key of Remembrance: A Study of Chaucer's Poetics* (New Haven and London, 1963). Chute tells us that the "introduction to his tale bears no relation to his tale at all" and that the story of Constance "was never right for Chaucer." She holds that the tale is "alien to Chaucer's particular brand of genius" (pp. 245–46). Payne speaks of it as "a one-dimensional elaboration of morality into sentimentality . . . a moral statement which will be immediately apprehensible emotionally and nearly incomprehensible by any rational or intellectual faculty" (pp. 163–64). As I attempt to show, the tale is most decidedly *not* intended to appeal to reason, but to another aspect of human experience.

4. *PMLA* 68 (1953), 572–616.

5. Trivet was fond of having his villains fall with a satisfying crash. Alla kills his wicked mother by cutting off her head and hewing her body to pieces as she lies naked in her bed. Chaucer substitutes "Alla, out of drede, / His mooder slow" (ll. 893–94).

6. Block, "Originality," p. 581.

7. Ibid., p. 592.

poor art. Since he was writing in the tradition of the saint's legend, what was more natural than that he should have wanted to make it a masterpiece of its kind and therefore accentuated the religious element? Since he was also writing about human beings, what was more natural than that he should have attempted to make them lifelike? To expect of Chaucer that he should have written a credible saint's legend is, after all, to expect the impossible—even for him.[8]

Even this meticulously effective source study ends with an apology, which is perhaps unnecessary. The drift of scholarly comment is then as follows. Wood and David attempt to make too strong a point from a particular notion of the tale; Block's open-ended, contradictory notions of the structure are more productive. The reading of the tale as inadequate because it is "medieval" and/or a saint's life can, I think, be dismissed. A saint's legend does not appeal to credibility, nor are its events ordered by reason. It appeals to faith, by means of showings forth of God's power, through and for His chosen ones. There is a tension within the tale, and within the teller; I hope to show that the basis for the tension that is seen in all the Man of Law's "matter" has an altogether different base,[9] and that almost every contradiction in the several introductions to the tale can be explained.[10]

8. Ibid., p. 616.

9. I have so far neglected to deal with Morton Bloomfield's excellent study "The Man of Law's Tale: A Tragedy of Victimization and a Christian Comedy," *PMLA* 87 (1972), 384–90. Bloomfield makes a suasive argument for the Man of Law's Tale as a tale of pathos, which, like the Clerk's Tale, the Physician's Tale, and others, presents difficulties for the modern reader. Bloomfield's delicate treatment of what is indeed an alien genre for some literary critics certainly offers a valid reading of the tale in and of itself, and opens a question that is essential for students of medieval literature to consider most carefully. To develop my views on his discussion of the pathetic would be to enter upon another and far longer critical essay, the basic argument of which would be that Bloomfield is too modest in his claims for the genre. He seeks to breed sympathy for this sort of literature, not to convert a large audience to its enjoyment; he has certainly an enthusiastic supporter in me. Though Bloomfield takes us close to the center of the tale's appeal, however, I view it somewhat differently in the context of the Man of Law as speaker. The tale's effect is modified by the relationship it bears to the teller. While the tale offers a first-rate example of the pathetic, it resonates in other ways in the particular context of the Man of Law.

10. The sole exception is perhaps the single phrase "I speke in prose" (l. 96).

I

The following elements must be dealt with in any complete discussion of the Man of Law and his tale; the division into
sections is my own:

1. The Prologue portrait (I.309–30).[11]
2. Words of the Host to the Man of Law and his reply (II.
   1-45).
3. What has been described as the Man of Law's discussion
   of Chaucer and his poetry (II.46-98).
4. The Prologue itself, an apostrophe to poverty, followed
   by praise of rich merchants, which leads us into the tale
   (II.99–133).
5. The tale itself (II.134-1162).[12]

The placement of the Man of Law's Tale is essentially the
same in all of the manuscript traditions. It occurs as fragment B^1
(Robinson's II), immediately after the Knight-Miller-Reeve-
Cook's *incipit*. Our expectations are therefore quite high, for it is
clear that after the Knight's Tale, Chaucer followed a descending line from the exquisite and daring parody of courtly
values in the Miller's Tale through the vicious seaminess of the
Reeve's Tale to the abortive beginnings of yet another piece of
bawdry. A new start was required. Once again, Harry Bailly
chooses a man of high station as his teller.[13] One must, I think,
accept the equation of the Sergeant of the Law in the General
Prologue with the Man of Law—to my knowledge, no one has
seriously questioned this identification. Certainly, the lawyer is
an impressive figure, at least equal to the Knight in social position. As Manly pointed out a long time ago, Burke's *Peerages*
ranked sergeants immediately after knights bachelor; sergeants
took precedence over Companions of the Bath. In their profes-

11. All citations are from F. N. Robinson, *The Works of Geoffrey Chaucer*,
2d ed. (Boston, 1957).

12. I exclude the epilogue from discussion on the authority of J. M.
Manly and E. Rickert, *The Text of the Canterbury Tales* (Chicago and London,
1940), who tell us, "When Melibeus was transferred to Chaucer himself and
the Summoner involved in the quarrel with the Friar, this endlink ceased to
have any proper function and became a mere vestigial organ, a kind of ver-
miform appendix" (II, 189–90).

13. I quite arbitrarily assume in this statement that the Host "fixed" the
first draw. There is, of course, much to support this claim on the basis of his
character, as displayed elsewhere.

sional roles, these officers of the law had still higher status. They processed ahead of both the attorney general and the solicitor general, they were not required to remove their head coverings in the presence of the king, and they were addressed in royal writs as *vos*.[14] So much for a sergeant's station; more important are the distinctive characteristics Chaucer accords *this* sergeant in the General Prologue. He is rich and skilled in his profession; and other indications are given. It is always difficult to pin down Chaucer's art, and particularly hard to do so in the cameo forms of the Prologue portraits. One thinks of the multiple resonances of *worthy* in the Knight's description, the Friar's *solempne* quality, and the perfect bringing back to order of the Squire by his act of filial and feudal piety described in the last line of his portrait, "and carf beforn his fader at the table." Jill Mann has recently provided us with a study of social classes in the General Prologue, and her conclusions on Chaucer's Man of Law support the notion of a delicate balance between reference to previously established satirical tradition on the one hand and the present reality of Chaucer's own lawyer on the other.[15] The element that strikes me as most obvious in the Sergeant is *tension*. Chaucer as narrator, in whatever persona, does not display the generous enthusiasm that marked his descriptions of the Monk, Friar, Prioress, and others.[16] In the case of the Sergeant, the surface of the character is twice lifted:

> Discreet he was, and of greet reverence—
> He *semed* swich, his wordes weren so wise . . .

14. See J. M. Manly, *Some New Light on Chaucer: Lectures Delivered at the Lowell Institute* (New York, 1926), pp. 31–35.

15. *Chaucer and Medieval Estates Satire* (Cambridge, 1973), discussion of the Sergeant of Law, pp. 86–91. Mann's excellent critique deserves to be read in full, but a few of her summary statements are apposite here. "We recognise," she tells us, "the same kind of ambiguity that circumvented moral criticism of the Monk and the Friar, and the same tendency to suggest rather than to state, to transfer a characteristic from factual to linguistic status." In summary, Chaucer avoids *any* precise delineation of his character in terms of traditional satire, and Mann sums up the accomplishment best by saying, "To suggest a front without giving away the reality is a feat which Chaucer manages with dexterity."

16. I avoid entirely the complex question of irony in the portraits mentioned.

Nowher so bisy a man as he ther nas,
And yet he *semed* bisier than he was.   [ll. 312–13, 321–22]

Though suspicion is raised, no specific cause for uneasiness is given.

Let us turn to the introduction, or perhaps more accurately the introductions, to the tale. Harry Bailly, in a rare mood of reflection, muses: "los of tyme shendeth us. . . ." He turns to the Man of Law, addressing him in legalistic language: "Acquit-eth yow now of youre biheeste. . . ." The Man of Law answers, picking up the joke and extending it further, in a short dig at Chaucer—the only time that another pilgrim breaks the fictional situation, intruding a kind of reality into the exchange. David[17] would have us believe that these lines are the central revelation of the Man of Law, and claims that "different artistic impulses are at work . . . the handling of the Host and the Man of Law in the headlink and in the lively Epilogue to the tale continue the impulse toward realism, drama, and satire. . . . The tale is . . . an example of the moralized romance. . . ."[18] The assumption seems once again to be that Chaucer is "good" when he writes in modern modes, less good when he works in a supposedly "medi-eval" form. In a sense, the tension that Block saw in the tale itself is here externalized, so that the surrounding matter, intro-duction and end link, are effective literature, the tale mere ro-mance. David's further extensions in characterizing the Man of Law are still more difficult to accept. To David, the lawyer is "an ill-informed and pretentious literary critic [in his discussion of Chaucer's poetry]"[19] and "something of a fool and perhaps also something of a knave . . . who turns out to have extremely straitlaced notions about literature and tells an impeccably moral tale."[20] The further assumption is that "those who insist most loudly on morality in art are often morally insensitive."[21] This is a heavy charge to lay without proof positive, and it is by no means the only interpretation of the Man of Law.

Let us look at what is present in the text. So far, I have

17. David, "Man of Law vs. Chaucer."
18. Ibid., p. 218.
19. Ibid., p. 220.
20. Ibid., p. 219.
21. Ibid., p. 221.

discussed the status of the Sergeant and interpreted the force of the dual *semed* as causing a tension between surface and interior appearance and reality, if you will, in the Prologue portrait. The first section of the introduction to the tale has been characterized as a kind of heavy humor, Host and Man of Law bantering ponderous legal terminology. David has interpreted the very next section, lines 46–98, as a serious statement of poetic values; I respectfully disagree. The Man of Law is clearly in a mood of heavy humor as he turns to Chaucer:

> For swich lawe as a man yeveth another wight,
> He sholde hymselven usen it, by right;
> Thus wole oure text. But nathelees, certeyn,
> I kan right now no thrifty tale seyn
> That Chaucer, thogh he kan but lewedly
> On metres and rymyng craftily,
> Hath seyd hem in swich Englissh as he kan
> Of olde tyme, as knoweth many a man;
> And if he have noght seyd hem, leve brother,
> In o book, he hath seyd hem in another. [ll. 43–52]

This is the *only* treatment of Chaucer's work in the large. The scope narrows, to Ceys and Alcione and tales of lovers, which correspond in part to *The Legend of Good Women*. We move from the general topic of Chaucer's work to the specifics of lovers.[22] The most significant point about this series is that it centers on the sufferings of women and their fidelity—fairly natural secular prefigurations of what we are to have in the tale. The next lines are more interesting, for the lawyer moves on to recount what Chaucer did *not* tell, the highly specific and unnatural torments of Canacee:

> That loved hir owene brother synfully;
> (Of swiche cursed stories I sey fy!)

22. It is confusing to note that of the women mentioned, eight are not in *The Legend of Good Women*, and two that are in that work (Cleopatra and Philomela) are left out of the tale. The reasonable supposition is that Chaucer was still working on *The Legend of Good Women* when this part of the introduction to the Man of Law's Tale was written. A detailed discussion of this question is out of place here, though of course such a discussion is of interest to students of the *Legend*.

How that the cursed kyng Antiochus
Birafte his doghter of hir maydenhede,
That is so horrible a tale for to rede,
Whan he hir threw upon the pavement.   [ll. 79–80, 82–85]

As the lawyer tells us, these are *unkynde abhomynacions*,[23] of
which Chaucer would not write, and which the lawyer *wol noon
reherce, if that I may*. This is where we have been heading: from a
humorous opening to a jocular if ponderous swing at Chaucer,
to a relevant but highly selective and highly colored aspect of
Chaucer's work, to specific unnatural offenses that are brought
up for no real logical or sequential reason.

The tone of horror and fearful indignation is continued in
the following apostrophe, a prime passage from Innocent III,
the start of his specific catalog of the anxieties that beset human-
kind. Poverty, therefore, might be seen as a particular specter,
which the lawyer strives against in his professional life, both for
his clients and for himself. The final apostrophe is extremely
apt. Riches are a goal, and merchant venturers in particular
provide a transition to a tale of those of high station in ancient
days.[24]

23. A check of J. S. P. Tatlock and A. G. Kennedy, *Concordance to the
Complete Works of Geoffrey Chaucer and to the Romaunt of the Rose* (Washington,
D.C., 1927; reprinted Gloucester, Mass., 1963), reveals that these are fairly
heavy words; "abomination" and "abominable" appear with some frequency in
the Pardoner's and Parson's descriptions of sin, and Troilus, when offended,
sees Criseyde often as *unkynde*.

24. See R. E. Lewis, "Chaucer's Artistic Use of Pope Innocent III's *De
Miseria Humane Conditionis* in the Man of Law's Prologue and Tale," *PMLA* 81
(1966), 485–92. His point on the poverty–wealth sequence here is well taken:
"The praise of wealthy men, coming as it does so soon after his criticism of
poor men, shows clearly where the sympathies of the Man of Law lie, and this
is further reinforced by two other details: first, one of the two lines that
Chaucer adds to the passage on poverty from *De Miseria* is 'Be war, therefore,
er thou come to that prikke [i.e., state of poverty]!' (l. 119); and second, where
Pope Innocent scorns both poor *and* rich, Chaucer reverses both the tone and
details of the original and scorns only the poor. The Man of Law's speeches on
poverty and wealth are similar in tone to the Reeve's discourse on old age in his
own prologue, and I would suggest that, just as the Reeve's words help to
characterize the Reeve, so the Man of Law's words serve to characterize further
a side of his own character that has already been mentioned in the General
Prologue: his concern with wealth" (p. 487).

II

With this view of the character of the Man of Law in mind, we can now approach the function and form of the tale and its suitability to the teller. Briefly to recapitulate Block's study, the tale was lifted to the level of a saint's legend by the exclusion of particularizing detail and by the addition of a number of apostrophes that make for a higher rhetorical tone. A closer look at some of these added rhetorical pieces shows that they have more specific functions. Many point up the cruel quality of life and the control that the stars have over men. In this vein, we have the outburst in lines 295–315, which starts:

> O firste moevying! crueel firmament,
> With thy diurnal sweigh that crowdest ay
> And hurlest al from est til occident
> That naturelly wolde holde another way . . .

The address to the murderously unregenerate pagan Sultaness and the high pathos of Constance at her trial are at the same pitch of intensity.[25] Instances such as these can be multiplied, but I think that most readers of the poem would accept the thesis that the temporal context in which Constance exists is cruel. It is perhaps best described by Egeus at the darkest point of the Knight's Tale:

> This world nys but a thurghfare ful of wo,
> And we been pilgrymes passynge to and fro.   [ll. 2847–48][26]

As R. E. Lewis has pointed out,[27] two passages in the Man of Law's Tale are not present in Trivet, lines 421–27 and 1132–38. Both point up the transitory quality of earthly joy and establish the motion.

> O sodeyn wo, that evere art successour
> To worldly blisse, spreynd with bitternesse!

25. Ll. 358–78 and 645–58 respectively.
26. The allusion to the Knight's Tale will be developed shortly; it is no accident that both Egeus and the Man of Law choose to resonate to the kind of tension between the world and the spirit which was most dramatically developed by Innocent III.
27. "Chaucer's Artistic Use."

The ende of the joye of oure worldly labour!
Wo occupieth the fyn of oure gladnesse. [ll. 421–24]

Yet another interjection of the Man of Law provides his solution
to the dark universe in which Constance must function. The
lines in question come at the opening of the second part of the
poem, when Constance is being set adrift by the Sultaness. The
passage is particularly important because the lawyer is answering possible objections to the nature and manner of his heroine's
survival. In doing so, he invokes figures in the iconographical
series of the Help of God, Daniel in the lions' den, Jonah in the
whale, the Hebrews passing through the Red Sea, and others:

Men myghten asken why she was nat slayn
Eek at the feeste? who myghte hir body save?
And I answere to that demande agayn,
Who saved Danyel in the horrible cave
There every wight save he, maister and knave,
Was with the leon frete er he asterte?
No wight but God, that he bar in his herte.

God liste to shewe his wonderful myracle
In hire, for we sholde seen his myghty werkis;
Crist, which that is to every harm triacle,
By certeine meenes ofte, as knowen clerkis,
Dooth thyng for certein ende that ful derk is
To mannes wit, that for oure ignorance
Ne konne noght knowe his prudent purveiance.

Now sith she was nat at the feeste yslawe,
Who kepte hire fro the drenchyng in the see?
Who kepte Jonas in the fisshes mawe
Til he was spouted up at Nynyvee?
Well may men knowe it was no wight but he
That kepte peple Ebrayk from hir drenchynge,
With drye feet thurghout the see passynge.

Who bad the foure spirites of tempest
That power han t'anoyen lond and see,
Bothe north and south, and also west and est,
"Anoyeth, neither see, ne land, ne tree"?
Soothly, the comandour of that was he
That fro the tempest ay this womman kepte
As wel whan she wook as whan she slepte.

Where myghte this womman mete and drynke have
Thre yeer and moore? how lasteth hire vitaille?
Who fedde the Egipcien Marie in the cave,
Or in desert? No wight but Crist, sanz faille.
Fyve thousand folk it was as greet mervaille
With loves fyve and fisshes two to feede.
God sente his foyson at hir grete neede. [ll. 470–504]

The popularity of this series was immense; not only are these basic images of early Christian art, but they can be traced to an early Judaic base. These figures appear in early liturgy as well and are central to the *Ordo commendationis animae*, a prayer for the dying used by the Roman church. I have traced the history of these images of the theme of the Help of God elsewhere, and have also pointed out that there is good reason to suspect that Constance can be seen as a *direct* representation of the ultimate figural reduction of the theme.[28] To quote from C. R. Morey on the funerary iconography of the early Christian church: "The content of deliverance is further simplified by a type that vies with Jonah in popularity—the orant woman, personification of prayer and heavenly beatitude, so abstract that we find her sometimes represented on the epitaph as a man, precluding thus the possibility of a portrait."[29]

What we have, then, is an assertion of faith in terms of images of power. This is the rationale for the narrative, the mode of the saint's life, and the link between the tale and a basic stratum of Christianity. *This* is the Man of Law's assertion, but his is no serene acceptance. If I am right, his castings about in the various layers of the introduction reflect an inner tension, already hinted at in the Prologue portrait. The tale does arrive at a solution, but it is more a grasping at a simplistic answer than an act of affirmation that reflects anything like a state of spiritual well-being on the part of the Man of Law.

Chaucer's Man of Law is troubled by a vision of life that sees evil very readily. He has sought satisfaction in striving after

28. "Chaucer's Use of the Theme of the Help of God in the *Man of Law's Tale*," *Neuphilologische Mitteilungen* 71 (1970), 239–43.
29. *Early Christian Art* (Princeton, 1941), p. 63.

prosperity, and though he has reached the ultimate in his profession, he has not found peace. If I may be permitted to combine my impression of a life at law in the Middle Ages and my discussions with friends in the legal profession, the darkness of the Man of Law's philosophy and his desperate hope do not make him evil, but rather reflect the kinds of activity that constitute the bulk of a lawyer's professional life. Even a fully moral man cannot but be sometimes appalled at the constant succession of gain and greed, human pain in legal tribulation, and maneuvering of fact and principle in order to protect a client's interest which play so large a part in a lawyer's life. In the tumult of the late fourteenth century a lawyer would probably have had even more experience with the raw aspects of life—prosecution for debts and "rape" played a role even in Chaucer's own affairs. If I am correct, then, the projection of self in the Man of Law's Tale is an inversion of what we would expect from the *type* of sergeant at law; instead of the polished product of a well-furnished mind set in terms of unassailable logic, we have a reassertion of the values of primitive Christianity, and the base on which the whole is structured is a series that is a part of the very roots of Judeo-Christian imagery. The lawyer's worldly wisdom provides the background of evil against which the action takes place; his uncertain hope in the divine gives us the unquestioning faith of his heroine; his sensitivity to human nature makes Constance a believable and pitiable woman in anguish, as well as the *figura* of the theme of the Help of God.

The parallels between the Man of Law and the Knight are close. Both are troubled by such questions as predestination, the horrors of life in this world, the apparent futility of human effort, and both resort to ultimate appeals to the very essence of Christian faith. But the Knight presents a detailed history of one who only through a long process of time and extraordinary strains on his basic beliefs can come to understand the ultimate wisdom of Egeus, and to accept, though sorely tried by affliction, the implications of the Boethian chain of love. The Lawyer gives us no such progress, but rather grasps firmly and desperately at a single basic fact—God saves the faithful in need —while the entire tonality of *his* questionings of fate, predestination, and the ubiquity of suffering strain against his assertion of salvation, not for Constance but for himself.[30]

It may be that Chaucer wrote the various layers of introduction to the Man of Law's Tale at different times; it may be that he originally intended a revision or limitation of the introduction, but stayed his hand. His intention is not known; if I have provided an explication of this complex structure, I have succeeded in my attempt. We surely have an effective tale of the pathetic in the story of Constance,[31] but in the context of the Man of Law as teller, it is also a revelation of an acutely troubled intelligence, perhaps seeking salvation through the tense and forceful assertion of a simple faith to which the Man of Law cannot give either intellectual or emotional assent.

30. It is no accident that the questionings of fate and destiny in the Knight's Tale are voiced by the two brother-suitors, while the Knight himself can confront the eternal question of the fate of the just pagan and accept that his understanding cannot cope with such matters. See ll. 2809–16. The sublimation that Boccaccio provided for Arcite (Giovanni Boccaccio, *Teseida*, ed. Salvatore Battaglia (Florence, 1938), Book XI, ll. 1–24) is, of course, reserved by Chaucer for use elsewhere, when Troilus achieves his gently ironic distance as one of the bases for the complex ending of *Troilus and Criseyde*.

31. To follow Bloomfield's characterization, see n. 9, above.

9

Chaucer and "Pite"

Douglas Gray

Pembroke College, Oxford

As any reader of Chaucer can see, the words *pite* and its near-synonym *routhe* appear so frequently that no-one would hesitate to include them in any list of the author's favourite words. The complex of ideas and suggestions embodied in the word *pite* is not only interesting in itself but is of considerable importance in understanding Chaucer's moral sensitivity in all its humanity, variety, and subtlety. Surprisingly, the topic has not often been discussed.[1] This essay attempts to isolate a few aspects of the subject and to follow up a few of its ramifications.

An obvious, though humble, starting-place is the short poem traditionally entitled *A Complaint of Pitee*. It is not usually admired by modern critics—"in this early work," says Professor Clemen, "Chaucer displays little originality; he is still held fast by the conventional language of love employed in French formal lyric verse."[2] The lyric is both conventional—Chaucer was certainly not the first to think of the image of Pity buried in a heart —and stylised. But it is a polished example of its kind, written with ease and eloquence, and the simple allegorical situation is handled with a happy blend of elegy and argument. What is

1. Gordon Hall Gerould, *Chaucerian Essays* (Princeton, 1952), chap. 5, "The Serious Mind of Chaucer"; and J. W. Kleinstück, *Chaucers Stellung in der mittelalterlichen Literatur* (Hamburg, 1956), chapter on *Pitie*.
2. Wolfgang Clemen, *Chaucer's Early Poetry* (London, 1963).

[173

important from our point of view is that here *pite* is a virtue seen exclusively in the context of a love-situation, a virtue which the beloved lady should show to her suppliant lover. Chaucer finds Pite dead "and buried in an herte," her hearse surrounded by Beaute, Lust, Jolyte, and others ("withouten any woo, as thoughte me") "confedered alle by bond of Cruelte," Pite's contrary and enemy. He will endure with "trouthe" though he is tormented by desire:

> This is to seyne, I wol be youres evere;
> Though ye me slee by Crueltee, your foo,
> Algate my spirit shal never dissevere
> Fro youre servise, for any peyne or woo.
> Sith ye be ded—allas, that hyt is soo!—
> Thus for your deth I may wel wepe and pleyne
> With herte sore, and ful of besy peyne. [ll. 113–119][3]

The background to this concept of *pite* (beyond the courtly verse of Chaucer's own time) is to be found in the *Roman de la Rose*. There, in the first part, Franchise and Pitié intercede for the dreamer with Dangiers (or Daunger). Crueltee is the aspect of Daunger which the suppliant lover sees. Daunger is a *vilain;* in the English version he appears thus:

> With that sterte oute anoon Daunger,
> Out of the place were he was hid.
> His malice in his chere was kid;
> Full gret he was and blak of hewe,
> Sturdy and hidous, whoso hym knewe;
> Like sharp urchouns his her was growe;
> His eyes reed sparclyng as the fyr glowe;
> His nose frounced, full kirked stood,
> He com criand as he were wood. . . . [ll. 3130–38]

(In the Morgan manuscript of the French poem he is represented with a great club.) He relents and allows the dreamer to have the comradeship of Bialacoil. In Jean de Meun's continuation there is a splendid allegorical battle between Pitié and Daunger. Pitié fights not with a sword but a misericorde dripping with tears.

3. All references to Chaucer are from the edition of F. N. Robinson, *The Works of Geoffrey Chaucer*, 2d ed. (Boston, 1957).

Her shield is of solace (*alegement*) adorned with sighs and complaints, and she weeps as she fights. This unusual method of assault is irresistible—the *vilain* is quite overcome by the floods of tears.

Pite as a desirable and benevolent aspect of the beloved lady's "landscape of the heart" is indeed rather done to death by the courtly poets. The modern reader's interest is quickened more often by the bizarre and extreme or ironic cases. In one famous poem, Chartier's *La Belle Dame sans merci* (which provided a title for Keats and provoked a literary quarrel in its own day), the lady is so "daungerous" and piti-less that her lover actually dies. It is perhaps worth remarking, however, that like some other aspects of this somewhat maligned poetry, the notion of *pite* has some recognisable relationship with human emotion. This is immediately obvious when we see it in the more realistic contexts of Chaucer's non-allegorical poems. In *Troilus and Criseyde* the struggle between "Pity" and "Daunger" in Criseyde's heart is presented with an extraordinary sense of actuality. Troilus's agony before he is shown *pite* bursts out in his tortured first words to Criseyde:

> In chaunged vois, right for his verray drede,
> Which vois ek quook and therto his manere
> Goodly abaist, and now his hewes rede,
> Now pale, unto Criseyde, his lady dere,
> With look down cast and humble iyolden chere,
> Lo, the alderfirste word that hym asterte
> Was, twyes, 'Mercy, mercy, swete herte!' [III.92–98]

This lover's plea for *pite* is found again and again in Chaucer's poetry. Thus (to choose two examples at random) the royal tersel in *The Parlement of Foules* pleads, "My deere herte, have on my wo som routhe," and in the Franklin's tale, where at the beginning Dorigen has had pity on Arviragus, she "hath swich a pitee caught of his penaunce." Later (V.972–78) the squire Aurelius pleads with her in words which recall those of Troilus and the noble tersel:

> For wel I woot my servyce is in vayn;
> My gerdon is but brestyng of myn herte.

Madame, reweth upon my peynes smerte;
For with a word ye may me sleen or save.
Heere at youre feet God wolde that I were grave!
I ne have as now no leyser moore to seye;
Have mercy, swete, or ye wol do me deye!

A modern reader certainly finds this kind of language strange. Professor Clemen says, "Today we find it hard to understand the position that *Pite* . . . occupied in the medieval hierarchy of values connected with love. The modern conception of love no longer recognises 'compassion' as one of its main forces; but this feeling played a most vital role in medieval wooing and relationships."[4] It seems to me, however, that though the words may not be the same, the emotions and the emotional situations may not be so strangely different. "Compassion" may not here be a happy gloss for *pite*. *Pite* in love was no doubt often a conventional thing (rather in the way that Pandarus's "joly wo" makes conventional and trivial the divided soul and the anguish of spirit of the love-poets). Elsewhere, though, *pite* has some of the wider connotations we shall discuss later. Where *daunger* may suggest disdain, a holding back, a defensive refusal of love, *pite* may imply a giving of one's self, a generous self-sacrifice, an emotion which is both intensely human, an expression of benevolence and nobility of soul, and which is related to spiritual qualities of charity and mercy. It is a natural expression of that noble love which overflows from the "gentle heart" and which is a "shadow" of the cosmic love binding together the universe. In Book III of *Troilus and Criseyde*, where this love finds its finest expression, the climax of Criseyde's *pite* for Troilus comes when, in Chaucer's phrase, she "opened her heart."

The concept of *pite* in human love is presented by Chaucer in a variety of contexts and in a variety of tones. It is an accurate reflection of his continuing interest in the complexities and mysterious paradoxes of love and passion. In *The Legend of Good Women* there are some exemplary stories of misguided and tragic *pite* shown by women to faithless men. In the legend of Dido, for

4. Clemen, *Chaucer's Early Poetry*, p. 184.

instance, the narrator is moved to exclaim (the passage is Chaucer's own invention):

> O sely wemen, ful of innocence,
> Ful of pite, of trouthe, and conscience,
> What maketh yow to men to truste so?
> Have ye swych routhe upon hyre feyned wo,
> And han swich olde ensaumples yow beforn?
> Se ye nat alle how they ben forsworn? [ll. 1254–59]

Indeed, in this story, Dido herself is reduced to pleading for mercy from her lover, a plight whose sadness and bitterness would be the more striking to an audience accustomed to the patterns of courtly poetry:

> She falleth hym to fote and swouneth ther,
> Dischevele, with hire bryghte gilte her,
> And seyth, 'Have mercy! and let me with yow ryde!' [ll. 1314–16]

In a very different context in the Miller's tale, the student, "hende" Nicholas ("as clerkes ben ful subtile and ful queinte," says the narrator somewhat archly) makes a sudden and violent pass at Alisoun, and even in the grip of his very physical passion remembers something of the lover's language of *pite:*

> And prively he caughte hire by the queynte,
> And seyde, 'Ywis, but if ich have my wille,
> For deerne love of thee, lemman, I spille.'
> And heeld hire harde by the haunchebones,
> And seyde, 'Lemman, love me al atones,
> Or I wol dyen, also God me save!' [ll. 3276–81]

Her immediate reaction, as we might expect, is one of an instinctive animal *daunger*, and with one delicious phrase she teasingly reproves him for his distinctly "uncourtly" gesture:

> And she sproong as a colt dooth in the trave,
> And with hir heed she wryed fast awey
> And seyde, 'I wol nat kisse thee, by my fey!
> Why, lat be', quod she, 'lat be, Nicholas,
> Or I wol crye "out, harrow" and "allas"!
> Do wey youre handes, for youre curteisye!' [ll. 3282–87]

[177

It is one if the minor comedies of the situation that "hende" Nicholas does in fact find more courtly methods of wooing more effective:

> This Nicholas gan mercy for to crye,
> And spak so faire, and profred him so faste,
> That she hir love hym graunted atte laste . . .   [ll. 3288–90]

At a much more solemn moment at the end of the Knight's tale (I.3075–89) Theseus begs Emilye to have *pite* on "gentil" Palamon:

> 'Suster', quod he, 'this is my fulle assent . . .
> That ye shul of youre grace upon hym rewe,
> And taken hym for housbonde and for lord . . .
> Lat se now of youre wommanly pitee.
> He is a kynges brother sone, pardee;
> And though he were a povre bacheler,
> Syn he hath served yow so many a yeer,
> And had for yow so greet adversitee,
> It moste been considered, leeveth me;
> For gentil mercy oghte to passen right'.

The rational tone of the duke's plea, the hint of theological undertones in the association of *pite* with grace, the application of the adjective *wommanly* to *pite*, suggest perhaps that we are moving towards a wider concept of *pite*. We shall in fact see *pite* occurring in non-erotic contexts, and indeed emptied of all erotic suggestions. Nevertheless, its connection with love, which I have been at pains to emphasise, remains of fundamental importance. It is time, however, to pause for some etymologising.

Pity, like *piety*, comes from Latin *pietas*. In Chaucer's English the forms and senses of the words were not differentiated as sharply as in ours. *Pietas* meant "piety" with respect to gods, conscientiousness, scrupulousness, and, with respect to one's kin, country, or benefactors, duty, dutifulness, affection, loyalty, gratitude, etc. One of the great images of filial "piety" in classical literature is Aeneas carrying his old father from the destruction of Troy. In the story of Griselda, the heroine cares for her aged father with what Chaucer calls "greet reverence and charitee." The French version here has *pitie*, taken from Petrarch, who thinking of classical usage calls it *pietatis officium*. In general, *pietas* suggests (a) duty, or moral obligation, and (b) natural affection (as of parents for children, children for parents), a sense which is important for later English uses. In later Latin *pietas* was extended to mean gentleness, tenderness, pity, compassion.

Of the senses of "pity" recorded by the *NED* as current in Chaucer's time, the following seem especially relevant to the enquiry: (1) "The quality of being pitiful; the disposition to mercy or compassion; clemency, mercy, mildness or tenderness." (Two of the illustrative quotations are especially revealing: Caxton's "Pyte is no thyng ellis but a right grete wylle of a debonary herte for to helpe alle men," and a fifteenth-century gloss of *humanus* as "fulle of pytie.") (2) "A feeling or emotion of tenderness aroused by the suffering, distress, or misfortune of another, and prompting a desire for its relief; compassion, sympathy" (the quotation from Hoccleve, "Pite . . . is . . . To help him þat men sen in meschif smert" shows how easily these two senses may overlap or coalesce). The *NED*'s senses (3) "a ground or cause for pity; a subject of condolence . . . or . . . regret," and (4) "a condition calling for pity" may serve to remind us of the interesting fact that "pity" in this time may signify either the emotion itself or the object or cause of the emotion. This "double" meaning is marked in the ME adjective *pitous*, which may mean "full of pity," "compassionate," etc., or "exciting, appealing for, or deserving pity; moving to compassion; affecting, lamentable," etc.

If we examine the various uses of *pite* in Chaucer's poetry, three important points quickly become obvious. There is, firstly, invariably a close connection between *pite* and *gentilesse*, nobility of soul. The two are almost inseparable; it is as if wherever there is true *gentilesse* there will be *pite*, and vice versa. At the very beginning of the Knight's tale the "eldest lady" of the company of wretched women asks Theseus for mercy:

> Have mercy on oure wo and oure distresse!
> Som drope of pitee, thurgh thy gentillesse,
> Upon us wrecched wommen lat thou falle. [ll. 919–21]

Theseus, like a *gentil* knight, at once responds:

> This gentil duc doun from his courser sterte
> With herte pitous, whan he herde hem speke.
> Hym thoughte that his herte wolde breke. . . . [ll. 952–54]

Later in the tale, when Theseus finds Arcite and Palamon fighting (one of them a banished exile, the other an escaped prisoner), he tempers justice with mercy at the request of the queen and "all the ladies":

> And alle crieden, bothe lasse and moore,
> 'Have mercy, Lord, upon us wommen alle!'
> And on hir bare knees adoun they falle,
> And wolde have kist his feet ther as he stood;
> Til at the laste aslaked was his mood,
> For pitee renneth soone in gentil herte. [ll. 1756–61]

This last is obviously one of Chaucer's favourite lines, for he repeats it in the Squire's tale (V.479), prologue F of *The Legend of Good Women* (l. 503)—and, typically, in a much more ironic context in the Merchant's tale (IV.1986). While the idea is found in other places (e.g. in the Franklin's tale (V.1514–24), Aurelius has "greet compassioun" for Dorigen's plight, and his *pite* produces an act of *gentilesse*), it is given its fullest expression in the passage in the Squire's tale. Canacee sees the grief of the falcon—"wel neigh for the routhe almoost she deyde"—and out of her compassion offers help, whereupon the bird replies:

> Right in hir haukes ledene thus she seyde:
> 'That pitee renneth soone in gentil herte,
> Feelynge his similitude in peynes smerte,
> Is preved alday, as men may it see,
> As wel by werk as by auctoritee;
> For gentil herte kitheth gentillesse . . .' [ll. 478–83]

It does, as Robinson says, recall "the familiar doctrine of the poets of the 'dolce stil nuovo' that Love repairs to the gentle heart"[5] (cf. *Troilus* III.5); *pite* is linked with love as an expression of the overflowing generosity of spirit of the noble heart. At the

5. Robinson, ed., *Works*, p. 675.

same time, *pite*—and love—may be shown to have a rôle in wider social relationships. Theseus goes on in his speech to hint at some ethical and political implications:

> Upon a lord that wol have no mercy,
> But been a leon, bothe in word and dede,
> To hem that been in repentaunce and drede,
> As wel as to a proud despitous man
> That wol mayntene that he first bigan.   [ll. 1773–80]

We may note in passing how he calls the "despitous" man *proud;* in Chaucer's works humility is a dominant characteristic of those of gentle and *pitous* heart. The point Theseus is making about the proper behavior of a lord is something of a *topos.* The Parson, in his discussion of the signs of gentilesse, tells us (X.465; in the section *de Superbia*):

> Another is to be benigne to his goode subgetis; wherfore
> seith Senek, 'Ther is no thing moore covenable to a man of
> heigh estaat than debonairetee and pitee'.

Pite is a virtue expected of a good knight, of one who might aspire to be called a "flower of chivalry." It is also expected of a ruler. This is a favourite topic in books of advice for rulers, and "mirrors" for princes. Gower in the *Confessio amantis* (VII.3118 ff.) makes *Pite* the fourth point of Policy (it was the virtue shown to mankind by God when he sent his son to take flesh of Mary):

> Pite may noght be conterpeised
> Of tirannie with no peis;
> For Pite maketh a king courteis
> Bothe in his word and in his dede.
> It sit wel every liege drede
> His king and to his heste obeie,
> And riht so be the same weie
> It sit a king to be pitous
> Toward his poeple and gracious
> Upon the reule of governance,
> So that he worche no vengance,
> Which mai be cleped crualte.
> Justice which doth equite
> Is dredfull, for he noman spareth;

> Bot in the lond wher Pite fareth
> The king mai nevere faile of love,
> For Pite thurgh the grace above,
> So as the Philosophre affermeth,
> His regne in good astat confermeth.

Canacee's encounter with the falcon in the Squire's tale reveals a second important characteristic of *pite*. The falcon goes on to say,

> I se wel that ye han of my distresse
> Compassion, my faire Canacee,
> Of verray wommanly benignytee
> That Nature in youre principles hath set.   [ll. 484–87]

Pite is a natural affection, which "runs" especially in the tender hearts of women. The queen of Theseus in the Knight's tale, when Palamon and Arcite are discovered, "anon, for verray wommanhede, / Gan for to wepe, and so dide Emelye, / And alle the ladyes in the compaignye" (ll. 1748–50). One of the considerations that moves Theseus to show mercy is that his heart "hadde compassioun / Of wommen, for they wepen evere in oon" (ll. 1770–71). At the end of the tale, as we have seen, he appeals to Emily's "wommanly pitee." *Pite* may also be an expression of the affection which parents feel for children. The prioress describes the distraught mother of the "litel clergeon" seeking her child:

> With moodres pitee in hir brest enclosed,
> She gooth, as she were half out of hir mynde,
> To every place where she hath supposed
> By liklihede hir litel child to fynde.[6]   [ll. 593–96]

Finally, *pite* is a generous, outgoing, abundant emotion, "a readiness to feel compassion for suffering," and, indeed, it sometimes becomes virtually synonymous with "compassion." It is a deeply intense emotion. Such is Canacee's reaction when she understands the words of the falcon:

> And wel neigh for the routhe almoost she deyde.
> And to the tree she gooth ful hastily,

6. Cf. also Melibee VII.975, Phys. T. VI.209–11.

And on this faukon looketh pitously,
And heeld hir lappe abrood . . .   [ll. 438–41]

And when she gives voice to her feelings she says vehemently,

Ye sle me with youre sorwe verraily,
I have of yow so greet compassioun.   [ll. 462–63]

Similarly, in the Man of Law's tale (II.528–29), the constable and his wife are profoundly moved by the sufferings of Custance, washed ashore in Northumberland:

The constable hath of hire so greet pitee,
And eek his wyf, that they wepen for routhe.

Another good example, in a more complex context, occurs in the legend of Hypermnestra (*Legend of Good Women* 2678 ff.), where the heroine is forced by her father to kill her husband. In a brief but remarkable scene we are shown her tormented by the conflicting claims of *pite* and of terror—terror of meeting death at the hands of her father and terror of the knife she must use:

The nyght is wasted, and he fyl aslepe.
Ful tenderly begynneth she to wepe;
She rist hire up, and dredfully she quaketh,
As doth the braunche that Zepherus shaketh,
And hust were alle in Argon that cite.
As cold as any frost now waxeth she;
For pite by the herte hire streyneth so,
And drede of deth doth hire so moche wo,
That thryes doun she fyl in swich a were . . .

In the discussion of *pite* in human love we have already noticed some cases where more distinctly religious overtones were present. The same is true in some cases of *pite* in its more general senses. Possibly the phrase in the Knight's tale, "som drope of pitee," suggests both tears of compassion and the traditional religious imagery of grace as a gently descending dew. In a passage in *Melibee* against avariciousness (VII.1615–25), " 'The goodes,' he [Tullius] seith, 'of thyn hous ne sholde nat been hyd ne kept so cloos, but that they myghte been opened by pitee and debonairetee' that is to seyn, to yeven part to hem that han greet nede," *pite* is beginning to sound like the *amor proximi* which is

[183

part of the conception of *caritas*. The Parson associates it with *misericorde* (X.805)—the remedy of avarice is "misericorde, and pitee largely taken," "misericorde folweth pitee in parfournyng of charitable werkes of misericorde," "the speces of misericorde been, as for to lene and for to yeve, and to foryeven and relesse, and for to han pitee in herte and compassioun of the meschief of his evene-Cristene." It was *pite* for man, says Gower, that caused God to send his son to take flesh and redeem mankind. *Pite* is sometimes explicitly related to the *pite* which Christ showed for man. Such *pite* was the expression of love, for medieval devotional tradition always saw the redemption of man as a supreme act of love. "Love was our lord's meaning," says Julian of Norwich. And Julian in her work uses the bold (though not unique) image of Christ as a loving mother. In later medieval iconography, Caritas came to be represented by the figure of a mother with children.[7]

In Chaucer, there are a few cases where Christ's *pite* is directly referred to. The Parson (X.885–90) speaks of "the lawe of Jhesu Crist, that is lawe of pitee," and earlier (255), he says that the fifth "point" that ought to move a man to contrition is the remembrance of Christ's passion—

> For, as seith Seint Bernard, 'Whil that I lyve I shal
> have remembrance of the travailles that oure Lord Crist
> suffred in prechyng; his werynesse in travaillyng, his
> temptaciouns whan he fasted, his longe wakynges whan he
> preyde, hise teeres whan that he weep for pitee of good
> peple . . .'.

The same idea lies behind a reference to the cross in the Man of Law's tale (II.452):

> hooly croys,
> Reed of the Lambes blood ful of pitee.

Pite is also a traditional characteristic of the Virgin Mary, the *mater misericordiae* (in the *ABC* she is given the traditional title "of pitee welle"). It appears in the invocation to Mary at the beginning of the Second Nun's tale (VIII.50–56):

7. Cf. R. Freyhan, "The Evolution of the *Caritas* Figure," *Journal of the Warburg and Courtauld Institutes* 9 (1948), 68–86.

Assembled is in thee magnificence
With mercy, goodnesse, and with swich pitee
That thou, that art the sonne of excellence
Nat oonly helpest hem that preyen thee,
But often tyme, of thy benygnytee,
Ful frely, er that men thyn help biseche,
Thou goost biforn, and art hir lyves leche.

Pite—compassion, sympathy for those in distress—is a dominant characteristic of Chaucer's own narrative art. It manifests itself in his attitudes to characters and their situations as well as in the explicit statements and comments of his narrators. He will often alter his originals in order to elaborate a moment of great pathos or of high emotional pitch. There is a small but characteristic example of this in the incident in the Knight's tale referred to earlier where the eldest lady of the company of womens pleads for mercy. She swoons, "with a deedly cheere, / That it was routhe for to seen and heere." Chaucer has added this swoon, to point the pathos of the scene. It is of course very often the case that such *pite* co-exists in a delicate and mysterious balance with other more ironic or comic tones. There is a fine and elaborate scene of sorrow at Arcite's death. Characteristically, Chaucer has added the outcry of the women:

'Why woldestow be deed', thise wommen crye,
'And haddest gold ynough, and Emelye?' [ll. 2835–36]

"Shrighte Emelye, and howleth Palamon"—it is one of those extreme scenes of emotion at which Chaucer excels. Some of the lines which he adds, however, have a subtle ambiguity, which while never destroying the intensity of the pathos, hint at other perspectives and registers:

What helpeth it to tarien forth the day
To tellen how she weep bothe eve and morwe?
For in swich cas wommen have swich sorwe,
Whan that hir housbondes ben from hem ago,
That for the moore part they sorwen so,
Or ellis fallen in swich maladye,
That at the laste certeinly they dye. [ll. 2820–26]

Equally characteristic, however, are the intense and heartfelt expressions of *pite* which he is quick to utter. In the legend of Ariadne (*Legend of Good Women* 2179–84), he dismisses Theseus curtly and turns with affection to the heroine:

> Me lest no more to speke of hym, parde.
> These false lovers, poysoun be here bane!
> But I wol turne ageyn to Adryane,
> That is with slep for werynesse atake.
> Ful sorwefully hire herte may awake.
> Allas, for thee myn herte hath now pite!

In the legend of Dido (*Legend of Good Women* 1341–45) he shrinks from recording her last lament:

> And thus, allas! withouten his socours,
> Twenty tyme yswouned hath she thanne.
> And whanne that she unto hire syster Anne
> Compleyned hadde—of which I may nat wryte,
> So gret a routhe I have it for t'endite. . . .

The most famous of all his expressions of *pite* is that fine statement of compassion for the unfortunate Criseyde (*Troilus*, V.1093–99):

> Ne me ne list this sely womman chyde
> Forther than the storye wol devyse.
> Hire name, allas! is punysshed so wide,
> That for hire gilt it oughte ynough suffise.
> And if I myghte excuse hire any wise,
> For she so sory was for hire untrouthe,
> Iwis, I wolde excuse hire yet for routhe.

The last two books of *Troilus* are perhaps the most impressive example of Chaucer's pathetic style—far more moving than Boccaccio's "stilo assai pietoso," mature, restrained, eloquent, and compassionate. The tragedy of the lovers is treated with clear-sighted understanding and a compassion as intense as that which Dante felt for the doomed lovers Paolo and Francesca— for *pite* (*di pietade*) he "fell down as a dead body falls."

Since it is impossible to do justice to a work of such complexity here, I confine myself to an excursus on two of Chaucer's less popular works, where the overflowings of the generous emo-

tions of *pite* may seem to some modern readers excessive. It will
have become obvious by now that in situations which excite *pite*,
tears flow very freely. In a philosophical tale like *Melibee*, weeping is soberly discussed (VII.985), and moderation is advised.

> This Melibeus answerde anon, and seyde, 'What man', quod he,
> 'sholde of his wepyng stente that hath so greet a cause for to wepe?
> Jhesu Crist, oure Lord, hymself wepte for the deeth of Lazarus hys
> freend'. Prudence answerde: 'Certes, wel I woot attempree wepying
> is no thyng deffended to hym that sorweful is, amonges folk in
> sorwe. . . .' The Apostle Paul unto the Romayns writeth, 'Man shal
> rejoyse with hem that maken joye, and wepen with swich folk as
> wepen.' But though attempree wepyng be ygraunted, outrageous
> wepyng certes is deffended. Mesure of wepyng sholde be considered,
> after the loore that techeth us Senek: 'Whan that thy frend is deed',
> quod he, 'lat nat thyne eyen to moyste been of teeris, ne to muche
> drye; although the teeris come to thyne eyen, lat hem nat falle . . .'.

But in a *pitous cas* the vast majority of Chaucer's characters do
not think of St. Paul or of Seneca and his *mesure*, but weep as
Melibee wept. That the lamentation could be long or un-
restrained—"shrighte Emelye, and howleth Palamon"—should
not surprise us, for there is much evidence in art, in descriptions
of funerals,[8] etc., that in everyday medieval life emotions of
grief were directly, and sometimes extravagantly, expressed.
Froissart imagines Richard II in prison weeping bitterly, wring-
ing his hands, and cursing the hour that he was born; the Tudor
writer Cavendish describes a tearful scene when Wolsey takes
leave of his faithful servants. One royal grief left an elegant
memorial in the series of Eleanor crosses erected by Edward I to
mark the resting-places of his queen's body, another destroyed a
palace—Richard II demolished the palace of Sheen, where his
queen had died.

After the Physician has ended his tale of Virginia (VI.288
ff.), the Host is deeply moved:

> 'Harrow!' quod he, 'by nayles and by blood!
> This was a fals cherl and a fals justise . . .

8. Cf. J. Huizinga, *The Waning of the Middle Ages* (London, 1924), p. 6.

[187

> Algate this sely mayde is slayn, allas!
> Allas, to deere boughte she beautee! . . .
> Hire beautee was hire deth, I dar wel sayn.
> Allas, so pitously as she was slayn! . . .
> But trewely, myn owene maister deere,
> This is a pitous tale for to heere.'

It is indeed a "pitous tale." In my view, one of Chaucer's most remarkable achievements—though it has rarely been recognised —is in this curious and interesting type of story. The works I have in mind are the stories of Constance and Griselda. These have close connections with a number of medieval stories and romances (in English, for instance, *Emare, Le Bone Florence de Rome, The King of Tars,* and others), many of which are "test" stories exhibiting and extolling the virtues of Constancy, Patience, or Endurance. Some are close to moral exempla (the Host calls the Man of Law's tale a "thrifty" tale). Most interestingly, they are often "sentimental" works. They make their moral point by means of sentiment or pathos; they present their audience with the pitiful sight of goodness in a cruel and oppressive world. I should prefer to call such stories the "literature of tears" or the "literature of sensibility," since "sentimental" is now rather too easily used simply as a term of abuse. It is not hard to see how this has come about. Writing of this type deals with simple, ordinary emotions—the love of a mother for her child, the pity felt for a defenceless and falsely accused woman, etc.—and this is the source both of its greatest strength and of its greatest weakness. "Ordinary" or simple emotion may all too easily become merely trite. And, on the other hand, this kind of writing is not content with the simple portrayal of sentiment or of sentimental scenes. It strives to involve the reader, to make him participate (and it is therefore essential for success in this mode that the writer should be confident and assured in his relationship with his audience—as both Chaucer and Dickens seem to have been). It sometimes indulges the emotions—there is often some degree of enjoyment in the expansiveness and the intensity of the emotions. This is easily misused—the emotional response invoked and expected may be too vast for the fictional situation, "too great for the occasion," "inappropriate to the situation." Sentimentality would therefore often be the result of an elementary failure in decorum. The natural impulse of the modern reader is to distrust the direct and powerful appeal to emotion which is central to this mode of writing; he prefers an indirect or oblique approach, and tends to shy away from the direct presentation of strong and simple feelings. Whether he is right or not, his attitude seems to have been much rarer in earlier times.

Some of the older meanings of "sentiment" or "sentimental" come close to capturing the qualities of these medieval "romances of tears": "sentiment" in the sense of a "refined and tender emotion; exercise or manifestation of 'sensibility' . . . appeal to the tender emotions in literature or in art"; "sentimental" in its eighteenth-century sense "characterised by or exhibiting refined and elevated feeling," or (of literary compositions) "appealing to sentiment; expressive of the tender emotions. . . ." Some of the older meanings of "sensibility" are also relevant: "quickness and acuteness of apprehension or feeling; the quality of being easily and strongly affected by emotional influences; sensitiveness" (or eighteenth–nineteenth century) "capacity for refined emotion; delicate sensitiveness of taste . . . readiness to feel compassion for suffering, and to be moved by the pathetic in literature or art." Some readers will already be thinking of the extended (and ironic) portrait Chaucer gives us of a medieval lady who has in no small degree a "capacity for refined emotion," the Prioress (I. 142–50):

> But, for to speken of hire conscience,
> She was so charitable and so pitous
> She wolde wepe, if that she saugh a mous
> Kaught in a trappe, if it were deed or bledde.
> Of smale houndes hadde she that she fedde
> With rosted flessh, or milk and wastel-breed.
> But soore wepte she if oon of hem were deed,
> Or if men smoot it with a yerde smerte;
> And al was conscience and tendre herte.

Pathetic or emotional writing was of course not unknown in antiquity—parts of Seneca's tragedies and of Ovid's *Heroides* come immediately to mind—nor in the earlier Middle Ages—

Hroðgar weeps as he takes leave of Beowulf, Roland weeps at the death of Oliver. [9] But from the twelfth century the poets take a more conscious interest in the refinements of emotion and in the intricacies of sentiment, and show a greater willingness to linger over pathetic scenes. Students of the religious literature of the high and late Middle Ages will of course be familiar with the pervasive "affective" style which seeks to involve the reader's emotions directly in such piteous scenes as that of the crucified Christ. St. Francis, overheard lamenting, says that he goes through the world without shame, "lamenting the Passion of my Lord." Margery Kempe in the fifteenth century is moved to roar and cry by the sight of the dead Christ in a *pietà*, or *pite* as it is significantly called in Middle English.

The "literature of tears" is not found so extensively in secular forms, but it is certainly there. Marie de France is one of the earliest and one of the best practitioners of "sensibility" in stories of love. Many of her lais are suffused with a gentle and pathetic melancholy. There is a touching scene in *Laustic* where the lady takes up the body of the dead nightingale:

> La dame prent le cors petit;
> Durement plure . . .

In *Fresne* she delicately tells an emotional story of a foundling who falls into a situation of the kind Griselda found herself in, endures, and finds happiness at the end. In *Eliduc* we have a very fine example of a "pitous tale." Here the hero finds himself loved by two ladies with a love that is equally "fine" and true—his wife, and a princess, Guillardun, whom he has met in a distant land (Marie makes the most of the exquisite blend of joy and grief which they have to endure). On hearing by accident that Eliduc is married, Guillardun falls into a swoon. She is thought to be dead, and her body is placed in a chapel. Eliduc bids her a touching farewell, and keeps returning to gaze at her. Eliduc's wife notices his sorrow, hears of his visits, and goes to the chapel. As she looks she is filled with sorrow. Marie then "points" the scene with a fine sentimental-symbolic incident. A weasel runs across the princess's body and a servant kills it with

9. Cf. L. Beszard, *Les Larmes dans l'épopée* (Halle, 1903).

a blow of his staff. The weasel's mate comes out and tries to make the body stand up:

—Quant ne la pot fere lever
Semblant feseit de doel mener—

but she brings a red flower from the wood which when it is placed in the mouth of the dead animal immediately revives him. The same flower is then used to resuscitate the maiden. The wife is filled with joy, and with a *gentilesse* which a modern reader cannot but find a little extreme, generously decides to enter a convent so that Eliduc and the princess may be married. (We might note, incidentally, that the theme of a "supposed death" has, in a variety of forms, been popular in this kind of story from *Apollonius of Tyre* to *The Winter's Tale*.) The best English non-Chaucerian example of a "romance of sensibility" is *Sir Orfeo*, where the emotions are simply and delicately handled— there is a very touching recognition scene in the wilderness between husband and supposedly dead wife:

ȝern he biheld hir, and sche him eke,
Ac noiþer to oþer a word no speke,
For messais þat sche on him seiȝe,
þat had ben so riche and so heiȝe,
þe teres fel out of her eiȝe. [ll. 321–25]

Other romances, *Torrent of Portyngale, Eglamour, Octovian, Triamour*, which are related to the Constance story, handle the *pitous* elements, such as the casting out of a falsely accused heroine, in a rather crude and melodramatic way.

The best of all these English versions of the Constance story is certainly the Man of Law's tale. Chaucer has greatly expanded the story of Trivet, giving it an ample eloquence, and consistently stressing the "pitous" scenes. In this leisurely tale the narrator's presence is constantly felt. He "intervenes," addresses the characters, prays for his heroine, comments on the events, and gradually builds up that intimate relationship with the audience that is necessary for a "tale of tears." At one emotional point (II.645–51) he makes a very effective appeal to his audience's own experience:

Have ye nat seyn somtyme a pale face,
Among a prees, of hym that hath be lad
Toward his deeth, wher as hym gat no grace,
And swich a colour in his face hath had,
Men myghte knowe his face that was bistad,
Amonges alle the faces in that route?
So stant Custance, and looketh hire aboute.

When Constance first leaves her father and Rome, what was a mere hint in Trivet, "with great sorrow and weeping and crying and complaining" is expanded into a full-scale "pitous" scene extending over several stanzas. The narrator stresses the sorrowful outcome of the event ("the woful day fatal is come," etc.), draws our attention to Constance's feelings ("with sorwe al overcome") and appearance (she is "ful pale"), and makes his own sad comment:

Allas! what wonder is it thogh she wepte,
That shal be sent to strange nacioun. . . .   [ll. 267–68]

Then Constance is given a short speech of farewell, a simple dramatic device which not only makes more vivid the "pitous" nature of the "cas," but also allows a hint of her own steady, pious constancy to emerge. The narrator brings what has now become a very emotional scene to a climax with a series of rhetorical comparisons:

I trowe at Troye, whan Pirrus brak the wal,
Or Ilion brende, at Thebes the citee,
N' at Rome, for the harm thurgh Hanybal
That Romayns hath venquysshed tymes thre,
Nas herd swich tendre wepyng for pitee. . . .   [ll. 288–92]

This pattern, with a number of subtle variations, is followed throughout the many tribulations of the unfortunate heroine. Constance ("this innocent") is sometimes almost a falsely accused saint; in one dramatic scene she prays "with ful pitous voys" to the cross, the emblem of suffering, "reed of the Lambes blood ful of pitee." There is a very affecting scene when she makes her final departure from England with her child. As usual there is the merest hint in Trivet which has become the germ of an elaborate "pitous" scene (ll. 835–75). Constance's humble patience and fortitude shine through her prayer to Mary (ll. 845 ff.):

> . . . Thy child was on a croys yrent.
> Thy blisful eyen sawe al his torment;
> Thanne is ther no comparison bitwene
> Thy wo and any wo man may sustene. . . .
>
> Rewe on my child, that of thy gentillesse,
> Rewest on every reweful in distresse.

Yet at the same time she is a distraught mother, "with a deedly pale face":

> Hir litel child lay wepyng in hir arm,
> And knelynge, pitously to hym she seyde,
> 'Pees, litel sone, I wol do thee noon harm'.
> With that hir coverchief of hir heed she breyde,
> And over his litel eyen she it leyde,
> And in hir arm she lulleth it ful faste. . . . [ll. 834–39]

Here her simple phrases are in striking contrast to the passionate grief of the bystanders. At the end of her prayer, her emotions break out:

> 'O litel child, allas! what is thy gilt,
> That nevere wroghtest synne as yet, pardee?
> Why wil thyn harde fader han thee spilt?' . . . [ll. 855–57]

And at last, after a simple symbolic action ("therwith she looked bakward to the londe, / And seyde, 'Farewel, housbonde routheless!' " [ll. 862–63]), she takes her child into the ship.

This type of story does not usually have a tragic ending: The happy resolution is normally brought about by a recognition scene or a reunion scene, which were obviously relished by the authors, and presumably by the audience. There is often a great overflowing of emotion; the reunited may swoon or weep for joy. Chaucer can use these scenes to evoke the sudden and overwhelming change from despair to happiness, and the mixed, deep emotions of the encounter. In the scene between Constance and her father, Chaucer describes this complex of emotions by the happy phrase "pitous joye." He handles the resolution of the tale superbly; the exigencies of the plot demand two successive

[193

reunion scenes. They are nicely differentiated, and soberly and eloquently written. The use of the child to bring about the reunion of Constance and Alla (1051 ff.), and the emotional power of the meeting, make the scene one which Dickens would have been proud to have written.

> Whan Alla saugh his wyf, faire he hire grette,
> And weep, that it was routhe for to see;
> For at the firste look he on hire sette,
> He knew wel verraily that it was she.
> And she, for sorwe, as doumb stant as a tree,
> So was hir herte shet in hir distresse,
> Whan she remembred his unkyndenesse.
>
> Twyes she swowned in his owene sighte;
> He weep, and hym excuseth pitously. . . .
> But finally, whan that the sothe is wist
> That Alla giltelees was of hir wo,
> I trowe an hundred tymes been they kist,
> And swich a blisse is ther bitwix hem two
> That, save the joye that lasteth evermo,
> Ther is noon lyk that any creature
> Hath seyn or shal, whil that the world may dure.

It seems to me that Chaucer is the great master of this kind of literature in the Middle Ages. But whereas the Man of Law's tale, although it is not usually a favourite with modern critics, is admired, it is rare to find a favourable mention of another story with the same combination of eloquence and sentiment—the Clerk's tale of the marquis Walter's cruel testing of his patient wife, Griselda.[10] It is an extraordinary example of the genre, and does present genuine difficulties. Modern readers are revolted by the cruelty of the situation and the way in which Griselda's patient goodness is carried to what seem inhuman extremes. It seems to have been popular in the Middle Ages (and

10. There is an intelligent and interesting study by A. C. Spearing, "Chaucer's Clerk's Tale as a Medieval Poem," in his *Criticism and Medieval Poetry*, 2d ed. (London, 1972). Other useful studies are James Sledd, "The Clerk's Tale: The Monsters and the Critics," *Modern Philology* 51 (1953–54), 73–82; and Elizabeth Salter, *Chaucer: The Knight's Tale and the Clerk's Tale* (London, 1962).

later), and was probably regarded as a moving and pathetic story, though there are hints of disbelief. Originally a folk-tale, it appears in literary form as the last story of the *Decameron*; Dioneo, who tells it, is moved to reflect at the end that Gualtieri "perhaps might have deemed himself to have made no bad investment, had he chanced upon one who, having been turned out of his house in her shift, had found means so to dust the pelisse of another as to get herself thereby a fine robe." Petrarch's Latin prose version was made about twenty years later; he describes the differing reactions of his friends—one was so moved by the story that he could not continue but had to hand the book to one of his retinue, but the other was quite unmoved, not believing that there ever lived a wife so patient and submissive.

As in the Man of Law's tale, the "pitous" aspects of the story are emphasised (there is already a hint of this in the French translation of Petrarch which Chaucer used), but here the process is more gentle and austere. The Clerk's tale has almost nothing of the extensive amplifications or the rhetorical elaboration of the Man of Law's tale. The treatment is consistently simple and unadorned, as befits both the subject—the humble Griselda is no emperor's daughter—and the teller (who has been enjoined not to display his rhetorical skills). Like the Man of Law's tale it is a kind of secular saint's life. There are many echoes of religious themes and language; Chaucer, as Professor Salter points out, 'emphasises the almost symbolic nature of Griselda's poverty'.[11] Above all, however, he emphasises the human aspects of Griselda's plight. The few additions he makes to the Petrarchan story nearly all tend in this direction. He rarely misses a "pitous" hint or detail in his sources, and deliberately attempts to increase the pathos of the situation. The scene in which her daughter is taken from her by order of the marquis (IV.519–74) is an impressively emotional one in the originals. Chaucer's cruel "sergeant" who performs the deed is made slightly more terrifying—"out the child he hente / Despitously," and Chaucer (more than the French version) makes the most of a Petrarchan anaphora:

11. Salter, *Chaucer*, p. 44.

Suspecious was the diffame of this man,
Suspect his face, suspect his word also;
Suspect the tyme in which he this bigan. . . .   [ll. 540–42]

He takes pains to stress the profundity of her maternal affection. She sits "meke and stille" as "a lamb," not showing any emotion, but by one phrase the Clerk suggests how much is pent up within her:

But atte laste to speken she bigan.

She meekly prays the sergeant to allow her to kiss her daughter,

And in hir barm this litel child she leyde
With ful sad face, and gan the child to blisse,
And lulled it, and after gan it kisse.   [ll. 551–53]

Chaucer's phrases, "in hir barm," "litel child," "ful sad face," "lulled it," are delicately increasing the pathos of the scene (Petrarch and the French simply say: "tranquilla fronte puellulam accipiens, aliquantulum respexit, et simul exosculans, benedixit . . ." / "de plain front prist son enffant et le regarda un pou et le baisa et beneist"). His adjective "sad" for "tranquilla" is an especially happy choice, for it sets up a subtle, hovering ambiguity —"steadfast, constant," "grave, serious," "expressive of sorrow." The narrator, following Petrarch, emphasises the strain on *modres pite:*

I trowe that to a norice in this cas
It had been hard this reuthe for to se;
Wel myghte a mooder thanne han cryd 'allas!'   [ll. 561–63]

Touchingly, Griselda begs the sergeant to bury the child's body somewhere so that it should not be torn by animals. Chaucer suggests wonderfully the cruel suppression of outward emotion; she says "mekely" and simply to the sergeant, "Have heer agayn youre litel yonge mayde."

A similar technique is used in the fine scene (ll. 813–96) in which, finally, Griselda herself is sent away to make room for a new wife. In a long and moving speech to her husband she contrives to control her emotions, but Chaucer succeeds in giving the impression that she is almost at breaking point:

'But ther as ye me profre swich dowaire
As I first broghte, it is wel in my mynde
It were my wrecched clothes, no thyng faire,
The whiche to me were hard now for to fynde.
O góode God! how gentil and how kynde
Ye semed by youre speche and youre visage
The day that maked was oure mariage!'   [ll. 848–54]

The final strained, pathetic exclamation is Chaucer's own invention. She applies to herself the scriptural verse "Naked out of my fadres hous . . . I cam, and naked moot I turne agayn" (ll. 871–72), and in a "pitous" descant upon this her own feelings overflow:

Lat me nat lyk a worm go by the weye.
Remembre yow, myn owene lord so deere,
I was youre wyf, though I unworthy weere.   [ll. 880–82]

Finally, when all is resolved, we are given the tears of *pitous joye* in a recognition scene. It is done with tact and simple eloquence. Griselda "ferde as she had stert out of a sleep":

Whan she this herde, aswowne doun she falleth
For pitous joye, and after hire swownynge
She bothe hire yonge children to hire calleth,
And in hire armes, pitously wepynge,
Embraceth hem, and tendrely kissynge
Ful lyk a mooder, with hire salte teeres
She bathed bothe hire visage and hire heeres.

O which a pitous thyng it was to se
Hir swownyng, and hire humble voys to heere!   [ll. 1079–87]

Again, one feels that this is a scene which would have impressed Dickens.

The story of Griselda seems to me to be an excellent, if extreme, example of the "pitous tale," but in general critics disagree violently with that friend of Petrarch's who was overcome by emotion. "It is too cruel, too incredible a story," says Professor Coghill;[12] Lounsbury says that the central idea is too re-

12. Nevill Coghill, *The Poet Chaucer* (Oxford, 1949), p. 139.

volting for any skill in description to make it palatable;[13] and so on. We need to remember that its origins are in a folk-tale which may well have concerned a mortal wife and a supernatural lover; it still has something of the curious inevitability of the fairy-tale. It is also important to recall that it is an exemplary story, and that medieval moral tales of this type often make their point by means of extreme situations (and by a very partial analysis). It is perhaps also worth pointing out that not only were "test" stories popular at the time, but gifted story-tellers in the Middle Ages seem to have been attracted to such extraordinary stories, possibly because of the challenge that they presented. It is surely significant that the Griselda story attracted three of the greatest medieval authors. In an exemplary tale such as this, a narrow principle of verisimilitude is not of much help. It would be very interesting to have a psychological account of Walter's twisted motives, but it would be irrelevant to this kind of tale. We are simply presented with certain *données*—which include the facts that Walter is suddenly possessed by this extraordinary desire to test his wife, and that Griselda's actions are virtuous. As Professor Sledd says, it is "a secular saint's legend, in which extreme cruelty and extreme long-suffering had to be pictured without arousing disgust for brutality or contempt for the absurd . . . to destroy the extremes in the Griselda story would be to destroy its effect, but a wrong treatment could make these same extremes either ludicrous or sickening."[14] Chaucer's technique is a bold one—on the one hand the extremes are intensified—the Clerk is more severe on Walter's black humour than Boccaccio or Petrarch and Griselda's *pitous cas* is fully developed and heightened—while on the other the story is, within limits, humanised and given some probability. The narrator quietly establishes a relationship of trust with his audience (and comes close to hinting that he too finds the story disquieting), and there is what Sledd calls "at least a partially successful effort . . . to transform the generally improbable into the specifically probable"[15]—we are told of the political pressure on Walter to

13. Thomas R. Lounsbury, *Studies on Chaucer, His Life and Writings* (London, 1892), p. 341.
14. Sledd, "The Clerk's Tale," pp. 78–79.
15. Ibid., p. 79.

marry, of his self-will and secrecy (this is established early); the contrast between Griselda's absolute poverty and nobility of soul and her lord's absolute power, magnificence, and lack of true *gentilesse* is emphasised; we are told of the doubts of her father, Janicula, about the marriage.

This brings us to the second line of attack on the Clerk's tale, which is to say that these attempts of Chaucer to humanise a cruel and incredible story only make it worse: "the humanism of Boccaccio has been applied to material that cannot bear such a load . . . what was meant as magical has become monstrous."[16] This is rather fully developed in a study of the poem by Professor Salter. But her arguments raise some difficulties which are, to my mind, unnecessary. It is true that there are religious echoes in the tale, but is it quite true to say that "the basic intent of the story is religious"? The "moral" that she quotes,

> for that every wight, in his degree,
> Sholde be constant in adversitee [ll. 1145–46]

is not exclusively or specifically "religious." The story, while it is "sounynge in moral vertu" is in that strange area between "secular" and "religious"; it might more fairly be described as "moral" or "ethical." To treat the story as a "religious fable" is to invent difficulties. Professor Salter thinks that Chaucer's attempts at "pathetic realism" get him into trouble: "The *Tale* is constantly pulled in two directions . . . the human sympathies so powerfully evoked by the sight of unmerited suffering form, ultimately, a barrier to total acceptance of the work in its original function,"[17] i.e. as a "religious fable." This, however, rests on the assumption that its "original" function is that of a "religious fable." It is just as reasonable to take the tale as the Clerk tells it, as an extraordinary "pitous tale" of suffering and goodness, which has religious overtones, and from which a clear moral and exemplary pattern can be seen to emerge. Chaucer cannot resist, she says, becoming increasingly critical of Walter. By making him into a "character" Chaucer loses Walter's "symbolic authority, either for good or for evil: and this authority is

16. Coghill, *The Poet Chaucer*, p. 140.
17. Ibid., p. 50.

exactly what he needs if he is to justify, or to refuse to justify, his apparently wanton acts of cruelty." Griselda refers to him at the end to the children as "youre benygne fader"—how can we see him thus, she argues, without "some 'heightening' of Walter's role, for instance, an indication that his conduct is to be judged by standards *other* than those of real life." Our dilemma is clearly defined, she argues, by the lines (932 ff.) which compare Griselda's trials and virtues to those of Job—'the biblical reference forces our attention to the divergence between that story and this. The awesome, mysterious power which permits Job's correction and chastening is presented as beyond question or criticism. . . . Walter, on the other hand, has been so vividly and adversely presented to us, that we are inclined—indeed, encouraged—to believe in his heartlessness rather than in his inscrutability. And yet his role is not envisaged as that of the sanctioned Tempter, Satan, in the *Book of Job*. . . .' This is not convincing. The comparison to Job is simply to another patient, virtuous sufferer, and there is no need for the whole story to be parallel. Walter is not God, nor a sanctioned Satan. God is no doubt there in the background of the Clerk's tale, allowing suffering, but there is no reason at all—theological or literary— why we should admire, respect, or regard as awesome, mysterious, or inscrutable the immediate agent who causes the suffering. This does not affect the moral point about the value of patience at all. Significantly, the Clerk speaks of Fortune—"the adversitee of Fortune al t'endure" (l. 756), and he is echoed by Walter "I rede yow t'endure / The strook of Fortune or of aventure" (ll. 811–12), and Fortune's hostile acts are often irrational, malicious, and unjust. (Chaucer does not in this tale make explicit the philosophical question of why the innocent are allowed to suffer, as he does in the Man of Law's tale, where there is perhaps a greater sense that God is "in control"). It seems to me that the clash between "religious fable" and "pathetic realism" is non-existent.

Part of the modern reader's difficulty is that neither the virtue of Patience, nor the assumption that it is beneficial, has much standing today. It is worth pointing out that Chaucer refers to and discusses the quality a number of times. The Franklin, praising the "gentil" and temperate marriage of Dorigen and Arviragus, says that it is a "high virtue," and that it "venquysseth . . . Thynges that rigour sholde nevere atteyne" and that one should therefore "learn to suffer" (he is echoing the adage *vincit qui patitur*). The Wife of Bath in her harangue makes a wonderfully cynical use of the doctrine of patience in love. But the most interesting parallel to the Clerk's tale is in *Melibee*, where the idea that "pacience is a greet vertu of perfeccion" is vehemently urged. Prudence quotes many authorities, including St. Paul (whose words [l. 1290], "Ne yeldeth nat harm for harm, ne wikked speche for wikked speche; but do wel to hym that dooth thee harm, and blesse hym that seith to thee harm," are surely being put into practice by Griselda in her simple and humble way when she refers to Walter as "youre benigne fader") as well as the patience of Christ himself (l. 1500): "nevere cam ther a vileyns word out of his mouth. Whan men cursed hym, he cursed hem noght; and whan men betten hym, he manaced hem noght." The modern reader is often rightly disturbed by what he considers the extreme passivity of the virtue, the abandonment of action, which he suspects may easily lead to adulation of suffering in itself. In earlier times, however, the idea of Patience could have a much more active and positive aspect. Melibee makes the natural objection to Prudence's arguments—if he should humble himself before his enemies he would lose his honour. In answer she quotes Solomon (l. 1715): "whan the condicioun of man is plesaunt and likynge to God, he chaungeth the hertes of the mannes adversaries and constreyneth hem to biseken hym of pees and of grace"—and in this case her advice proves correct, for patient goodness begets patient goodness. This is the optimistic view of the Clerk's tale. This active aspect of patience is very clear in some Renaissance iconography. Pope Leo X had as his *impresa* Patience victor of Chance,[18] not the aggressive *fortezza* of *The Prince*, but a passive, contemplative—and victorious—*fortezza*. The idea is also given visual form in a sixteenth-century emblem of Jean Cousin,[19] *Fortunae Patiaentia Victrix*, in which Fortune, her wheel and bow broken, is tram-

18. Cf. R. Wittkower, "Patience and Chance," *Journal of the Warburg and Courtauld Institutes* 1 (1937–38), 171–77.

19. Jean Cousin, *Le Livre de fortune. Recueil de deux cents dessins inédits de Jean Cousin*, ed. L. Lalanne (Paris, London, 1883).

pled down by the figure of Patience, unarmed save for a helmet and a shield which has protected her from Fortune's slings and arrows. We should probably see Constance's and Griselda's patience in this more positive and heroic way. It is interesting that the Parson in another philosophical treatment of the virtue (he points out that the old pagans commended and used the virtue of patience) quotes the philosopher (X.660):

> Pacience . . . is a vertu that suffreth swetely every mannes goodnesse, and is not wrooth for noon harm that is doon to hym. The philosphre seith that pacience is thilke vertu that suffreth debonairely alle the outrages of adversitee and every wikked word. This vertu maketh a man lyk to God, and maketh hym Goddes owene deere child, as seith Crist. This vertu disconfiteth thyn enemy. And therefore seith the wise man, 'If thow wolt venquysse thyn enemy, lerne to suffre'.

The concept of patience is a broad one, having something of the quality of wisdom, and something of the quality of Fortitude (the Parson later cites "constance," "that is stablenes of corage" as one of the species of Fortitude), a heroic quality of endurance and self-sacrifice. Indeed, under the name of fortitude or endurance it is not so strange to the modern reader, and has found some memorable expressions in modern literature; possibly the figure of Lena Grove, in Faulkner's *Light in August*, might be thought of as a modern equivalent to the heroically suffering and enduring heroines of medieval tales of tears.

I would not wish to claim too much for the Clerk's tale. It certainly does not have the colour, variety, or depth of Chaucer's greater works. Its marvellous extremes are a far cry from the balance and humane maturity of *Troilus*. Yet it is not as simple as it has been sometimes presented; Mr. A. C. Spearing has very convincingly argued that it is characterised less by harmony than by tension, a tension which arises, to my mind, not from an opposition of "religious fable" and "human realism," but from the narrator's intense *pite* for Griselda and his horror of the cruel test imposed upon her by the extraordinary whim of Walter. The tale may not have many of those characteristically bold clashes of tone which we admire so much in Chaucer's best work—in general it is marked by a graceful simplicity and eloquence. Yet other perspectives are present in the outspoken and critical compassion of the narrator, and also in his relationship to the wider discussion of marriage and authority among the pilgrims. This bursts out into the open in the brilliant Envoy, which has never failed to win approval. It does not seem to me to be quite accurate to describe it as "a marvellously versified ironical disclaimer," for its effect is not at all to obliterate the preceding tale. Both the ironical Envoy and the "pitous tale" which precedes it are, poetically speaking, equally valid. Chaucer, as he so often does in his mature work, encourages us to entertain paradoxical or conflicting emotions at the same time. It is perhaps a little like a later, and simpler, example in Perrault's *Fairy Tales*, where the "second morality"—that it may be, for example, of some advantage to have godmothers and godfathers as well as the gifts of nature—suggests an intrusion of another more world-weary point of view. In the end, the Clerk contrives to combine the attitudes of Dioneo and of Petrarch with his own critical intelligence and compassionate *pite*.

Pite in its many manifestations, and the "pitous tale" or literature of tears, are obviously only a part of Chaucer's total achievement, but I hope that the preceding pages have shown that they should be taken seriously, and that to the many laudatory phrases which are applied to our greatest medieval poet we should add that old gloss—*humanus, fulle of pytie.*

10

Make Believe: Chaucer's Rationale of Storytelling in *The House of Fame*

Geoffrey T. Shepherd

UNIVERSITY OF BIRMINGHAM

Story in literature occupies something of the place of tune in music. Tune or melody is what is first sought in music and what ultimately is abstracted and remembered: the beginning and the end; it does not fill the middle ground where performers and critics gather. It is of course notoriously difficult to treat tune directly or informatively. It is perhaps as difficult to talk usefully about story. One of Tolkien's achievements as scholar, critic and writer is to have drawn attention again to the importance of story as the mysterious heart of literature.

No doubt a story is a communication which the storyteller thinks worth making, and which, if he is successful, the listener thinks has been worth attending to. But the listener is not satisfied entirely by a purely formal succession and arrangement of words. He is attending to something that lies beyond the verbal signs that project it. The story is in some way different and separable from a telling of it: it can be delivered in word, film, mime, comic strip, etc.—in all sorts of hot and cold media. What then gives identity, structure and coherence to a story? What authenticates its integrity?

"It is at any rate essential to a genuine fairy-story . . . that it should be presented as 'true.' "[1] Most people will agree with Tolkien's judgment, even if they would wish to examine further his explanation that truth in story depends upon a coherence and consistency within a "secondary world" produced by a successful "sub-creator." Fairy-stories of all stories bring this problem of "truth" into sharpest focus, for in them fantasy is most pervasive. But a presentation of "truth" seems indeed essential to any successful storyteller. But what makes a story worth telling and listening to is plainly not truth in the content of the story in any of our ordinary meanings of truth.

It may be a philosophical problem; but it is also literary, and can be discussed in literary terms. In *The House of Fame* Chaucer dealt with these matters, and in such a way as to illustrate the puzzlement of a gifted practitioner and the slippery and shifting character of the questions themselves. It may be wondered whether he ever answered them to his own satisfaction; but the discussion is subtle and still instructive. Chaucer serves us well, for at least in his surviving pieces he was almost nothing but a storyteller, with an extraordinary variety of skills and an extraordinary interest in the mechanics of storytelling. He was of course concerned with the primal art, not with later modifications in novel-writing. He told stories at a time when, though he himself had a peculiar personal interest in establishing and preserving a fixed text, yet his narratives were still controlled by methods of composition which relate to face-to-face telling. He could not rely upon the authority and persuasiveness that print possesses by reason of its visible rationality and its public objective existence. Nor was he sustained by a convention of realism in narrative which has dominated attitudes towards fiction in the last two hundred years and which has worked to obscure or blur some fundamental puzzles about storytelling.

Nowadays *The House of Fame* is presented in three books. The division derives from the printed editions by Caxton and Thynne and is not marked in the MSS. But the transitions in story are indicated by separate invocations and new beginnings

1. Tolkien, "On Fairy-Stories," *Essays Presented to Charles Williams*, ed., C. S. Lewis (Oxford, 1947), p. 45.

in narration, and the division into books is entirely acceptable in a printed text. As we have it, *The House of Fame* consists of an analogical introduction about dreams; a space-travel fiction; and an account of the two houses of fame. Then rather abruptly the piece breaks off—apparently it was left unfinished. We can speculate how it could or should end, but not to our present purpose.

Fame is the theme of the poem. Personifications of Fame had been presented of old by Virgil, Ovid and Statius. In the Renaissance she was to be apotheosised into Glory. Chaucer's own lady Fame rules in her house as no shining figure. She is a grotesque, with her outfit of wings, her innumerable eyes and ears and tongues—a comically flamboyant assemblage of heterogeneous elements to make a concept vivid and memorable. Nobody was expected to give this lady Fame any imaginative reality as a personage. Fame is shown as the consequence and completion of utterance. She is not the reputation acquired by an author so much as the public recognition given to what he is talking about. Fame is what remains in the memory of what has been said about people or events. What remains may be reliable, influential, false or nothing at all. Fame is in part then the actual delivery of the material; it is also whatever remains of what has been said. It is the substance of story and the intention and outcome of storytelling.

Fame is Chaucer's theme. He starts with dreams. The problems of organising dreams into words and of interpreting them give him easy models for examining the claims to sense and coherence made in storytelling. What status has a dream? he asks. How do you assess its authenticity? Are dreams streams of fantasy? Do their images cohere into an argument or are they already shaped according to a deeper secret meaning? "Why this a phantom, why these oracles, I know not." How can we recognise that some dreams are more significant than others? How credulous should we be in general and in particular? Rapidly Chaucer runs through a whole series of questions of this kind and does not stay for an answer. Instead he commits himself and his story to the guidance of Morpheus, the god of dreams. The poet will allow the dream to explain itself as he narrates it. We should attend to the tale and not to the interpreter.

So the dreamer recounts his dream of the story of the founding of Troy by Aeneas—for medieval Englishmen the greatest and most potent secular story they knew. Who would deny the authenticity of this story? The dreamer describes the series of paintings on a temple wall which illustrate the episodes of Virgil's narrative. It takes him some three hundred lines of verse; but two hundred of these deal with the one episode of Queen Dido, persuaded into love by Aeneas and then by him miserably deserted. Chaucer's elaboration here suggests his interests. Dido's problem was rather like Chaucer's own. How should you make and take a story? It was Aeneas's account of his adventures that had won Dido's heart, as Chaucer explains. She had judged him worthy simply from his story about himself and from the way he told it. In the event she was much too credulous. She was completely taken in by his words. She at least had attended too much to the tale and too little to the intention of the teller. The poet, free from his source ("Non other auctour alegge" I.314) elaborates on Dido's pitiful discovery of the deceit practised on her. The burden of her complaint is

> O, have ye men such godlyhede
> In speche, and never a del of trouthe? [ll. 330–31]

Are good stories well-told simply a means of beguiling the credulous? How should she have distinguished the truth from the appearance of truth when it was presented so winningly? Women especially, Dido concludes, are born to be exploited thus, for they never master the arts of speech and effective skills of interpretation.

Chaucer has not quite done with the sorrowful Dido. By a story she was misled, by words deceived. And after her betrayal, he tells us, she becomes the subject of her own story. Stories of her unlucky fame run through the land. "O wicked fame" that so entrapped her one way in life, and in another after death. Many other people have suffered similarly: you can read about them in books and hear about such cases daily. Once started, a story true or false has a self-generated power of extension. Report and rumour fly off in all directions. Any author, even Chaucer, can spin things out further. Perhaps something solid lies at the heart of the expanding fog curling into fantastic shapes and dissolving images. But it is very difficult to be sure. It is the storyteller's problem and his listener's, as well as poor Dido's.

The dreamer describes the paintings on the walls and concludes his account of the *Aeneid*. He leaves the temple and suddenly finds himself in the middle of a desert, a nothingness. There is no sign of life anywhere around, no contact with a real world.

> 'O Crist!' thoughte I, 'that art in blysse,
> Fro fantome and illusion
> Me save!' [ll. 492–93]

Even in this greatest story of Troy is there "never a del of trouthe" but only a "godlyhede in speche"? Must the storyteller be as credulous as he requires his audience to be, able to do no more than sketch fictions out of fantasies? Such questions are by the end of Book I implicit in Chaucer's narrative.

Book II begins with the resolve to enquire further. The dream is recognised by all the signs to be "an avisyon"—a high and important dream in which men look for a meaning. The poet seeks Venus's aid, and the Muses', and also makes a strange summons to his own intelligence:

> O Thought, that wrot al that I mette,
> And in the tresorye hyt shette
> Of my brayn, now shal men se
> Yf any vertu in the be,
> To tellen al my drem aryght.
> Now kythe thyn engyn and myght! [ll. 523–28]

Thought presumably is that activity which processes the matter of story, conjoins it with meaning and makes it intelligible.

In this book of theory, Geoffrey the dreamer becomes an agent in the story. He is snatched up by the eagle and when he recovers his wits in his upper flight, he is told that the expedition is all designed for his profit. Geoffrey had wondered at first whether he was to be stellified: "Loo, this was thoo my fantasye" (l. 593). The eagle corrects him; indeed throughout their acquaintance the eagle has repeatedly to call Geoffrey back from his fantasies. The real purpose of the outing is simple. The faithful poet who has for so long written poems at command has never really found out what happens to the lovers for whom he writes. Geoffrey the poet sits at home reading his books, never properly understanding what happens in the great world. Now is his chance to learn. He is going to be shown what actually goes on.

It might seem at first sight that the eagle is offering access to a solid and lasting knowledge—to that real objectivity we nowadays sometimes ascribe to science and history—an obvious kind of material for a storyteller to make use of, we may think. It does not appear to have been nearly so obvious to Chaucer and his contemporaries. It is doubtful if any medieval storyteller thought he could make up a story from direct observation and reportage. First he had to establish a narrative organisation. The determination involved in literary imitation depended upon what Chaucer calls the "virtue of thought" that committed images to the memory: it did not depend upon or reside within the nature of things themselves. In this situation a medieval storyteller would get his schemes almost exclusively from pre-existing organisations of phrase and topic, from what we now loosely refer to as "oral tradition." But a fourteenth-century poet of Chaucer's flair and intelligence knew that the great mass of story which had oozed westward across Europe from the eleventh and twelfth centuries had become so desiccated, had been so ground away at, that now it was little more than an amorphous powder of incident, scene, motive and narrative device. The real sources of new narrative structures that were becoming available to English vernacular writers in the fourteenth century were those that could be extracted from books. French books were important. Beryl Smalley has drawn attention to the special importance of the "classicising friars" in England during the fourteenth century. Such men processed material which English writers were to use increasingly.[2]

But in theory at least there was another way of discovering how to organise material: through special revelation. If an outer reality could suddenly break through the existing verbal author-

2. Beryl Smalley, *English Friars and Antiquity in the Early Fourteenth Century* (Oxford, 1960).

isations, then a new principle might emerge, bringing with it a fresh understanding of what was going on in earth, hell and heaven. Of course that is what a medieval writer using a dream convention in narration pretends he has access to: he pretends to be composing in such a way that his authorisation cannot be challenged. Usually he knows very well that he has no such access to special revelation; nor would he seriously claim he had. It was a device for shelving ultimate responsibility. Chaucer uses the device readily enough; but without any sense of truth-fulness, such revelations

> I certeinly
> Ne kan hem noght, ne never thinke
> To besily my wyt to swinke
> To knowe of hir signifiaunce
> The gendres. . . . [ll. 14–18]

But at some length in Book II he explores the claims of special knowledge as a "theory of imagination" offering a guar-antee of fiction. This is what the eagle has to offer, as authorised messenger from the supreme god Jove revealing and dispensing (at some length) a wisdom which can discern causes and inter-pret signs. The eagle can authenticate this new knowledge by experience, that is, not by going back to the books of the great clerks, but by individual testimony and demonstration. Geo-ffrey submits to this new method of instruction for a while as he is carried up through the heavens, but somewhat mockingly. He perceives, sensibly enough, that in the end this stimulating in-struction based on direct intuition can do no more than confirm the authority of the same old books. He allows that he has had the promised real experience. He speaks of it in terms that recall the experience of St. Paul on the Damascus road, and that expe-rience had been as vivid, novel and productive as any special revelation could ever be. But Geoffrey refuses to make more than a perverse and timid use of his "clere entendement." He cannot and will not learn the new stuff. Revelation only confirms him in his old habits, it does not open up new ways for him. It simply shows that the old writers, Martianus Capella and Alan of Lille, had got things right long ago. Geoffrey could have learnt by experience exactly where the stars are located. He excuses himself. "I am now too old. I can believe what other men have written about the stars just as well as if I had seen them for myself." So rebuffed the eagle gives up his attempt to educate Geoffrey and abandons him near the House of Fame.

Book III begins with an invocation to Apollo, not for the gift of the art poetical to aid the poet's expression, but to Apollo the god of light and science for intellectual understanding. The poet is concerned to produce good *sentence*—a true sense and just appraisal of what he sees. So in this Book Chaucer attempts a classification of stories and story material in the light of his argument in Books I and II. The main categories are distinguished by the delineation of the Temple of Fame and the House of Rumour.

The Temple of Fame stands on a foundation of ice, slowly melting against the sun, but on its northern side still preserving clearly the name and titles of the great. It is built of beryl, magnifying all images. Around the castle is a noisy crowd of minstrels, jugglers, jesters, harpers, pipers, trumpeters, all the popular entertainers who celebrate the great. These jostle outside. At the very entrance gather heralds and pursuivants. Thus from kings of arms to acrobats we have the whole range of publicists—and among them in late medieval England we should have to include most of the vernacular writers—the hangers-on of Fame, whose compositions are trivial, whose fictions are entertaining but ephemeral. At least this is how Chaucer sees them. These are the men who never expect and are never expected to enter the House of Fame, but who serve its needs.

But the dreamer, who displays a self-confidence that lifts him at least in his own presentation of himself well above his proper station in life, ventures inside. There sits lady Fame herself in state, growing and shrinking like Alice at the medicine bottle. Down the hall stand the giant pillars of the establishment presenting the stories which have the prestige of history, the poet-historiographers preserving the great deeds of the past. There on a pillar of iron stands Josephus the old who by his recital of the *gestes* of the Jews "bore up the fame of Jewerye." Another cluster including Statius and Homer bears up the massive fame of Troy. Among this group there was some dissension because

> Oon seyde that Omer made lyes,
> Feynynge in hys poetries,
> And was to Grekes favorable;
> Therfor held he hyt but fable . . . . [ll. 1477–80]

Even the *gestes* which constitute the solid monuments of fame, however well attested, cannot be absolutely guaranteed.

In succession, down the hall stand Virgil, Ovid, Lucan, Claudian and many more:

> The halle was al ful, ywys,
> Of hem that writen old gestes,
> As ben on trees rokes nestes;
> But hit a ful confus matere
> Were alle the gestes for to here. [ll. 1514–18]

The dreamer is not too reverential, but he admits that it is through the written compositions of these poet-historiographers that men's deeds can win a certain permanence. These are the great authors who give fame to men, though not necessarily the truth about them, although fame may have all the appearance of truth, and in time may well be taken for truth.

A series of different companies enters the hall to seek their dispensations. The first seeks a fame commensurate with good works performed. "No," says lady Fame, "you shall have oblivion." The second company makes a similar request. "No," says Fame, "you shall be slandered." The third group surprisingly receives what is asked for. Lady Fame continues with her judgments. All the decisions are presented to seem unfair, unexpected and completely arbitrary. The storyteller, whose role it might be to fulfil these decisions, would have small scope to do justice to his matter or to tell the truth. He has no direct access to truth.

The dreamer has nothing to gain by stopping in the House of Fame. His concern is with more ordinary story material, with "tidings," with news. There is no opportunity of gathering news in the House of Fame. There, story is already distorted and hardened into history.

Outside down in a valley lies Domus Dedaly, the place of tidings, a revolving house of wickerwork like a cabin in a Russian fairytale, made of twigs, some green, some dead, some dying. Into this wicker cage all rumours and gossip stream. Nothing is permanent there, for everything exists at the whim of *Aventure*—chance and fashion together—and *Aventure* is the mother of tidings. It is the world of instant journalism, full of noise and scraps of news. But all the information is unreliable, distorted, exaggerated, unattested, unattestable, truth and lies inextricably commingled and often self-cancelling. Nothing has a fixed form. Everything is as unbelievable as believable with the unadmitted status of fiction as well as of firsthand experience. All these bits of news jostle to fly off to the lady Fame to fulfil their destinies. What they seek is a purveyor who can project them into some kind of appropriate form, however, impermanent. This is the material we may assume that all those minstrels and jugglers outside the gate of the House of Fame will handle, if it is ever to be handled at all.

What is the *sentence* then, which Chaucer was after in Book III? Instructive it may be, but it is somewhat depressing. Storytelling, what is called nowadays "imaginative literature," is presented as a lowgrade intellectual activity: certainly it does not exist on any level of truth regarded as an adequation of representation and fact. Aspects of truth may be mixed in with lies but, as they cannot be distinguished one from another, the effect is bound to be deceiving. The disreputable fragility of the House of Rumour is clearly apparent. Tit-bits of gossip, mixed motifs and topics in themselves do not make a credible story. At the edge of the age of print, oral tradition is insubstantial when the principles of organisation are no longer felt to be valid.

Stronger claims might be made at first sight for the documents of revelation—Chaucer was not of course thinking of the Bible—but of European vision literature, once associated with holy men, Fursey, Drihthelm, Tundale, later with Dante, and in his own time in the fourteenth century with a swarm of apocalyptics and pseudo-visionaries, including some of the alliterative poets. The eagle of Book II spoke for all of them, and Geoffrey had not been convinced.

What Chaucer accepted provisionally was the authority of the old poet-historiographers. He admits without investigation their authority. English culture of his time offered him no means of testing their weight and authenticity. They exist in an inviolable aura of splendour, stable and immensely respectworthy. If any human composition could be authentic, here it was. These books even offered a model of aspiration and a distant standard for a vernacular poet.

But in the form in which this programme of imitative classicism was available to Chaucer it afforded a limited basis for inventive storytelling. Its authority rested on an enclosed and uncertainly inscrutable tradition. One impression in *The House of Fame* is of squawking confusion—of rooks' nests in the trees: even the tale of Troy is doubtful if you collate the famous authors. Chaucer lived in a sceptical age and often his own scepticism goes very deep. From the treatment given to the eagle it might seem that Chaucer himself was sceptical about the possibility of knowledge, about the reality of revelation, about the evidence of the senses, about any accurate and coherent representation of the nature of things. On first reflection, life-as-lived as related by any vernacular writer begins to look like a tale told by an *idiota*—by a totally unlearned man, an illiterate who does not know even the alphabet of reality; and what the storyteller can say signifies nothing.

Yet this is not the effect that *The House of Fame* produces, nor was it Chaucer's intention to produce such an effect. Chaucer was certainly not indulging in a blatant paradox that might attract a modern nihilist—of giving a successful demonstration in the form of a story that no effective story is possible, offering as story a non-story with never a deal of truth in it. Certainly he has told a lengthy story which is complex, bizarre, well-fitted together and sufficiently entertaining. However fantastic the material, the story is put together by a narrator who has perfectly maintained a reasonable development in the argument and exercised cool sense and common standards of judgment. Whatever ironies or mockeries we may find, they never eliminate a certain weight and dignity in the narration and an impression of a serious intention. *The House of Fame*, it can be suggested, shows a rationale of storytelling rather than a dismissal of the whole business. If the familiar chronology of Chaucer's works is accepted we can see *The House of Fame* as liberating Chaucer as a storyteller for his future achievement.

The operations of Fame disguise the issue. All human life and all human activities offer material for making stories, but the question is how to gather, select and shape verbalisations of this flux of existence into satisfying organisations, each with a simplified but appropriate argument—what Chaucer called the *knotte* of a story (*Canterbury Tales*, Squire's Tale V(F) 401) and later practitioners will call a story-line. It is the problem of turning tidings into story, of getting cohesion and some truthfulness into a jumble of information. Chaucer allows that the storytelling process cannot directly produce anything like absolute truth. But a coherent and convincing story can be made with some confidence. It needs luck to do it. Reports exist in abundance, and something substantial can make its way into a narrative, although much must inevitably be lost. Successive storytellers who tell more or less the same story act as a succession of filters. What is required in every telling is a lucky combination: the right narrator, the right audience and the right occasion. Slowly then through re-tellings, tidings will set firm as story. The truth that emerges may seem entirely contingent. But that is not strictly accurate. For the truth that emerges eventually is the necessary truth. Things will be said to have happened this way, because this is the way that they are required to be seen to have happened. History, the story about men, is then the necessary truth that emerges out of contingencies: "And this is storial soth, it is no fable" (*Legend of Good Women* 702). *Vox populi*, the stories that people tell and want to hear told again and again, are in the long run very similar to the record of truth, *vox dei*. History becomes the story that is told everywhere, at all time, by all men. This is why the great old books are to be accepted and followed. This is why tidings need to be processed to winnow the fruit from the chaff. Thus in sum, Fame embodies a rather curious blend of an appreciation of history and an awareness of the strength of oral tradition.

There is no simple word in Chaucer for what we should call truth in story—a conformity between personal narrative and an objective registration of events. As a result, Chaucer does not make that over-sharp disjunction we make between fact and fantasy. Instead, with most medieval writers, he distinguishes narratives by the different levels of disclosure of truth. Some narratives disclose a great deal, but not the whole (except the Bible of course, and that cannot disclose all truth to any individual reader); some disclose very little truth at all. But the art of narrative is essentially the same for all kinds of narrative: rhetoric is open and uncommitted as a technique, and deals with all opinions and probabilities possessing less or more truth. Throughout the Middle Ages into the Renaissance, the rhetoric of narrative is applied alike to history, story and fable, and in each case seeks to establish the best case possible for truthfulness.

What then is the truth that story contains? It is not our kind of truth. No medieval storyteller relied on an ultimate truth of fact and measured his achievement by it. Individually observed experience, which was as far as he could take experimentation, was known to be deceiving: it needed to be checked against collective wisdom. There are however two concepts in early English which can be brought together to overlap and replace our modern expectation of truth in story: the concepts expressed by Chaucer's *sooth* and *trouthe*. *Sooth* is axiomatic truth, what is given, known and accepted as circumstantially true; it is often expressed proverbially; its reference is often moral or social. Many of Chaucer's generalisations out of human experience are "sooth to say." The *sentence* of a story will be *sooth*. *Sooth* resides in the import of the tale not in the narrative detail. *Trouthe* is not truth either. It remains much closer in meaning to the other derivative "troth." *Trouthe* refers to personal worth and reliability, to what is nowadays spoken of as credit-rating. In storytelling it will be that which guarantees that what the teller says can be believed. In rhetorical terms, it is what Aristotle referred to as *ethos*.

Sooth and *trouthe*, archaic forms as they are, suggest useful concepts in dealing with the permanencies of storytelling. The medieval storyteller standing on this ground can make a good case. If we insist on seeking the truth in story, a modest medieval narrator would have referred us first to its *sooth;* but we should have been invited to make that kind of judgment about the story when we had heard it through: as the Nun's Priest invited serious enquirers to find a moral in his tale if they were so minded. The authority and moral force of the story lies outside the composition and delivery of it, just as the force and authority of an act of parliament lies outside the lawyer's production of the bill.

But if a medieval narrator was less effacing, or if he were pressed harder on his own attitude to the story, then he could be expected to respond, perhaps with some distress of countenance: "But when I tell you something, don't you trust me? What my author says, so say I. I take my author as trustworthy, why should you not also credit what I say?" He would have switched his explanation from *sooth* to *trouthe.*

The interrogation of the narrator may be perfunctory, but the answers are not altogether naive. They reveal an understanding of the methods of storytelling which is often buried in modern critical and legal discussion of realistic fiction, pure fantasy, or pornography and libel, of all the unresolved problems of the interrelation of morality and technique. *Sooth* and *trouthe* have a convenience in drawing attention to the face and obverse of a writer's position at any time. To tell a story effectively an author must establish his credit with his audience: his telling must generate *trouthe.* The audience must be prepared to believe what is told them. Chaucer's account of audience reaction during *The Canterbury Tales* always assumes that an audience will be credulous. *The House of Fame* itself would seem to be making an extreme claim on its audience in this respect, even while the poem explores the interaction of credibility in story and credulousness of the audience.

We live in a world which officially seeks to discredit rumour-mongering and credulity on the scale envisaged in *The House of Fame*. We have gone far beyond any medieval audience in developing devices against belief. Indeed during the last phase of European history we have encountered the egotistically sublime claims of Romantic artists—our modern eagles—to a special private revelation by invoking 'that willing suspension of disbelief'. Thus we can reassure ourselves, whenever we wish, that we have defused the deceiving power of fiction by treating it as a merely esthetic, strictly non-utilitarian form of discourse. Many of our favourite critical activities, our searches for symbols, ironies, masks, forms of alienation, are means whereby we rebut an author's direct claim on our assent: we practise not to believe him.

As a result of these defensive manoeuvres we usually undervalue the part that credulity still plays in hearing stories. Coleridge's *obiter dictum* on a "willing suspension of disbelief" has passed too little examined into critical orthodoxy. The neatness of the phrase and the extensive explanatory power we give it epitomise the problem without solving it. The phrase (the summary of a story) has generated a context of credibility out of all proportion to its original intention, and has through repetition emerged as an axiomatic truth. We may coldly suspect that the phrase has been over-interpreted. Consciously not to believe disbelief when we are told something: to take up and maintain two negative attitudes simultaneously so positively—that is no easy mental feat. One may suppose that few people engage in these acrobatics or even try to when they read works of fiction. It may be suspected that they do something much simpler—what they are invited to do. They surrender to the story. They agree to make believe it. And this is no exceptional activity. Most people will allow that there is something in ordinary life very like what Walter Bagehot referred to as an innate "animal nature to belief," whereby man as both a rational and social animal manifests a marked tendency to accept what he is told. Doubt in itself is not a necessary sign of social and moral health.

It may be that medieval people in general retained longer and stronger this gift of credulousness. But it would seem that a response of credulity is inalienably entailed in the activity of speech. A predisposition to believe what one is told may be essential for the establishment and maintenance of human society and for the development of human thought. This readiness to accept testimony appears to continue to operate whenever a person is told something, unless a positive check is introduced, something which activates an intrusive judgment to cut across the current story. A natural instinctive credulity appears to be a reality in the study of language and literature which we need to discover again.

A storyteller is aware of the audience, and many of the checks hindering willing acceptance can be avoided: a story can be adjusted to fit other stories or to accommodate fresh material: the judgment can be invited to operate only on heavily pre-conditioned material; moreover an active self-adjusting rapport can be maintained between teller and audience and tale, by which emergent discrepancies can be subdued. The efficient narrator can produce something like primitive credulity in his audience. Good medieval storytellers did this. Perhaps all good storytellers do this. In many ways medieval storytelling is a more obviously normative activity than self-conscious novel-writing.

But there is an obverse which we may also tend to under-value when we take our norms from novels. A storyteller can expect to be believed, but the credulousness of an audience presents its own problems. A total credulity inhibits the communi-cation of a particular meaning, as the dreamer discovered in the House of Rumour. Might not a totally credulous audience be-lieve anything and everything, the wildest and most inconsistent stuff? It was impossible to make any sense of what was being said by the houseful of gossips. No clamorous insistence on *trouthe* can successfully deny the countervailing demand for *sooth*.

Normally a medieval author is not a free and independent agent in composition, because some part of his work in estab-lishing *sooth* belongs to those who have commissioned the story, and some part is transferred to the audience in his telling of it. A participatory formulation of a story is immediately obvious to anybody present at an oral storytelling. But all audiences, and every solitary reader, play some active role in giving shape as well as meaning to the story which they willingly receive. The truth of story is closely related to their prejudices, memories and perception as well as to the author's intention and technique.

The longer Chaucer went on composing, the more completely he liberated himself from the restriction of a single voice of *trouthe* imposed by oral tradition. At the same time, the greater authority his *trouthe* acquired, the more voices he could speak in, so that he came to depend more and more upon his audience for the completion of the *sooth* of his stories. In *Troilus and Criseyde*, after the climax of love, Chaucer comments on the story:

> But soth is, though I kan nat tellen al,
> As kan myn auctour, of his excellence,
> Yet have I seyd, and God toforn, and shal
> In everythyng, al holy his sentence;
> And if that ich, at Loves reverence,
> Have any word in eched for the beste
> Doth therwithal right as youreselven leste.
>
> For myne words, heere and every part,
> I speke hem alle under correccioun
> Of yow that felyng han in loves art,
> And putte it al in youre discrecioun
> To encresse or maken dymynucioun
> Of my langage, and that I yow biseche.
>
> [III, 1324–36]

The matter may come from my author; but the trustworthy storyteller mediates it to the listener who takes the meaning and finds its *sooth*. Together they are moving towards approximate truth. Story exists in this complementarity. Viewed from either position, from the teller's or the listener's, the story seems to have an independence and an existence of its own. For Chaucer, it is his author's and his audience's; for his audience, it belongs to the teller. Like language itself, with narrowed reference and increased complexity of organisation, story has thus an institutional character: it displays something of the autonomy, solidity and permanence that the eagle claimed for all the utterances of men. Perhaps that is why a story can seem as anonymous, as distinct and memorable as a tune.

I I

Moral Chaucer and
Kindly Gower

Rosemary Woolf

SOMERVILLE COLLEGE, OXFORD

C HAUCER'S apostrophe to Gower as "moral"[1] and Coleridge's
reference to the "innate kindliness" of Chaucer's nature[2] have
had a distorting effect upon much modern criticism of these two
authors. It is known, but too often ignored, that when Chaucer
saluted Gower as "moral" he was thinking of him as the author
of the versified moral handbook, the *Mirour de l'omme*, and probably also of the *Vox clamantis*, a lengthy complaint against the
times; the *Confessio amantis* was as yet unwritten. Chaucer therefore did not mean that Gower was "moral" in the modern sense
any more than that Strode (a then well-known Thomist philosopher and logician) was "philosophical" in the sense that this

1. *Troilus and Criseyde*, V.1856, Geoffrey Chaucer, *The Works of Geoffrey
Chaucer*, ed. F. N. Robinson, 2d ed. (London, 1966), p. 479. Unless otherwise stated this is the edition used throughout for references to Chaucer's
works or for quotations from them.

2. S. T. Coleridge, *The Table Talk and Omniana* (London, 1917), p. 294.
It is worth noting that this view of Chaucer was repeated by Matthew Arnold,
who referred to Chaucer's "large, free, simple, clear yet kindly view of human
life" ("The Study of Poetry" in *The Complete Prose Works of Matthew Arnold*, IX,
ed. R. H. Super (Ann Arbor, 1973), 174, and this characterisation of Chaucer
is at least to some extent related to Arnold's famous charge that Chaucer was
lacking in "high seriousness."

epithet now has when applied to people. Nevertheless, the term "moral" has been reserved for Gower both by his admirers and by his detractors. The latter find in it a good reason for describing the *Confessio amantis* as dull, whilst the former have breathed new life into the term "moral" by associating it with the recognition that Gower's ideal of love in the *Confessio* was happy married love not the supposed courtly love code.

Coleridge's emphasis upon the kindliness of Chaucer probably arose from a blindness to Chaucer's use of irony, particularly perhaps in the Prologue to *The Canterbury Tales;* but its propriety has also to be considered in a historical context. When the most recent and the most eminent satirist known to Coleridge was Pope, it might seem appropriate to him that a poet, who was so notably free from asperity and personal malice, should be described as having a kindly nature. The danger to criticism arises only when this view is perpetuated as a truism amongst critics, and furthermore when an overt contrast is made between kindly and tolerant Chaucer and moral Gower.

Gower, as the author of the *Confessio amantis*, has of course some claim to be called moral in the Chaucerian sense. Some of the stories told in the *Confessio* are not feigned exempla (in the sense that the stories in *The Legend of Good Women* are feigned saints' lives) but genuine exempla, deriving from a well-established didactic tradition, and exceptionally well-told: good examples are *The Trump of Death* and *The Three Questions*, both of which bear upon the levelling power of death, a subject that always moved Gower imaginatively.[3] Similarly, though less certainly, Chaucer has some claim to demonstrating a kindly nature in his works in that some of his insights into human behaviour are perceptively tender rather than ironically acute: indeed, if Chaucer were being contrasted with another of his great contemporaries, Langland, kindliness might well be distinguished in him, though even then only as one of many traits. However, despite the possibility of these claims, it is not at all certain that

3. For lists of analogues to these exempla see *Gesta Romanorum*, ed. Hermann Oesterley (Berlin, 1872), s.v. *Drei Fragen*, p. 723, and *Todestrompete*, p. 736.

Chaucer and Gower, who knew each other well and must have benefited from each other's comments on the art of poetry, should be isolated as a historical pair, one kindly the other moral. Indeed, when they are considered as a pair, it may be more illuminating to reverse the labels and call them kindly Gower and moral Chaucer.

That a narrative writer should display a keen moral sense may in literary terms be either good or bad. Gower's willingness to absent himself from didacticism in the *Confessio* is obviously at an elementary level of criticism good in that it allows him to tell powerful stories, such as those, for instance, of Albinus and Rosamund or of Horestes, without care for their lack of didactic value. But more interesting than these tales of appalling crimes and appalling acts of revenge, which would shatter the penitential framework if too closely attached to it, are the stories where Gower could have adhered to the traditional moral views which he expounds elsewhere, but has chosen to eschew them. At times this suspension of moral judgment works well, liberating a fresh and illuminating sympathy for his characters; at other times it leaves the story flaccid, the controlling moral pattern of the source being disregarded. All the stories to be examined are concerned with love and in a true penitential work most of them would therefore find a place under the various subheadings of lust. But, as has often been noticed, Gower, when he reached the last of the seven deadly sins, abandoned his traditional method of dividing each sin into five branches (each illustrated by one or more exempla), and instead confined himself to the sin of incest, chiefly illustrated by the inordinately long story of Apollonius of Tyre. Stories which could have served to illustrate all five branches are, however, scattered through the work, attached to the moral frame in a variety of ingenious ways. By a tradition commonly (though not invariably) followed, lust was divided into the following branches of sin, arranged in order of gravity: sexual acts against nature (i.e. those that could not lead to procreation); incest, which had an element of the unnatural since it violated the reverence due between father and child and by extension between other members of the

[223

family; rape; adultery; fornication.[4] It is worth bearing this medieval classification in mind because it does not necessarily correspond with the views of modern readers and certainly does not
accord with the modern criminal law.

Gower seems to be alone among medieval vernacular narrative writers in his willingness to deal with or touch upon the
subject of homosexuality (which of course comes under the first
heading) and equally remarkably to do so with sympathy. It is
worth noting first of all a surprising but imaginative touch that
Gower has invented in the story of Achilles and Deidamia. In
the original, which is part of the *Achilleid* of Statius,[5] Achilles
feels repugnance when compelled by his mother to dress in
women's clothes and to adopt a womanly manner. He becomes
manifestly satisfied with this attire only when he finds that the
disguise will serve as a stratagem to bring him close to Deidamia, with whom he has fallen in love. Gower makes his
Achilles more youthful and less consciously a man. Initially,
dressed as a girl, he pays no attention, 'And he was yong and tok
non hiede'; later, taught feminine graces, he becomes positively
pleased:

> Achilles, which that ilke while
> Was yong, upon himself to smyle
> Began, whan he was so besein.[6]

It was of course not Gower's intention to portray Achilles as a
homosexual: shortly afterwards he shows Achilles's masculinity
asserting itself in both amatory and martial instincts. But he has
created for Achilles a moment of sexual indeterminacy which is
much more psychologically striking than the straight-forward
conventional responses described by Statius.

Gower also borrowed a full-length story of homosexuality

4. For this order and its justification see Thomas Aquinas, *Summa Theologica* II.ii, q. 154, a.12.

5. Statius, *Achilleid*, ed. O. A. W. Dilke (Cambridge, 1954), pp. 41–43.
For knowledge of the *Achilleid* in the Middle Ages see Paul M. Clogan, *The
Medieval Achilleid of Statius* (Leiden, 1968).

6. Book V, ll. 3011–13, John Gower, *English Works*, ed. G. C. Macaulay,
Early English Text Society (hereafter EETS), 81, 82 (London, 1899–1902),
III, 29. This edition is used throughout for references to and quotations from
the *Confessio amantis*.

from the *Metamorphoses*.[7] The outline of the plot is the same in both works: Iphis, daughter of Telethusa, is brought up as a boy, because her father had ordered that if a girl was born she must be put to death; when grown, Iphis is betrothed to Ianthe and the dilemma is resolved when the gods transform Iphis into a man. The later stages of the story are recast by Gower in order to achieve a different moral patterning. In Ovid, Iphis at the age of thirteen finds the marriage arranged and her proposed bride Ianthe in love with her (believing her to be a man). To her horror Iphis is aware that she returns this love and in an eloquent monologue she laments this strange passion, one alien to animals and worse than the monstrous love of Pasiphaê for the bull. Iphis is appalled at what has befallen her, and the reader is correspondingly appalled.

By contrast Gower denies to Iphis any recognition of her predicament. The age of the arranged marriage is lowered from thirteen to ten[8] and in this child-marriage the two for a time remain loving but unaware that their marriage cannot be a normal one. When their period of innocence was about to end, Cupid took pity on them and, in order that they might continue to love but within the natural law, transformed Iphis into a man. By removing conscious moral responsibility from the protagonist Gower has obscured the moral issue, and by some unclear generalisations (nature, it would seem, can constrain to unnatural acts), he further absolves from blame. His one explicit acknowledgement of the sin in his statement that Cupid hates that which is against nature carries far less moral weight than does Iphis's understanding of her own situation in Ovid. Both in terms of narrative and moral strength the story has become much more lightweight in Gower's hands: the potentiality for tragedy is lost; in place there is a certain delicacy and tenderness.

In telling stories about incest Gower is of course not alone in

7. *Confessio amantis* IV.451–505; *Metamorphoses* IX.666–797.
8. The usual minimum age given by the canonists for marriage was fourteen for a boy and twelve for a girl; on English custom cf. William Lyndwood, *Provinciale* (Oxford, 1679), p. 272. For further discussion and references cf. H. A. Kelly, *Love and Marriage in the Age of Chaucer* (Ithaca and London, 1975), p. 182 and n. 17.

the Middle Ages: indeed incest, whether committed, threatened, or narrowly avoided is a common medieval theme. It is to be found, not only in the re-telling of stories of classical origin, but also (perhaps often borrowed from these prototypes) in some of the most widespread of medieval tales, such as that of the legend of Pope Gregory[9] and in some versions of the Constance story (though not in Trivet's account followed by both Chaucer and Gower). Where Gower is remarkable therefore is not that he tells the story of Apollonius of Tyre in Book VIII,[10] but that earlier he had related the tale of Canace and Macareus with compassion, achieving this end by recasting his source in the *Heroides*.[11] Some changes were of course inevitable in the adaptation of Canace's letter to her brother (after their incestuous relationship has been discovered) into a continuous narrative, but it is clear that Gower used these opportunities to invest the whole tale with a sense of pathos, which in Ovid had been reserved for one part of it only, namely the murder of the baby.

Though Gower on this occasion says nothing about the age of the lovers, he manifestly intends to convey the same impression of innocent youthfulness as he had done in the tale of Iphis. In Ovid, Canace fully understands and powerfully laments the relationship that there had been between her and her brother:

> Cur umquam plus me, frater, quam frater amasti,
> et tibi, non debet quod soror esse, fui?[12]

9. Cf. *Die mittelenglische Gregoriuslegende*, ed. Carl Keller (Heidelberg, 1914), and Margaret Sclauch, *Chaucer's Constance and Accused Queens* (New York, 1927). The theme of unintended incest between mother and son whether committed as in the story of Pope Gregory or narrowly avoided as in *Sir Degarré* probably derives from the story of Oedipus known in the Middle Ages from the beginning of the *Thebaid* of Statius and of its romance derivative the *Roman de Thèbes*, ed. Léopold Constans, I, Société d'anciens textes français (Paris, 1890).

10. In his history of the pagan gods in Book V Gower also tells a brief story (of at present unknown origin) of how Cupid lay with his mother Venus, he being blind and she "unwis." This is part of a generally censorious summary of classical mythology.

11. *Confessio amantis* III.143–336; *Heroides*, Epistle xi.

12. *Heroides*, ed. Grant Showerman, Loeb Classical Library reprints (Cambridge, Mass., 1963), p. 134.

In the *Confessio* Canace pleads her innocent unawareness to her father: "That I misdede yowthe it made." To justify this plea Gower had invented a past for the brother and sister in which they grew up in isolated companionship, childish love thus turning into sexual love without their recognising the change. Again Gower is obscure in his extenuating generalisations: in this instance "kinde" and love overrule "the lawes of nature" (since "kinde" and "nature" are synonymous, it would seem that nature here has a part in overruling nature).[13] In Ovid incest remains an abominable sin and therefore Aeolus in commanding his daughter to commit suicide appears to impose a harsh but inevitable penalty. It is only in ordering that the baby be cast out to be devoured by animals that Aeolus inhumanly exceeds the laws of tragic justice, and it is for the innocent baby that Ovid contrives that the reader shall feel pity. In the *Confessio*, however, the killing of the baby is postponed in time and entirely subordinated to the fate of Canace. It is she who is seen primarily as the pathetic and helpless victim of her father's fury and her own sin thus becomes trivial in comparison with the savagery of Aeolus (indeed the tale is told as an exemplum against wrath). In this story, as in that of Iphis, Gower has skilfully and deliberately worked against the moral pattern of his original, worked against the didactic teaching of his age, and furthermore worked against the moral assumptions of all other medieval stories on the same type of subject.

It will be apparent from the story of Canace and Macareus that Gower is skilful and agile in manipulating the seeming rigidity of his moral framework. Had Gower attached the tale to the frame by its primary theme, he would have been compelled to place it in Book VIII alongside that of Apollonius, and he would then have been compelled to condemn the lovers. By fastening it through a subordinate element he achieves an ingeniously won moral freedom for himself. This device is even more noticeable in Gower's numerous tales of rape, which are scattered through at least four of the books (excluding Book VIII

13. Macaulay's comments on the relationship between *kinde* and the *lawe positif* (Gower, *English Works*, note to III, 172) are superseded by the discussion of this point by Kelly, *Love and Marriage*, pp. 141–44.

on lust). This arrangement was clearly dictated primarily by the requirement of diversity rather than by the intention to effect an unexpected distribution of sympathies: thus the story of Lucretia is included in Book VII under the heading of chastity as a virtue in princes, whilst that of Tereus and Progne appears in the book on avarice, rape here being classified as a vice of lovers who take by strength that which is withheld from them. But stories of rape, which are less horrific than that of Tereus, are fastened to the frame in a neutral way. The much-told story, for instance, of the begetting of Alexander by Nectanebus is told as an illustration of sorcery as a branch of gluttony and the emphasis of the story is correspondingly more upon the marvellous than the wicked; similarly the story of Mundus and Paulina is related in Book I under the heading of hypocrisy (in this context deceptive disguise) as a branch of pride.[14] In this tale Gower shows an unexpected sympathy for Mundus, but he has not had to recast his source in order to justify this sympathy for a mitigating reference to the irresistibility of love was included in it. This dependence upon a source perhaps explains why Gower's sympathetic extenuation of Mundus's behavior does not carry conviction in the way that his sympathy for the potentially homosexual and the incestuous lovers had done.

The origin of the story is in the *Antiquities* of Josephus.[15] In this version the explanation at the end that Mundus was given a more lenient sentence than the others involved in the stratagem, "quod amoris vehementia deliquisset," makes sense, for Mundus is no more than a helpless and lovesick youth, and the ruse of his disguising himself as the god Anubis is devised by the freedwoman Ida in order to save his life: it is she therefore and the conniving priests, who have allowed the temple to be desecrated, that are sentenced to death; Mundus fittingly is merely banished. In subsequent versions, however, including that in the *Speculum historiale* of Vincent of Beauvais (in all probability Gower's source),[16] the figure of Ida and all other mitigating

14. *Confessio amantis* I.761–1059.
15. *Antiquitates Iudaicae* XVIII.7 (Cologne, 1534), p. 190.
16. *Speculum maior* IV.4 (Venice, 1591), p. 75. Macaulay's note on the sources of this story has been corrected in the Oxford D. Phil. thesis of H. C.

circumstances have vanished though the milder penalty and the reason for it remain. The moral patterning of the story thus becomes distorted, particularly if one considers it alongside that of Lucretia, for instance, in which Tarquin is traditionally villainous, and it is therefore not surprising that Godfrey of Viterbo in his *Pantheon* (a work known to Gower) recast the story, omitting the reference to the compelling power of love and having Paulina commit suicide.[17] Gower, however, follows the gentler ending: Paulina, having lamented her defilement, is comforted by her husband, and Mundus, unlike the priests, has his life spared, "For Love put reson aweie / And can noght se the rihte weie." Until that moment, however, Mundus's cold-blooded stratagem and his subsequent taunting of Paulina had seemed morally repugnant, and it is difficult for the reader to see why the passions that overcame Mundus should be so much more simply and gently described than those that moved Tarquin (cf. V.3998–4900). The explanation undoubtedly lies in the respective sources, but, though Vincent had referred to the *vis amoris*, Gower would have done better not to repeat him. In his efforts to penetrate with an unscolding eye into the depths and ramifications of human weakness, Gower from time to time accidentally debases some of the key terms of his poem. "Love" in the story of Mundus seems to be equivalent to "kinde" in other contexts, and in some of these other contexts "kinde" is apparently reduced to its most restrictive meaning of sexual instincts. This debasement is undoubtedly not intended but it represents a serious flaw in the poem. Chaucer (as we shall see) at times also debases some of his recurring terms but he does so with sharp awareness and for a moral purpose.

It would be tediously time-consuming to investigate all the stories in the *Confessio* in which Gower related either neutrally or sympathetically stories that in Christian terms involve the sins of either adultery or fornication; but there is one in each category that may be briefly mentioned. The first is the tale of the

Mainzer, "A Study of the Sources of Confessio amantis of John Gower" (1967; Bodley MS d.Phil.d. 4209), pp. 93–96.

17. Ed. G. Waitz, MGH, *Scriptorum*, XXII (1872), 153. Gower refers to the *Pantheon* in Book VIII, 1.272.

king and his steward's wife, borrowed from the *Roman des sept sages*.[18] The story is told as an exemplum against avarice in love and serves this purpose very well, for the steward, who is indignantly banished by the king, firstly has married his wife for her wealth and secondly procures her for the king's bed on payment of a hundred pounds. What is curious is that a happy ending is contrived by the king adulterously—indeed bigamously—marrying the steward's wife. The moral presuppositions of the story resemble the sentimental conventions of some of the best French or Anglo-Norman romances of the twelfth century, wherein there might be a rightness in mutual, requited love that annulled the obligations of a marriage that was wretched and loveless. Careful and sensitive writers, however, such as Chrétien de Troyes in *Cligés* and Marie de France in *Guigemar*, delay the marriage of the lovers, which provides the happy ending, until the first husband has died. Gower, concerned for the happiness of the well-meaning king and unhappy wife, provides a bigamous marriage to expunge the ugliness of the steward's actions. Sensitive moral judgment has manifestly deserted Gower at this point.

Yet more curious from the moral point of view is the story of Iphis and Anaxarete, borrowed from the *Metamorphoses* and told under the heading of sloth in love.[19] Despite its theoretical appropriateness as an exemplum, both Gower's choice of the story and his treatment are remarkable. According to Ovid, Anaxerete was a young man of low birth who fell irresistibly in love with Iphis, a princess. Unable to refrain, he made known his love, and Iphis, who was more cruel than the sea and more hard than iron or rock, did nothing but scorn and mock him. Anaxarete in despair committed suicide, and, as Iphis unemotionally watched the funeral procession, the gods turned her into a statue, so that she who in life had been stony-hearted, fittingly became all stone. This unimpressive story is given point in the *Metamorphoses* in that it is related by the god Vertumnus (disguised as

18. *Confessio amantis* V.2643–2825; *Le Roman des sept Sages de Rome*, ed. Leroux de Lincy (Paris, 1838), pp. 51–54. Mainzer, "Study," pp. 204–7, notes that Gower probably drew also upon English versions of this work.

19. *Confessio amantis* IV.3515–3684; *Metamorphoses* XIV.698–761.

an old woman) to Pomona, whose love he wishes to gain. As part of a seductor's persuasions the tale falls into place. Robbed of its cynical context and told as a warning against despondency in love, the story underwent radical changes.

In Gower's version the social positions of the protagonists are reversed: Iphis is now a maiden of humble birth, Anarexete a prince. Though Iphis no longer has any arrogant reasons to reject his love, she does so "to save and kepe hir wommanhiede"; nevertheless after Anarexete has committed suicide she distractedly reproaches herself for being the cause of his death and for not having shown *pite*, and the gods transform her into a statue out of compassion for her grief. The epitaph engraved upon the marble tablet at the sepulchre, however, points the Ovidian moral: women should take warning from this statue, which was once of flesh and blood and showed no pity. Gower tells the story with feeling but its moral outlines are extraordinarily fuzzy: his one attempt to sum up and strike a balance, "He was to neysshe and sche to hard," is inadequate. Gower's attempt here to sentimentalise the cynical, to sympathise with characters for whom the plot forbids sympathy, is a failure. "Moral" Gower would surely have recognised the material as intractable and would not have sought to transform it.

Gower's abstentions from received morality and his observations of human weakness which are often uncritically kind may reasonably be demonstrated by choosing appropriate examples. To attempt to prove the strength and subtlety of Chaucer's moral imagination within short space is difficult, for one of the most striking characteristics of his narrative technique is the effect of continuous moral probing and of a sure and delicate sense of decorum, which never fail unless Chaucer contrives a deliberate breach. It is only in his overt classical imitations, notably *The Legend of Good Women* and the Physician's tale and the Manciple's tale in *The Canterbury Tales*, that Chaucer tells stories that conflict with Christian moral principles in what is on the whole a serious, unquestioning way. But even in these he shows a moral awareness and moral scruples alien to Gower. In the telling of these tales he has in the first place a moral advantage over Gower. Since he is a poet highly conscious of genres and consequently of the different moral codes appropriate to them, he can suspend ordinary moral judgment simply by indicating a classical setting for his tales. The reference to Titus Livius as a source in the first line of the Physician's tale, for instance, inhibits us from asking whether a father had the right to kill his daughter. But so many genuine exempla had acquired the trappings of a Roman setting that this kind of moral indicator was not available in the *Confessio*.

In the second place in *The Legend of Good Women* Chaucer spatters the stories with oblique allusions and ironic hints which undercut the surface morality.[20] Two examples will illustrate this. Through their re-telling of classical stories Chaucer and Gower are committed to the non-Christian view that in some situations (particularly those in which a woman has been betrayed or violated) suicide is either apt or admirable. Though Gower ostensibly tells the story of Pyramus and Thisbe as a warning against suicide (as a part of homicide), the matter is lightly treated, and it would appear to be the hasty imprudence of a lover's suicide that is at issue. Other stories of suicide, including that of Lucretia, are manifestly untouched by the moral so faintly drawn and applied only to the suicide of unhappy lovers. When Chaucer, however, tells the story of Lucretia, the only example of suicide in *The Legend* which might seem legitimate in Christian terms (Jerome, for instance, had considered it so), Chaucer allusively hints that it was wrong:

> Nat only that these payens hire comende,
> But he that cleped is in oure legende
> The grete Austyn, hath gret compassioun
> Of this Lucresse, that starf at Rome toun.

Chaucer in other words slyly goes out of his way to refer us to the *De Civitate Dei* which furnished a *locus classicus* for the view

20. It has been plausibly argued that there are many odd, deflationary touches in *The Legend of Good Women* which reflect Chaucer's awareness of his own presentation of the characters as Love's martyrs with the traditional view of the *accessus* and *scholia* that it was Ovid's intention to blame 'foolish love'; for this argument see M. C. Edwards, "A Study of Six Characters in Chaucer's *Legend of Good Women* with reference to Medieval Scholia on Ovid's *Heroides*" (Oxford thesis, 1970; Bodley MS B.Litt.d. 1589).

that neither virgins nor wives should commit suicide after rape, with specific reference to the story of Lucretia.[21] Many or most of Chaucer's audience would of course not have recognised the significance of the mention of Augustine's name; but to anyone attuned to Chaucer's style his statement that pagans praised Lucretia and Augustine felt pity for her would rightly arouse the suspicion that Augustine pitied but did not approve. There is a more subtle moral conscience at work here than in Gower.

A slightly different example is that of Chaucer's moral good taste in his treatment of the story of Tereus and Progne. This story of horror had first been told by Ovid and then in twelfth-century romance style by Chrétien de Troyes.[22] Chaucer, recognising that this story could not be told with lightness of touch and as an illustration of the sufferings of helpless women adopts the clever strategy of lapsing into a kind of mumbling reluctance to tell it and indeed stops short. Gower, however, persists to the end, unaware that some softening of detail will scarcely make Ovid's account of Philomela's vengeance (she kills her son and feeds his flesh to Tereus) any the less appalling, whilst his excusing of her in that she was "as who seith, mad / Of wo," is a pathetically insufficient moral reaction. Milton was later to use a comparable story, that of the vengeance that Atreus took upon Thyestes, as a metaphor for the Fall: the eating of the fruit was a "Thyestean banquet." The morally horrific was of course within

21. Robert W. Frank, Jr., *Chaucer and the Legend of Good Women* (Cambridge, Mass., 1972), p. 97 and notes 7 and 8, has argued strongly for Chaucer's entirely eulogistic presentation of Lucretia. Whilst the evidence of note 8 is important, however, the argument of note 7, i.e. that Chaucer derived Augustine's name from the *Gesta Romanorum*, is unconvincing. *Oure legende* is undoubtedly the *Legenda aurea*, in which as part of an etymological exposition of the name the term *magnificus* is used (cf. edition of Th. Graesse, [Leipzig, 1850], p. 549). Either *grete* is a translation of *magnificus* (it appears in Caxton's translation) or *magnus* may be a manuscript variant. Like the appellation "the grete" the statement that Augustine had "gret compassioun" of Lucretia is not to be found in the *Gesta Romanorum*. The *De Civitate Dei* does, however, provide a source in that two chapters before that on Lucretia, Augustine says of virgins who committed suicide after being raped, "Ac per hoc et quae se occiderunt, ne quicquam huius modi paterentur, quis humanus affectus eis nolit ignosci?," I.xvii, CCSL, XLVII, p. 18.

22. Chrétien de Troyes, *Philomena*, ed. C. de Boer (Paris, 1909).

Milton's range; it was beyond Chaucer's, but he knew it and through mock contortions of authorial boredom evaded the issue; only Gower, unaware of the morally perilous nature of his material, stolidly and weakly completed the story.

Chaucer's serious treatment of love and of its sinful complement lust can best be illustrated from three of the most famous parts of *The Canterbury Tales*, the Merchant's tale, the Franklin's tale and the Wife of Bath's prologue. The depiction of lust in the Merchant's tale is extraordinarily forceful and for Chaucer forthright. In the Middle Ages it was an accepted view of canon lawyers and other moralists that a husband could commit adultery with his wife. This is a view unlikely to command immediate acceptance in the present age and it is therefore the more remarkable that the Merchant's tale can instantly persuade one of the truth of this. The story normally used by medieval writers to illustrate this doctrine was that of Tobit: Gower tells it as an illustration of the virtue of chastity as a point of policy for princes.[23] But the biblical narrative of how Sarah's first six husbands had their necks wrung by the demon Asmodaeus because on the wedding night they approached Sarah lecherously is too bizarre to be morally convincing. But the union of January and May is plainly an instance of this teaching, and that this point was in Chaucer's mind can be seen from the way in which he makes January deny it, "A man may do no synne with his wyf," adding a preposterous reversal of the persuasive image, used in the Parson's tale, that a man can sin with his wife just as he can harm himself with his own knife.[24] When January asserts this to be impossible his folly is unmistakable: there are few commoner accidents.

In the first part of the tale in which Chaucer draws eclectically from many works for arguments for and against marriage a dominant source for the praise of marriage is the wedding service itself. The service is concerned to assert the dignity and significance of the sacrament: marriage was the first sacrament instituted for man and it was instituted by God himself; it makes

23. *Confessio amantis* VII.5307–81: for discussion cf. Kelly, *Love and Marriage*, pp. 275–78.
24. Robinson, ed., *Works*, p. 256.

man and wife one flesh; above all, as the special nuptial blessing (reserved for first marriages only) describes, it is a figure of the relationship between Christ and the church.[25] The marriage between January and May, however, is clearly an outrageous travesty of the meaning of the sacrament. Contrary to Chaucer's narrative custom, the religious ceremony is itself described though the contemptuous style draws attention to the discrepancy between the mysterious meaning of the service and the intentions of the participants. The marriage feast too is described and also mocked by the apparently auspicious presence of Venus, though its inauspiciousness is also indicated by the casual manner in which Venus, lyrically dancing before the married couple, wounds another man with passion for the bride.

This lengthy description of Christian rite, secular pomp, and pagan allegory focuses the reader's attention upon the idea of marriage. That January is a lecherous old man who degrades this idea by using the sacrament as a means of buying himself a young wife is entirely plain. It may not, however, be quite so evident that May enters into the marriage in almost as tarnished a state: it is only gradually that one becomes aware of a conspicuous omission in the narrative, namely the lack of a statement that May was married against her will. Parental compulsion is of course a stock theme in the *chansons de mal mariées*, whilst in one of Chaucer's immediate sources for the earlier part of the tale, Boccaccio's *Ameto*, the nymph is married against her will to an old man though she longs for (and later obtains) a young and beautiful husband.[26] In such a highly-wrought work it is exceptionally unlikely that Chaucer intended this meaning but forgot to insert the required mention of it. This understanding is confirmed by the narrator's twice-repeated refusal to tell us what May thought. This rejection of authorial omniscience seems heavy-handed if its only point is to indicate

25. *Sarum Manuale*, ed. A. Jefferies Collins, Henry Bradshaw Society 91 (1958), 44–59; *Manuale et processionale ad usum insignis Ecclesiae Eboracensis*, Surtees Society 63 (1875), 24–40.

26. *Sources and Analogues of Chaucer's Canterbury Tales*, ed. W. F. Bryan and Germaine Dempster (London, 1941), p. 339; for the full story see the same work published under the title *La Comedia delle ninfe fiorentine* in Giovanni Boccaccio, *Tutte le opere*, ed. Vittore Branca, II (Milan, 1964), 772–81.

May's maidenly revulsion at January's obscene embraces: but it
is sinisterly acute if intended to suggest that May had cold-
bloodedly made a bargain and that what she felt was a calculated
acquiescence in the price she had to pay for all the legal documents conferring January's property upon her, documents so
abundant that it would have taken the narrator too long to enu-
merate them. It may be worth noting that the first time that the
narrator reveals May's feelings is when she is said to feel "pitee"
for Damian, in a context where the word can be nothing but a
euphemism, and where it is almost instantly repeated in one of
Chaucer's most beautiful recurring lines, "Lo, pitee renneth
soone in gentil herte," but this time occurring in a conjunction
which makes the whole passage a shady *double entendre*.

Whilst the nastiness of the relationship of January and May
and its almost sacrilegious violation of the significance of Christian marriage is exposed in a variety of ways in the Merchant's
tale, its most brilliant expression is through the much-discussed
image of the enclosed garden. This garden has often been associated with the Garden of Eden, the *hortus conclusus* of the *Song of
Songs*, and the garden of love described in many medieval romances.[27] Whilst none of these associations can be excluded it is
the last two that are the most telling. That January's garden is
intended to recall the *hortus conclusus* is made clear by January's
invitation to May to come forth ("The gardyn is enclosed al
aboute") in a speech redolent of the erotic imagery of the *Song of
Songs*. But in the Middle Ages this was reserved for its mystical
meanings, the love between Christ and the church or the love
between Christ and the Blessed Virgin. January's use of it therefore once more indicates that which his marriage so vilely presumes to be a figure of, whilst at the same time stressing that this
garden is also a travesty of the enclosed garden of the Blessed
Virgin's virginity. The reversal of the allegorical significance of
the garden of the *Song of Songs* is made addedly obscene by the
adjunct of 'the smale wyket', naturalistically required of course,

27. Cf. Kenneth Kee, "Two Chaucerian Gardens," *Mediaeval Studies* 23
(1961), 154–62. An association has also been made with Susannah's garden
(Alfred L. Kellogg, "Susannah and the *Merchant's Tale*," *Speculum* 35 [1960]),
275–79, but this is less likely.

but recalling an image often associated with the *hortus conclusus*, that of the *porta clausa* of *Ezekiel*, 41.2 through which no man will pass, but the Lord has passed through it.[28] Through this gate pass both January and Damian.

The blasphemous parody of marriage is thus symbolised by the blasphemously obscene garden. But the garden could also be called obscene without reference to religious imagery. Its disagreeableness is at first hinted at in the superficially innocuously rhetorical statement that Priapus, though he was god of gardens, could not have described its beauty. Priapus, however, was also the ithyphallic deity whose statue had a prominent place in the temple of Venus in *The Parlement of Foules*.[29] That it is this suppressed aspect of Priapus that is paramount in the Merchant's tale becomes plain a few lines further on where it is revealed that January had devised this garden as a place for lovemaking. This transference of the conjugal relationship from the marriage-bed to the garden again emphasises its unnaturalness: unnatural, not because medieval poets invariably restrained the union of lovers to the bedchamber, but because the garden setting was reserved for love which was most natural, tender, and beautiful. The scene in *Cligés*, for instance, where Cligés and Fenice make their couch in a walled garden, lying on the sward beneath a tree in full leaf and blossom, is an idyllic scene of romance. The sweetness and living naturalness of the garden reflects the quality of their love.[30] The arrangement in the Merchant's tale is the exact reverse of this, and to emphasise the point Chaucer gives little description of the garden. What the reader chiefly remembers of it are the two necessary props for

28. For these images and their association see Yrjö Hirn, *The Sacred Shrine* (London, 1958), pp. 311–12, and Anselm Salzer, *Die Sinnbilder und Beiworte Mariens* (reprint, Darmstadt, 1967), pp. 15–16 and 26–28.

29. Lines 253–56, and cf. notes p. 795. The association of Priapus with an obscene statue was probably as common in the Middle Ages as it was in antiquity. The tradition could have been transmitted, for instance, by the *Etymologies* of Isidore or by Servius's note on *Georgics* IV.111; for the latter references see Hans Herter, *De Priapo*, Religionsgeschichtliche Versuche und Vorarbeiten 23 (Giessen, 1932), 77.

30. Cf. "Les romans de Chrétien de Troyes." Edités d'après la copie de Quiot. T. 2. *Cligés*, ll. 6305–36, publié par A. Micha, CFMA (Paris, 1957), pp. 192–93.

the action: the bush behind which Damian lurks and the pear-tree into which May and Damian so grotesquely climb.

Whilst the emphasis in the Merchant's tale is upon the corrupt nature of the marriage, it is equally shown that the supposedly courtly affair between May and Damian is equally vitiated. In contrast, for instance, to some of the lays of Marie de France, such as *Yonec* or *Guigemar*, the presence of an old and jealous husband does not release the young wife into a love that is ardent but innocent.[31] These lays of Marie provide a sure moral backcloth for the relationship between the young lovers in the Merchant's tale for Marie's lays reveal a very sure, delicate, and moral sensitivity whilst not conforming precisely to traditional Christian morality. Marie allows a romantic, aesthetically satisfying escape from the kind of marriage that January procures, but in the Merchant's tale Chaucer deliberately blocks this escape. The relationship between wife and young lover is as gross and distasteful as the relationship between husband and wife.

There is of course no moral doctrine in the Merchant's tale with which Gower would not have agreed. Not only are passages in praise of marriage scattered through the *Confessio* but Gower's French *Traitié* also praises it in specifically Christian terms. The difference between Gower and Chaucer lies in their illustration of the doctrine. Gower in the *Traitié* summarises briefly many of the tales told at leisure in the *Confessio;*[32] but sensational tales from Ovid, such as that of Tereus, are too outlandish to convince the reader that the dignity of marriage should not be violated. In contrast Chaucer has contrived a notable image of vice, perhaps more notable than any in Spenser.[33]

31. For the texts see Marie de France, *Lais*, ed. A. Ewart (Oxford, 1952), pp. 82–96 and 3–25, and for illuminating commentary Ernest Hoepffner, *Les Lais de Marie de France* (Paris, 1935), pp. 72–94.

32. "Traitié pur essampler les amantz marietz," *French Works*, ed. C. C. Macaulay (Oxford, 1899), pp. 379–92. In this poem, stories such as that of Mundus and Paulina (p. 386) are briefly re-told without sympathy.

33. It is certainly far more morally powerful than Spenser's imitation of it in the episode of Malbecco and Hellenore in the *Faerie Queen* III.xi, where the transformation of Malbecco into some kind of loathsome bird, personifying jealousy, is more melodramatic but not as insidiously horrible an end as January's degraded and deluded exit from the garden.

The strong element of comedy in the tale has the effect of puri-
fying it from any prurient effect, but in no way undoes its black
analysis of a polluted marriage which no conventions of time or
place block off from daily life.

An attempt to demonstrate that Chaucer's narrative poetry
is controlled by a very fine, analytical moral imagination is
difficult, for Chaucer's best tales do not offer a flat, uncon-
troversial surface as do Gower's. With the exception of the Pardoner's tale, the Merchant's tale is the only one dealing with vice
of which one could firmly assert that it was not formed by an
imagination always guided by a kindly understanding of human
weakness nor by a sensibility which always preferred to sympathise with the sinner than to condemn the sin.[34] Critical interpretations of the Franklin's tale and of the Wife of Bath's prologue are not likely to yield such consent: an examination of
them is nevertheless useful in that both of them manifestly turn
upon crucial moral issues and in both of them Chaucer made
additions which clarify his moral intention.

The Franklin's tale is often seen as an idyllic little narrative,
important within the design of *The Canterbury Tales* in that it
both resolves the marriage debate (presumably an artificial issue
which pre-occupies the pilgrims but would have been taken
light-heartedly by Chaucer's audience) and also provides an ide-
alisation of marriage which complements the savage examination
of it in the Merchant's tale. In order to achieve these effects
Chaucer has handled the story and characterisation in a far more
sensitive way than Boccaccio had done in the *Filocolo*. But by his
more sensitive telling of the story Chaucer has allowed a host of
moral questions to arise: should Arveragus have decided that
Dorigen should commit adultery in order to keep her promise?

34. This is not the first essay to find the Merchant's tale moral in intent;
cf. for instance the excellent analysis leading to this conclusion by E. Talbot
Donaldson, "The Effect of the *Merchant's Tale*" reprinted in *Speaking of Chaucer*
(London, 1970), pp. 30–45, but it is perhaps the first to do so without some
betrayal of astonishment. I have throughout avoided the controversy of
whether or not the tale was originally intended for another speaker: this would
be relevant only if anyone were to argue that the tale could not be moral
because the Merchant was not a moral person: this would seem to me in itself
an unacceptable type of argument.

Should Dorigen have made the promise in the first place and in the second place was she bound to keep it? Had Aurelius a right to assume that a promise had been made and to regard it as binding? Since the story in the *Filocolo* is an example in a *demande d'amour* some of these questions are implicit in the tale in order that they may later be extracted and analysed, but the manner of the telling does not permit them to become live issues in the course of the narrative;[35] other questions, such as the rightness of Arveragus's decision, are ignored by Boccaccio, but are unavoidable in a reading of the Franklin's tale.

Obviously the answers to all these questions turn upon the nature of Dorigen's promise. On this issue Flametta in the *Filocolo* argues lucidly: as a married woman the lady had no right to make this promise, and, though she did, it was null since it contradicted her marriage vow; furthermore Tarolfo (Aurelius) was not notably generous, since his generosity consisted solely in restraining his libidinous desires and that a man should do anyway.[36] It may be added that outside the world of romance Dorigen's promise was not binding for another reason, namely that a promise to commit a sinful act should not be kept: this was the common teaching of the church.[37] Chaucer, as he wrote the tale, dealt skilfully with this awkward moral problem, namely that for the sake of the plot Dorigen's promise must be regarded as binding, yet Christianity, commonsense, and his source all indicated that it was not. His revisions show a mind still at work upon the moral problems that he had created by adapting Boccaccio's brief and cynically told story to a gentler, more idealistic moral ambience.

For a modern audience perhaps the most difficult element to accept is Arveragus's decision that his wife keep her word by committing adultery. It is of course possible to see this as part of a pattern in *The Canterbury Tales*. The lecherous and jealous January is horribly possessive of his wife's body; the noble and

35. Giovanni Boccaccio, *Tutte le opere*, ed. Vittore Branca, I (Milan, 1967), 396–410.
36. Ibid., p. 408.
37. E.g. *Summa Theologica* II.ii, q. 89, a. 7, and Robert Mannyng, *Handlyng Synne*, lines 2805–2902, EETS, 119 (London, 1901–3), 99–102.

generous-minded Arveragus is too liberal. Between these two extremes there is an unstated mean which a medieval audience familiar with an Aristotelian ethical scheme would have recognised as existing.[38] Furthermore Chaucer sought to gain sympathy for Arveragus in his decision by having him burst into tears at the moment that he makes it. The agonising cost is plain. Nevertheless the fact that modern misgivings are not an anachronistic reaction is shown by Chaucer's insertion of lines 1493–98, preserved only in Ellesmere and one other manuscript:[39]

> Paraventure an heep of yow, ywis,
> Wol holden hym a lewed man in this
> That he wol putte his wyf in jupartie.
> Herkneth the tale er ye upon hire crie.
> She may have bettre fortune than yow semeth;
> And whan that ye han herd the tale, demeth.

Chaucer here gives his narrator a blustering tone and inconsequential argument: But this dramatically uneasy attempt to deflect judgment reassures the reader that Chaucer is aware of the perilous nature of the material that he is handling.

A similar moral tact is seen in the handling of Dorigen. From the start Chaucer had presented her more sympathetically than Boccaccio had done. Long space—indeed unduly long space—had been given to her thoughts of suicide (in the *Filocolo* these had been briefly expressed to her husband) and her condition for accepting Aurelius as a lover had been made to seem more human and natural, less sophisticatedly capricious, than in Boccaccio. Nevertheless Chaucer's revisions show that he was not satisfied that these modifications were sufficient and he therefore made two additions affecting her, both of them

38. For Chaucer's reference to the mean in *The Legend of Good Women*, F 164–65, and Kelly, *Love and Marriage*, p. 285.

39. John M. Manly and Edith Rickert, *The Text of the Canterbury Tales* (Chicago and London, reprint 1967) II, 308. Their reference to Ellesmere "picking up" lines 1493–98 presumably implies a belief that these lines were added in the margin of the exemplar of Ellesmere, and it seems reasonable to suppose that like lines 1541–44 and lines 1000–1006 (on which see following footnotes) this was an addition made by Chaucer.

slightly misplaced in most manuscripts and therefore in the familiar printed texts. One is lines 1541–44 (which should follow line 1550)[40] in which the narrator by warning other women to be beware by Dorigen's example by implication rebukes her:

> But every wyf be war of hire beheeste!
> On Dorigen remembreth, atte leeste.

Since the tale turns upon the fragile romance convention that an oath must in all circumstances be kept, no specific disavowal of this can be made within the story. Chaucer, however, has taken the opportunity to condemn the initial giving of the promise, as the story permits and morality demands: in the revised text it is only after this that the audience may be given the assurance that Dorigen and Arveragus lived happily ever after.

The other and more remarkable addition consists of lines 1001–5, which should follow line 998:[41]

> For wel I woot that it shal never bityde.
> Lat swiche folies out of youre herte slyde.
> What deyntee sholde a man han in his lyf
> For to go love another mannes wyf,
> That hath hir body whan so that hym liketh?

Even in its present slightly illogical position this passage is remarkable in bluntly laying bare the unromantic aspect of any romanticised adultery. In its proper place, however, it makes yet plainer that the promise was made, as the narrator says, "in pley," for instantly after making it, Dorigen demonstrates incontrovertibly that the keeping of it, even from Aurelius's point of view, must be without happiness or decency. This is in effect an explicit statement of what Aurelius is later to learn.

It might seem that this last addition would cast an unpleasing shadow over Aurelius's conduct but Chaucer had already contrived to absolve him from responsibility. In the *Filocolo* Tarolfo recognises the lady's answer as a rebuff, but nevertheless sets off to try to fulfil the condition and resolves neither to rest nor to return until he has done so. In the Franklin's tale Aurelius's mind is fixed more upon the impossibility of

40. For the argument that these lines are an addition and misplaced in many manuscripts see Manly and Rickert, *Text*, II, 314.
41. See previous footnote.

the task set than of the implied rejection. He falls therefore into a fit of love-sickness, and having elaborately called upon the gods for help, helplessly swoons; his brother (a newly invented character) puts him to bed, where he remains wretchedly for two whole years. It is the brother, distressed by Aurelius's incurable sickness, who devises the plan of seeking help from the Orleans clerk and who accompanies Aurelius upon this quest. Here one can see Chaucer doing simply and on a small scale what he had done intricately and on a large scale in *Troilus and Criseyde*. In the latter he had shifted responsibility for the consummation of the love-affair from Criseyde to Pandarus (and ironically from Pandarus to Fortune). In the Franklin's tale he neatly shifts responsibility from Aurelius to a hitherto non-existent brother: Aurelius himself is too sick with love to take any initiative. Of course there remains a strong moral implication in the tale that adulterous love is wrong. Dorigen rightly shows no *pite* to Aurelius although he appeals for it sincerely, and Aurelius, offered a woman who comes weeping and with her husband's consent, apparently learns to "unlove." But though the moral is plain, Chaucer has contrived that the characters should be guilty of nothing except a little foolishness.

The Wife of Bath's Prologue has often been taken to show Chaucer at his most tolerant, genial, and kindly: indeed there is a tendency to talk of the Prologue as though it were the medieval forerunner of Molly Bloom's soliloquy. But the Wife of Bath is not characterised by a vital, spontaneous expression of female sexuality: on the contrary she is made to consider her sexual capacity as a commercial asset. There is evidence elsewhere in medieval literature and also in historical records that a young woman might marry a prosperous old husband, her wealth then enabling her in her almost inevitable widowhood to marry a young husband.[42] Such a situation depicted in literature would normally arouse censure.[43] If the Wife of Bath escapes censure,

42. This pattern has been observed in the transmission of the land-holdings of peasants, cf. R. J. Faith, "Peasant Families and Inheritance Customs in Medieval England," *Agricultural History Review* 14 (1966), 91. I am indebted to Miss Barbara Harvey for this reference.

43. Cf. *Piers Plowman*, ed. W. W. Skeat (reprint, Oxford, 1924), B. IX, lines 160–63, where the abuse of marrying a widow for her property is linked with that of an old man marrying a young woman.

[243

it is not because Chaucer has made such conduct seem a tolerable human failing, but rather because the Wife of Bath has accumulated riches by marrying not one old husband but four. This unrealistic excess turns her into a grotesque figure, far larger than life, and one who therefore eludes any simple moral response. The Wife of Bath's venal use of sex is further accentuated by her demanding of actual payments before rendering the "marriage debt," the latter phrase expressing one of the less congenial elements in the medieval view of marriage and one which Chaucer pointedly makes characteristic of the Wife of Bath's apologia for her life. It was Chaucer's first intention to underline the theme of the relationship between sex and money by having the Wife tell a fabliau in which a calculating woman should both cuckold her husband and contrive to make him pay for the cuckolding. In terms of narrative diversity Chaucer's rearrangement whereby this tale was relegated to the Shipman and the Wife of Bath with brilliant unexpectedness provided with a debased romance rather than a fabliau was superb. But it carried with it a danger, namely that one or two touches, such as the passage in which the Wife recalls the past with courageous nostalgia, might seem to colour the whole, and that the reader would carry away with him the remembrance of the beautiful, though in context inapposite line, "Allas! allas! that evere love was synne!" rather than, for instance, the brutal grossness with which the Wife responded to her husband's reproaches to her for seeking a lover, "Ye shul have queynte right ynogh et eve."

That Chaucer was aware of the danger can be seen from his addition of lines 619–26 to the text:[44]

> Yet have I Martes mark upon my face,
> And also in another privee place.
> For God so wys be my savacioun,
> I ne loved nevere by no discrecioun,
> But evere folwede myn appetit,
> Al were he short, or long, or blak, or whit;
> I took no kep, so that he liked me,
> How poore he was, ne eek of what degree.

44. Manly and Rickert, *Text*, II, 191–92. Of the five additions there listed this is the only one which substantially changes the moral tenor of the Prologue.

As we have seen, an inevitable corollary in literature of a young woman marrying an old husband was that she would take a young lover, and that the Wife of Bath had done so even more than once had been indicated in the General Prologue, where she had had five husbands, "Withouten oother compaignye in youthe," and had been implied throughout her own Prologue. But this explicit statement of total promiscuity has a coarsening and alienating effect. Chaucer has used the same device here as in the Merchant's tale. Even if a woman has married an old husband of her own choice, there may still be some residual sympathy for her if she takes a young lover, but not, as with May, if she copulates with him up a tree, and not, as with the Wife of Bath, if she takes innumerable lovers without discrimination. Within context of course this addition does not make the Wife of Bath a repulsive figure but it does counteract any tendencies to take a romantic or sentimental view of her.

If the Wife of Bath is compared with her (and May's) descendents in Dunbar's *Tua Mariit Women and the Wedow*, one can see why as a literary figure she remains attractive despite the repulsiveness of her actions. For Dunbar's figures have become degraded by their experiences whilst the Wife of Bath remains triumphantly undegenerate. But the explanation is surely not that Chaucer thought that a mercenary or promiscuous use of sex would not degrade but rather that as a poet he had a rare and happy gift, namely that he could touch pitch without being defiled. In the *Tua Mariit Women* the effect of indulgence in repellent detail and the unmistakably prurient tone induce disgust but deflect the leader's judgment from moral precision, whilst in the Wife of Bath's Prologue the generally wholesome tone enables the sin to stand out undisguised. In Gower compassion for the sinner sometimes spills over into a blurring of the sin. This does not happen in Chaucer's poetry, and the Wife of Bath's Prologue in particular would be a lesser achievement if Chaucer had not succeeded in combining an amused sympathy for this highly literary though seemingly lifelike figure with a recognition that she exemplifies to a heightened and grotesque degree a misuse of female sexuality and marriage.

PART THREE

I 2

The Lord of the Rings as Romance

Derek S. Brewer

EMMANUEL COLLEGE, CAMBRIDGE

I

My argument will be circular: both that to understand *The Lord of the Rings* we have to understand the true nature of romance; and that romance can be understood as the kind of thing that *The Lord of the Rings* is: a familiar dilemma in literary studies, which, like life itself, require that we make an initial leap of faith, or at least, of sympathy. The popularity of *The Lord of the Rings* shows that many sensible people uncorrupted by literary prejudice find the jump easy to make; but there are also those who with the best will in the world cannot give themselves to the work. The reason in many cases seems to me to be that they do not recognise that *The Lord of the Rings* is not a novel. Novel and romance are often taken nowadays to be much the same kind of thing, except that romance is inferior; it is taken to be debilitating, unrealistic wish-fulfilment, or abstract fantasy, whereas the novel shows life as it truly is, in all its concrete tragic elements.

The contrary seems to me true: that romance and novel are essentially opposed forms, and that they tend to represent dif-

[249

ferent kinds of outlook, just as they employ different types of literary device, and of course arouse different kinds of expectation. To explore these differences fully would take a book that has yet to be written[1]—Tolkien apart—but some brief comment on them may help to clarify some observations on *The Lord of the Rings*.

Novel and romance of course resemble each other in being extended narratives, but in this respect they resemble epic poetry and history as well. The romance appears later than epic and history in classical antiquity, if we regard as the first romances those deeply implausible late Greek and Latin rhetorical fictions of love and adventure, with happy endings, which seem to have developed in the second and first centuries B.C. (though the examples are from the second or third centuries A.D.) and which modern critics miscall novels.[2] In both defence and attack of such works we see the same conflicting attitudes as exist over *The Lord of the Rings*. One might go further back into antiquity and find something of the prototype of romance in *The Odyssey*. Northrop Frye has made the characteristically happy distinction between those who are naturally *Iliad* critics, and those who are naturally *Odyssey* critics—critics of tragedy, or of its natural opposite, romance.[3] The latter are nowadays a small and unfashionable band of critics, though I suspect they represent the vast majority of common readers who take pleasure in *The Lord of the Rings*. The Greek and Latin romances have many points of interest, and one very notable point is that for all their apparatus of educated rhetoric, and their refusal to take themselves quite seriously on the surface as plausible fictions—or *because* of these characteristics—they have close relations with myth, folktale, dream, and religious cult—with the world of Psyche, indeed, as in the latest, most famous, example.[4]

1. Though I still have hopes.
2. See, for example, *Three Greek Romances*, trans. with an introduction by Moses Hadas (New York, 1953); P. G. Walsh, *The Roman Novel* (Cambridge, 1970). In this, and the notes that follow, I can make no attempt at a full range of reference.
3. N. Frye, *A Natural Perspective* (New York, 1965). I have slightly adapted this, since what he and the Middle Ages call comedy seems to me more appropriately to be called romance.
4. The story of Psyche in *The Golden Ass* by Apuleius: cf. e.g. R. Mer-

After the Dark Ages romance is resumed in the West most vigorously by Chrétien de Troyes, whose true greatness is only slowly coming to be recognised and explored by criticism. We are slowly becoming aware of the profound significances that Chrétien is capable of evoking through the symbolic patterns of his stories. In so great a writer we can also find, as so often in romance generally, a sharp local realism and a subtle or open comedy, but these are subordinate, either as representation of the world of natural appearances, or as mockery, to the deeper, more inward, significances. Chrétien makes particularly effective use of the theme of the Quest, by a young man, who proves himself, and wins his love, and establishes himself in society. Such romances are the literary equivalent of what the anthropologists call *rites de passage*. The characteristic *passage* of romance is from untried youth to adulthood, emergence from (or rejection of) the rule of parents, then establishment of the self, and of a stable relationship with the beloved. The theme is transition, and therefore the natural subject-matter of romance, especially at this period, is adventure and love. This is why it has a happy ending, because the nature of the transition expressed by the *rite de passage* is to come successfully through to the other side. The happy ending is imaged as marriage, because marriage at once signalises union with the beloved and establishment in society. The underlying substance of the transition is very often conflict with parents and the discovery of sexuality, but this can take many forms, and we note again that this is the substance of much dream, folktale, and myth. A very interesting variant on the theme in the ancient Judaic tradition is the story of the young David. He proves himself by killing Goliath (who at one level may be regarded as a hostile father-figure—as may Saul himself in some aspects). David is accepted by the people and indeed marries the princess (Micah), as in all good folktale and romance. But in ancient Hebrew society love was not associated with sex as it came to be in the western European Middle Ages, and the loving relationship which David establishes is not with a woman but with Jonathan. Nor can anyone imagine David as a sexual pervert. Those who have not lived in warrior societies

kelbach, "Eros and Psyche," *Philologus* 102 (1958), 103–16, and R. Merkelbach, *Roman und Mysterium in der Antike* (Munich, 1962).

(and it is worth remembering that both Tolkien's generation and mine have been unusual among scholars in having done so) may easily underestimate the deep attachment that may exist between comrades in arms. Love does not need sex. The attachment between Frodo and his Company, and especially between him and Sam, must have been paralleled many times in the two World Wars.

Just as the passage from youth to adulthood may take many forms, we may note that of the two great passages of our lives, into adulthood, and into death, romance may also take the second passage as its subject. The story of Cupid and Psyche may draw some of its power from its confrontation with death. The other notable secular attempts at the same creative confrontation are Shakespeare's last plays, truly called romances. Nor can the Resurrection itself be forgotten here. We may look ahead a little at this point and suggest that whatever else *The Lord of the Rings* is ultimately "about", it is certainly "about" death, as Tolkien himself said, in the BBC Television programme about him.

To return to Chrétien, he must be seen as attempting a representation of the individual emerging into the world, which is seen from the point of view of the hero. In this sense his romances are representations of a dynamic psychic progress, but they are not psychological studies in our sense, nor studies of the "world" as it appears to that abstract observer for whom, since the seventeenth century, works of fiction have increasingly been written. It is worth remarking that the weakest chapter in that stimulating book, Erich Auerbach's *Mimesis,* is the one criticising Chrétien.[5] Once again, it is for the usual reason that romance is condemned: because it does not offer that impersonal close verbal representation of material "social" "reality", offered to an unlocated observer outside the story, which it was Auerbach's purpose to trace as it developed in literature, and which was for him, as nowadays for so many critics, the only criterion of literary worth.

That representation of things "as they are", which goes deeper than "realism," for it concerns deeply materialistic cause and effect, is best called naturalism. It began to develop in the Italian Renaissance with Humanist thinking and it eventually

5. Erich Auerbach, *Mimesis,* trans. W. R. Trask (Princeton, 1953).

linked up with, if it was not part of, the scientific revolution of the seventeenth century which led directly to the Industrial Revolution and the technological world we know today. In literary matters we can see this tremendous cultural change imaged very early in the natural ambivalence with which men of a realist bent regarded romance—in England, most notably, Chaucer.[6] Ariosto in the early sixteenth century in Italy is another. The Humanist picaresque novel—truly so called, for its naturalist basis—in Spain in the mid-sixteenth century is perhaps the first clear expression[7] of thoroughgoing naturalism, which reaches its first climax, and demonstrated opposition to romance, in *Don Quixote*. *Don Quixote* itself, being parodic, is not a novel, but it so to say shows that the novel is not only possible, but necessary. It is very much a product of Humanist, or as it is better and more precisely termed, Neoclassical, thought and feeling, which ultimately produces the novel in the eighteenth century, and along with it a closely literalistic ideal of literary language, which rejects such romance modes as hyperbole, variable style, comedy mixed with seriousness, sententious wisdom, and the whole apparatus of rhetoric.[8] From the late seventeenth century onwards Neoclassical naturalism has dominated literary ideals notwithstanding isolated protests, as by Blake, or Hurd, or uneasy practitioners, like Dickens, or the subjectivism of the Romantics which did not in fact challenge the dominant naturalism.

Of course the human needs represented by romance always continue, and literary or sub-literary forms emerged, as romance was displaced, which tried to satisfy the need. It is surely no mere co-incidence that the fairy tale appears in the late seventeenth century when romance as a literary form dies.[9] Nor is

6. I have tried to suggest something of this ambivalence and its roots in Chaucer in my Gollancz Memorial Leture, 1974, *Towards a Chaucerian Poetic* (Oxford, 1975).

7. A. A. Parker, *Literature and the Delinquent* (Edinburgh, 1967), especially pp. 5–6, 20.

8. I have argued this in more detail in "Some Observations on the Development of Literalism and Verbal Criticism," *Poetica*, Sanseido, Tokyo, 2 (1974), 71–95.

9. See *The Classic Fairytales*, ed. with introductions by P. and I. Opie (London, 1974).

Tolkien's interest in the fairy tale an arbitrary accident of taste. Nor is the contemptuous tone that has become attached to the expression "fairy tale" an accident, any more than is the use of the word "romance" to mean a lie which developed in the late seventeenth century.

So much for an historical sketch to account for some of our literary concepts. At the present time, we may finally remark, we are, as *The Lord of the Rings* constantly re-iterates, at the end of a period. Nothing seems clearer than that a major cultural phase, dominated by a special quality of science, and in art by a broadly Neoclassical view of order and imitation, began roughly in the sixteenth century and closed roughly in the first half of the twentieth. It had its beginnings before, and much of it continues fragmentarily now. But that Age of the World is ended. *The Lord of the Rings* paradoxically (and of course symbolically) laments its passing while in its own nature it shows that it has passed. To summarise, the novel is, as art, the dominant literary form of that Age. It is distinguished by its self-enclosed form and its aim to create naturalistic illusion or mimesis (the novel of the seventies may be a different matter). *The Lord of the Rings* is in fact, like its progenitors, the romances of William Morris, much affected by this novelistic aim, where Tolkien's genius is weakest. But romance, in itself, and as found in *The Lord of the Rings*, is intrinsically different. If it "imitates" anything it imitates the movements of the imagination in search of its own integrity, the movements of the will, the search for love, for personal relationship with others, the passage from childhood to adulthood, the confrontation with death. Of course the events of romance are similar in their general nature to those events in the world that we know or have heard of; and the people who take part in them are roughly, or schematically, like those we meet or might meet; and we need to be able to "believe" in the story. But we do not need to believe that the story is likely in ordinary life for us to be deeply engaged in it, to be moved and illuminated, any more than we need such belief in our own dreams to be shaken by them, or in Shakespeare's plays, or in Grimm's fairy tales, or many other literary works, to recognise their importance to us. The "reality" pointed at is not that of ordinary appearances.

Romance, or as we should perhaps say from now on, romances, for there are many different kinds, tend to develop their own rules, to create their own world. Characters may well be simple, schematic, and of that world, not ours; events often have a broader sweep and may be exaggerated in scale as the language may be hyperbolical. The setting may be remote in space or time, or frankly invented. All sorts of conventions may be different. In a good romance we are in a world closely associated with dream, folktale, myth, and which has the same spontaneous appeal to the natural understanding, uncorrupted by Neoclassical literary criticism, as have those experiences. Like them, too, romance is susceptible of literary interpretation into more rationalistic, if by definition less powerful, terms, provided we are patient and sympathetic. To put it another way, the value of dream, folktale, myth, and romance, consists in their symbolic power, whereby they engage the mind and feelings on several different levels at once; generating propositions (to put it once again in rationalistic terms) about many aspects of life apparently unrelated to the central fiction. The capacity to create and respond to symbolic systems is one of the main elements in human relationship and individual human existence. The claim for *The Lord of the Rings* is simply that it constitutes a fiction which, with whatever weaknesses and shortcomings, has symbolic power.[10] And this power corresponds to human needs and desires.

II

It is natural that the archetypal romance theme should be the Quest, which is both search and transition. The Quest images so much of what we experience. It is easy for our imaginations to translate space into time, passage over ground to passage through time. Our burgeoning (and recurring) needs and desires are easily imaged as a long seeking for journey's end, either as an achievement in itself, or as a sought-after person, or

10. It may be worth emphasising that by symbolism here I do not mean that direct correspondence between unreal "symbol" and some "real," other object, outside the fiction, which is sometimes called allegory. Tolkien explicitly, and entirely convincingly, denied allegorical significance to *The Lord of the Rings*. The Ring does not "mean" something else other than it is. The symbolism in *The Lord of the Rings* is inherent in its whole structure.

as the ending ambivalence of death. Tolkien uses the Quest magnificently in *The Lord of the Rings*. The whole immense story is strung out on Frodo's journey. Moreover, Tolkien has given the Quest a paradoxical twist that amounts to genius. Frodo already has the Ring, the instrument of power that earlier, less sophisticated ages might have sought. His quest is to destroy it, in the only place where that can be done, its place of origin.

One of the fine things in *The Lord of the Rings* is the increasing horror of Frodo's journey, especially after he and Sam are on their own. The effectiveness of the journey is partly found in the interweaving of the adventures of the other members of the Company with those of Frodo, and Tolkien shows great skill in inventing significant and varied narrative events; but the main power, naturally enough, lies with the Ring-bearer himself. The paradox of this particular quest is that what is most wanted is most against the grain. Not only must good struggle against evil: not only must Frodo labour through miserable physical circumstances: but there is for the hero a struggle within himself, to do what he must do, but can hardly bear to do. No subtle or realistic characterisation is needed to show this situation, yet it reaches down into our deepest sense of identity. Tolkien is extraordinarily good at creating that visionary dreariness in the world, that sinking of the heart that comes, for example, to an unprofessional soldier, when the orders for the attack are received, but which recurs often enough in ordinary existence, from the most trivial examples to the greatest. We have to do something, of our own choice, that we do not want to do. There is in human consciousness a deep sense that the ultimate goodness of the universe requires an ultimate sacrifice of the self that would usually seem to be the ultimate personal disaster. While this consciousness is most profoundly articulated among stories in that on which Christianity is based, it is not limited to specifically religious people. Many soldiers, to whom the adjective "religious" would be the last that it would occur to one to apply, have shown it. One of the paradoxes of the twentieth century has been the readiness of many Communists to martyr themselves to achieve the materialistic paradise of the future that they could never enjoy. Like all noble things, self-sacrifice may be corrupted, but perception of its necessity, even where it is not acted upon or lived up to, is a remarkably commonplace, though profound, spiritual insight. Self-sacrifice is most poignant when it is entirely solitary; when apparently no one can ever know of the lonely painful deed that has been ungladly volunteered, and that has apparently been of no avail. This solitary heroism is Frodo's, and the more convincing in that Tolkien does not totally isolate him physically, since Sam remains with him for various purposes of the narrative. But Frodo becomes progressively withdrawn even from Sam. In the last stages of the journey to the Crack of Doom Tolkien succeeds in creating the sense of physical difficulty and cost that romance sometimes fails to achieve. He realises most vividly the appalling landscape, the aching struggle towards the repellent yet desired objective, barely relieved by the blessed brief oblivion of exhausted sleep. This is a hopelessness which is not despair; an assertion of the will which denies the self. No doubt Tolkien's war-experience contributed to the imagery, but it is of the nature of literature to enable us to create such experiences in our own minds out of the very much smaller, but perhaps not less significant events, in our own individual lives, when any kind of moral and physical achievements have been sought. Very little in life is achieved without some self-sacrifice and some strain. One of the virtues of romance is that its remote adventures can so well symbolise quite ordinary and usual predicaments.

Tolkien achieves the final perfect twist to the Quest when he makes Frodo, at the very brink of success, relinquish it. This seems to me a fine comment on the feebleness of the human will. Then Gollum springs forward, the despised, hated, barely tolerated, yet pitied enemy, and bites off both ring and finger, to fall himself into the Crack of Doom. Even evil may do good in its own despite, may even be given a pitiful satisfaction. It is a splendid narrative turn, unexpected yet true, full of interest in itself, yet also symbolically significant of a view of life. It is entirely within the rules of the romance, yet entirely translatable into the terms of our own world.

One of the notes this episode sounds, both within the romance and within life, is the strange hinted sense that things are "meant," as we say: more explicitly, that behind the flux and pain of events there is a providential order. It is a witness of Tolkien's tact that this sense is never more than hinted. One of the most effective moments when he does this is splendidly Wordsworthian and nineteenth-century-romantic, when Frodo and Sam are almost at the end of their tethers in the dreadful land of Shadow, and Sam, keeping watch, "saw a white star twinkle for a while. The beauty of it smote his heart, as he looked up out of the forsaken land, and hope returned to him. For like a shaft, clear and cold, the thought pierced him that in the end the Shadow was only a small and passing thing: there was light and high beauty for ever beyond its reach" (standard hardback edition, III, 199). Tolkien is never afraid of a cliché, but this seems to me also a true and deep perception, resting on a feeling for and a conception of the nature of the world that supports much romance. It is very wide-spread in the book, very consoling, and very typically nineteenth-century European, though resting on deep foundations. Its obverse is the hatred of industrialism. The natural descriptions have little geological, botanical, or zoological substructure, and there is no sense of the huge benefits that industrialism has brought to the human race. So it is a very one-sided, though genuine, intuition, arising out of a feeling that the world is part of a whole of which we too are part; and the world is not simply to be ruthlessly exploited, for to destroy it is to destroy ourselves. Our recently acquired vivid sense of this at a national level is some validation of the nineteenth-century literary feeling for nature.

This very contemporary feeling "for the environment" is only one instance of how the romance of *The Lord of the Rings*, for all its apparent archaism, can hit off, as millions of readers know, a strongly contemporary feeling, once we leave aside the demands of the novel, which may well be paradoxically more intrinsically old-fashioned than *The Lord of the Rings*. Another example is that very sense of apocalyptic anxiety which is a notable quality of our times. Tolkien evokes it again and again. "The shadow of these times" is the constant note of the Council at Rivendell, and that note continues to be struck. The Battle of the Pelennor Fields, which is one of the great climaxes, is called by Theoden, who will himself be killed in it, "the great battle of our time, in which many things shall pass away" (III, 74). And although the battle is won, and Frodo's own quest succeeds, Gandalf says that "though much has been saved much must now pass away." "The Third Age of the World is ended" (III, 249). Lothlórien, that marvellous recreation of the Earthly Paradise, is itself doomed to pass away, as the elves also must depart. Aragorn himself is the last of the Elder Kindred. Moreover, no guarantee is given that the triumph over Sauron is any kind of enduring success over evil. Other evil may come. Sauron himself, though the mightiest single power in the book, the source of the evil and engineer of disaster, is only a servant (III, 155). Tolkien evokes at key moments a sense of the cosmic struggle between good and evil whereby pain and defeat and loss continually recur, and we are left in no doubt of the climactic nature of Frodo's quest.

A sense that disaster is almost or quite upon us is not unusual. It is one of the ingredients of ordinary life, as is anxiety. Most dreams are anxious. But surely that sense is more widespread today in the West than ever before, and Tolkien has finely registered it, without succumbing to the nihilism or fatalism, or totalitarianism, that often enough accompany it in modern life.

Tolkien's romance comes nearer home even than this. As in all good romance, the creation of an imaginative world is also a creation of generalised psychological images of the personal human situation. Traditional literature, involving myth, folktale, dream, is often peculiarly powerful in this, and Tolkien is particularly happy in calling on such resources. They can be summarised under two main heads: the confrontation with death, and the romance of childhood or early adolescence, both potent and valid sources of popularity.

Tolkien himself said that *The Lord of the Rings*, "like all big stories," is a story about death. Here is one source of the feeling of anxiety, which *The Lord of the Rings* creates. We are more uncertain about death nowadays than ever before. An anthropologist who has analysed modern British and American society observes how much of a taboo we impose upon the very mention of death, yet cannot leave it alone in all sorts of depraved cultural manifestations, notably, many modern films. He refers to the *pornography of death*.[11] Our problem is that as human beings we have a need deeper than hunger or sex to find in our experience a significance that transcends yet contains ourselves. Hunger and sex themselves are only part of that need. To live at all implies that we have found at least some partial satisfaction, as for food and water. Yet we must die, and one of our enduring problems is to reconcile our own percipience and sense of purpose, our own sense of significance, with the death which cancels them out. Death is the intersection of significance with negation. Perhaps not surprisingly death's most potent symbol is a cross: significantly and symbolically, with a cross we show that a way is barred, and that an answer is wrong. Yet the way that is barred is the way we have to go. Death casts doubt on, or, if it is absolute, totally refutes, any values in which it is sensible for us to take any interest. So it is normal to feel that death is, we may say, a bad thing. The traditional syndrome is that Sin brought Death into the World and all our Woe. Christianity claims that death is overcome, but this has always been a lesson that we need a lot of teaching, and in every age serious literature has confronted the problem afresh. *The Lord of the Rings* has a number of real deaths, and a number of death-demons, notably the barrow-wight, the king of the Ring-Wraiths, and Shelob. Here again the most effective presentation is Frodo's acceptance of death in the journey to the Crack of Doom. But I sometimes wonder if the story has not failed a little in the presentation of death. Frodo must survive, even if only in the burned-out half-life that is all that remains to him. But should Gandalf have been resurrected? Are the rules of the romance, or of the symbolic language, not broken? I should also have liked to see Gwaihir, the rescuing eagle, a little better justified. Even more, I am sure that too many of the Companions survive. War should take a heavier toll even of generals. Boromir is of course sacrificed, but it is a pretty question which others should have gone. I think Merry should have died even as he killed the Nazgul king of the

11. G. Gorer, *Death, Grief and Mourning in Contemporary Britain* (London, 1965).

Ring-Wraiths. I am afraid that the admirable Gimli too should have gone at the gates of Mordor. And Sam Gamgee, the best batman (i.e. officer's servant) the world has ever known, obviously deserved the martyr's crown. He should have struggled with Gollum and fallen into the Crack of Doom. But apart from the unduly fortunate careers of the Companions, the romance seriously images the brave and necessary confrontation of death with great variety and power, so as to strengthen our sense of the possibility of enduring the human predicament.

We may go further than this. The death-images are not only overcome, they are also accepted when they come in peaceful ways. The calm departures to the West over the sea recognise that death may be a release and a blessing: they give another side to destruction and negation, an image of that further transition all must make, a verbal rite of the final passage.

But the crucially fascinating core of the romance is concerned with the transitions of early life, of which indeed the consciousness of death is an integral part. It is probably in adolescence that most people fully recognise for the first time the possibility of death, a recognition which is part of growing up. It is very significant that the Hobbits, who are at the centre of consciousness of *The Lord of the Rings* are Halflings, half as high as men, their actual age being unimportant and sex of no overt significance (itself one of the great charms of *The Lord of the Rings*). Imaginatively they represent the emergence of the individual from childhood into realms of responsibility and danger. The cosy domesticity of the Shire, though to my taste embarrassingly rendered at the beginning of *The Lord of the Rings*, is absolutely vital as representing the comfortable childish home from which everyone must be forced out, as much by friendly/formidable father-figures like Gandalf as by sinister intruders. As we grow up we come to realise that nowhere is safe.

The departure from the Shire and from Bree into a strange and uncertainly hostile environment, where vague figures of evil are chasing one, where the way is lost through tangled thickets, yet one may be watched, and one may even be guided; where strange men much taller and older than oneself, facetious and impenetrable, offer help; and where one commits errors by

sheer carelessness and inattention; all this is a marvellous evocation of the world when one is young. The whole story images
one's nightmares and one's hope of doing doughty deeds in a
grown-up world where the girls are rare, queenly, and remote
(or at least were when Tolkien and I were young), the men
admirable or evil; and where there are really rough characters
who speak in an uneducated way, and who may well, if they
catch hold of you, knock you about and carry you off, as the
Orcs do Pippin and Merry. Fortunately one's Aragorn-father
and friends will sleeplessly search for one, tirelessly speeding
after one in seven-leagued boots; and in the countryside folk are
kinder, and speak slower, than in the rough industrial towns.

The psychological dimension might be explored a good deal
further than is possible here. Tolkien can evoke, often by turning to traditional literature, some images powerful in the minds
of ages, such as the Earthly Paradise. There is both ancient
depth and a fresh inventiveness in his creation of non-human,
non-animal creatures, elves, dwarves, Ents, fairies, that embody
perceptions and impulses that the naturalistic novel has long
since laid aside. One aspect of this to be noted is that such
figures may, in the language of psychoanalysts, be regarded as
split-off characteristics of the hero himself.[12] In one sense the
whole story is Frodo's dream of growing-up and dying: if
Frodo's, ours too. The superb creation of Gollum is a clear
instance of this. He is especially Frodo's *alter ego*, Frodo's own
doubt, fear, suspicion, greediness, selfishness, cowardice. We
have all got our Gollums. Gollum is always being suppressed
and rejected, but always there. It is impossible to get rid of him.
He cannot be killed. He must not be approved of, must not be
liked, but must, in a sense, be loved. It is always possible that he
may suddenly achieve the supremacy, and if he does a part of us
perishes and the rest lives only a half-life. With his capacity to
achieve images of such psychological penetration it does not
matter if Tolkien is no great hand at ordinary old-fashioned
novelistic character-depiction.

12. For the concept, devised by Freud and Jung, see, as a convenient
modern summary, *Dreams and Dreaming*, ed. S. G. M. Lee and A. R. Mayes
(Harmondsworth, 1973).

There is a profusion of father-figures, good and bad, in *The Lord of the Rings,* and of course the important thing is that Frodo achieves independence of them all, even of Aragorn. Mother-figures are less notable. Goldberry and Galadriel are aspects of the Good Mother, but somewhat faint. The Terrible Mother, an archetype as potent as the Good Mother, is perhaps to be observed in the huge, ancient, horrible, engulfing spider Shelob, who is also seen as a death-image.[13] The Crack of Doom is itself perhaps fundamentally a repellent image of the engulfing sexuality that civilization must repudiate. In one sense, one might say almost seriously, Freud got it wrong: far from wishing to marry their mothers, most men are desperately anxious to get away from them. Romance and folktale are full of escapes from the wicked witches and stepmothers who represent the mother, just as the giants and monsters represent the father. The hero has to escape from the domination of his parents and to establish relationships with his peers. It is probably a cultural and personal accident whether his peers are men or women, Jonathan or Juliet, as far as the life of the imagination is concerned.

Though it is worthwhile to emphasise that aspect of Romance which is the literary equivalent of the *rite de passage,* and to emphasise both the passage to adulthood and the passage to death, in each case involving loss and gain, sorrow and joy, those emphases need not exclude other elements in *The Lord of the Rings* which this essay has not been concerned with; nor exclude the fact that we do not live our lives in a single linear sequence. We always have to fight our battles and win our loves and meet our death over and over again. *The Lord of the Rings* itself shows this simple truth often enough. Hence the importance of repeated rituals and of the renewals of literature. Good and evil; death and suffering; joy and rebirth; moral effort and defeat and victory; the love of family and friends; all continue

13. For the composite archetypal image of the Mother see E. Neumann, *The Great Mother,* trans. R. Manheim (London, 1955). C. R. Stimpson in her indignant and unsympathetic account, *J. R. R. Tolkien,* Columbia Essays on Modern Writers, No. 41 (New York and London, 1969), complains, along with much else, that Tolkien has a "regressive emotional, pattern" because he is "irritatingly, blandly, traditionally masculine" (p. 18). The same might be said of Shakespeare.

throughout our lives, though perhaps we feel them at their greatest intensity in the confrontations and discoveries of adolescence. That most of us go on living after adolescence is some evidence of the at least partial success of our major transition, and some justification of the general optimism, of the happy ending, that romance is so often accused of presenting as a false picture of life. It is some justification, too, of that other remarkable characteristic of *The Lord of the Rings* among modern literature, that it is a story of innocence tested and of virtue successful, not fugitive and cloistered, but having borne the heat and burden of the day.

13

The Gospel of Middle-Earth according to J. R. R. Tolkien

William Dowie

SOUTHEASTERN LOUISIANA UNIVERSITY

L IN Carter is right when he says that one either reads Tolkien with rapt fascination or puts down the book after the first thirty pages. What is amazing is that enough people were fascinated by the 1,300 pages of *The Lord of the Rings* for over a quarter of a million copies to be sold in a ten-month span.[1] Other writers achieve popularity and admiration as well as critical acclaim; but the Tolkien books breed a kind of fierce discipleship that seeks to proselytize the unenlightened. Many popular stories are made into movies these days; but few are trumpeted on buttons. "Frodo Lives" proclaims more than simple enjoyment and cult-ish interest. It is a sign that readers have been touched by the aspirations and themes of fairyland, especially by the "oldest and deepest desire . . . the Great Escape: the Escape from

This is a revised form of an article that originally appeared in the *Heythrop Journal* 15, no. 1 (January 1974), 37–52.

1. Lin Carter, *Tolkien: A Look behind the Lord of the Rings* (New York, 1969).

Death."[2] The religiosity of devotion to the Tolkien works cannot be separated from the religiosity of the realm of his imagination. His journey through the region of *Faërie,* or what he likes to call "the Perilous Land," is indeed an excursion into the beyond, the "wholly other," in Rudolf Otto's terms, which fills "the mind with blank wonder and astonishment."[3]

In *The Lord of the Rings,* however, there is no talk of gods, mysticism, or religion.[4] Nor is this surprising for, as Tolkien himself observed, "It is man who is in contrast to fairies, supernatural . . . whereas they are natural, far more natural than he" ("On Fairy-Stories," p. 12). Yet the Tolkien volumes convey a sense of the unfathomable mystery of life at its deepest points. The Perilous Land is a domain rich in enchantment, fantasy, and magic and yet so consonant with one's experience of life's depths that one could not expect the full dimensions of the actual world to be any smaller; for, as Tolkien believes, the art of writing is a secondary creation and "we make still by the law in which we're made" ("On Fairy-Stories," p. 49).

The religiosity of Tolkien's trilogy is neither conceptualized nor dogmatized within the story. Yet the sense of the sacred is present in blood and symbol and theme. It is the unvocalized

2. J. R. R. Tolkien, "On Fairy-Stories," in *Essays Presented to Charles Williams,* ed. C. S. Lewis (Oxford, 1947), pp. 80–81; reprinted in Tolkien's *Tree and Leaf* (London, 1964), pp. 11–70. Subsequent references are to the 1964 edition.

3. R. Otto, *The Idea of the Holy* (London, 1958), p. 26.

4. In the appendix there is a reference to the "One" (Tolkien, *The Lord of the Rings,* 2d ed., 3 vols. [London and Boston, 1966], III, 317), explanation of the Valar as "the Guardians of the World" (ibid., pp. 314–17) and of the word "vala" as meaning "angelic powers" (ibid., p. 401). However, next to nothing is made of these figures within the story itself. There are also many songs and invocations to Elbereth as a special intercessor for Elves and their friends. However, her power is not out of continuity with the many other powers in and about Middle-Earth, such as that of wizards and spells. Basically religion as such is lacking because there is nothing like worship. See Richard Purtill, *Lord of the Elves and Eldils* (Grand Rapids, Mich., Zondervan Publishing House, 1974), pp. 115–33, for a fine account of the various supernatural powers in the trilogy. He concludes that the religious element "is muted and in the background" (p. 133).

religion of man in touch with nature and the cosmos, sharing in what Mircea Eliade calls the "cosmic liturgy."[5] The disagreement over whether Tolkien's eschatology is guided more by Christian or by Norse ideology[6] misses the point that Tolkien plunges into the sacrality of the natural; he delves into basic human emotions and a symbolic structure that is so widely distributed over cultural boundaries that it can be called fundamentally human symbolism. The stories evoke participation in a secular religion—that is, a religion in which all is sacred because all things, even the most natural, are related to one another and to a founding transcendence. Mircea Eliade's remarks on the profane are so appropriate, they can serve as an accompanying text in reading Tolkien:

> For religious man, nature is never only "natural"; it is always fraught with a religious value. This is easy to understand, for the cosmos is a divine creation; coming from the hands of the gods, the world is impregnated with sacredness. It is not simply a sacrality *communicated* by the gods, as is the case, for example, with a place or an object consecrated by the divine presence. The gods did more; *they manifested*

5. Mircea Eliade, *The Sacred and the Profane* (New York, 1959), p. 179.

6. See Gunnar Urang, "Tolkien's Fantasy: The Phenomenology of Hope" (Christian) and Charles Moorman, "Now Entertain Conjecture of Time" (Norse), both in *Shadows of Imagination*, ed. Mark Hillegas (Carbondale, Ill., 1969). Also favoring the Christian interpretation are: Sandra Miesel, "Some Religious Aspects of *Lord of the Rings*," *Riverside Quarterly* 3, no. 3 (August 1968), 209–13; Edmund Fuller, "The Lord of the Hobbits," *Tolkien and the Critics*, ed. Neil D. Isaacs and Rose A. Zimbardo (Notre Dame, Ind., and London, 1968), pp. 17–39; Willis B. Glover, "The Christian Character of Tolkien's Invented World," *Criticism* 13 (Winter 1971), 39–53; Clyde S. Kilby, "Mythic and Christian Elements in Tolkien," *Myth, Allegory and Gospel*, ed. Edmund Fuller, et al. (Minneapolis, 1974), pp. 119–43; Paul Pfotenhauer, "Christian Themes in Tolkien," *Cresset* 32, no. 3 (January 1969), 13–15; Dorothy Barber, "The Meaning of *The Lord of the Rings*," *Mankato State College Studies* 2, no. 1 (February 1967), 38–50; R. J. Reilly, *Romantic Religion: A Study of Barfield, Lewis, Williams, and Tolkien* (Athens, Ga., 1971), pp. 190–211; and Purtill, *Lord of the Elves.* William B. Ready, "The Tolkien Relation," *Canadian Library* 25, no. 2 (September 1968), 128–36, sees the story embodying a more humanistic type of religion.

the different modalities of the sacred in the very structure of the world and of cosmic phenomena. [The Sacred and the Profane, p. 116][7]

Eliade specifies what he means when he says that the earth is "transparent" for religious man, for "it presents itself as universal mother and nurse. The cosmic rhythms manifest order, harmony, permanence, fecundity. The cosmos as a whole is an organism at once *real, living,* and *sacred. . . ." (The Sacred and the Profane,* p. 117).

The Lord of the Rings is basically a rural book, even something of an ecological tract. The companions travel through forests, over mountains, marshes, and down rivers pursuing their quest. They are in contact with the rhythms of nature and the significance of places and events in a way that is impossible for man in the era of mass production and urban construction. Things have meaning for Frodo and his companions, things that looked at from afar might be called natural hierophanies. The principal of these which Tolkien employs are special places, stones, rings, narrow passes, underground tunnels, moon and sun, night and day, trees and foliage, ship and sea, and the changing seasons.

The experience of space as nonhomogeneous is germinally a religious experience of the sacred, for to recognize a qualitative difference in places implies an ordering by degree of importance. That place experienced as most real becomes then an absolute in relation to which one can arrange his universe. It becomes holy, a ground of being, allowing man to valorize the

7. Gunnar Urang, *Shadows of Heaven: Religion and Fantasy in the Writing of C. S. Lewis, Charles Williams and J. R. R. Tolkien* (Philadelphia and London, 1971), p. 105, mentions Eliade in reference to the symbol of the tree in his fine chapter on Tolkien. Sandra Miesel speaks of Tolkien's paradisal man and uses Eliade's *Myth, Dreams, and Mysteries* in explanation. Willis Glover uses Eliade to say that pagan myth is cyclic in contrast to Tolkien's saga. Since the original publication of my article, Clyde Kilby applies two of Eliade's characteristics of myth, paradigmatic gesture and paradisal symbolism, to *The Lord of the Rings;* and Randel Helms, *Tolkien's World* (Boston, 1974), pp. 5, 81, also applies the notion of "archetypal gesture" from Eliade's *Cosmos and History* to Tolkien's story. Oddly enough, none of these critics apparently have noticed, beyond their particular references, the far-reaching applicability of Eliade's research to Tolkien.

rest of his world. Whereas "the profane experience . . . maintains the homogeneity and hence the relativity of space," Eliade explains that "settling in a territory," on the contrary, "is equivalent to founding a world," and building a home or a city is "in the last analysis equivalent to consecrating it" (*The Sacred and the Profane*, p. 23). The spot becomes a paradigm of creation and involves a communal affirmation of its value. For the hobbits the Shire is this special kind of place. Leaving it is a great sacrifice, and the thought of return is a constant refrain of their journey. But each visited city and territory has this kind of consecrated individuality for the inhabitants. Rivendell, Lórien, Rohan, and Gondor are all sacred areas of peace and defense against the forces of chaos and destruction without. This is what the conflict of the story is all about: the power of the Dark Lord of Mordor is seeking to break down the border of lands, and control the West as one vast homogeneity. The struggle, granted that each land is a cosmos, assumes mythic proportions; for

> any attack from without threatens to turn it into chaos. And as "our world" was founded by imitating the paradigmatic work of the gods, the cosmogony, so the enemies who attack it are assimilated to the enemies of the gods, the demons, and especially to the archdemon, the primordial dragon conquered by the gods at the beginning of time. An attack on "our world" is equivalent to an act of revenge by the mythical dragon, who rebels against the work of the gods, the cosmos, and struggles to annihilate it. "Our" enemies belong to the power of chaos. *Any destruction of a city is equivalent to a retrogression to chaos. Any victory over the attackers reiterates the paradigmatic victory of the gods over the dragon (that is, over chaos).* [*The Sacred and the Profane*, pp. 47–48]

The Shire and all the parts of the West suffer such a threat of chaos. Frodo tells the Elf Gildor at the outset of his long journey, "I knew that danger lay ahead, of course; but I did not expect to meet it in our own Shire. Can't a hobbit walk from the Water to the River in peace?"[8] The answer naturally is no, not until something is done to confront and defeat the forces of the

8. Tolkien, *The Lord of the Rings*, I, 93. Subsequent references are included in the text. (The page numbers can be correlated with the one-volume edition by adding 4 in Vol. I, 418 in Vol. II, and 758 in Vol. III.)

primordial dragon, the Dark Lord of Mordor, who rules, by the iron hand of power, a place void of fruitful vegetation, growing thorns, spread with swamp marshes, and peopled by filthy orcs. As Gandalf tells the Hobbits, Sauron's "power is again stretching out over the world! We are sitting in a fortress. Outside it is getting dark" (I, 238). All the nine companions of the Fellowship of the Ring must temporarily assume a nomadic stance in the world for the sake of their important quest, but all except Gandalf have a place to return to, if and when the mission is accomplished. Legolas is an elf of the forest; Gimli a dwarf of the mountain. For each of these two, his kind of place is the most real. Part of the secondary interest of the journey is to watch the interplay between the two, which will result in a mutual respect for the kind of place that the other feels at home in. They each plan to share the splendors of their special kind of world with the other.

Gandalf is the one pilgrim who has no home. The others share his lot temporarily, and Frodo becomes more and more like him, but the wizard alone from first to last takes up that special symbolic posture of wanderer. Eliade explains a significance of this lot:

> If possessing a house implies having assumed a stable situation in the world, those who have renounced their houses, the pilgrims and ascetics, proclaim by their "walking," by their constant movement, their desire to leave the world, their refusal of any worldly situation. . . . Those who have chosen the Quest, the road that leads to the Center, must abandon any kind of family and social situation, any "nest," and devote themselves wholly to "walking" toward the supreme truth, which, in highly evolved religions, is synonymous with the Hidden God, the *Deus absconditus*. [*The Sacred and the Profane*, pp. 183–84]

All of the Nine take a "walking" attitude for the duration of their mission. The hobbits sing the old dwarf-song:

> With foes ahead, behind us dread,
> Beneath the sky shall be our bed,
> Until at last our toil be passed,
> Our journey done, our errand sped.

> We must away! We must away!
> We ride before the break of day! [I, 116.]

Eventually they all hope to return home; even Aragorn, the Strider, who has been on the road for so long, has a kingdom which he is to come into. Frodo, on the other hand, increasingly resembles Gandalf in his nonrootedness, until at the end he cannot settle down in the Shire happily ever after, as do Sam, Pippin, and Merry. Frodo lives with Sam and his bride Rosie for a while, but before long he tells Sam that he must be moving on to the Grey Havens with Gandalf. Sam tearfully objects, "I thought you were going to enjoy the Shire, too, for years and years, after all you have done" (III, 309). But Frodo has been too long a ring-bearer and too deeply hurt to settle down. On their last ride together, Sam hears Frodo singing the old walking song, but with new words added:

> Still round the corner there may wait
>   A new road or a secret gate;
> And though I oft have passed them by,
>   A day will come at last when I
> Shall take the hidden paths that run
>   West of the Moon, East of the Sun. [III, 308.]

The final journey, of course, is a very special one. For it is taken by ship across the great sea. The image significantly proclaims not simply the end of Gandalf, Frodo, and Bilbo, but their passing over to a new land, the definitive land that is cut off from the Shire and all the western lands by a great gulf. The leave-taking is sad because of the parting of friends, but a profound peace prevails: "And the ship went out into the High Sea and passed on into the West, until at last on a night of rain Frodo smelled a sweet fragrance on the air and heard the sound of singing that came over the water. And then it seemed to him that as in his dream in the house of Bombadil, the grey rain-curtain turned all to silver glass and was rolled back, and he beheld white shores and beyond them a far green country under a swift sunrise" (III, 310). Wanderers in life, the company finally go toward the absolute haven across the sea, presumably to share in the wholeness and immortality that is signified by the far West, the undying lands.

Natural rhythms and phenomena foster a sensitivity to the Other that is characteristic of the Middle-Earth folk. When at a crucial and bleak point in the battle of Helm's Deep, Gamling says to Aragorn, "Dawn is not far off. . . . But dawn will not help us, I fear," Aragorn responds, "Yet dawn is ever the hope of men" (II, 142). And later, when the city of Minas Tirith is under great internal and external threat, "a cock crowed. Shrill and clear he crowed, recking nothing of wizardry or war, welcoming only the morning that in the sky far above the shadows of death was coming with the dawn" (III, 103). The moon is also a hierophany of hope for the hobbit in touch with nature. In their lonely journey to Mordor, Frodo and Sam reflect this responsiveness. Frodo says:

> "Night will be on us soon. How beautiful the stars are, and the Moon!"
>
> "They do cheer the heart, don't they?" said Sam looking up. "Elvish they are, somehow. And the Moon's growing. We haven't seen him for a night or two in this cloudy weather. He's beginning to give quite a light."
>
> "Yes," said Frodo; "but he won't be full for some days. I don't think we'll try the marshes by the light of half a moon." [II, 218]

In the periodic disappearance and reappearance of the moon, what is revealed inchoately to the hobbits is "not only that death is indissolubly linked with life but also, and above all, *that death is not final, that it is always followed by a new birth*" (Eliade, *The Sacred and the Profane*, p. 157).

Symbols of passage, initiation, rebirth abound in the course of the story. The hobbits leave the Shire by a thick-set iron gate that "shut with a clang" after they passed through; and "the sound was ominous" (I, 121). When they are rescued by Tom Bombadil from the Barrow-wights he expressed their liberation in terms evocative of baptism: "You've found yourselves again, out of the deep water. . . . Be glad, my merry friends, and let the warm sunlight heat now heart and limb! Cast off these cold rags! Run naked on the grass . . ." (I, 155). The company is led by Gandalf into the dark underground mines of Moria, where he is killed by the Balrog only to reappear again in the forest of Fangorn. And to penetrate into Mordor, Sam and Frodo must endure the climb up the Straight Stair and the Winding Stair as well as the crawl through Shelob's tunnel. Before he can come into his kingdom, Aragorn feels impelled to travel to Minas Tirith through the Halls of the Dead. Eliade notes the frequency of symbols of dangerous passage in mythology and ancient societies, declaring that in initiatory contexts,

> death signifies passing beyond the profane, unsanctified condition, the condition of the "natural man," who is without religious experience, who is blind to spirit. The mystery of initiation gradually reveals to the novice the true dimensions of existence; by introducing him to the sacred, it obliges him to assume the responsibility that goes with being a man. Here we have a fact of the first importance: for all archaic societies, access to spirituality finds expression in a symbolism of death and a new birth. [*The Sacred and the Profane*, pp. 191–92]

A further symbol of the triumph of life is the cosmic tree, which is related of course to the whole renewal of nature that begins in spring and blossoms into summer. As Eliade points out, "for religious man, the appearance of life is the central mystery of the world," for "human life is not felt as a brief appearance in time, between one nothingness and another; it is preceded by a pre-existence and continued in a postexistence" (*The Sacred and the Profane*, p. 147). Because this mystery of the inexhaustible presence of life is bound up with the rhythmical regeneration of nature, the tree became a central symbol in religious traditions. So in *The Lord of the Rings* the figure of the tree carries something of this same mythic significance when the Eagle sings to the people of Gondor:

> And the Tree that was withered shall be renewed,
> and he shall plant it in the high places,
> and the City shall be blessed. [III, 241]

The Quest of the Fellowship of the Ring took one year. They set out in early fall, endured the bitter and bleak days of winter when it seemed the dark might of Mordor was unconquerable, and triumphed at the budding of spring. Aragorn ritualistically uproots the old and withered tree of the palace of Minas Tirith and then "planted the new tree in the court by the fountain, and swiftly and gladly it began to grow; and when the month of June entered in it was laden with blossom" (III, 250). The year after the completion of the mission and the destruction of Sauron, the West enjoys the Year of Great Plenty:

> Spring surpassed his [Sam's] wildest hopes. His trees began to sprout and grow, as if time was in a hurry and wished to make one year do for twenty. In the Party Field, a beautiful young sapling leaped up: it had silver bark and long leaves and burst into golden flowers in April. It was indeed a *mallorn*, and it was the wonder of the neighborhood. In after years, as it grew in grace and beauty, it was known far and wide and people would come long journeys to see it: the only *mallorn* west of the Mountains and east of the Sea, and one of the finest in the world.
>
> Altogether 1420 in the Shire was a marvellous year. Not only was there wonderful sunshine and delicious rain, in due times and perfect measure, but there seemed something more: an air of richness and growth, and a gleam of a beauty beyond that of mortal summers that flicker and pass upon this Middle-earth. [III, 303]

The very idealness of the special tree and the richness of the year—"beyond that of mortal summers"—invites an archetypal interpretation. Life is dominant and ultimate.

One symbol or another would not perhaps mean much in a tale as long as *The Lord of the Rings;* but the pervasive importance of the seasons, the great tree, the moon, the dark passage, the night and morn, the ship across the sea, and the special place makes one realize that Tolkien has indeed rooted his tale in the symbolic consciousness of naturally religious man. Natural hierophany is a major mode of his approach toward the transcendent.

Another of Tolkien's ways of unobtrusively exploring the sacred is to embody certain moral and intellectual themes of the Christian vision in a context that has no explicit trappings of religion. This, in some way like C. S. Lewis's *Out of the Silent Planet* and *Perelandra*, allows a fresh emotional contact with ideas that might otherwise be categorically prejudged. Gunnar Urang calls this "repaganizing," using Tolkien's own description of *Beowulf.*[9]

The sense of vocation initiates the quest of the ring for Frodo Baggins. He complains to Gandalf, "I am not made for perilous quests. I wish I had never seen the Ring! Why did it come to me? Why was I chosen?" Gandalf explains that the reason was not because of special merit on Frodo's part; nevertheless "you have been chosen, and you must therefore use such strength and heart and wits as you have" (I, 70). This recognition of being chosen or called to a special task is at the heart of the Christian life. Elrond confirms the council's sense of vocation when he tells them of "the purpose for which you were called hither. Called, I say, though I have not called you to me, strangers from distant lands. You have come and are here met, in this very nick of time, by chance as it may seem. Yet it is not so. Believe rather that it is so ordered that we, who sit here, and none others, must now find counsel for the peril of the world" (I, 255). So, although the meeting seems merely fortuitous, Elrond makes it clear that an ordering and a directing is operating behind the scenes. Frodo and the rest of the fellowship must struggle to live up to this vocation.

Suffering, as a necessity of life and an integral part of personal growth, is bound up with the task. Frodo, as well as the others, foresaw the danger involved in their quest, but the difficulty increases the further along they go. As he and Sam cross the marshes near Mordor, "Frodo seemed to be weary, weary to the point of exhaustion. He said nothing, indeed he hardly spoke at all; and he did not complain, but he walked like one who carries a load, the weight of which is ever increasing" (II, 238). Every man, in the Christian vision, must carry the heavy weight of his own cross. It is part of his possible moral greatness that he suffer—even a great deal:

> The last stage of their journey to Orodruin came, and it was a torment greater than Sam had ever thought that he could bear. He was in pain, and so parched that he could no longer swallow even a mouthful of food. It remained dark not only because of the smokes of

9. *Shadows of Heaven*, p. 120.

the Mountain: there seemed to be a storm coming up, and away to the south-east there was a shimmer of lightnings under the black skies. Worst of all, the air was full of fumes; breathing was painful and difficult, and a dizziness came on them, so that they staggered and often fell. And yet their wills did not yield, and they struggled on. [III, 217]

Frodo, Sam, and the whole company overcome mountainous difficulties and finally reflect that splendor of courage through hardship. But up until the end, the possibility of turning back, giving up, and keeping the Ring remains open. Freedom of will is a constantly affirmed theme. Boromir succumbs to the desire for power and breaks the fellowship by trying to snatch the Ring from Frodo. And Frodo himself feels the pull of the Ring as he is tempted to use it for his own sake: "The two powers strove in him. For a moment, perfectly balanced between their piercing points, he writhed, tormented. Suddenly he was aware of himself again. Frodo, neither the Voice nor the Eye: free to choose, and with one remaining instant in which to do so. He took the Ring off his finger" (I, 417). Even after all Sam had suffered for Frodo, the power and temptation of the Ring is so strong that Frodo interprets Sam's offer to help carry it as an attempt to steal it from himself. He repents and apologizes, realizing that no one is immune from the lure of the Ring.

Behind the whole struggle against the forces of Mordor and the internal struggle to fulfil personal tasks is the implication that there is such a thing as good and evil. The men of the West can go to battle with such fierce intensity against the orcs and the winged Nazgûl because while they are set in their course of power and destruction, they are wholly evil, given over to their own self-love and to the service of their Dark Lord. Because the opposition is stark, violence is necessary and good. War in *Faërie*, unlike war in reality, possesses no ambiguous shades of gray. However, it is by this heightening of the contrast between good and evil that *Faërie* affirms the presence of the antinomy in real life as well. Neither values nor morality are relative in Middle-Earth. As Aragorn tells Éomer, "Good and ill have not changed since yesteryear; nor are they one thing among elves and dwarves and another among Men. It is a man's part to discern them, as much in the Golden Wood as in his own house" (II, 41).

In spite of the amount of war in *The Lord of the Rings*, there exists still a strong moral compassion for enemies who are in any way capable of reformation. Bilbo has spared Gollum in *The Hobbit*, and Gandalf tries to teach Frodo the same lesson: "It was Pity that stayed his hand. Pity, and Mercy: not to strike without need. And he has been well rewarded, Frodo. Be sure that he took so little hurt from the evil, and escaped in the end, because he began his ownership of the Ring so. With Pity" (I, 68–69). Frodo learns well and spares the same Sméagol later in the story, with the result that he is instrumental in the successful destruction of the Ring and Mordor. Even the traitor Saruman is allowed to go free by the Ents, and afterward spared by Gandalf and, at last, by Frodo, who says, "He is fallen, and his cure is beyond us; but I would still spare him, in the hope that he may find it" (III, 299). Battle against true evil has done the opposite of hardening Frodo. When he returns to the Shire, he is positively pacific. He orders that no hobbit be killed even if he has gone over to the other side, for "no hobbit has ever killed another on purpose in the Shire, and it is not to begin now. And nobody is to be killed at all, if it can be helped" (III, 285). When some violence proves necessary, Frodo "had not drawn sword, and his chief part had been to prevent the hobbits in their wrath at their losses, from slaying those of their enemies who threw down their weapons" (III, 295–96).

The morality of law and power embedded in the story is also basically Christian. Law is necessary, but it is not absolute. In fact, one must always be prepared to act upon the rationale behind the law rather than follow its letter. Otherwise the men of Rohan could never have allowed the company free access across their land. As Aragorn tells the riders, "I do not think your law was made for such a chance. . . . Aid us, or at the worst let us go free. Or seek to carry out your law" (II, 41). The same necessity for choosing the spirit over the letter occurs when the lord Denethor orders his wounded son to be placed on the funeral pyre. Pippin tells Beregond that he must "choose between orders and the life of Faramir" (III, 101).

[277

As far as power is concerned, it is the realm of the Dark Lord. The way of the Fellowship is the way of renunciation of power. The story constantly sounds the theme that the great deed must be accomplished humbly. The big advantage that Frodo and the fellowship have against Mordor is that Sauron cannot foresee what they are trying to do because he could not imagine anyone willing to destroy the means of ruling others. As Gandalf says, "That we should wish to cast him down and have *no* one in his place is not a thought that occurs to his mind. That we should try to destroy the Ring itself has not yet entered into his darkest dream" (II, 100). Yet the hope of the company is slim because they must also fight the enemy directly, and this, the field of power, is the very home ground of evil. In war alone, the good would be defeated; but with the great labor of the humble ring-bearers, there is hope. Elrond instructs the original council that "neither strength nor wisdom will carry us far upon it. This quest may be attempted by the weak with as much hope as the strong. Yet such is oft the course of deeds that move the wheels of the world: small hands do them because they must, while the eyes of the great are elsewhere" (I, 283). For Gandalf, Galadriel, Boromir, or even Aragorn to have accepted the Ring would have been disastrous; for, although they would have begun with good works, the corruption of absolute power would have set in. The implications of a Ring whose possession without corruption is impossible for any king or wise man are obvious: the use of such power belongs elsewhere, to some being alone who transcends the mortality of even *Faërie*. The greatest achievement within the story is the destruction of the Ring by the Hobbit-bearers. It is only through the humble that the mighty are confounded.

Along with these moral themes, certain ontological implications of *The Lord of the Rings* also belong to the warp and woof of Christian tradition. These include notions of fellowship, kingship, providence, prophecy, prohibition, festivity, and eucatastrophe.

A foundation for more than one of these themes is the recognition of self-insufficiency. Initially this leads to the need of fellowship, of community. The undertaking of the book, the destruction of Sauron and the Ring, is attempted from the nucleus of a nine-member Fellowship of the Ring. They progress only by mutual aid: Gandalf's leadership, Sam's devotion, Aragorn's tracking, and so on. The final battle depends upon the last-minute aid of first the riders of Rohan and then Aragorn's forces to the besieged city of Minas Tirith. And still that is not enough; The Ring-bearers must also succeed. And their triumph depends on their mutual love. As the Ring burdens Frodo more and more toward the end, Sam must shoulder much of the weight by taking care of his master. Their relationship is caught in the picture of Sam "propped against the stone, his head dropping sideways and his breathing heavy. In his lap lay Frodo's head, drowned deep in sleep; upon his white forehead lay one of Sam's brown hands, and the other lay softly upon his master's breast. Peace was in both their faces" (II, 323). He must carry Frodo up the final slope of Mount Doom. With a "new strength" and a "new sense of responsibility" Sam takes Frodo right up to the edge of the fire.

Yet even that is not enough. For the final dissolving of the Ring, Frodo needs a force more mysterious than fellowship. Frodo has wanted all the while to cast the Ring into the fire, but at the end he cannot. Only because Sméagol happens to be still around and is able to snatch Frodo's ring finger, is the deed finally accomplished; for Sméagol somehow trips off into the fire with his newly won treasure. At the end, chance is needed. But the sense throughout the book is that the force at work is more purposeful than chance or blind fate.[10] Even at the beginning of the quest, one senses vaguely a providence at work behind the scenes. Gandalf refers to the "strangest event in the whole history of the Ring so far: Bilbo's arrival just at that time, and putting his hand on it, blindly, in the dark" (I, 65). Elrond had spoken of the calling together of the council by "chance as it may seem. Yet it is not so. Believe rather that it is so ordered" (I, 255). Later Frodo senses a guiding hand in the background when he literally finds himself volunteering to carry the Ring; he

10. I agree with Patricia Meyer Spacks's fine analysis of providence in the story, in her "Power and Meaning in *The Lord of the Rings*," in *Tolkien and the Critics*, ed. Isaacs and Zimbardo, pp. 87–90.

"wondered to hear his own words, as if some other will was using his small voice" (I, 284). And so on, up to the very edge of Mount Doom, where Sméagol, who might have been killed at any one of the many times during the story, is still around to cause the destruction of the Ring, accidentally, at the very moment when the forces of the West are hard pressed at the gate of Mordor.

The extent of dependence in Middle-Earth reaches out to the longing for and need for a king. The king will restore order, and rule in peace and wisdom. As Frodo tells Bilbo after Aragorn has taken his rightful role, "I'll come back soon: it won't be dangerous any more. There is a real king now, and he will soon put the roads in order" (III, 266). Kingship is not easily assumed; Aragorn had to prepare for it through arduous tasks and over long years. But once his labors are accomplished, his right recognized, and his time ripe, he comes into his kingdom. Faramir, after Aragorn healed his wounds, awakes with immediate recognition of the king: "My lord, you called me. I come. What does the king command?" (III, 142), thus expressing the great yearning of the people of the West—consonant with the Christian vision of man fulfilled only through dependence and humility. As Gerardus van der Leeuw observes: "Since kingly potency is no personal capacity, all conceivable salvation is expected of it. The king's powers ought to overflow. . . . As a genuine saviour the king also heals." Thus "the king . . . is a god. . . . Power has become embodied in a living figure. . . . The institution of kingship signifies, indeed, a forcible and thorough change in human life: everything was waste and misery, but now all is well. Once again the breath of Spring is wafted: 'What a Happy day! Heaven and earth rejoice'."[11] But kingship cannot be dissociated from community. It is only after the people have answered the question, "Shall he be king and enter into the City and dwell there?" (III, 245) with a resounding "yea" that Aragorn assumes the throne. Great rejoicing erupts now that the people can bend their knees to a genuine ruler once again.

11. G. van der Leeuw, *Religion in Essence and Manifestation* (London, 1938; reprint New York, 1963), pp. 117, 120.

Instances of prophecy, prohibition, and festivity are common in *The Lord of the Rings*—implying the existence of a transcendent realm outside ordinary time and power. The men of the council of Elrond put great trust in a prophetic song which they only barely understand:

> Seek for the Sword that was broken:
>   In Imladris it dwells;
> There shall be counsels taken
>   Stronger than Morgul-spells.
> There shall be shown a token
>   That Doom is near at hand,
> For Isildur's Bane shall waken,
>   And the Halfling forth shall stand.   [I, 259]

Prophecy operates, as does prohibition, in a region free of time and its consequent limitations of ignorance. It implies mysterious contact with this other realm. Tolkien talks in his essay "On Fairy-Stories" of the "great mythical significance of prohibition," the "Thou shalt not—or else thou shalt depart beggared into endless regret" ("On Fairy-Stories," p. 33), as being part of even the most innocent nursery tale. It bespeaks the inscrutable domination of otherness, for it operates beyond the boundary of the rational. So when Bilbo ventures against Gandalf's warning into the elves' forest, he pays for it with considerable trouble.[12] On a much more far-reaching level, the violation by the Numenoreans of the ban against inhabiting the Undying Lands led to the casting of Numenor into the sea and the removal of the Undying Lands from the circles of the world. In this case, the source of the prohibition is the Valar (III, 315).

The hobbits are a very festive group, willing to accept any good excuse for a celebration. Bilbo's birthday party is a gala affair. The meeting at Elrond's is marked by a feast. And, of course, there is the final festivity at Minas Tirith. This capacity for festivity has a profound religious significance, for by it one makes a commitment both to a historical world and to a moment of ideal parousia that anticipates the hopeful future. As Harvey

12. Tolkien, *The Hobbit* (London, 1937; reprint New York, 1966), pp. 149ff.

Cox says in his *The Feast of Fools:* "The religious man is one who grasps his own life within a larger historical and cosmic setting. He sees himself as part of a greater whole, a longer story in which he plays a part. Song, ritual, and vision link a man to this story. . . . Festivity periodically restores us to our proper relationship to history and history-making. It reminds us that we are fully within history but that history also is within something else."[13] And van der Leeuw notes that transitional rites such as "birth, naming, initiation, marriage, sickness and recovery, the start and end of a long journey, the outbreak of war and conclusion of peace, death and burial, are all points of contact between Power and life, and hence must not merely be experienced and then remembered, but must actually be celebrated."[14] Song and festivity are important to the hobbits because these activities heighten the special moments of contact with Otherness, join the present to the past, and look forward to the ideal future.

Which brings us to the happy ending. *The Lord of the Rings* is a joyful book. Even at the darkest times Gandalf and Aragorn encourage a hope that all will come out well, along with a realization that it might not. When Bilbo and Frodo discuss the ending of Bilbo's book, the older hobbit says that "books ought to have good endings. How would this do: and they all settled down and lived together happily ever after?" (I, 287). According to have good endings. How would this do: *and they all settled down and lived together happily ever after?"* (I, 287). According evidence, if you will) universal final defeat and in so far is *evangelium*, giving a fleeting glimpse of Joy, Joy beyond the walls of the world, poignant as grief" ("On Fairy-Stories," p. 60).[15] The triumphant panoply of Aragorn the good king assuming his rightful throne and the Ring-bearers being escorted to his right and left is one of the most joyfully thrilling moments in fiction. Sam cried out:

13. Harvey Cox, *The Feast of Fools* (Cambridge, Mass., and London, 1969), pp. 14, 46.
14. *Religion in Essence and Manifestation*, pp. 192–93.
15. Reilley, *Romantic Religion*, pp. 207–11, nicely relates Tolkien's essay to his fiction on this point of eucatastrophe.

"O great glory and splendour! And all my wishes have come true!" And then he wept.

And all the host laughed and wept, and in the midst of their merriment and tears the clear voice of the minstrel rose like silver and gold, and all men were hushed. And he sang to them, now in the Elven-tongue, now in the speech of the West, until their hearts, wounded with sweet words, overflowed, and their joy was like swords, and they passed in thought out to regions where pain and delight flow together and tears are the very wine of blessedness. [III, 232]

The happy ending of the story—what Tolkien calls the necessary eucatastrophe—trumpets a hope that the impressive suffering of tragedy and the brief interlude of comedy are not the ultimate stuff of life. Curiously enough, Tolkien picks Lewis's term *joy* as a hallmark of the fairy story—a joy that goes beyond even hope, for "the peculiar quality of the 'joy' in successful fantasy can thus be explained as a sudden glimpse of the underlying reality or truth," and the "joy which the 'turn' in the fairy story gives . . . has the very taste of primary truth. (Otherwise its name would not be joy.)" ("On Fairy-Stories," p. 63). The glimmering turn of *The Lord of the Rings* contains both the taste of primary truth and a simultaneous image of an ultimate kingdom in which the Lord will be capable of holding even the mightiest Ring without self-corruption and with the obedient love of all his subjects.

The Lord of the Rings is a deeply religious work because it plunges into the sacrality of the natural. The trilogy has no mention of God as such, nothing like worship, and no hint of organized religion; and in this sense it could be readily incorporated into the corpus of modern literature which operates within the experience of a *Deus absconditus*. But Tolkien's whole creation of the perilous realm of Middle-Earth is an effort to transport us from a positivist, mechanist, urbanized, and rationalist culture into one in which man is in contact with his own desires and the significance of the cosmos around him. Tolkien asks: "Why should a man be scorned if, finding himself in prison, he tries to get out and go home: Or if, when he cannot do so, he thinks and talks about other topics than jailers and prison-walls? The world outside has not become less real because the prisoner cannot see it" ("On Fairy-Stories," p. 54). Eschewing the methods of allegory and explicit religiosity used by C. S. Lewis in his secondary worlds, Tolkien accomplishes his escape by means of natural hierophany, the broader ontological themes of fairy story, and the morals embedded in the quest of the Ring. Much of the latter two are based upon Christian experience.

Tolkien has helped us to understand the peculiar religious nature of his story in some private remarks on its revisions. In a letter to his friend Robert Murray, S. J., who had read the unpublished manuscript and commented how "without a word about religion, the book is all about grace," Tolkien answered,

> I think I know exactly what you mean by the order of grace; and of course by your references to Our Lady, upon which all my own small perception of beauty both in majesty and simplicity is founded. *The Lord of the Rings* is of course a fundamentally religious and Catholic work; unconsciously so at first, but consciously in the revision. That is why I have not put in, or have cut out, practically all references to anything like 'religion', to cults or practices, in the imaginary world. For the religious element is absorbed into the story and the symbolism. However that is very clumsily put, and sounds more self-important than I feel. For as a matter of fact, I have consciously planned very little; and should chiefly be grateful for having been brought up (since I was eight) in a faith that has nourished me and taught me all the little that I know; and that I owe to my mother, who clung to her conversion and died young, largely through the hardships of poverty resulting from it."[16]

Tolkien's words confirm my thesis that *The Lord of the Rings* is religious, not overtly but by means of natural symbolism and absorbed Christian tradition (both unconscious influences). Like Tolkien's explicit disavowal of allegorical intention in his last published comment on *The Lord of the Rings*, the "Foreword" to the one-volume edition of 1968 (pp. 9–12), this letter reveals how Tolkien's imagination was so thoroughly and naturally religious that he needed in revision to prune its unconscious ex-

16. In Robert Murray, S. J., "A Tribute to Tolkien," *The Tablet* 5, no. 227 (15 September 1973), 879–80.

pressiveness. The desires, values, and patterns of life which are part of *The Lord of the Rings* manifest the sacredness of life and challenge the limits set upon human aspiration by the "rawness and ugliness of modern European Life" ("On Fairy-Stories," p. 56; we may add "American"). The success of Tolkien's endeavor is attested by his popularity across the boundaries of formal religiosity.

14

Creation from Philology in *The Lord of the Rings*

T. A. Shippey

St. John's College, Oxford

I N the Foreword to the second edition of *The Lord of the Rings*[1] Professor Tolkien remarked that the unpublished work from which his trilogy grew was "primarily linguistic in inspiration" —a remark supported both by the extensive Appendices to *The Lord of the Rings* and by his own further, reported statements: "The invention of language is the foundation. The 'stories' were made rather to provide a world for the language than the reverse." The trilogy is "to me, anyway, largely an essay in 'linguistic esthetic'. "[2] Such observations have been extraordinarily unpopular with literary critics. In his now-notorious review of 1956,[3] Edmund Wilson quotes the statements given above, but assumes that they are automatically self-disqualifying; a work written on those principles could never be more than a "philo-

1. J. R. R. Tolkien, *The Lord of the Rings*, 2d ed. (London, 1966). Future references are to this edition, by volume and page. Pagination is identical in the American edition of the same year, by Houghton Mifflin, Boston.

2. These remarks are quoted in Edmund Wilson's review referred to below. Wilson says that Tolkien made them in "a statement prepared for his publishers."

3. Edmund Wilson, "Oo, Those Awful Orcs!" *Nation* 182, no. 15 (14 April 1956), more readily available in Wilson's collection *The Bit between My Teeth* (London, 1966), pp. 326–32.

logical curiosity." Neil D. Isaacs, rather later, confesses that Tolkien's remarks about philology cannot be ignored, but thinks them "offhand," they "need not be taken too seriously"; another contributor to the same volume of critical essays thinks that the only professional way to begin is by ignoring all appendices, runes, etc. as simply "fascinating trivia"; and yet a third, while mentioning Wilson disapprovingly, nevertheless goes on to argue that *The Lord of the Rings* cannot be a "philological game" because it is so evidently moral, serious, imaginative, and personal. Philology, however, cannot be personal. "No one ever exposed the nerves and fibers of his being in order to make up a language; it is not only insane but unnecessary."[4] All these remarks—and many others—much underrate the importance of philology and linguistic studies, so often thought, by literary critics, to be self-evidently "scholarly hobbies," unconnected with (indeed probably perversions of) "the eternal verities of human nature."[5]

In fact it is not hard to see that many elements in *The Lord of the Rings* are obviously "linguistic in inspiration"; that these are by no means the least significant elements, even for those who quest doggedly after meanings; and that in any case (as Tolkien himself remarked)[6] some of them have given perhaps "more pleasure to more readers" than anything else in the trilogy.

A start can be made by noticing Professor Tolkien's attitude to dictionaries, in particular to the *New English Dictionary on Historical Principles* (later renamed the *Oxford English Dictionary*). This work, in its many volumes and supplements issued from 1888 to the present day, is a great collective achievement of many members of the Oxford English Faculty, to which Tolkien belonged for nearly forty years; and he himself assisted in

4. The three references are to articles in *Tolkien and the Critics*, ed. Neil D. Isaacs and Rose A. Zimbardo (Notre Dame and London, 1968). They are, respectively, Neil D. Isaacs, "On the Possibilities of Writing Tolkien Criticism," pp. 1–11; Roger Sale, "Tolkien and Frodo Baggins," pp. 247–88; R. J. Reilly, "Tolkien and the Fairy Story," pp. 128–50.

5. The dichotomy is offered by Lin Carter, *Tolkien: A Look behind The Lord of the Rings* (New York, 1969), pp. 93–94.

6. In the last footnote to his lecture, "English and Welsh," printed in *Angles and Britons: O'Donnell Lectures* (Cardiff, 1963), pp. 1–41.

its compilation for a while. Yet it has been remarked[7] that Tolkien's attitude to it was not entirely favourable, or serious. In *Farmer Giles of Ham*, for instance[8] (the only one of Tolkien's short fictions to resemble the trilogy and *The Hobbit* in matter or manner), the word "blunderbuss" is mentioned. "Some may well ask," writes Tolkien, "what a blunderbuss was. Indeed, this very question, it is said, was put to the Four Wise Clerks of Oxenford, and after thought they replied: 'A blunderbuss is a short gun with a large bore firing many balls or slugs, and capable of doing execution within a limited range without exact aim. (Now superseded in civilized countries by other firearms.)' " Farmer Giles's blunderbuss, however, does not fit the definition; and Tolkien evidently found the parenthetic remark at best comic in its equation of civilization with better guns. But the definition is that given by the *OED*, and the Four Wise Clerks of Oxenford must be, as Professor Kocher has said, the dictionary's four editors, Murray, Bradley, Craigie, and Onions. This is not the only occasion when Tolkien showed that he had read the dictionary's definitions and found them wanting: in the essay "On Fairy-Stories,"[9] with which most evaluations of *The Lord of the Rings* rather misguidedly start, Tolkien noted an error in the *OED* entry under *fairy*. John Gower is quoted as saying of a young man that he appears "as he were a faierie"; but what Gower wrote, Tolkien observed, was "as he were of faierie," that is, "as if he were come from Faërie." *Fairy*, then, in the sense "supernatural being of diminutive size," is both more modern and (as Tolkien evidently thought) less respectable than the dictionary editors realised.

Since Tolkien could so obviously be provoked by dictionary entries, it makes sense to look at the definitions offered by the *OED* for the independent races that contribute so much to the

7. By Paul Kocher, *Master of Middle-Earth: The Achievement of J. R. R. Tolkien* (Boston, 1972; reprinted Harmondsworth, 1974). The reference is on page 161 of the Harmondsworth edition.

8. This story can be found most conveniently in *The Tolkien Reader* (New York, 1966).

9. Also to be found in *The Tolkien Reader*, as well as in Tolkien, *Tree and Leaf* (London, 1964). The basis of the essay was a lecture delivered in 1938.

charm of the Third Age: elves, dwarves, ents, and (if one substitutes "entertainment-value" for "charm") orcs. For connoisseurs of *The Lord of the Rings* they make sad but interesting reading. Under *dwarf*, for instance, we find:

> "1. A human being much below the ordinary stature or size; a pygmy
> b. One of a supposed race of diminutive beings, who figure in Teutonic and esp. Scandinavian mythology and folk-lore; often identified with the elves, and supposed to be endowed with special skills in working metals, etc."

There are several points at which Professor Tolkien's dwarves, like Farmer Giles's blunderbuss, surpass the definition offered. They are of course great craftsmen; but they are by no means "diminutive," though short; and they are distinct from elves by language, race, habits, and temperament. The slight slur in the word "supposed" and the promotion of "human pygmy" to the status of main sense are further evidences of the gap between sharply delineated fantasy and vague (indeed slightly bored) reality. There is no doubt that Tolkien did read this entry, for from the time of *The Hobbit*[10] he used the archaic plural "dwarves," and (*Lord of the Rings*, III, 415) showed a fondness even for "dwarrows" or "dwerrows": the reason for this is given in the *OED*'s long note on the word's "interesting phonetic processes." It seems likely that the entry was also an irritant, and that by using the archaic plural Tolkien was making a conscious effort to escape from modern forms, with their feeble conceptions of mythology, "the sillier tales of these later days," as he says (III, 415, once more). One might say the same of the entry under *elf*. This time the dictionary does give a mythological sense as the main one: "The name of a class of supernatural beings, in early Teutonic belief supposed to possess formidable magic powers. . . . They were believed to be of dwarfish form, to produce diseases of various kinds, to act as *incubi* and *succubi*, to cause nightmares, and to steal children, substituting changelings in their place." It goes on to observe that though fairies are

10. Future references are by page to *The Hobbit*, 3d ed. (London, 1966).

less Teutonic than elves, "In modern literature, *elf* is a mere synonym of FAIRY, which has to a great extent superseded it."

Tolkien's dislike for the word "fairy" is well-known. He does not seem to use it after page 11 of *The Hobbit*, while "On Fairy-Stories" contains an attack (once again) on the *OED* entry *fairy*, and especially on the idea it presents of tininess, of fairies hidden in cowslips and the like. The Lord of the Rings therefore attempts to reverse the supersession of the word "elf," as also to contradict its modern associations with maleficence and child-stealing. Perhaps most of all, Tolkien refuses to follow the *OED* in its circular definition of *elf* by *dwarf* and *dwarf* by *elf*: as has been noted,[11] the distinctiveness of the races is in *The Lord of the Rings* a major theme.

It would, of course, be both "insane" and "unnecessary" to write a thousand-page epic in contradiction of half-a-dozen dictionary entries! But the entries have a significance beyond themselves. They are an authoritative representation of modern opinion (or at least of opinion in Tolkien's youth and maturity). And they show a continuing insensitivity to the power of those literary works to which Tolkien devoted his working life. The word "dwarf," for instance, can hardly fail to evoke, for an Icelandicist, such violent and remorseless scenes as that of the Everlasting Battle, the *Hjaðningavíg*, in Snorri Sturluson's *Prose Edda*.[12] The viking Hethinn has stolen the princess Hildr from her father Hǫgni; but the King Hǫgni pursues them to Háey in the Orkneys. Hildr tries to mediate between her raptor-husband and her father, but the pride of the former will not let him submit in appropriately humble terms. Only as the armies meet does he offer peace to his kinsman; but his father-in-law replies that he has offered too late, "for now I have drawn the heirloom of Dáin, which the dwarves made (*Dáinsleif, er dvergarnir gerðu*), which must kill a man every time it is drawn and never yields in the stroke and no wound heals where it makes a scratch." Like most vikings, Hethinn is not impressed by descriptions. But we

11. By Paul Kocher, *Master of Middle-Earth*, chap. 5.

12. Future translations are my own, from *Edda Snorra Sturlusonar*, ed. Finnur Jónsson (Copenhagen, 1931).

are. Here and elsewhere,[13] the craftsmanship of the dwarves is associated with their noble but unforgiving spirit, a major strand in Tolkien's characterisation of the race (as in the costly and painful vengeance of Thráin, Náin, and Dáin for Thrór, *Lord of the Rings*, III, 354–57), but one long passed from common knowledge. In early literature, too, the dwarves are associated with the dangerous, strife-breeding hoards of which Tolkien makes so much in *The Hobbit*, often mentioning the "dragon-sickness," the "bewilderment" to which Bilbo's companions are liable; and of course with the fatal ring Andvaranaut. But it is enough to say that Tolkien's conception of the race is as much re-creation as new invention.

The elves, however, present more of a problem. In line 112 of *Beowulf*, for instance, they appear in odd company. The poet has said that the monster Grendel comes of the race of Cain, the primal murderer; and of this race too come all misbegotten creatures, *eotenas ond ylfe and orcneas*.[14] The *eotenas* are giants, as in Tolkien's Angmar place-name the Ettenmoors; *ne* in *orcnéas* seems analogous to Gothic *naus*, a corpse, while *orc* may come from Latin *Orcus*, Hell, the underworld. Elves or *ylfe* are then unequivocally hostile, like murderers, giants, or the *draugar*, the walking dead of Scandinavian story. They are also responsible for "elf-shot" and "elf-sickness"—dangerous creatures. But in the poem *Judith* the heroine is *ides ælfscinu*, "a woman beautiful as an elf." It is common also to find the word "elf" as a luck-element, presumably, in Anglo-Saxon names: Ælf-red, Ælf-wine, Ælf-helm, Ælf-gifu, etc. In Laȝamon's *Brut*, furthermore (the Middle English poem which perhaps preserves most of Old English lore and sentiment), King Arthur is taken by the elves (*aluen*) as soon as he is born, and given great gifts; when he is wounded in the last battle he says:

And ich wulle uaren to Aualun, to uairest alre maidene,

13. For instance, with the sword Tyrfing at the start of *The Saga of King Heidrek the Wise*, ed. and trans. (perhaps coincidentally) by Christopher Tolkien (London, 1960). The saga also contains a riddle-match and some revealing place-names.

14. Quotations and line numbers from *Beowulf*, ed. Friedrich Klaeber, 3d ed. (Boston, 1950). Translations are my own.

to Argante þere quene, aluen swiðe sceone,
and heo scal mine wunden makien alle isunde. . . .

"And I will go to Avalon, to queen Argante, fairest of all maid-
ens, the very beautiful elf; and she shall heal all my
wounds. . . ."[15] Laȝamon has added this to the story of his usual
sources, Geoffrey of Monmouth and Wace (who wrote in Latin
and French respectively). It seems to represent some popular
and native belief.

The problem then is that elves are of a dual nature: beautiful, lucky, beneficent, curative, but also dangerous, malignant.
It is evident that in *The Lord of the Rings* Tolkien has set himself
to solve this puzzle by presenting a situation from which the
mixed feelings of early Englishmen might naturally (if wrongly)
have arisen. Thus *his* elves take Frodo for cure in much the same
way as Laȝamon's took Arthur; and their beauty is everywhere
stressed (as in the dwarf Gimli's dispute with the Rider Éomer).
But even in Middle-Earth their reputation is not always good.
Thus Boromir (I, 352) balks at entering Lothlórien, the elves'
wood, for in Gondor "it is said that few come out who once go
in; and of that few none have escaped unscathed." His brother
Faramir is later wiser (II, 288) but gives Sam Gamgee the
chance to expound the elves' dangerousness: " 'I don't know
about *perilous*,' said Sam. 'It strikes me that folk takes their peril
with them into Lórien, and finds it there because they've
brought it. But perhaps you could call her perilous, because
she's so strong in herself. You, you could dash yourself to pieces
on her, like a ship on a rock; or drownd yourself, like a hobbit in
a river. But neither rock nor river would be to blame.' " Danger
and beauty co-exist. The reason for Boromir's fear of never coming out is also clarified at I, 404, where the Fellowship proves to
have lost track of time, as is traditional for those in fairy-hills.
They have come under the spell, or glamour, of elvish immortality; to immortals time flows rapidly. The Riders of Rohan, finally, express Anglo-Saxon attitudes in this as in so much
else, using "elvish" to mean "uncanny, mysterious, not to be
trusted." "Are you elvish folk?" says Éomer suspiciously (II,

15. Lines 4070–72 of *Selections from Laȝamon's Brut*, ed. G. L. Brook (Oxford, 1963). The translation is my own.

34). "They are elvish wights," say the bystanders at III, 59. "Let them go where they belong, into the dark places, and never return. The times are evil enough." Their surly know-nothingness—they are speaking of Aragorn, king-to-be—is a perfect repetition of the scandalised, ignorant, and dishonourable suggestion of the bystanders in *Sir Gawain and the Green Knight*, line 681, that Arthur should not have let Sir Gawain keep his word, but should have kept him at home:

> And so had better haf ben þen britned to noȝt,
> Hadet wyth an aluisch mon, for angardeȝ pryde.

"That would have been better than being broken to nothing, being beheaded by some elvish man, through vanity and pride!"[16] Tolkien's elves, then, not only repeat ancient literature but offer to explain it. There is a certain depth in their characterisation—especially as regards their effect on men. This appears to have come from long consideration of the discrepancies uncovered by philology.

In such passages ancient knowledge begins to turn into new creation. This is increasingly evident with at least three of the other intelligent species in *The Lord of the Rings:* orcs, ents, and hobbits. Of these orcs are naturally the simplest case. There is an entry under *orc* in the *OED*, but its main sense is "whale" or "seal," from Old Norse *orkn*, as in the Orkneys, "the seal islands." Tolkien rejected this in the Preface to *The Hobbit:* "Orc is not an English word." But in the sixteenth century the word was imported into English from Italian *orco*, meaning "ogre" or "giant." Tolkien might have known it from Ariosto. Middle-Earth is remarkable, however, for the absence in it of references to Latinate languages or peoples;[17] even Gondor is not very like

16. Lines 680–81 of *Sir Gawain and the Green Knight*, ed. J. R. R. Tolkien and E. V. Gordon, corrected edition (Oxford, 1930). The translation is my own.

17. There is only one evident exception to this, Bilbo's offensive relations the Sack*ville*-Bagginses. It may be noted that Bag End, which is where Bilbo lives, is a direct translation of *cul-de-sac,* the French phrase used for some reason in official English to replace the native idiom "dead end." It is typical that Tolkien should translate the phrase, perhaps finding the French import annoying and patronising—like the *Sack*ville-Bagginses themselves.

Rome. It seems more probable that in coining the word "orc" Tolkien is looking back, not to the Renaissance, nor to Blake,[18] but to the curious elements in the Anglo-Saxon compounds *orc-néas* (mentioned above) and *orcpyrs oððe heldeofol*, "orc-giant or hell-devil," as the *OED* puts it. "Orc," then, he seems to imply, is not an English word but *might have been* if it had happened to survive; its status is much the same as the forgotten plural "dwerrows." Its Englishness, moreover, explains his final preference for it over the word "goblin," used throughout *The Hobbit* but tainted by its Latinate etymology.

As a race, the orcs are simply and obviously characterised—too obviously, some have thought. The ents are more commonly admired for the originality of their conception. They are immensely old, wise, and strong, but also passive and tree-like: the least human of the intelligent species of Middle-Earth. But they too draw some part of their inspiration from a philological puzzle. "Ent" is definitely not an English word, there being no relevant entry at all in the *OED*. It is, however, an Anglo-Saxon word, and it means in most cases "giant." Both Nimrod and Goliath were *entas*. The disapproving use of it by biblical translators and commentators is belied, however, by the irritatingly vague use of it in heroic and elegiac poetry to mean just a vanished race, a race of builders. The Swedish King Ongentheow, in *Beowulf*, wears an "entish helm," and the sword with which Beowulf beheads Grendel's mother is the "former work of ents." But stone is their most common material. The ents made the dragon's den in *Beowulf*, the ruined walls of *The Wanderer*. Most strikingly, they made the cities mentioned in the first two lines of the Cottonian *Maxims*, that mysterious set of "gnomic verses" which still presents very evident puzzles to Anglo-Saxon scholars. The lines run:

> Cyning sceal rice healdan. Ceastra beoð feorran gesyne,
> orðanc enta geweorc. . . .

King shall guard kingdom. Cities are to be seen from far off,

---

18. Blake used the word "orc," and is suggested as a source by Randel Helms, *Tolkien's World* (London, 1974), pp. 76–80. *Beowulf* and the *O.E.D.* are, however, more prominent in Tolkien's world than Blake.

skilful (*orthanc*) work of giants (*enta*). . . ."[19] It will be remembered that in *The Lord of the Rings* the stone tower in the
middle of Isengard, where Saruman is besieged by the ents, is
called Orthanc, glossed by Tolkien (II, 160) as meaning either
"Mount Fang" or "The Cunning Mind"; the half-line of the
Cottonian *Maxims* has suggested to Tolkien both the name of the
tower and its association with the race. One might go further
and suggest that the true stimulus for Professor Tolkien was the
term's very vagueness: they are a race people have heard of, but
never seen, gigantic in size (or so one guesses from their surviving artefacts), but very definitely *gone*—unlike elves,
dwarves, ettins, or trolls, all accepted as contemporary hazards
by early English or Norse writers. Of course the main thing we
learn about the Ents from Fangorn is that they have lost the
Entwives, and that as a result there will never again be any
Entings: the race is doomed to extinction, just as the elves are (I,
380) to "dwindling." In Middle-Earth, however, Orthanc might
survive them, to be called vaguely by the Riders the *enta geweorc*.
Their name for wisdom might also survive. When Fangorn
meets the hobbits Pippin and Merry the first thing he does is to
run over in his mind a set of gnomic verses (II, 67), very similar
to those of the *Maxims*, to see where the hobbits fit. In doing so
he again hints at Tolkien's inspiration for the ents; and offers a
kind of explanation (otherwise lacking in Anglo-Saxon studies)
for the purpose of such poems—they are mnemonic, the card-
indexes of a race with long memories.

But the hobbits, of course, do not fit in Fangorn's list, and it
is this race which is most evidently an original creation by Tolkien, the starting-point, furthermore, of the entire Middle-Earth
cycle. "In a hole in the ground there lived a hobbit." This is the
sentence, as the story goes, that came unbidden into the professor's mind to start the whole creative process.[20] Could any-

19. The poem can be found conveniently edited and translated in *A Choice
of Anglo-Saxon Verse*, ed. R. Hamer (London, 1970).

20. I know no source for this but Oxford gossip. Since this essay was
written, however, Humphrey Carpenter has given a more detailed (but still
inevitably incomplete) account of the genesis of *The Hobbit* and the Middle-
Earth cycle in *J. R. R. Tolkien: A Biography* (London, 1977), especially pp.
176–79.

thing be more spontaneous, less philological? To this there are perhaps two replies. One is that having invented the word Tolkien felt obliged to give it an etymology, and to embed that deep in the structure of linguistic correspondences that holds Middle-Earth together. The explanation is given in note 1 to Appendix F on page 416 of *The Return of the King*: "hobbit" is a worn-down form of "*holbytla*," a feasible though non-existent Anglo-Saxon compound, "hole-dweller." The first line of *The Hobbit* is then a simple tautology: "In a hole in the ground there lived a hole-liver." Was this neat etymology, given on the *last* page of the trilogy, present unconsciously in the author's mind as he wrote the *first* words of *The Hobbit?* Perhaps not. But, as most critics agree, the word which "hobbit" is most likely to remind one of is "rabbit."[21] And that word, too, presents us with a puzzle.

It is a very familiar word, learnt in childhood along with fox, wolf, bear, rat, hare, frog, and so on. But where all these other animals are well-authenticated natives with proper Anglo-Saxon names (respectively, *fox, wulf, bera, ræt, hara, frogga*), "rabbit" never occurs in Anglo-Saxon at all. Nor is this a case (as with Brock the badger) of a nickname (*badge-ard*) replacing an older word (*brocc*). Rabbits were just not known in the world of Northern antiquity, being imports of perhaps the thirteenth century. Yet they do appear in Middle-Earth, quite prominently in Book iv, chapter 4, "Of Herbs and Stewed Rabbit." Why did Tolkien allow this anachronism? Why, indeed, did he reinforce it with those even later imports from the New World, potatoes (the speciality of Gaffer Gamgee, I, 30) and "pipeweed" or to-bacco (the hobbits' only technological innovation, I, 17–18, II, 163, et passim)? The anachronisms cannot be accidental. They suggest an admission by Tolkien that there are products of modernity acceptable even in an ideal world: new things which nevertheless *fit*. And hobbits appear to be in this category. Their attitudes are, if not modern, at least early twentieth century; they are furthermore evidently English, by habits and by history;[22] in the Northern and archaic company of elves and trolls

21. It occurred to Edmund Wilson, "Oo, Those Awful Orcs!" and to more than one critic in the Isaacs and Zimbardo collection.

22. In the Prologue to *The Lord of the Rings* we learn that they are good-humoured, fond of food, uninterested in education, by no means beautiful. In

and ettins they are immigrants, anachronisms, intruders. And yet from the start they have drawn their charm from a blend of total novelty and near-familiarity; neither their name nor their behavior seems out of place. It is therefore possible that the word "rabbit" *was* an element in the conception of "hobbit," though more from its etymology than its meaning. Hobbits *are* novel, but that novelty need be no more apparent to us than the simply philological discrepancy between a word like "rabbit" (no English ancestor), and words like "otter" or "weasel" or "mouse" (derived by true descent from *otor, wesle, mus*). The invented etymology of *holbytla* is then only a further sop to the rationalising mind.

Dwarves, ents, orcs, hobbits: all are words or forms that are not in the English language, but could be, or ought to be, or would have been had the language developed more obviously from ancient literary texts. A large part of Professor Tolkien's inspiration seems to come from long brooding over such cruxes as *ylfe ond orcnéas, hadet with an aluisch mon, orðanc enta geweorc, Dáinsleif er dvergarnir gerðu.* This is not a mode of composition very familiar to literary critics, or likely to be much favoured by them. But to deprecate it is to miss the importance of the philological crux. These are, after all, the only way into a thought-world once too familiar for explanation but now nearly too dead for recovery (as Tolkien rather wryly notes in Appendix D, III, 385). That world, of the Northern imagination, still possesses an unusual power for many (as Tolkien's friend C. S. Lewis has almost too personally testified).[23] And the whole of Tolkien's working life must have accustomed him to the way in which tiny, even pedantic points of philology can lead to the most certain and sweeping conclusions about that world *and the way that people lived in it.* This point is often forgotten or never

the story as a whole we find that they have great powers of endurance, though little aggression. This mixture of vice and virtue recalls a traditional, if old-fashioned, English self-image. Like the Anglo-Saxons, the hobbits emigrated in three tribes from the East, one of these tribes coming from a district called "the Angle." But in the Shire the hobbits forgot their history, as the English, in post-Conquest England, forgot theirs.

23. C. S. Lewis, *Surprised by Joy* (London, 1935). See especially chaps. 5, 7, 11.

known. But there are few chains of reasoning more compelling than that, for instance, which led Tolkien from certain points about vowel-length in words descended from Anglo-Saxon weak verbs of Class II, to the conclusion that in England at some period after the Norman Conquest there must have existed a people who had not been Gallicised but had retained and developed their native tongue even for literary purposes. What they wrote was "not a language long relegated to the 'uplands' struggling once more for expression in apologetic emulation of its betters or out of compassion for the lewd, but rather one that has never fallen back into 'lewdness,' and has contrived in troublous times to maintain the air of a gentleman, if a country gentleman."[24] The soil that bred this language was probably Herefordshire, on the western march of England. But it sounds also strangely like the Shire of the hobbits, another comfortable and backward relic of forgotten empire. The imaginative road to the Shire, in short, leads through weak verbs; the road to Middle-Earth lies between the lines of the *OED*.

At this point one may pause to consider a natural reply to the method of inference used so far. Source-study is always speculative, as has often been said, even if the pursuit of words and names is likely to be more successful than that of themes or ideas. But in any case it may be useless. Even if Tolkien did invent elves and ents in the sort of way that has been suggested, what would this matter to the millions of readers of *The Lord of the Rings* who have never even heard of *Beowulf* or Snorri's *Edda*, let alone worried about their difficult places? Or, to put it in more correct critical language:

> [O]ne function of Tolkien criticism should be to shift the emphasis from extraliterary aspects of the trilogy and its audience to a consider-

24. J. R. R. Tolkien, *Ancrene Wisse* and *Hali Meiðhad,"* *Essays and Studies* 14 (1929), 104–26. Tolkien's other long article, "*Sigelwara land,"* in *Medium Ævum* 1 (1932), 183–96, and 3 (1934), 95–111, also probes the hard word *Sigelwara* to find the meaning of its probable ancestor, *Sigelhearwa*. Tolkien remarks at the end that such searches are bound to be inconclusive, but useful as providing "dim and confused" glimpses of "the background of English and northern tradition." In the oblivion that all but swallowed the entire race of *Sigelhearwan* and the gentlemen of Hereford, Tolkien must have thought, there was room for any number of *holbytlan*, and many Shires.

ation of the work itself . . . for all the insight they might contribute it seems to me that [exterior approaches] would only add to the framework within which interior critical investigation might go on . . . the ultimate function of criticism is to render judgment on a work of art.[25]

Judge not, lest ye be judged, one might reply. But it is at any rate fair to inquire what function philology has, not for the author of *The Lord of the Rings*, but for its ordinary reader.

The answer must surely be, that the lore with which the trilogy is studded works overwhelmingly to produce that sense of depth and consistency which distinguishes *The Lord of the Rings* even from more academically respectable fantasies, such as Mervyn Peake's. Only a few examples need be given. The cloaks of Lórien, for instance, are one of the best-realised minor props in the story. They cannot protect their wearers, but they do provide excellent camouflage: "It was hard to say of what colour they were: grey with the hue of twilight under the trees they seemed to be; and yet if they were moved, or set in another light, they were green as shadowed leaves, or brown as fallow fields by night, dusk-silver as water under the stars" (I, 386). No wonder that Pippin asks, "Are these magic cloaks?"—to be told that they are not, though they are, once again, "elvish." The clue to their conception lies in the word "fallow," used in the quotation above; for though this now means "temporarily uncultivated," it descends from Anglo-Saxon *fealu*, a colour-word meaning variously yellow (like sand), russet (like apples), grey (like the sea), not to mention green, gold, pale, bay, and other alternatives. The scholarly answer[26] is that instead of communicating a particular colour or hue, as we now assume, the Anglo-Saxon word is one of a set dealing with brightness, a set much better developed in Old than in modern English. The general reader does not know or notice this. What he does realise, though, is that the cloaks help to define the elves, exemplifying their peculiar harmony with nature, and the respect they extend to inanimate objects—a respect so great that it may turn inanimate to animate, as with the trees of Fangorn (II, 71), and

25. N. D. Isaacs, "On the Possibilities of Writing Tolkien Criticism."

26. Given most recently by N. D. Barley, "Old English Colour Classification: Where Do Matters Stand?" *Anglo-Saxon England* 3 (1974), 15–28.

which makes the cloaks very nearly, just credibly responsive to the wishes of their wearers.

There philology is being *used*. A more wide-reaching example is the character Saruman. His name is Anglo-Saxon *searu-man*, "the cunning man," an appropriate name for a wizard.[27] But like *fealu*, *searu* presents a problem for Anglo-Saxonists. On the one hand it is applied to skilfully made artefacts, in *Beowulf*, of jewels, clamps, and armour. When Beowulf speaks first to King Hrothgar the poet remarks approvingly (lines 405–6):

> on him byrne scan
> searonet seowed   smiþes orþancum.

"On him his armour shone, the cunning net sewed by the crafts of the smith." One might note the connection of *orþanc*, once again, with *searo*, forerunning Saruman's living in the tower of Orthanc. But the use of *searo-* is favourable, indeed relishing. The monster Grendel's glove, however, into which he stuffs the corpses he feeds on, is not so attractive. Still, it is *searobendum fæst*, "held by cunning clasps." Elsewhere the poet uses the prefix even less neutrally, as when Hama flees the *searoniðas*, "crafty enmities," of wicked King Eormenric. In the Old English *Rhyming Poem*,[28] to complete the word's range, it is said of an evil character, *sinc searwade*, "treasure deceived him (?) treasure corrupted him (?)." As usual, the puzzle lies behind the word. But it also contributes to the character. Saruman relies less on will-power and more on mechanical contrivance than any other major personality in *The Lord of the Rings*. "He has a mind of metal and wheels," says Fangorn (II, 76); he appears to have invented gunpowder or something like it at II, 142, and a kind of napalm some thirty pages later; and in "The Scouring of the Shire" he approaches symbolism closer than anyone else in the story. What he stands for, evidently, is modern, industrial man. This section has on occasion been found unconvincing and un-

27. *Searu* is the West Saxon form most often found in Anglo-Saxon texts. But neither Tolkien nor *Beowulf* came originally from Wessex, and with typical punctilio the Anglian form *saru* has been restored. See also II, 123, *Herugrim* for *Heorugrim*.

28. To be found in *The Anglo-Saxon Poetic Records*, ed. G. P. Krapp and E. V. K. Dobbie, III (New York, 1936).

helpful as an analysis of recent history or the modern predicament, and certainly the references to socialism, or communism, are unexpected in Middle-Earth, where evil characters have no need of ideologies. Still, the reader takes the point. Just as the elves' respect for nature is mirrored in their works, so his machines come to be mirrored in Saruman's mind. Corruption comes from the objects and the attitude. Nowadays we would use words like "exploitative," "manipulative," but these would ring false in Middle-Earth—as we might have expected, they are inventions of the nineteenth century. Their meaning is latent, however, in Anglo-Saxon *searu*, and the temptation that gives rise to them can be, and is, fairly integrated into the thought-world of Saruman, the ents, the elves, the Riders.

It will be seen that Tolkien's attitude to words is very different from that of a modern critic. The critics think that man is master: that poets and artists use words originally, individually, for their own inner purposes. Tolkien feels that words have a life of their own, which continues irrespective of rough treatment from time and careless speakers. His names for things and people are often just (just?) old words. Thus Beorn, the were-bear of *The Hobbit*, comes from the Anglo-Saxon poetic word for "man," *beorn*, which at an earlier date meant also "bear"; of course the were-bear belief is deeply entrenched in Northern legend, e.g. in Beowulf, Beo-wulf, "the wolf of the bees," the honey-stealer—the bear. The Wild Men of Drúadan Forest are called Woses (III, 105) as an explanation of or apology for the garbled line 721 of *Sir Gawain and the Green Knight*. Smaug the worm takes his name from the mysterious *sméah-wyrm*, "penetrating worm," of the Anglo-Saxon *Leechbooks*, for *smáugr* would be in Norse to *sméah* in English as *dráumr* to *dréam* or *gláumr* to *gléam*—a regular formation, though one that does not happen to be recorded. Gollum's first name, Sméagol, is from the same root, Norse and English *smjúga*, *smúgan* "to creep," Old English *sméagan*, "to enquire"—Sméagol means "the Snooper." Gríma Wormtongue is so called (*pace* Lin Carter) not from Anglo-Saxon *grimena*, "caterpillar" but from *gríma*, a word meaning at once "helmet, mask," and "ghost, spectre." The dual meaning is shared by medieval Latin *masca*, testifying to an ancient fear, perhaps, of things without faces. It is a threatening word, like

Dernhelm, the alias chosen by Éowyn, translated for us by Tolkien at III, 116—"the helm of her secrecy had fallen from her." One is tempted to run on. Tolkien's linguistic manoeuvres are fascinating in themselves, like his pedigree of the kings of Rohan, nearly all the names of which are Anglo-Saxon words for "king," *except the first*, Eorl the Young, an ancient word which, in the Eddic poem *Rígspula*, seems to look back to a time before kings were invented, when all men were Jarl, Karl, or Thræl, earl, churl, or slave. But the substantive point is that through *The Hobbit* and *The Lord of the Rings*, words are used for names: not to save thought, but because the author feels a deep assurance that the words will do the work they always did—they will sound right.

There are more scholarly ways of putting the point just made, and Tolkien in his time made fun of them;[29] for the point contradicts a long-standing linguistic tenet that sound and sense are separate, that onomatopoeia cannot explain the growth of language. But Tolkien evidently felt that there was more to words than sound: there was sound-patterning, and there was also history, a process in which peoples and lands and languages all grew up together. He put the case in his little-read O'Donnell lecture "English and Welsh,"[30] in which he guardedly and learnedly avoided the by-paths of "folk-memory" and "native instinct" into which analytic explanations are drawn. But *The Lord of the Rings* shows what he meant in a better because more discursive way. It is instructive to remember how often characters in the trilogy react to the *sound* of languages which they do not know. At II, 112, Aragorn "began to chant softly in a slow tongue unknown to the Elf and the Dwarf; yet they listened, for there was a strong music in it. 'That, I guess, is the language of the Rohirrim,' said Legolas; 'for it is like to this land itself; rich and rolling in part, and else hard and stern as the mountains. But I cannot guess what it means. . . .' " There is a more un-

29. For instance on page 36 of his O'Donnell lecture already cited.

30. See above, n. 6. This lecture has been little read by academic critics, but, as often, the Tolkien fans have been wiser. In a short piece in the *Tolkien Journal* 3, no. 1 (1967), 9–11, "Tolkien as Scholar and Artist," Clyde S. Kilby makes good use of the lecture, and it is mentioned on other occasions in *Mythprint*, *Orcrist*, and similar magazines.

expected scene in Rivendell (I, 267) when Gandalf reads the words of the Black Speech written on the Ring: "The change in the wizard's voice was astounding. Suddenly it became menacing, powerful, harsh as stone. A shadow seemed to pass over the high sun, and the porch for a moment grew dark. All trembled, and the Elves stopped their ears." Gandalf is rebuked by Elrond, not for threatening them with what the words mean, but for expressing them in that particular language. By contrast, Elvish is used repeatedly in the trilogy as a password (III, 189), as a talisman (II, 329), even as an inspiration (II, 338–39)—for Sam in the spider's den "cried in a language which he did not know. . . . And with that he staggered to his feet and was Samwise the hobbit, Hamfast's son, again!" It is Sam too—by no means a scholarly character—who responds to the ring of the unfamiliar elvish and dwarvish place-names in the mines of Moria (I, 330). "I like that!" he says, "I should like to learn it." His response to language, like Merry's at the muster of Rohan in III, 65, instructs us in what should be our own. We do not need to know the languages to realise they have a history and an individual character; we need not know where the words come from to catch something of their effect.

In fact readers of *The Lord of the Rings* probably understand, half-consciously, a good deal more than they appreciate. The hobbits' speech sets up a standard of naturalness. Against this the Riders' is solemn and old-fashioned, often rather straightforward grammatically, though without losing a certain ceremoniousness. (See especially II, 34 ff., III, 58.) Much of their cultural history is indicated by this duality—they are aristocratic (unlike the hobbits), but unsophisticated (unlike the men of Gondor). The odd words they use serve first to show their difference from the longer-established peoples of the West, but in any case soon begin to make sense; if one does not know that *dwimor* is Anglo-Saxon for "nightmare, illusion, sorcery," Éomer's remark that Saruman is "dwimmer-crafty" (II, 39) may present a difficulty, though Tolkien translates it at once—"both cunning and dwimmer-crafty, having many guises." But by the time that one has learnt that Dwimordene means Lothlórien, the wood of "deceit" (II, 118), and Dwimorberg the Haunted Mountain (III, 59), Éowyn's "Begone, foul dwimmerlaik!" at

III, 116, seems exact and appropriate. (This last is a word, like
aluen, used by Laȝamon.) Meanwhile, in the background to the
Hobbit-Rider contrast, there is the language of dwarves and
northern men (Old Norse, as the Riders' is Old English), which
gives us Durin, Dáin, Gimli, and the other dwarf-names, as also
Gandalf, Smaug, the Wargs, and Glamdring, Gandalf's sword.
We can see that this is related to Westron and the Riders'
speech, for Gandalf is a name accepted by both peoples; it seems
nevertheless harsher and sterner in sound, appropriate to the
"dour" and "thrawn" dwarvish character—we project on them
the popular characteristics of Scots and Northumbrians. To all
this the Black Speech is entirely alien,[31] marked off by its use of
grammatical suffixes (durbatulûk), its apparent post-positions
(burzum-ishi, Saruman-glob), its constant back-vowels and con-
sonant-clusters (Lugbúrz, Nazgûl, Ufthak, Gorbag, Uglúk,
etc.). To our ears also it sounds thick, guttural, clumsy.

There are potentially scores of such discriminations and rec-
ognitions in *The Lord of the Rings*. Some of them are explained in
the Foreword to the second edition, and in Part II of Appendix
F, the places where Tolkien makes in most detail his extraordinarily elaborate claim to be, not the author, but a translator of something written originally in quite different languages. The pose has proved annoying to many, but at the
centre of it lies a compliment: Tolkien assumes that we are all
responsive to cultural history as expressed in language, even if
we just realise that words sound "queer" or have a "style" (III,
413). The reactions of most readers suggest that the compliment
was justified. And the use of old words, unexplained words,
words from different languages, has a further purpose: to suggest that Middle-Earth is as big and old as our real world, that it
is full of odd corners where half-known peoples speak their own
tongues and live their own lives, and that its history is full of

31. My colleague, Mr. Edwin Ardener, has remarked that the Ring inscription sounds like a garbled form of the start of the Lord's prayer in one or
other of the Slavonic languages, for instance Czech, "*Otcě náš kterýž jsi v ne-
besich,*" Serbo-Croat "*Oče naš koji si na nebesima.*" This point, of course, can only
be about the sound of languages, and must by no means be drawn into
allegory.

unknown patches where one can guess at events only through the blur of language-relationships. Tolkien said of *Beowulf* that its "illusion of historical truth and perspective . . . is largely a product of art."[32] This is self-evidently true of *The Lord of the Rings*. It need only be added that its illusions are particularly attractive in their solid-seemingness, and are largely the product of linguistic art.

Two areas in which this art is exercised may be noted, simply to re-exemplify the contribution of minor details to the overall effect of the trilogy. One is place-names. Nearly all the characters of *The Lord of the Rings* like to explain place-names. Fangorn can hardly take a drink without observing (II, 73), "Part of the name of this place might be Wellinghall, if it were turned into your language. I like it." Later he gives us Derndingle. Celeborn sends off the Fellowship (I, 389) to "the Tindrock, that we call Tol Brandir" and then to "the Nindalf, the Wetwang as it is called in your tongue." The names sound queer and old, or foreign, and there seems to be no arguing about them, any more than there is about Beorn and the Carrock in *The Hobbit*, page 125. "He called it the Carrock, because carrock is his word for it. He calls things like that carrocks, and this one is *the* Carrock because it is the only one near his home. . . ." Gandalf has put his finger on the essential quality of place-names: to most people they do not *mean* anything, they simply *are*. They therefore help most particularly to weigh fantasy down with reality; why would one invent them (we feel vaguely) if their referents did not exist? But of course place-names at one time always *did* mean something, and the meaning of most of those mentioned so far can readily be discovered from E. Ekwall, *The Oxford Dictionary of Place-Names*, in its various editions from 1936 to 1960. Can anything of that meaning survive? Tolkien, with his tendency to stress relationships between lands and languages and peoples, evidently thought so. And the Shire, at least, seems to be characterised very largely, in all its variety and joviality and general muddy-footedness, by the names of places by no means directly relevant to the story. Breehill,

32. J. R. R. Tolkien, "*Beowulf*: The Monsters and the Critics," *Proceedings of the British Academy* 22 (1936), 245–95.

Chetwood, Crickhollow, remind us that the hobbits are im-migrants;[33] to an English ear Haysend, Bamfurlong, and the Withywindle sound irresistibly rustic, though by no means alien; Nobottle and Hardbottle may sound funny. But then so do the Farthings, and the English reader may then think un-easily of the Yorkshire Ridings, and reflect how little he knows of his own country's history, how often it shows itself in garbled names. The Shire sounds real. So, to a lesser extent, does the rest of Middle-Earth. The cultists' map-making instinct (shared of course by hobbits) is not in the end inappropriate.

Place-names, however, contribute only broadly to literary effect. One can be more precise about those other familiar re-positories of archaic words and ideas, proverbs. These, too, stud *The Lord of the Rings* in scores, often surprising the reader with their switches on the proverbial expressions of the present. "All that is gold does not glitter," writes Gandalf (I, 182), reversing the common saying, though with evident good sense; "Need brooks no delay," says Éomer, "yet late is better than never," and he puts a grim twist on familiarity (III, 110); Éowyn says (III, 77), "Where will wants not, a way opens," and her poetic, alliterative re-phrasing of "Where there's a will there's a way" exposes suddenly the epic solemnity of the Riders' culture. "Where there's a whip there's a will," say the orcs (III, 208). One might think, too, of the blacksmith's merry "No news is bad news" in *Farmer Giles of Ham*, "A worm won't return." But though proverbs, like place-names, are interesting one at a time, Tolkien can also use them to make broader points at particular places. There is a vein of ironic comedy in the proverbs of Bree, for instance (I, 165 ff.), which shows up better than words the town's complacent self-centredness. Barliman Butterbur greets the hobbits with that stalest and most overtly untruthful of say-ings, "It never rains but it pours" (as if there was no such word as "drizzle"). Then, feeling the need of a gloss, he adds, "we say

33. They contain misunderstood Celtic elements as well as the obvious Anglo-Saxon ones; see *Lord of the Rings*, III, 414, and Ekwall's *Dictionary of Place-Names*. Several of the Shire place-names are local to the Oxford area, e.g. Buckland, Bree (from Brill), Withywindle (from Withybrook and perhaps Windsor). *Farmer Giles of Ham* gives joking etymologies to the nearby villages of Worminghall and Thame.

in Bree" (as if it wasn't said everywhere). A few pages later he offers a real novelty, but a rude one—"there's no accounting for East and West, we say in Bree, meaning the Rangers and the Shire-folk, begging your pardon." The point is not lost on the Shire-hobbits. Pippin retaliates at I, 183, with "handsome is as handsome does, as we say in the Shire." And even Gandalf seems to have guessed what happened, when he defends Butter-bur at I, 233, qualifying his "he can see through a brick wall in time" with "(as they say in Bree)."

The proverbs of Rohan have a very different ring. It should be noted that in all the early encounters between members of the Fellowship and Riders of Rohan, the Riders take a risk. Éomer lends Aragorn a horse (II, 41); the gateward does not arrest Gandalf and the others, though he knows they are unwelcome (II, 113); three pages later Háma lets Gandalf carry his staff. Each man knows that he may be blamed, or executed, for what he does, since authority in Rohan is monarchic; but it is not despotic, and the Riders are not intimidated. Their attitude is summed up by Háma's "in doubt a man of worth will trust to his own wisdom," a virtual translation of the Danish coast-guard's saying in lines 287–88 of *Beowulf*, "*Æghwæþres sceal scearp scyldwiga gescad witan*," "in all things a sharp warrior must know how to discriminate." Tolkien has also taken from *Beowulf* the way in which proverbs may be used ironically—"Seldom does thief ride home to the stable"; aggressively—"news from afar is seldom sooth"; or to suggest hidden knowledge—"the wise speak only of what they know" (all to be found in II, 113–18). In the whole of that discussion there is a strong sense of dangerous tension underlying surface politeness; for this the proverbs are a safety-valve. They remind us that King Théoden is both barbar-ian and gentleman.

Many more examples could be cited, of proverbs, or place-names, or indeed of the use of nursery-rhymes. But the central point should be clear: *The Lord of the Rings* is full of hidden references, which work no doubt for those who notice them as references, but work just as well for those who do not. The sense of depth, truth, solidity, consistency, which nearly all readers agree is projected by the trilogy, stems from its substrata of ancient and modern lore. One further point may be made, both generally and from the Rohan passages just discussed. Though Tolkien pretends that he is a translator using Old English and Welsh and Old Norse simply for convenience, so that we are *not* to think that "the Rohirrim closely resembled the ancient English . . . except in a general way"[34] his claims are not even emotionally true. The social patterns of the Rohirrim doorguards and gatewards resemble those of the characters in *Beowulf* down to minute detail. And Tolkien used his ancient languages not because they helped to give a cultural outline to Middle-Earth (though that is what they do), but because he loved them. They were in his mind from the first,[35] and stayed in even if they had to be rationalised. As he testified himself: "Languages (like other art-forms or styles) have a virtue of their own. . . . Welsh is beautiful. . . . O felix peccatum Babel!"[36]

In the preceding pages it has been suggested firstly how Professor Tolkien's "inspiration" might indeed have been "linguistic," and secondly how the trilogy's "esthetic" might be seen as linguistic as well. It is also possible to remark, relatively briefly, on the help that language gives us in understanding the "meaning" of *The Lord of the Rings*, even its "mythology"—the quest of so many commentators!

It is now extremely common to talk about Tolkien's *"religious*

34. *Lord of the Rings*, III, 414. The thing in which they are most unlike the Anglo-Saxons is of course their love of horses. But while historical Anglo-Saxons were almost self-willed in their refusal to develop cavalry, the poetry contains many appreciative references to horses. Tolkien might have noted, for instance, the rare word *éored*, which he uses at II, 37. In the gnomic verses of the *Exeter Book* this seems to have been intended by the poet, but the scribe did not understand it and wrote instead the commoner word *worod*, "warband." *Éored*, then, is a word like *orc* or *sigelhearwa*: rare, old, suggestive of a lost tradition.

35. As one can see from the early comment, *Hobbit* p. 62, that "Glamdring" and "Orcrist" are elvish names, when they are in fact Northern (though neither exactly English or Norse). Tolkien seems to have conceived the dwarvish milieu originally as being Old Norse—the names are from the Eddic poem *Voluspá*—and to have evolved the rationalisation of "outer" and "secret" languages only later, see III, 415.

36. O'Donnell lecture, "English and Welsh." The whole lecture deserves to be read, for instance for its claims about the emotional effect, not of Gothic literature (of which none survives) but simply of Gothic words.

vision of reality," to translate *The Lord of the Rings* "into Augustinian terms," to say that the White Tree of Gondor "may be taken to refer to the Cross," etc.[37] At its worst this kind of criticism seems to be written by cultural monoglots, forced continually to assimilate unfamiliar ideas to their own preoccupations: thus tunnels are Freudian symbols of fertility, or alternatively of corruption, Frodo is a "perfect androgynous Adam," hobbits (in spite of their rabbit stews (II, 263), broiled bacon (II, 166), cold chicken, pork pies, and roast mutton, all mentioned in *The Hobbit*) are *vegetarians;* and so, unfortunately, on.[38] But such comments do at least direct us to what is evidently a difficult and important element in *The Lord of the Rings*, its relationship with the Christianity in which the author himself believed.

The problem may be stated simply. There are no references to Christianity in *The Lord of the Rings*, and much of its thought-world seems to be absent; even if Tolkien did say later, "Gandalf is an angel,"[39] Gandalf neither looks like one, talks like one, nor has the powers that would customarily be attributed to one. It is hard to be sure of a thousand-page story with no concordance, but words like "angel," "hell," "heaven," "soul," seem to be used sparingly if at all. No-one speaks of Judgment Day. No-one mentions God, or gods. Yet there are pervasive hints of other-worldliness and providence. Gandalf shows repeatedly that he believes in an organising power: he says that Bilbo was *meant* to find the Ring (I, 65), that this was not just "a strange chance" (I, 263, and again III, 360), that the orcs' capture of Pippin and

37. The first reference is to Robley Evans, *J. R. R. Tolkien* (New York, 1972); the next two to articles in *Tolkien and the Critics*, respectively Charles Moorman, "The Shire, Mordor, and Minas Tirith," pp. 201–17, and Mary Q. Kelly, "The Poetry of Fantasy: Verse in *The Lord of the Rings*," pp. 170–200.

38. All these suggestions are offered by writers in the Isaacs and Zimbardo collection; some of them are repeated from one essay to the next.

39. This is reported by Edmund Fuller, "The Lord of the Hobbits," pp. 17–39 of *Tolkien and the Critics*. Perhaps Tolkien was thinking of that rather untypical angel who appears at the start of Book II, canto 8, of Spenser's *Faerie Queene*. It has to be said that Tolkien has encouraged such identifications by his remark in *The Road Goes Ever On* (London, 1968), p. 65, that the invocations of Elbereth "and other references to religion in *The Lord of the Rings* are frequently overlooked."

Merry was too useful to be simply luck (II, 99–101). He is supported (I, 137) by Tom Bombadil, with his "just chance brought me then, if chance you call it." Hints could hardly be broader! Several characters also seem to believe in life beyond the grave, including the narrator. He says that Aragorn never returned to Cerin Amroth "as living man" (I, 367)—he did, then, as a dead one? Bombadil dispatches the Barrow-wight "till the world is mended" (I, 154), King Théoden says as he dies, "I go to my fathers" (III, 117), Thorin Oakenshield in *The Hobbit*, pp. 300–301, goes "to the halls of waiting to sit beside my fathers, until the world is renewed." Aragorn looks forward to some similar renewal on his deathbed (III, 344). But with all this there is no sign of organised religion, priesthood, or temples. Even the Riders, who might be expected from their cultural level to show superstition, have nothing except the place-name Dunharrow—which would, if it existed in modern English, be taken to mark a former pagan sanctuary. There *is* a religious map of Middle-Earth, but it is mostly blank—a striking, and unrealistic, phenomenon, which demands to be explained, not explained away.

The evident literary analogue to this situation is *Beowulf*—a work whose problems underlie *The Lord of the Rings* almost to the extent that *Paradise Lost* underlies C. S. Lewis's *Perelandra*.[40] The 3,182 lines of the epic contain getting on for seventy references to God or Hell or Doomsday, to Cain or to the Flood, enough to make it obvious, both from their number and their type, that the poet was as firm a Christian and Catholic as Tolkien himself. But there are no references in the poem to Christ: or to the Incarnation, the Resurrection, the Crucifixion. The poem has devils, but neither saints nor angels. Modern critical explanations for this astonishingly consistent restraint on the part of the poet are as complex as they are diverse. Fortunately we know Professor Tolkien's attitude to the problem, for it lies near the heart of his famous British Academy lecture for 1936, "*Beowulf*: The Monsters and the Critics." The main aim of this

40. "He has rewritten, or rather recreated *Beowulf*": so Douglass Parker, "Hwaet We Holbytla," *Hudson Review* 19 (1956–57), 598–609. Among other interesting points, Mr. Parker notes parts of some of the etymologies discussed here, though without remarking their roots in ambiguity or crux. I would not agree, for instance, that *searumann* means "man of treachery" *tout court*.

lecture was to defend the monsters from charges of irrelevance or triviality: but this was done by pointing to their role in the Northern mythology of "ancient England and Scandinavia" as the enemies of gods and men. Even when, with Christianity, belief in the gods faded, belief in monsters did not. And even though English Christians, like the *Beowulf*-poet, might feel assured that the monsters would not win in the end, they could still believe that the monsters and all they stood for ("Chaos and Unreason") were going to win "in Time . . . within Time . . . within the limits of human life." To these feelings of despair the "heroic temper" opposes "the theory of courage, which is the great contribution of early Northern literature"—the theory which says that even when the hero knows infallibly that he is going to lose (to the monsters, to Chaos, or to Time), he fights on and thinks his defeat "no refutation." So, to put it bluntly, Beowulf, though a pagan, is felt to have achieved something in killing the dragon in spite of its being "the end of Beowulf and of the hope of his people"; the poet, meanwhile, though a Christian, is able to look back at the pagan past without horror and to see in its defeat "something permanent and something symbolical."

Many difficulties remain. But at least two points emerge from the lecture which are of significance for commenting on *The Lord of the Rings*. One is that we do wrong to rummage in the trilogy for references to the Cross or the heavenly Jerusalem: if a Christian like the *Beowulf*-poet did not need to include them (and this was Tolkien's view, though not everybody's), then Tolkien himself might present an age of noble, pre-Christian mono-theism with a clear conscience. His characters are not Christians, yet, but they are not criticised for it either. It is true that the term "heathen" is used reprovingly in *The Lord of the Rings*, at III, 99, and III, 129, both referring to the same incident, the suicide of Denethor. But even for this there is a Beowulfian analogue, since in lines 175–88 of that poem the author also lets his feelings show and castigates the Danes for idol-worship, calling them "heathens" for the only time in the poem.[41] But in

41. In Appendix C to his British Academy lecture, Tolkien declared that he thought the attitude of these lines so alien to the rest of the poem that they were probably interpolations. If the Denethor episode does imitate them directly, he must later have changed his mind.

both works religion is normally not sharply defined—if pervasively present.

The second point, meanwhile, is that we do right to stress in the trilogy its references to *defeat*. These are obvious enough. From an early stage it is plain that the elves, at least, have little hope of an entirely satisfactory end to the war: when the Ring is destroyed their own power will fade and they will dwindle to extinction. Aragorn's elf-wife in the end loses immortality and lies in Cerin Amroth (III, 344) "until the world is changed, and all the days of her life are utterly forgotten." These events in any case follow a familiar pattern. Galadriel calls history "the long defeat" (I, 372), and Elrond says (I, 256), "I have seen three ages in the West of the world, and many defeats, and many fruitless victories." In a fully Christian society these remarks might require more explanation, and still more would Gandalf's "I am Gandalf, Gandalf the White, but Black is mightier still" (II, 103). As it is, though, we accept such remarks as helping to define heroism. These characters from the Northern world naturally hold to "the theory of courage"; they fight not because they expect ultimate victory but because (*mutatis mutandis*) they are men not monsters. Their courage is also not without some effect, even a great effect, as is proved by the reign of Aragorn and the golden age of the Shire; Elrond qualifies the adjective "fruitless" quoted above, and Gandalf says often enough that though one cannot foresee the future (III, 155), yet one has a duty towards it (I, 280): "We should seek a final end of this menace, even if we do not hope to make one." One can say only that such deliberate and clear-sighted valour, neither hopeful nor desperate, has been one of the particular charms of *The Lord of the Rings* in the present day. It gives special weight to Tolkien's death-scenes (Boromir, Théoden, Thorin Oakenshield, Aragorn, and Arwen); it is at least partly a historical re-creation; and it would be entirely destroyed by any too-near approach of salvation or omnipotence.

Any presentation of heroism causes problems, however, for our un-heroic, or anti-heroic age; we are reluctant to believe that it exists or that it is not by nature vicious. Tolkien salves modern embarrassment to some extent by presenting events largely through the modernistic and un-ambitious eyes of the Hobbits, who (though "tough in the fibre," determined, and self-sacrificing) are rarely allowed to be militarily *aggressive*. (When they are, as at I, 339, "One for the Shire!" or II, 47, "Good old Merry!" one may well feel a certain uneasiness.) Critics have reacted on the whole by praising the hobbits, especially in Book vi, very much more than the heroes, especially in Book v, and they may be right to do so. Tolkien, however, unlike most of his critics, was able to see to what extent such reactions are accidents of time and culture rather than "eternal verities" (as they have been called). He gives us a final critique of heroism through his central character; and a clue to what is permanent about it through the character's name, Frodo.

Hobbit-names are explained rather carefully in Appendix F (III, 413), where Tolkien informs us that they fall into two types. Some male hobbits were given "high-sounding" appellations from the heroic past, translated for English readers into the old Gothic or Frankish names which we now know but very rarely use—names like Fredegar, Meriadoc, Peregrin. But mostly they received "names that had no meaning at all in their daily language. . . . Of this kind are Bilbo, Bungo, Polo, Lotho," and so on. To which category does "Frodo" belong? Tolkien, surprisingly, does not mention this name in the Appendix. But he *does* say that although names like "Bilbo" have been simply retained from hobbit-language, he has made one regular change to them, which is to anglicise them "by altering their endings, since in Hobbit-names *a* was a masculine ending, and *o* and *e* were feminine." "Bilbo", then, represents earlier "Bilba"; "Frodo", correspondingly, must have been "Froda." Now "Froda" is not a meaningless name at all, but a hero-name from the dimmest reaches of Northern legend. It is mentioned once in *Beowulf*, line 2025, where Beowulf is reporting to his own king that the king of the Danes has betrothed his daughter to one Ingeld, "the noble son of Froda," *gladum suna Frodan*. Beowulf does not think, however, that the marriage will be a success; there is an old grudge between Ingeld's people and the Danes, and (heroic) human nature will not be able to forget it. It is generally agreed that Beowulf's gloomy prophecy was meant to be accurate; the attempted revenge of Ingeld was a famous theme of Northern literature. Tolkien had a low opinion of Ingeld, calling him "thrice faithless and easily persuaded"[42]—a slave, in short, to social convention. But he mentions Froda once or twice with some respect.[43] Naturally one cannot be sure either of how Tolkien reconstructed the Froda legend or of what the truth of the matter may have been: the references to Froda in ancient story are more than normally confusing. But it is at least guessable that Froda was killed by the Danes, and that this is Ingeld's grudge. It is also striking that (as is agreed by Saxo Grammaticus and Snorri Sturluson)[44] there was once a Danish king called Frotho, or Frothi, who was famous for his peace-making: he was the king who ruled at the time of Christ's incarnation, when (as Milton recalls) war ceased temporarily throughout the world. But this Frithfrothi, or "peace-Frothi," did not die peacefully: because he gave no rest to the giantess slaves who ground out his gold and peace and prosperity they ground out first an army to kill their master, and then salt to sink the killers' boat—and that is why the sea is brine. One can say only that behind these stories there may be the faint image of an anti-hero, a man who tried in pagan times to make peace, but who failed, both personally (for he was killed), and ideologically (for his son returned to the ways of feud and revenge, while even his name faded almost entirely from English memory).

Something of all this hangs over Tolkien's Frodo. He too turns increasingly to pacifism. Though he resists the Nazgûl and stabs the Moria troll, he refuses repeatedly to kill Gollum; and in Mordor he throws away his weapons (III, 214), declaring ten pages earlier, "I do not think it will be my part to strike any blow again." In the Battle of Bywater, too, he does not draw his sword (III, 295), and his main role is to protect the hobbits' prisoners. It is, ironically, natural that his reputation should suffer. Peregrin and Meriadoc, the large and "lordly" hobbits,

42. In "*Beowulf*: The Monsters and the Critics," p. 258.

43. Tídwald (the more sensible of the two speakers) mentions the time "when Fróda fell, and Finn was slain," in "The Homecoming of Beorhtnoth Beorhthelm's Son," *Essays and Studies* 38 (1953), 1–18, also available in *The Tolkien Reader*, pp. 1–24.

44. See *The First Nine Books of Saxo Grammaticus*, trans. O. Elton with introduction by F. York Powell (London, 1894), pp. 205–10; and *Edda*, ed. Jónsson, pp. 135–38.

are much respected, but Sam is "pained" to notice how little people care about Frodo's greater deeds (III, 305). The moral is that even hobbits prefer an aggressive brand of heroism, if they can get it; peacemakers are not good story-material. This seems to be true of the ancient Northern Froda, whose story has vanished much more completely than that of his vengeful son. It is true of the hobbit Frodo, who founds no noble family in the Shire, and drops out of popular legend much more completely even than his uncle Bilbo, who at least survives to posterity (I, 51) as "mad Baggins."[45] And yet Frodo is the hero of *The Lord of the Rings*. Tolkien presents in him a modern ideal, but suggests by his name that it was also, to some, an ancient one. Peacemakers might be admired in heroic societies, and aggressors are in peaceful ones. Though customs change, this elemental opposition is permanent.

Frodo's victory, then, is shadowed by a sense of loss and pain, as all victories are in Middle-Earth. But sorrow is itself qualified by the temporary and local, but nonetheless genuine happiness that falls on the West for the lifetimes of Rosie Cotton and Aragorn; as also by the vaguer suggestions of a final providence. What has happened is that Tolkien has succeeded in blending suggestions from the optimistic Christian mythology and the tragic Northern one, without impiety to the former or dishonour to the latter. Before he did it, the achievement must have appeared impossible. It is more than eleven hundred years since Alcuin asked his famous question, "What has Ingeld to do with Christ?", and in all that time his answer—"Nothing!"—has gone unchallenged.[46] Yet Frodo, though neither Ingeld nor Christ, is distantly if differently related to both.

45. One of Frotho's relations in Saxo's confused and unreliable story is Amlethus, "mad Hamlet."

46. Alcuin's remark is in a letter to the monks of Lindisfarne, *Alcuini Epistolae*, ed. E. L. Dümmler, in *Monumenta Germaniae Historica, Epistolae* IV (Berlin, 1895), p. 183. It is, however, a commonplace of *Beowulf* criticism. It is fair to add that Nikolai Grundtvig, the Danish Beowulfian and church-reformer, displayed a wish to accommodate the two figures which might have influenced Tolkien; he suggested, for instance, that the Nordic Ragnarök might symbolise the end of an age with Christ's incarnation, in terms reminiscent of Bombadil's "till the world is mended." See E. L. Allen, *Bishop*

The achievement may yet have significance for philosophers, as it has had charm for readers; for Tolkien's approach
was not in the end just historical, though it was scholarly. All
his life he made jokes about philologists who remained interested in words and words alone, who forgot that the words at
least at one time referred to realities; the herbmaster of the
Houses of Healing in *The Return of the King* is descended from
the "jabberwocks of historical and antiquarian research" in the
British Academy lecture. The true philologist, Tolkien seems to
say, may be seen in the parson of *Farmer Giles of Ham*, a tale
which has been seen (by Professor Kocher)[47] as exposing philologists and laughing at their "pretensions." It is true that the
parson is inclined to hide behind learned language when he gets
stuck with his runes; true also that he does not prevent the
peasants from freeing the dragon once it is beaten. But when
Tolkien writes that the parson with his booklearning ought to
have known better, his qualification—"Maybe he did"—turns
out to be near the truth. For the parson "was a grammarian, and
could doubtless see further into the future than others." He saw
far enough, anyway, to send Farmer Giles off on his second,
more successful encounter, and (as Professor Kocher might have
granted) *to make him take the rope that was needed to tie the treasure on
the dragon!*

If I may conclude with a short and wholly adventitious allegory: the grammarian parson is a Christian philologist; Farmer
Giles is the creative instinct; the dragon is the world of the
ancient Northern imagination; the rope is linguistic science. The
"Little Kingdom" of Ham is of course Middle-Earth. As for that
bold and overbearing tyrant, Augustus Bonifacius Ambrosius
Aurelianus Antoninus, from whom Farmer Giles and the
dragon so tolerantly declare their independence, he must surely
be either the demands of modern literature, or else any modern
literary critic.

Grundtvig: A Prophet of the North (London, 1949), especially chap. 4, "Odin and
Christ." Grundtvig is probably one of the mythological voices "(old voices
these, and generally shouted down)," whom Tolkien commends in his British
Academy lecture.

47. Kocher, *Master of Middle-Earth*, p. 163.

Handlist of The Published Writings of

J. R. R. TOLKIEN

COMPILED BY HUMPHREY CARPENTER

Juvenilia and poems published in magazines or anthologies have been omitted.

1922 *A Middle English Vocabulary*. Oxford; Clarendon Press, 1922. (Designed for use with Sisam's *Fourteenth Century Verse and Prose*. Separately issued for use with the 1921 edition of that book, in subsequent editions of which it appears as the glossary. It was also reprinted separately.)

1923 "Holy Maidenhood," *Times Literary Supplement*, Thursday, 26 April 1923, p. 281. (A review of Furnivall's Early English Text Society edition of *Hali Maidenhad*. Unsigned, but Tolkien's authorship is established by a reference in his diary.)

"Henry Bradley, 3 December 1845–23 May 1923," *Bulletin of the Modern Humanities Research Association*, no. 20 (October 1923), pp. 4–5. (Signed 'J. R. R. T.')

1924 "Philology. General Works," *The Year's Work in English Studies*, 4 (1923), 20–37. London: Oxford University Press, 1924.

1925 "Some Contributions to Middle-English Lexicography," *Review of English Studies*, 1, no. 2 (April 1925), 210–15. London: Sidgwick & Jackson, 1925.

"The Devil's Coach-Horses," *Review of English Studies*, 1, no. 3 (July 1925), 331–36. London: Sidgwick & Jackson, 1925.

Sir Gawain and the Green Knight, edited by J. R. R. Tolkien and E. V. Gordon. Oxford: Clarendon Press, 1925. (Reprinted many times. Second edition revised by Norman Davis, Oxford, 1967.)

1926 "Philology. General Works," *The Year's Work in English Studies*, 5 (1924), 26–65. London: Oxford University Press, 1926.

1927 "Philology. General Works," *The Year's Work in English Studies*, 6 (1925), 32–66. London: Oxford University Press, 1927.

1928 Foreword to *A New Glossary of the Dialect of the Huddersfield District* By Walter E. Haigh. London: Oxford University Press, 1928.

1929 "Ancrene Wisse and Hali Meiʒhad," *Essays and Studies*, 14 (1929), 104–26. Oxford: Clarendon Press, 1929.

1930 "The Oxford English School," *Oxford Magazine*, 48, no. 21 (Thursday, 29 May 1930), 778–82. Oxford: The Oxonian Press, 1930.

1932 Appendix I: "The Name 'Nodens' in *Report on the Excavation of the Prehistoric, Roman, and Post-Roman Sites in Lydney Park, Gloucestershire*. Reports of the Research Committee of the Society of Antiquaries of London, no. 9 (1932), 132–37.

"Sigelwara Land": Part I in *Medium Ævum*, 1 (December 1932), 183–96; Part II in *Medium Ævum*, 3 (June 1934), 95–111. Oxford: Basil Blackwell.

1934 "Chaucer as a Philologist: The Reeve's Tale," *Transactions of the Philological Society* (1934), pp. 1–70. London: David Nutt, 1934.

1936 *Songs for the Philologists* by J. R. R. Tolkien, E. V. Gordon, and others. Privately printed in the Department of English at University College, London, 1936. (A collection of humourous verses originally circulated in typescript at Leeds University. The verses are unsigned, but Tolkien was the author of "From One to Five," "Syx Mynet," "Ruddoc Hana," "Ides Ælfscýne," "Bagme Bloma," "Éadig Béo Þu," "Ofer Wídne Gársecg," "La, Húru," "I Sat Upon a Bench," "Natura Apis," "The Root of the Boot," "Frenchmen Froth," and "Lit and Lang.")

1937 "Beowulf: The Monsters and the Critics," *Proceedings of the British Academy*, 22 (1936), 245–95. London: Oxford University Press, 1937. (Reprinted in *An Anthology of Beowulf Criticism*, edited by Lewis E. Nicholson, University of Notre Dame Press, 1963; and in *The Beowulf Poet*, edited by Donald K. Fry, Englewood Cliffs, N.J., Prentice-Hall Inc., 1968.)

The Hobbit; or There and Back Again, London: George Allen & Unwin Ltd., 1937. (Reprinted in 1937, 1942, and 1946. From the second impression onwards, four colour plates were included. Second edition 1951; reprinted many times. Third edition 1966; reprinted many times. First U.S. edition 1938. Second U.S. edition 1958. Third U.S. edition, 1965; reprinted many times. Translated into and published in Swedish [1947 and 1962], German [1947 and 1967], Dutch [1960], Polish [1960], Portugese [1962], Spanish [Argentine, 1964], Japanese [1965], Danish [1969], French [1969], Norwegian [1972], Czech [1973], Finnish [1973], Italian [1973].)

1940 Preface to *Beowulf and the Finnesburg Fragment: A Translation into Modern English Prose* by John R. Clark Hall, revised by C. L. Wrenn. London: George Allen & Unwin Ltd., 1940.

1945 "Leaf by Niggle," *Dublin Review*, 432 (January 1945), 46–61. London: Burns Oates & Washbourne Ltd. (This short story was later reprinted—see below—and translated into Dutch [1971], Swedish [1972], and French [1974].)

1947 " 'Ipþlen' in Sawles Warde,"*English Studies*, edited by R. W. Zandvoort, Groningen, 28 (6 December 1947), 168–70. (In collaboration with S. T. R. O. d'Ardenne.)

"On Fairy-Stories," *Essays Presented to Charles Williams*, edited by C. S. Lewis, pp. 38–89. London: Oxford University Press, 1947. (Reprinted—see below—and translated into Swedish [1972] and Japanese [1973].)

1948 "MS. Bodley 34: A Re-collation of a Collation," *Studia Neophilogica*, 20 (1947–48), 65–72. Uppsala, 1948. (In collaboration with S. T. R. O. d'Ardenne.)

1949 *Farmer Giles of Ham.* London: George Allen & Unwin Ltd., 1949. (Later reprinted. Translated into Swedish [1961], Polish [1965], German [1970], Dutch [1971], and Israeli [date unknown].)

1953 "A Fourteenth-Century Romance," *Radio Times*, London, 4 December 1953. (Foreword to the BBC Third Programme broadcasts of Tolkien's translation of "Sir Gawain and the Green Knight.")

"Middle English 'Losenger,' " *Essais de Philologie Moderne (1951)*, pp. 63–76. Université de Liège, 1953.

"The Homecoming of Beorhtnoth Beorhthelm's Son," *Essays and Studies*, pp. 1–18. London: John Murray, 1953.

1954 *The Fellowship of the Ring: Being the First Part of The Lord of the Rings.* London: George Allen & Unwin Ltd., 1954.

The Two Towers: Being the Second Part of The Lord of the Rings. London: George Allen & Unwin Ltd., 1954.

1955 *The Return of the King: Being the Third Part of The Lord of the Rings.* London: George Allen & Unwin Ltd., 1955.

(Between 1954 and 1966 *The Fellowship of the Ring* was reprinted 14 times, *The Two Towers* 11 times, and *The Return of the King* 10 times. Second edition of all three volumes, 1966; reprinted many times. Paperback edition of *The Lord of the Rings* in one volume, 1968. First U.S. edition, 1954 [vol. I], 1955 [vols. II and III]. Second U.S. edition 1967. Ace Books edition, New York, 1965. Ballantine Books edition, New York, 1965. Translated into Dutch [1956], Swedish [1959], Polish [1961], Danish [1968], German [1969], Italian [1970], French [1972], Finnish [1973], Norwegian [1973], Portugese [Brazil, 1974], and Japanese [date unknown].)

Preface to *The Ancrene Riwle*, translated into Modern English by M. R. Salu. London: Burns & Oates, 1955.

1962 *Ancrene Wisse: The English Text of the Ancrene Riwle.* Edited from MS Corpus Christi College Cambridge 402 by J. R. R. Tolkien, with an introduction by N. R. Ker. Early English Text Society, Vol. 249. London: Oxford University Press, 1962.

The Adventures of Tom Bombadil and Other Verses from The Red Book. London: George Allen & Unwin Ltd., 1962. (Subsequently reprinted. Translated into Swedish [1972].)

1963 "English and Welsh," *Angles and Britons: O'Donnell Lectures*, pp. 1–41. Cardiff: University of Wales Press, 1963. (Published in United States by Verry, Lawrence, 1963.)

1964 *Tree and Leaf*. London: George Allen & Unwin Ltd., 1964. (Reprint of "On Fairy-Stories" and "Leaf by Niggle." Published in United States by Houghton Mifflin, 1965.)

1966 "Tolkien on Tolkien," *Diplomat*, 18, no. 197 (October 1966), 39. (Taken from a statement prepared by Tolkien for his publishers, this is a brief account of his life and his motives as a writer.)

The Jerusalem Bible. London: Darton, Longman & Todd, 1966. (Published in United States, New York: Doubleday, 1966.) (Tolkien is named as an editor of this work, but his only contribution was to make the original draft of the translation of the Book of Jonah, and even this was extensively revised by other hands before publication.)

The Tolkien Reader. New York: Ballantine Books, 1966. (A reprint in one volume of "The Homecoming of Beorhtnoth," "On Fairy-Stories," "Leaf by Niggle," "Farmer Giles of Ham," and "The Adventures of Tom Bombadil.")

1967 *Smith of Wootton Major*. London: George Allen & Unwin Ltd., 1967. (Subsequently reprinted. Second edition 1975. Published in United States by Houghton Mifflin, 1967. Translated into Afrikaans [1968], Dutch [1968], Swedish [1972].)

1968 *The Road Goes Ever On: A Song Cycle*. Poems by J. R. R. Tolkien, set to music by Donald Swann. London: George Allen & Unwin Ltd., 1968. (Published in United States by Houghton Mifflin, 1967).

(At the same time as the publication of *The Road Goes Ever On*, a long-playing record was issued by Caedmon Records (TC1231) entitled *Poems and Songs of Middle Earth*. On the record, William Elvin sings Swann's settings of Tolkien's poems, with the composer at the piano, and Tolkien reads some of his own verse.)

1969 Letter describing the origins of "The Inklings" in *The Image of Man in C. S. Lewis* by William Luther White, pp. 221–22. Nashville and New York: Abingdon Press, 1969. (Reprinted in Great Britain by Hodier & Stoughton, 1970.)

1975 *Sir Gawain and the Green Knight, Pearl, and Sir Orfeo,* translated into Modern English by J. R. R. Tolkien. Edited and with a Preface by Christopher Tolkien. London: George Allen & Unwin Ltd., 1975.

Critical works: A great number of critical writings on Tolkien's work have been published, especially in the United States. A comprehensive list of these up to 1968 is to be found in *Tolkien Criticism: An Annotated Checklist* by Richard C. West, Kent, Ohio: Kent State University Press, 1970.

Index

J.R.R. Tolkien, Scholar and Storyteller

Designed by Guy Fleming.
Composed by Imperial Litho/Graphics
in 11 point VIP Janson, 2 points leaded,
with display lines in Janson.
Printed offset by Thomson/Shore, Inc.
on Warren's Olde Style, 60 pound basis.
Bound by John H. Dekker, Inc.
in Holliston book cloth
and stamped in All Purpose foil.

Library of Congress Cataloging in Publication Data

Main entry under title:
J.R.R. Tolkien, scholar and storyteller.

Bibliography: p.
Includes index.
1. Tolkien, John Ronald Reuel, 1892–1973 — Criticism and interpretation —
Addresses, essays, lectures. 2. English literature — Middle English, 1100–1500 —
History and criticism — Addresses, essays, lectures. 3. Anglo-Saxon literature —
History and criticism — Addresses, essays, lectures. I. Tolkien, John Ronald Reuel,
1892–1973. II. Salu, Mary. III. Farrell, Robert T.
PR6039.032Z665   828'.9'1209   78-58032
ISBN 0-8014-1038-X